Grammar and
Conceptualization

Cognitive Linguistics Research
14

Editors

René Dirven
Ronald W. Langacker
John R. Taylor

Mouton de Gruyter
Berlin · New York

Grammar and Conceptualization

Ronald W. Langacker

Mouton de Gruyter
Berlin · New York 2000

Mouton de Gruyter (formerly Mouton, The Hague)
is a Division of Walter de Gruyter GmbH & Co. KG, Berlin

Library of Congress Cataloging-in-Publication Data

Langacker, Ronald W.
    Grammar and conceptualization / Ronald W. Langacker.
      p.   cm. − (Cognitive linguistics research ; 14)
    Includes bibliographical references (p.   ) and index.
    ISBN 3-11-016603-8 (alk. paper). − ISBN 3-11-016604-6
    (pbk. : alk. paper)
      1. Cognitive grammar.   2. Concepts.   I. Title.   II. Series.
    P165.L363   1999
    415−dc21   99-33328
                                                                        CIP

Die Deutsche Bibliothek − Cataloging-in-Publication Data

Langacker, Ronald W.:
Grammar and conceptualization / Ronald W. Langacker. −
Berlin ; New York : Mouton de Gruyter, 2000
    (Cognitive linguistics research ; 14)
    ISBN 3-11-016604-6

Printing: Werner Hildebrand, Berlin
Binding: Lüderitz & Bauer, Berlin
Printed in Germany

To Sheila

Preface

In the preface to *Concept, Image, and Symbol*, the predecessor of this book, I recounted the recent founding of cognitive linguistics as a self-conscious intellectual movement with an institutional basis. A decade later, cognitive linguistics is thriving. Its institutions are sounder, its adherents are steadily increasing in numbers worldwide, and its influence is more and more being felt in other disciplines. The volume of publications in cognitive linguistics has reached the point that keeping up with them all—even the ones I am aware of—is no longer a realistic objective.

During this period, the theory of cognitive grammar has greatly progressed as well. My own efforts have resulted in about forty substantial articles, either published or in press. An enormous body of material is therefore potentially available representing the articulation, refinement, and evolution of cognitive grammar since the last comprehensive statement of the framework appeared. However, this material is scattered around in a wide range of venues, so that not even assiduous readers in general and cognitive linguistics can be expected to have come across more than a fraction of it. The aim of this volume is thus to provide an accessible collection of representative and significant writings showing the continued development of the theory and further illustrating its application to diverse problems.

Just twelve papers have been selected for this purpose. Included are basic theoretical statements, analyses and descriptions of particular phenomena, as well as a preview of future research. All have been adapted to make this a cohesive work; the revisions range from slight adjustments to almost a complete rewriting. Besides formatting, the most significant changes have been the pruning of excessively redundant material and certain attempts at coherence and continuity. The result is naturally a compromise. In large measure, I believe that each individual chapter (and also the full volume) can be read and understood as a self-contained entity. At the same time, it is meant to be readable as an integral whole and is best appreciated in the context of previous publications. To facilitate cross-reference, I have thus adopted certain abbreviations: CIS for *Concept, Image, and Symbol*, as well as FCG1 and FCG2 for the two volumes of *Foundations of Cognitive Grammar*. I have also succumbed to the acronymistic proclivities of theoretical linguists in adopting CG for cognitive grammar.

The ordering of the chapters is more thematic than chrono-logical. The first three chapters are introductory, providing a basic description of the framework, discussion of its methodology, and illustrations of its application to some representative descriptive pro-blems. The next two chapters are extensive treatments of some foun-dational theoretical issues: the nature and implications of a usage-based approach, and the status and characterization of constituency. The six chapters that follow offer reasonably detailed descriptions of particular grammatical phenomena showing the need for a variety of constructs pertaining to conceptual structure. Chapters 6 and 7 deal with perspective and mental access; the former considers the role of conceptual reference points, while the latter examines the extensive parallelism between *per*ception and *con*ception. Chapters 8 and 9, respectively concerned with generic and habitual expressions and with pronominal anaphora, demonstrate the importance of positing multiple "planes" or mental spaces. Chapter 10 documents a common path of grammaticization involving subjectification and the attenuation of an agent's control. As a synchronic result, this diachronic process pro-duces "raising" constructions, analyzed in Chapter 11. Finally, some recurring themes are drawn together in the last chapter under the rub-ric "dynamic conceptualization", which is offered as a key to future developments.

Let me conclude by collectively acknowledging and thanking the many scholars and students who have contributed to this volume through their questions, comments, and criticisms, as well as through their own research.

Contents

Notes 377

References 401

Index 419

Chapter 1
Clause structure

The relation between grammar and meaning is probably the most crucial issue in current linguistic theory.* Even in the generative tradition, which has long and loudly proclaimed the autonomy of grammatical structure, semantic considerations have not only intruded but taken on progressively greater significance. This of course is perfectly unsurprising from the standpoint of *cognitive grammar*, which for many years has claimed that grammar and meaning are indissociable. This theory takes the radical position that grammar reduces to the structuring and symbolization of conceptual content and thus has no autonomous existence at all.

Actually, this position seems radical only through the distorting lens of formal grammatical theory. It is in fact both natural and alluring in view of the basic *semiological function* of language, which is to allow the symbolization of conceptualizations by means of phonological sequences. Granted this function, language necessarily comprises *semantic structures*, *phonological structures*, and *symbolic links* between the two. The central claim of CG is that nothing else is needed. The theory maintains that lexicon and grammar form a continuum, and that only *symbolic structures*—each residing in the symbolic linkage of a semantic and a phonological structure—figure in their proper characterization. It thus achieves a major conceptual unification, and further succeeds in reconciling the structural organization of language with its semiological function. It seems to me, then, that linguistic theorists should very much want to sustain this basic vision and should strive to demonstrate the viability of such a theory. Over the years, I and my students have tried to show that it does indeed afford an adequate and revealing description of linguistic structure.[1]

1. Basics of cognitive grammar

Least controversial is the symbolic nature of *lexicon*, by which I mean the fixed expressions of a language. As an inventory of basic conventions for linking meanings with phonological sequences, lexicon represents a distillation of shared human experience. A lexical item embodies the commonality in form and meaning observable across a substantial number of *usage events* (i.e. actual utterances in their full phonetic detail and contextual understanding). Its acquisition comes about through the *reinforcement* of recurrent features, the progressive *entrenchment* of whatever aspects of form and meaning are constant across events. It thus involves a process of *decontextualization*, whereby non-recurrent features are filtered out, as well as *schematization*, for it is only by abstracting away from specific points of fine detail that commonalities become apparent. For the most part, of course, the conceptions that achieve the status of lexical meanings are both psychologically natural and culturally salient. Their emergence through social interaction reflects not only their communicative utility for the description of shared experience, but also—and more fundamentally—the basic cognitive abilities which support and shape that experience.

1.1. Cognitive abilities

From research in cognitive linguistics, it appears that quite a number of such abilities are relevant to lexical semantics and to language structure more generally. We have, first, the inborn capacity for certain basic kinds of experience: we can experience a certain range of colors, pitches, tastes, smells, and tactile sensations; we have a notion of spatial extensionality in which spatial configurations can be manifested; we sense the passage of time; we undergo a certain array of emotions; and so on. I refer to these irreducible realms of experiential potential as *basic domains*. We have, next, various cognitive abilities that are applicable to any domain of experience and essential to the emergence of specific concepts (at successively higher levels of organizational complexity). We can, for instance, *compare* two experiences and register either their identity or any discrepancy between them. We can use one structure as the basis for *categorizing* another. We have the capacity for *abstraction* (*schematization*) and thus for conceiving of situations with varying degrees of specificity and detail. We are able to direct and focus our *attention*, and to structure scenes in terms of *figure/ground* organization (which is often reversible).

Less often noted are certain equally fundamental abilities that I consider crucial to linguistic semantics. One is the ability to *establish relationships*: to conceive of entities in connection with one another (e.g. for sake of comparison, or to assess their relative position), not just as separate, isolated experiences. This is linguistically important because relationships figure in the meaning of almost all expressions, many of which (e.g. verbs, adjectives, prepositions) actually *designate* relationships. We are also capable of *grouping* a set of entities— on the basis of similarity, proximity, or some other relationship—and manipulating that group as a unitary entity for higher-order purposes.[2] This dual process (grouping and manipulation as a unitary entity) amounts to *conceptual reification*, which populates our mental world with abstract "things" expressed by nouns. A further capacity is *mental scanning*, in which we trace a path through a complex structure. Here we exhibit great conceptual flexibility: we can scan *sequentially* through a static structure (e.g. in tracing the shortest route from one part of town to another), and can even view a changing situation holistically, in *summary* fashion (e.g. we can summarize the successive positions of a moving object and see them as a path-like entity with a definite "shape").[3]

Also fundamental to cognition and linguistic semantics are *image schemas* (Johnson 1987; Lakoff 1987) and *metaphor*. Image schemas include such notions as source-path-goal, container-content, center-periphery, linkage, force, and balance. They are highly abstract conceptions, primarily configurational, which are grounded in everyday bodily experience and play an essential role in structuring our mental world.[4] These schematic conceptions emerge in physical experience (experience with objects moving from source to goal along spatial paths, with actual containers and what they hold, etc.) and provide the basis for projecting it metaphorically to other conceptual realms. Metaphor is deemed essential to cognitive development. Though often regarded as merely a literary device (hence outside the scope of linguistic semantics), it is in fact pervasive in human understanding and independent of specific linguistic expressions. Metaphor is characterized as the conceptual phenomenon whereby a *target domain* is structured and understood with reference to another, more basic *source domain* (Lakoff and Johnson 1980). According to Lakoff (1990), the mapping between a source and a target domain always preserves *image-schematic structure*. It is these abstract configurational properties that the source imposes on the target (alternatively, they represent the perceived commonality that motivates the metaphorical projection).[5]

1.2. Lexical meaning

Returning now to lexicon, we can first observe that a typical lexical item represents a *complex category*: it does not have just one meaning, but a variety of related senses with varying degrees of entrenchment. These senses comprise a *network*, being linked by *categorizing relationships*, which are of two basic sorts. First, some senses arise by *extension* from other, more central values. The term *tree*, for example, is extended metaphorically from its *prototypical* value ('tall woody plant') to indicate various kinds of branching diagrams. Second, some senses *instantiate* (or *elaborate*) other, more schematic values. For instance, the prototypical and metaphorical senses of *tree* both instantiate the abstract conception of a 'brachiated entity' (this is the image-schematic commonality which motivates the metaphorical extension in the first place).

Let us next consider how any one conventionally established sense of a lexical item might be characterized. A basic tenet of CG is that lexical meanings cannot be sharply distinguished from general knowledge of the entities referred to. Our knowledge of a given type of entity is often vast and multifaceted, involving many realms of experience and conceptions with varying degrees of salience, specificity, and complexity. Our knowledge of trees, for example, subsumes physical properties (e.g. shape, height, color), biological characteristics (growth rate, root system, reproduction, photosynthesis, dropping of leaves), utility (wood, shade, food source), and numerous other specifications (forests, host for animals, how to cut one down, etc.). In principle, each of these specifications figures to some extent in the meaning of *tree*. A lexical item is not thought of as incorporating a fixed, limited, and uniquely linguistic semantic representation, but rather as providing access to indefinitely many conceptions and conceptual systems, which it evokes in a flexible, open-ended, context-dependent manner.[6]

The term *cognitive domain* is conveniently used for either a basic domain (as defined above) or a conceptualization of any kind or degree of complexity. We can say, then, that a lexical item evokes a set of cognitive domains as the basis for its meaning, and exhibits considerable flexibility in this regard. The access it affords is anything but random, however. First of all, the domains a lexical item invokes are primarily limited to those in which the entity it designates (i.e. its conceptual referent) figures directly (FCG1: 4.2.3).[7] As part of its conventional value, moreover, a lexical item *ranks* these domains: it accords them particular degrees of *centrality*, which in processing terms can be interpreted as likelihood and/or strength of activation. Expressions that invoke the same domains can nonetheless contrast semantically by virtue of their ranking. For instance, the domain of fish reproduction ranks more highly in *roe* than in *caviar*, even for those who know what caviar is made from. The conventional ranking a lexical item imposes may of course be adjusted in special circumstances.

The domains an expression invokes provide its conceptual *content*. Linguistic meaning does not, however, reside in content alone, for we are able to *construe* the same content in alternate ways, resulting in substantially different meanings. Though largely ignored in traditional semantics, construal is crucial for both semantic and grammatical structure.[8] It is a multifaceted phenomenon whose various dimensions reflect some of the basic cognitive abilities noted previously. They can be grouped under five general headings: *specificity*, *background*, *perspective*, *scope*, and *prominence*.

Specificity pertains to our capacity for conceiving and portraying an entity at varying levels of precision and detail, as illustrated by sets of expressions like *chianti > wine > beverage > liquid > substance* and *sprint > run > move > act > do*. Such hierarchies indicate that the process of schematization—required (as we have seen) for the acquisition of any lexical item—can be carried to different degrees.

Our ability to construe one structure against the *background* afforded by another has numerous linguistic manifestations. The broadest of these is categorization, in which the categorizing structure serves as background for assessing the target. In metaphor, likewise, the source domain provides the background for construing the target domain. Another kind of background is previous discourse, which figures in notions like focus and the given/new distinction. Also fitting under this rubric are the presuppositions embodied by many lexical items: *again*, for instance, portrays an event against the background of a previous occurrence, while *even* and *only* invoke a norm or expectation.

The term *perspective* subsumes a number of different factors. Some lexical items—e.g. *upstairs, outside, yesterday, soon*—incorporate a spatial or temporal *vantage point* as an inherent aspect of their meaning. In the absence of any contrary specification, the speaker's location is adopted as the vantage point by default. A second factor is *mental scanning*, which can be exemplified by the difference in meaning between *converge* and *diverge* in expressions like the following:

(1) a. *These two nerves converge just below the knee.*
     b. *This nerve diverges just below the knee.*

Both sentences describe the same, static objective situation. Their semantic contrast resides in how the *conceptualizer* scans through the scene: whether he traces a mental path inward, from the periphery to the central nervous system, or outward, from the center to the periphery. The same examples illustrate a third dimension of perspective. I say that an entity is construed *subjectively* vs. *objectively* to the extent that it functions asymmetrically as the *subject* vs. the *object* of conception.[9] The conceptualizer is thus construed subjectively in (1), and the nerve(s) objectively. Despite its pivotal role, the conceptualizer is not conceived as being part of the objective scene, nor as moving through it. His subjective motion does however determine whether the branching configuration is seen as an instance of convergence or of divergence.

   I define an expression's *scope* as the array of conceptual content it invokes (either typically or on a given occasion of its use). It thus comprises a set of cognitive domains, or those portions of active domains which are actually called upon and exploited for the purpose at hand. *Yesterday*, for example, requires for its temporal scope an expanse of time that includes both the time of speaking and the previous day; it need not encompass all of eternity, however. There is in fact good evidence that an expression's scope (in a given domain) is properly conceived as a bounded entity, even in cases where any specific line of demarcation would be arbitrary.[10] It is sometimes rather precisely delimited. In a partonymy like *arm > hand > finger > knuckle*, for example, the entity designated by each term (i.e. its conceptual referent) functions as the scope for the term that follows. Thus the conception of an *arm* provides the spatial scope for *hand*; likewise, the conception of a *hand* provides the spatial scope for *finger*, and *finger* for *knuckle*. With respect to spatial configuration, we observe a nesting such that the referent of one expression defines the *immediate scope* invoked for the characterization of the next.

   There are many sorts of *prominence* that have to be distinguished in linguistic analysis. Several of these have already been noted. One kind of prominence is the ranking of cognitive domains by a lexical item (e.g. the domain of kinship relations is central to the characterization of *aunt* but rather peripheral for *woman*). Along another axis, objectively construed entities—those placed "onstage", within the locus of viewing attention—have greater salience than "offstage" entities receiving a subjective construal. A further type of prominence is the status of being a conceptual referent. From the array of content it invokes, every expression selects some entity for designation, placing it onstage as the specific focus of attention. In the usual terminology of CG, an expression imposes a particular *profile* on the conceptual *base* subtended by its scope. The term *knuckle*, for instance, evokes as its base the conception of a finger, within which it profiles (designates) a certain subpart (any joint). The base for *aunt* includes a partial kinship network, which must at least subsume the reference individual ("ego"), a parent of that individual, and a female sibling of the parent; with respect to this base, *aunt* profiles the female sibling. These notions are sketched in Figure 1.1 (observe that heavy lines indicate profiling).

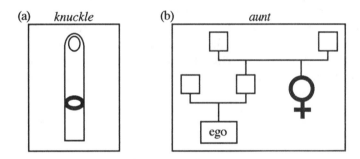

Figure 1.1

I emphasize that profiling is reference within a conceptualization, not in the "world".[11] A noun like *knuckle* or *aunt* can thus be characterized as having a profile, even though it names a *type* rather than a specific *instance* of that type (FCG2: part I). Furthermore, an optimal description of language structure requires a notion of conceptual reference in which not just thing-like entities but also *relationships* are capable of being profiled. The preposition *near*, for example, profiles a relationship of proximity (prototypically in space) between two entities. When used as an adjective, *yellow* profiles the relationship between a thing and a certain region of color space: it specifies that a color sensation associated with the thing (typically being induced by its outer surface) falls within that region. When used as a verb, *yellow* profiles a change through time in which the associated color sensation gradually enters the yellow region.

A relationship generally has one or more *focal elements*, normally describable as *participants*,[12] which stand out with special salience within the relational profile. The type of prominence they exhibit is hypothesized to be a matter of figure/ground organization. The most salient element—termed the *trajector* (tr)—is thus characterized as the *primary figure* within a profiled relationship. If a relationship encompasses a second focal element, it is called a *landmark* (lm) and characterized as a *secondary figure*. The choice of focal elements represents an important aspect of construal. It is not uncommon for expressions to invoke precisely the same conceptual content, and even to profile the same relationship, yet contrast semantically in terms of the trajector/landmark alignment they impose. Consider the semantic opposition between *in front of* and *in back of*, diagrammed in Figure 1.2. Each profiles the relation involving two focal participants (shown by heavy-line circles) wherein one participant stands in the line of sight (indicated by the dashed arrow) between a viewer (V) and the other participant. The only difference resides in the choice of trajector, which can be characterized as the entity being located. *In front of* takes the far participant as a landmark for purposes of locating the near participant, whereas *in back of* reverses these roles.

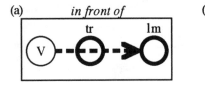 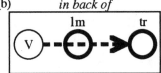

Figure 1.2

1.3. Lexical classes

Having surveyed various aspects of construal, essential for describing the individual senses of lexical items, let us now consider their grouping into classes. Basic lexical classes (i.e. noun, verb, adjective, etc.) are claimed in CG to be susceptible to semantic characterization. The recognition of semantic prototypes for these classes is, of course, quite common: a linguist does not risk ostracism by asserting the prototypicality of physical objects for the class of nouns, of properties for adjectives, etc. By contrast, the claim that these classes also have schematic characterizations—abstract semantic descriptions valid for all class members—runs directly counter to accepted linguistic dogma. There is, however, no real basis for this dogma other than a lack of imagination concerning the kinds of notions one might conceivably posit for this purpose. From my perspective, it is utterly implausible to suppose that something as fundamental and universal as the noun and verb classes would not reflect a rudimentary conceptual distinction. The usual mistake is to assume that such a distinction would have to reside in specific conceptual content, in which case viable definitions are indeed unavailable.[13] We have seen, though, that meaning is a function of both content and construal. It is in the realm of construal and basic cognitive abilities that we must seek the schematic characterization of lexical classes.

A lexical item's grammatical class is determined by the nature of its profile. *Aunt*, for example, is a noun because it profiles a kind of thing (even though a relation is crucial to its characterization), whereas *in front of* is a preposition because it profiles a certain kind of relationship. A particular class represents a complex category that takes the form of a network centered on a prototype.[14] Some of the network's nodes constitute extensions vis-à-vis more central values, and some are schematic with respect to others. I have come to believe that basic and universal linguistic notions—noun and verb being prime examples—have this privileged status precisely because they combine a cognitively salient prototype with a highly abstract schema reflecting a basic cognitive ability. Though itself schematic, the prototype is grounded in experience. It embodies a recurrent commonality so frequent in our everyday experience that it can reasonably be called a *conceptual archetype*. On the other hand, the most schematic characterization comprises cognitive abilities (presumably inborn) which make it possible for structured experience to arise in the first place. Initially manifested in the concrete experience giving rise to the corresponding archetypes, these abilities are subsequently applied to other, more abstract domains.

Consider first the noun class. Largely constituting this complex category are individual nouns, which serve as nodes in the network.[15] A noun is symbolic in nature, residing in the association between a meaning and a phonological shape; I refer to these as its *semantic* and *phonological poles*. Also serving as nodes in the network are schematic symbolic structures which represent—at different levels of abstraction—the commonality that various sets of nouns exhibit. The category prototype is one such structure, as is the highly abstract schema expressing what is common to the class of nouns overall. The archetypal notion defining the noun-class prototype is that of a physical object. The symbolic structure representing this prototype thus takes for its semantic pole the schematized conception of a physical object, which functions as its profile.[16] How do we then describe what all nouns have in common? We expect the overall noun-class schema to invoke the basic cognitive ability that enables us to conceive of physical objects in the first place. This can be identified as conceptual reification, our manifest capacity for grouping a set of entities and manipulating them as a unitary entity for higher-order purposes. Essentially automatic for physical objects (where the constitutive entities are overlapping "splotches" of material substance), it is more evident as a psychological phenomenon when applied to other sorts of elements (e.g. the letters of an *alphabet*) in the creation of non-prototypical nominal referents. A unitary entity resulting from conceptual reification is called a *region*, or alternatively—to avoid the spatial metaphor—a *thing*. At the most schematic level, a noun is thus characterized as an expression that profiles a thing.

The class of verbs is comparably arranged. Its prototype is the archetypal conception of an asymmetrical energetic interaction, specifically an event in which an agent does something to a patient. Among the basic cognitive abilities that figure in this notion, two are essential for characterizing the verb-class schema: the ability to establish relationships, and to scan sequentially through a complex structure. It is claimed that every verb profiles a *process*, defined as a relationship that evolves through time and is scanned sequentially along this axis. A process might also be called a *temporal relation*, where "temporal" refers to both its evolution through time and the sequential nature of its scanning. A non-verbal relational expression can then be described as profiling an *atemporal relation*. It may be atemporal by virtue of being scanned in summary fashion; I analyze infinitives and participles as imposing this kind of holistic perspective on the process designated by a verb stem. Or it may be atemporal simply because evolution through time is not intrinsic or central to the profiled relationship's characterization; relations of this sort are profiled by adjectives, adverbs, and prepositions. The basis for distinguishing these lexical classes lies in the nature of their focal participants. A preposition has two focal participants, its landmark being a thing. On the other hand, an adjective or adverb has just one participant with

focal prominence, the distinction hinging on whether that participant
— by definition the trajector—is a thing or a relationship.[17]
   A specific set of examples may help to clarify these notions.
Consider the use of *yellow* as a noun, as an adjective, and as a verb.
One of its nominal senses can be illustrated by the sentence *Yellow is
a warm color*. Here, as sketched in Figure 1.3(a), *yellow* profiles a
particular kind of thing, namely a region in color space (a range of
possible color sensations).

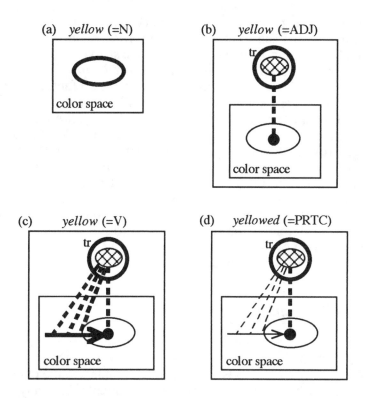

Figure 1.3

Figure 1.3(b) diagrams its adjectival meaning (as in *yellow paper*).
Observe that the same region in color space which is profiled by the
nominal sense of *yellow* functions in its adjectival sense as a kind of
relational landmark (although it lacks the prominence of a focal
element). The trajector is a thing (depicted as a circle), and the cross-
hatched ellipse represents a color sensation that is somehow associated with it (usually being induced by its outer surface). The facet of

the trajector that is most directly involved in the profiled relationship—its *active zone* with respect to that relation (Chapter 2)—is precisely the associated color sensation. Its manifestation within the landmark region of color space is what constitutes the profiled relation (shown as a heavy dashed line).

When *yellow* is used as a verb (e.g. *The paper yellowed*), it profiles a process in which the trajector's color gradually changes and enters the same landmark region. This processual value is diagrammed in Figure 1.3(c): the heavy-line arrow plots the change through time in the active zone's location in the color domain. We can now contrast this verbal sense, in which the profiled relation is followed sequentially in its temporal evolution, with the stative-adjectival meaning of the participle *yellowed*, as in *the yellowed paper*. The verb and the participle evoke the same conceptual content. In fact, the process profiled by the verb serves as the base with respect to which the participle is characterized—something can only be *yellowed* by virtue of having undergone the process of yellowing. Comparison of Figures 1.3(c) and 1.3(d) reveals that the semantic contrast resides in profiling (an aspect of construal). Within the process evoked as its base, the participle profiles only the final, resultant state; this makes it atemporal and hence non-verbal. Observe that, whereas the verb and the participle have the same content but different profiling, the adjective and the participle differ in content but profile the same relationship. A participle of this sort therefore constitutes a kind of adjective (since an expression's profile determines its grammatical class).

1.4. Symbolic complexity

In addition to their meanings and basic classes, there is one more aspect of lexical items that needs to be discussed: their *symbolic complexity*. An expression is symbolically complex to the extent that it is decomposable into smaller symbolic elements. We may distinguish two dimensions of symbolic complexity, the first of which is simply the number of component symbolic elements it contains. Along this parameter, a sequence of lexical items such as *sharp > sharpen > sharpener > pencil sharpener > electric pencil sharpener* displays progressively greater symbolic complexity. We tend to think of lexical items as relatively non-complex, consisting primarily of morphemes and secondarily of polymorphemic stems. But if lexicon is defined as the set of fixed expressions of a language, then in fact the vast majority of lexical items are symbolically complex, for in addition to derived stems they include a virtually limitless supply of compounds, idioms, formulaic expressions, standard collocations, and conventional phrasings of all sorts, irrespective of size and degree of regularity. When this full spectrum is taken into account, individual morphemes are fairly small in number and represent the limiting, degenerate case of lexical items whose symbolic complexity happens to be zero (FCG1: 1.2.2; Pawley 1985; Pawley and Syder 1983).

The other dimension of symbolic complexity is *analyzability*, defined as the extent to which symbolic components are discernible within a complex expression and recognized as contributing to its value. The very process of *fixation* by which composite expressions achieve the status of lexical items creates the potential for wielding them as pre-assembled wholes, without cognizance of their constitutive elements or the compositional relationships that permitted their assembly in the first place. Analyzability is clearly a matter of degree, even among expressions that are frequent, well-entrenched, and fully conventional. I have more confidence in the following introspective ranking, for instance, than in most well-formedness judgments: *diversifier > complainer > printer > computer > propeller > drawer*. While I almost invariably think of a *printer* as 'something that prints', I tend not to understand *computer* specifically as 'something that computes', and I virtually never regard a *propeller* as 'something that propels'. We thus observe a gradation that stretches from novel expressions (e.g. *diversifier*), which by nature exhibit full analyzability, to lexical items that lack it altogether, even though (as with *drawer*) they may have been complex in origin. Along this dimension as well, morphemes represent the limiting, degenerate case of lexical items whose symbolic complexity happens to be zero.

A symbolically complex expression—also termed a *construction*—can be characterized as an *assembly of symbolic structures*. One of these structures enjoys a privileged status, being foregrounded and representing the assembly's primary value, whereas the remaining structures have only a subsidiary, background function. The foregrounded element is called the *composite structure* because it usually incorporates the content of those in the background, referred to as *component structures*. Consider the derived verb *sharpen*, for example. The two component structures are *sharp* (an adjective) and *-en* (a schematic causative/inchoative verb). The composite structure subsumes both the semantic and the phonological content of these components: its semantic pole comprises the integrated conception of the specific causative/inchoative process of sharpening; and the phonological pole, which symbolizes this conception, is the full sequence *sharpen*. Figure 1.4(a) diagrams the construction's global organization. Observe that words in capital letters are used as mnemonic abbreviations for semantic structures, while phonological structures are given orthographically in lower case.

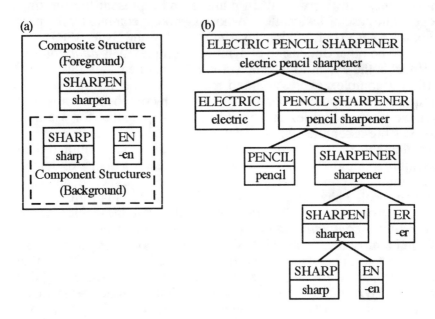

Figure 1.4

Sharpen has only minimal symbolic complexity. There is of course no inherent limit on how complex an expression might be symbolically, even a lexical item. An expression with more than two components usually groups them in some fashion, i.e. it exhibits *constituency*, traditionally represented by bracketing or tree structures. In CG, constituency reduces to a special kind of symbolic assembly involving multiple constructions: an assembly in which the composite structure of one construction functions as a component structure with respect to another construction. Thus *sharpen*, a composite structure with respect to *sharp* and *-en*, is also (along with *-er*) a component of *sharpener*. This pattern can naturally be repeated, yielding composite structures with progressively more elaborate semantic and phonological content; *sharpener*, for example, serves as one component of *pencil sharpener*, which is in turn a component of *electric pencil sharpener*. For complex structures of this sort, it is convenient to use a tree-like diagram, as in Figure 1.4(b), instead of the box notation of 1.4(a). This is merely a notational device, however—CG does not posit phrase trees as distinct formal objects or as an independent aspect of linguistic structure. The configuration in 1.4(b) is simply an assembly of symbolic structures, some of which are construed against the background afforded by others.[18]

Although a composite structure typically incorporates the content of its components, it is rather misleading to think of it as being constructed from them.[19] The meaning of a complex expression is typically (if not invariably) either more specific than any value regularly derivable from its components, or else it conflicts in some way with such values—i.e. it constitutes either an elaboration or an extension vis-à-vis its expected, "compositional" value. The reason is easy to discern. When a novel expression is first used, it is understood with reference to the entire supporting context. The speaker relies on this context, being able to code explicitly only limited, even fragmentary portions of the conception he wishes to evoke. Usually, then, the expression's conventionally determined import at best approximates its actual contextual understanding (the semantic pole of the usage event); it does not contain or convey the intended meaning, but merely furnishes the addressee with a basis for creating it (cf. Reddy 1979). Suppose, now, that the expression occurs with some frequency and gradually achieves the status of a lexical item. As it undergoes fixation, recurrent aspects of its meaning—including some of non-compositional origin—become entrenched and establish themselves as part of what eventually emerges as its conventional linguistic value.

For example, although a *pencil sharpener* is indeed 'something that sharpens pencils', this compositional value falls considerably short of its actual linguistic meaning. *Pencil sharpener* is conventionally understood as indicating a specific type of physical object, one with various properties not subsumed by the individual meaning of either *pencil* or *sharpener*. Of course, its ability to sharpen pencils is what we are most concerned with. So while the components and their compositional value fail to exhaust the composite conception, they do reflect important features of it, thus enabling an addressee who does not yet know the term to direct his attention to the proper element presented by the context. From this contextual support arise non-compositional aspects of meaning which are then established as part of the term's conventional import.

Since non-compositional specifications figure in our actual understanding of expressions at every stage (from initial use to full conventionalization), they must be recognized as falling within the legitimate scope of linguistic meaning and linguistic semantics. CG thus takes the position that complex expressions exhibit only *partial compositionality*. They do in fact manifest conventional patterns of composition: the relation a composite structure bears to its components is neither random nor arbitrary. But at the same time, a composite structure is not constructed out of its components, nor is it consistently or fully predictable.[20] Rather than *constituting* a composite structure, the component structures *correspond* to certain facets of it, offering some degree of *motivation* for expressing the composite conception in the manner chosen. And because the composite structure represents a distinct entity that is not in general reducible to its components, a construction is described as an assembly of symbolic structures.

A construction thus comprises multiple symbolic structures linked by correspondences, one structure being foregrounded with respect to the others. Consider the compound *jar lid*, diagrammed in Figure 1.5. The two component structures, *jar* and *lid*, are placed at the bottom to indicate their background status. Phonologically, each is a word, as represented by the ellipses labeled W. At the semantic pole, each is a noun by virtue of profiling a thing. *Jar* profiles a specific type of container, whereas *lid* designates the cover for a container of an unspecified nature (i.e. it evokes the schematic conception of a container as an unprofiled facet of its base).[21] The composite structure *jar lid* consists phonologically of a two-word sequence, the first word taking primary stress. Semantically, it profiles the cover for a jar in particular.

At each pole, correspondences link the component structures to one another and to the composite structure. Represented by dotted lines, the correspondences can be thought of as specifying how the components are *integrated* to form the composite structure, or alternatively, how the composite conception is *dissociated* into overlapping facets susceptible to individual symbolization. The phonological correspondences have the effect of identifying *jar* as the word immediately preceding *lid* in the temporal sequence. The semantic correspondences equate the schematic container evoked by *lid* with the specific container profiled by *jar*. To the extent that an expression is compositional and lends itself to the building-block metaphor, we can speak of assembling the composite structure from its components by

superimposing corresponding entities and merging their specifications. In general, however, the compositional value thus obtained will
at best approximate the actual composite structure, which bears to it a
relationship of either elaboration or extension. The discrepancy happens not to be very noticeable for *jar lid*, and in what follows it will
not be a prime concern.

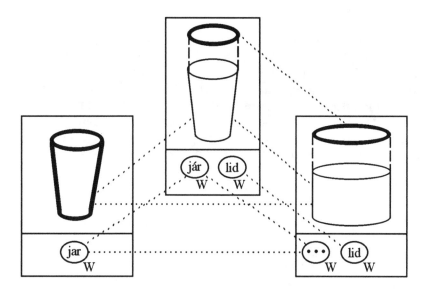

Figure 1.5

In a construction, the component and composite structures are
linked not only by correspondences but also by relationships of categorization. It is usual for one component structure to elaborate a
substructure of the other. In the case of *jar lid*, the schematic container
evoked by *lid* functions as an *elaboration site* (or *e-site*), being specified in finer detail by *jar*.[22] Moreover, both component structures can
be thought of as categorizing either the composite structure as a whole
or some facet of it. (I suggest, in fact, that the background/foreground
alignment of the component and composite structures reduces to the
inherent asymmetry between a categorizing structure and the target of
categorization.) In a typical construction, one component is schematic
with respect to the composite structure as a whole: they construe the
scene in the same fashion, particularly in regard to profiling, and differ only in the composite structure's greater specificity. The compo-

nent structure with this property is called the construction's *profile determinant*, since it has the same profile as the composite whole. From Figure 1.5, it is evident that *lid* functions as the profile determinant of *jar lid* (i.e. the composite expression's conceptual referent is the lid, not the jar).

1.5. Extension to grammar

We have focused thus far on lexicon, even though our main concern is grammar. A basic claim of the theory is that there is in fact no distinction: lexicon and grammar form a continuum, structures at any point along it being fully and properly described as symbolic in nature. By and large, the elements traditionally ascribed to grammar tend to be quite schematic (semantically and/or phonologically), whereas those assigned to lexicon tend toward greater specificity. Yet the difference is clearly one of degree, and any particular line of demarcation would be arbitrary. Numerous elements usually considered "grammatical"—e.g. modals, demonstratives, prepositions—are obviously meaningful in many of their uses.[23] At the same time, elements of undisputedly "lexical" status run the full gamut in terms of both specificity and concreteness, and some (e.g. *entity*, *property*, *have*) are at least as abstract as certain grammatical elements.

The fixed symbolic structures of a language are distributed in a multidimensional space whose major parameters are schematicity and symbolic complexity.[24] "Typical" lexical items (e.g. *sharpen*) tend to cluster in a certain region: they have only limited symbolic complexity, and are fairly specific both semantically and phonologically. Bearing in mind the absence of any rigid boundaries, we can next observe that various kinds of grammatical elements fall in other, complementary regions. A "grammatical morpheme" (e.g. the *-en* of *sharpen*) is symbolically non-complex and phonologically specific, but at the semantic pole it is quite schematic. The abstract symbolic structure that defines a grammatical class is schematic at the phonological pole as well. For instance, the noun-class schema is maximally non-specific phonologically, and the only semantic specification is that it profiles a thing (i.e. any result of conceptual reification). What about grammatical rules? The symbolic structures that serve in this capacity occupy the remaining region of the multidimensional space. They are not only schematic (at each pole) but symbolically complex as well.

No distinction is drawn in this framework between grammatical rules and grammatical constructions.[25] Rules are simply schematizations of symbolically complex expressions, or constructions, and can thus be described as *constructional schemas*. Abstracted from some array of specific expressions (both fixed and novel), a constructional schema is a template that mirrors their symbolic complexity and captures whatever commonality they exhibit. Sketched in Figure 1.6, for example, is the constructional schema that characterizes *jar lid* (Figure 1.5) as well as an open-ended set of other noun-noun compounds. It specifies that each component structure is a noun (i.e. it profiles a thing), as is the composite structure, whose profile corresponds to that of the second component. The profile of the first component corresponds to a thing that is associated with the second component's profile in some unspecified manner. Phonologically, the first component is equated with the word that directly precedes the second; it is further specified as bearing primary stress at the composite structure level. Comparison of Figures 1.5 and 1.6 reveals that they are precisely parallel except for the latter's greater schematicity.

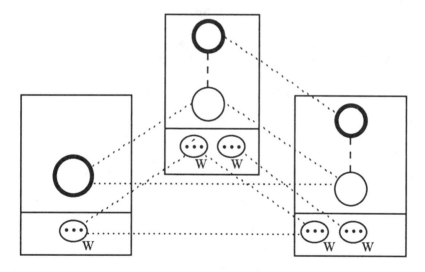

Figure 1.6

Constructional schemas emerge to represent the commonalities observable at any level of abstraction. They range from low-level schemas based on just a few, quite similar expressions (such as [N lid] for *jar lid* and *coffin lid*) all the way up to high-level schemas embodying the broadest possible generalizations (e.g. [X Y] for the class of all two-member compounds). Like lexical meanings, they form complex categories describable as networks centered on prototypes (cf. Lakoff 1987: case study 3). The nodes of such a network include complex expressions as well as constructional schemas, characterized at various levels of schematicity and linked by categorizing relationships of elaboration and extension. Networks of this kind thus incorporate a speaker's knowledge of not only grammatical patterns but also their exploitation in conventional usage. Granted minimal and reasonable assumptions about language processing, they account for both distributional restrictions and the sanction of novel expressions (CIS: ch. 10).

As we shift our attention from lexicon to phenomena traditionally viewed as falling within the province of grammar, the expressions to be accounted for are often novel in certain respects and tend to exhibit greater symbolic complexity than lexical items. The description of grammatical structure does not, however, require a substantially different approach or a battery of unrelated constructs, but merely elaboration and further application of notions already introduced in regard to lexicon. For instance, the same constructs needed for lexical semantics—domains, scope, background, perspective, profiling, etc.—also characterize the meanings of novel expressions, regardless of their size (phrases, clauses, entire sentences). The same notions that figure in the description of complex lexical items—e.g. correspondence, component vs. composite structure, profile determinant, elaboration site—apply to constructions and constructional schemas at any level of organization. I claim, moreover, that basic grammatical constructs, including those pertaining to clause structure, have semantic characterizations based on construal and conceptual archetypes.

Grammar resides in patterns of composition, which take the form of constructional schemas. Collectively, these patterns sanction the progressive assembly of expressions of any size and degree of symbolic complexity. At a given level of organization, a construction or constructional schema includes component and composite structures linked by relationships of correspondence and categorization. The composite structure is *foregrounded* in the dual sense of (i) being the target of categorization by the components, and (ii) being accessible to serve as a component (or categorizing) structure at a higher level of organization. We have seen that one component is usually schematic with respect to the composite structure as a whole and has the same profile (i.e. their profiles are linked by a correspondence); it is thus called the profile determinant. We have also noted that one component typically elaborates a salient substructure of the other (its elaboration site). More precisely, the e-site corresponds to the elaborating structure's profile and is schematic with respect to that structure as a whole.

These conceptual properties of a typical construction (or constructional schema) support the definition of certain traditional grammatical notions. First, a *head* is simply the profile determinant at a given level of organization. Consider the nominal expression *people with problems*. At one level of organization, the preposition *with* combines with the noun *problems* to form the prepositional phrase *with problems*. At this level *with* functions as the head, since the relationship it profiles is also profiled by the composite expression. Then, at a higher level of organization, *with problems* combines with *people* to yield *people with problems*. The head at this second level is *people*, since the conceptual referent of the full nominal is the people, not the prepositional relationship. We can next define a *complement* as a component structure that elaborates a salient substructure of the head. *Problems* is thus a complement of *with* in the phrase *with problems*: the head *with* profiles an atemporal relation between two focal participants, one of which—its landmark—is elaborated by *problems*. Conversely, a *modifier* is a component structure a salient substructure of which is elaborated by the head. *With problems* is thus a modifier of *people* in *people with problems*: the head is *people*, which elaborates the schematic trajector of the relationship profiled by the prepositional phrase.

It was noted earlier that a lexical item's grammatical class is determined by the nature of its profile: a noun profiles a thing, a verb refers to a process, a preposition designates an atemporal relation with a thing as landmark, etc. Comparable definitions can be offered for the classes associated with higher-level grammatical constituents, i.e. for notions like noun phrase, prepositional phrase, and finite clause. Although the characterization of these traditional categories makes reference to more than just profiling, it conforms to the basic claim of CG, in that only semantic, phonological, and symbolic structures are invoked. For example, a prepositional phrase is a construction—an assembly of symbolic structures—with a number of specific properties. First, its two component structures are a preposition and a noun phrase (each definable in semantic terms). Second, their phonological integration is such that the preposition (directly) precedes the noun phrase at the composite structure level. Third, the composite structure profiles the same relationship as the preposition (i.e. the preposition is the profile determinant, hence the head). Finally, the profile of the noun phrase corresponds to the preposition's landmark. The nominal is thus a complement of the preposition, whose landmark it elaborates.

I have suggested that the noun and verb classes are universal and fundamental to grammar because they represent the pairing of essential cognitive abilities with highly salient conceptual archetypes. The cognitive abilities afford schematic characterizations of the categories: conceptual reification in the case of nouns, and for verbs the capacity to establish relationships and to scan sequentially through a complex structure. Schematically, then, a noun profiles a thing (the result of conceptual reification), while a verb designates a process (a relationship scanned sequentially in its temporal evolution). The conceptual archetypes that initially manifest these abilities serve to define the category prototypes: the conceptual referent of a prototypical noun is a physical object, and for a prototypical verb, an agent-patient interaction. Each of these basic classes figures in the characterization of a higher-level constituent type that is likewise universal and fundamental to grammatical structure. The constituent types corresponding to nouns and verbs (their "maximal projections") are, respectively, a noun phrase and a finite clause. When due allowance is made for the intrinsic difference between things and processes, these two constituent types show extensive parallelism (FCG2).

Let us first consider a noun phrase, for which the term *nominal* is preferred in CG.[26] A nominal always profiles a thing, and is thus itself a noun under the broadest (most schematic) definition of that category. It is a noun with special properties, however. Whereas a simple lexical noun (e.g. *pencil*) merely names a *type* of thing, a nominal (*the pencil*; *this pencil*; *a pencil*; etc.) always designates an *instance* of some type.[27] Moreover, the profiled thing instance is always *grounded*, by which I mean that there is some specification of its relationship to the *ground* (i.e. the speech event and its participants). Grounding merits extended discussion (cf. Langacker 1985; CIS: ch. 12; FCG2: chs. 3, 6), but here we need only observe that a primary (and sometimes the sole) aspect of nominal grounding is a specification of (in)definiteness. Simple nouns and full nominals can thus be described as serving different cognitive/communicative functions. Lexical nouns effect the classification of our world into thing types, or basic "kinds" (cf. Wierzbicka 1988: ch. 9). On the other hand, nominals have the further discourse function of enabling the speaker and addressee to coordinate their mental reference to specific instances of those types. Like nouns, nominals are susceptible to both prototypic and schematic characterization. A nominal is prototypical when it profiles a physical object instance whose type is specified by a head noun and its grounding by another element such as an article, demonstrative, or quantifier. Schematically, a nominal is simply an expression that profiles a grounded instance of any thing type.

The relation between a noun and a nominal is precisely paralleled by that between a verb and a finite clause. By itself, a simple lexical verb (e.g. *wash*) merely names a process type, whereas a finite clause (*I washed it*; *You should wash them*; *Jill may not wash the cat*) profiles a grounded instance of that type. For finite clauses in English, the primary grounding elements are "tense" and the modals. A prototypical finite clause is one that designates an agent-patient interaction, where the agent is coded by the subject nominal, the patient by the direct object, and their interaction by the verb. Schematically, a finite clause is simply an expression that profiles a grounded instance of any process type. And just as a nominal is a special sort of noun (because it profiles a thing), so a finite clause qualifies as a verb (in the broadest sense) by virtue of designating a process.

2. Application to clause structure

Our objective in what follows is to examine more carefully the structure of finite clauses as conceived and described in CG.[28] Even in this brief survey, numerous complex and interrelated topics deserve consideration, including clause types, transitivity, grammatical relations, voice, case marking, and accusativity vs. ergativity. The key to understanding these phenomena is an array of conceptual archetypes that define the prototypical values of grammatical elements. Of course, these elements are also used for the coding of non-archetypal situations; abstract commonalities motivate extensions from the prototype. As with lexical items, therefore, the meanings of grammatical constructs represent complex categories, comprising multiple values linked by relationships of elaboration and extension to form a network.

2.1. Conceptual archetypes

Relevant to clause structure are numerous conceptual archetypes, some of which are incorporated as components of others. One set of archetypes related in this fashion includes, first, the conception of a physical object, next the conception of a physical object occupying a location in space, and finally that of an object moving through space (i.e. changing location through time). Another such hierarchy comprises the conception of a physical object, that of an object being in a certain state (or exhibiting a certain property), and that of its undergoing a change of state (or property). Conceptual archetypes also arise from varied sorts of bodily experience. In the mental sphere, they include the experience of perceiving, of thinking, and of feeling emotions. Especially significant in the physical realm is experience of a "force-dynamic" nature: muscular exertion, being subjected to forces, resisting and overcoming them, carrying out a physical action. Force is also crucial to the archetypal conception of one object impinging on another and causing a change.

A number of conceptual archetypes come together to form a complex archetypal notion that I call the *canonical event model*. One of its components is the *billiard-ball model*: the conception of physical objects moving around in space and impacting other objects, which undergo some reaction due to the force thereby transmitted. A second component, dubbed the *stage model*, is a reflection of perceptual (especially visual) experience. In the normal arrangment, we direct our gaze outward to a general locus of viewing attention—the "onstage region". Within this region, we focus our attention on specific objects and their interactions (just as we watch the actors in a play from our viewing position offstage in the audience). The canonical event model further subsumes two *role archetypes*, namely agent and patient. An *agent* volitionally carries out a physical action, being both the instigator and the source of energy. The term *patient* is used in a narrow sense to indicate an object that undergoes an internal change of state. Summarized in (2), the canonical event model therefore represents the normal observation of a prototypical action.

(2) [V ----> [... **AG ⇒ PAT** ...]]

V, AG, and PAT stand respectively for the viewer, the agent, and the patient. The dashed arrow indicates a perceptual relationship, and the double arrow an interaction involving the transmission of energy.

Whereas the outer brackets delimit the viewer's maximal "scope" (everything within the field of view), the inner brackets mark the on-stage region (the general locus of viewing attention). Finally, the import of the boldface type is that the agent-patient interaction is the specific focus of attention (which necessarily falls within the onstage region).

The linguistic import of the canonical event model is that it furnishes the prototypical values of various grammatical notions pertaining to clause structure. Prototypically, a finite clause profiles a process of this sort construed as constituting a single event. The prototypical role of a subject is that of an agent, and the typical direct object is a patient. The notion of transitivity involves a number of parameters (Hopper and Thompson 1980) all interpretable as reflecting some aspect of the canonical event conception (Rice 1987a). There is, then, a natural correlation between this idealized cognitive model and the structure of a transitive finite clause. When a canonical event is coded linguistically in the maximally unmarked way, the clausal head is a verb that designates the agent-patient interaction, the agent and patient being coded by the subject and direct object nominals, respectively. Non-focal participants peripheral to the profiled interaction, such as *Adam* in (3), are expressed as obliques.

(3) *In the garden, Eve sliced an apple for Adam.*

A clause-level adverb like *in the garden* specifies the global *setting* within which the profiled event occurs. This setting can be equated with the general locus of viewing attention, represented in (2) by the inner brackets. The linguistic analog of the viewer, finally, is the speaker (and secondarily the addressee), who conceptualizes the event in its setting and constructs the finite clause to express it. The viewer's position—offstage and external to the profiled interaction—corresponds to the unmarked character of third-person participants. Nevertheless, because a finite clause and the nominals it contains are grounded, the speaker and hearer do fall within its overall scope, the linguistic counterpart of the maximal field of view (the outer brackets in (2)).

Despite its privileged status, the canonical event model is only one of the conceptual archetypes for the coding of which languages tend to evolve a basic clause type. Corresponding to the archetype of a physical object moving through space is a clause in which the head is an intransitive motion verb, the subject codes the mover, and a locative complement specifies the source, path, or goal of the motion (e.g. *Joe walked to the store*). Reflecting the archetypal conception of an object simply being in a certain state is a special clause type in which an adjective expresses the essential content of the profiled relationship (*The apple is ripe*).[29] It is common for languages to develop a special clause type—often involving a "dative" or "indirect object" with subject-like properties—used primarily for relationships of mental experience (cf. Klaiman 1981; Smith 1993).

A language thus exhibits an array of basic clause types tailored for particular conceptual archetypes, which provide their prototypical values. From their prototypes, these clausal structures are extended and adapted for the coding of other kinds of situations in ways that are clearly motivated but are nonetheless matters of language-specific convention. To take just one example, two-participant relationships in the domain of mental experience (e.g. 'see', 'understand', 'want', 'love', 'ask', 'deceive', 'encourage') are treated differently by English and Samoan (Cook 1993a). English codes them by means of transitive clauses (*I see you; They want it; She encouraged me*), which constitute extensions vis-à-vis the prototype of an agent-patient interaction. The extension is motivated by an abstract commonality between, on the one hand, the transmission of energy from an active source (the agent) to a passive goal (the patient), and on the other hand, the notion of a mental path (of perception, directed emotion, or social influence) leading from a more active experiencer to a less active target. By contrast, Samoan codes these relationships by means of the same clause type used for spatial motion along a path to a goal.[30] Here the extension is motivated by the abstract commonality between a goal-directed path in the spatial and in the mental realms. Observe that all three conceptions—energy transmission, spatial motion, directed mental activity—instantiate the fundamental source-path-goal image schema. Hence the two languages, while starting from different physically grounded conceptual archetypes, nevertheless exploit the same image-schematic commonality to effect the metaphorical structuring and grammatical coding of these mental relationships.

By virtue of such extensions, a given clause type is conventionally applied to a broad variety of situations. Semantically it forms a complex category, a network of values centered on the prototype defined by the conceptual archetype that spawns it. A grammatical construct pertinent to the characterization of distinct clause types (or variants thereof) likewise represents a complex category subsuming a multiplicity of values. Consider the notion finite clause itself. If we have correctly described its prototype as profiling an agent-patient interaction construed as a single event, it nonetheless encompasses a wide array of values corresponding to other archetypes and the extensions they engender. As more archetypes and extensions are taken into account, definitions reflecting their commonality become progressively more schematic, so that ultimately—for the class overall—we can only say that a finite clause profiles a grounded instance of any process type. In similar fashion, the notion of transitivity assumes a different character when extended from physical energy transfer to the domain of perception, thought, and emotion. The most schematic definition of a transitive clause merely specifies the inclusion within the processual profile of two participants with the status of trajector and landmark, which are manifested by the subject and object nominals.

2.2. Grammatical relations

Recall that certain linguistic notions are taken to be fundamental and universal because they combine a salient prototype with a schematic characterization reflecting a basic cognitive ability. Among those notions are the grammatical relations subject and object. How best to define these relations is of course a vexed, contentious, and confusing issue. To sort things out, we must distinguish carefully among a number of possible grounds for definition, including case marking, grammatical behavior, syntactic configuration, semantic role, discourse function, and prominence.

   An initial question is whether the subject and object relations can in fact be defined in terms of something more basic, or whether they should be considered syntactic primitives (as in relational grammar). By its very nature, CG is committed to the former option. The claim that grammar reduces to assemblies of symbolic structures rules out the possibility of undefinable, purely "syntactic" primitives. Another question is whether these relations are actually universal, in view of the fact that there may be no grammatical behavior characteristic of putative subjects and objects in all languages, and that in certain languages grammatical rules make little if any reference to these notions (Foley and Van Valin 1977, 1984; Schachter 1976, 1977). This line of thought presupposes that particular grammatical behaviors (such as those described in Keenan 1976, Keenan and Comrie 1977) are properly invoked for the definition of subjects and objects. By contrast, CG takes the position that such behaviors are merely symptomatic of their characterization. Subjects and objects are

uniformly definable even for languages whose grammatical exploitation of these notions is very limited (FCG2: 7.3.1.4).

Assuming, then, that the subject and object relations are
universal and non-primitive, how can they be characterized? The traditional approach in generative grammar has been to define them in
terms of syntactic tree configurations: as an NP directly dominated by
S or by VP, respectively (Chomsky 1965). Because these configurations are not overtly manifested in all instances where subjects and
objects are recognized, this approach leads to derivations from hypothesized underlying structures in which the relations are consistently
represented. Such derivations are precluded in CG by the *content
requirement*, which specifies that the only units ascribable to a linguistic system are (i) semantic, phonological, and symbolic structures
that occur as parts of actual expressions, (ii) schematizations of permitted structures, and (iii) categorizing relationships between permitted structures. The generative configurational definitions run afoul of
the content requirement in two respects: by positing underlying structures not directly manifested in actual expressions; and by their reference to syntactic tree structures, conceived as autonomous formal objects (neither semantic, nor phonological, nor symbolic—cf. fn. 18).

The remaining factors are case, semantic role, discourse function, and prominence. I reserve the term *case* for overt morphological
means of signaling either the semantic role of nominals or their grammatical relations in a clause. Though morphological case marking
does concern us, it is clearly inadequate as a universal basis for the
actual definition of subjects and objects. The other three factors are
however relevant. More specifically, semantic role and discourse function serve to characterize the subject and object prototypes, whereas
a particular kind of prominence offers the only viable basis for a fully
general schematic characterization.

Consider first the prototypes. I have already made the suggestion—neither new nor overly controversial—that the semantic roles
agent and patient are respectively prototypical for subjects and direct
objects. It is also commonly stated that subjects, and perhaps even
objects, tend to be topics as well. According to Givón, for example, a
subject is the primary clausal topic, and an object, the secondary
clausal topic (1984:138). It stands to reason that subjects and objects
should assume this kind of discourse function. For one thing, the
elements unproblematically identified as subjects and objects are full,
grounded nominals. Whereas simple nouns merely furnish type specifications, nominals designate particular instances of those types and
function in discourse to coordinate mental reference to these in-

stances. Furthermore, the subject and object relations hold at the clausal level of organization,[31] and the clause is a basic unit of discourse.

I thus accept the validity of describing a prototypical subject as being both an agent and the primary clausal topic, and a prototypical direct object as both a patient and the secondary clausal topic. It goes without saying, of course, that the agent and patient roles are at best typical of subjects and objects, certainly not universal. Any schematic characterizations proposed as valid for all subjects and objects would have to be considerably more abstract. It should further be evident that the notion clausal topic stands in need of clarification.[32] Let us note just two basic options. On the one hand, the term may refer to an entity accorded a special kind of salience throughout an extended stretch of discourse—we might describe it as a *reference point* serving to situate, organize, and interpret the specifications of multiple clauses in an ongoing fashion. This is apparently what Givón has in mind, for he speaks of the subject as coding "the most important, recurrent, continuous topic". If defined in this way, however, topic status can only be part of the subject and object prototypes, since it can hardly be ascribed to every instance of either category. Alternatively, one might contemplate a weaker, essentially local definition whereby a clausal topic serves as a reference point only within the confines of a single clause. Such a description could very well be applicable to all subjects and objects, hence part of their schematic characterization. I believe, though, that it is indistinguishable from the schematic definition I will propose based on figure/ground organization.

In a given language, extensions from the prototype occur depending on the array of clause types that develop and the range of situations for which they are conventionally used. The semantic import of the subject or object relation is thus a complex category whose values include both specific roles the subject or object can assume and more schematic characterizations capturing the commonality that certain roles exhibit. Offering natural points of attraction for extension are a number of conceptual archetypes which, like agent and patient, pertain to the role of participants in a process.[33] One such archetypal role is that of an *instrument*: an object manipulated by an agent to affect another participant (hence a conduit in the transmission of energy). An *experiencer* is an individual engaged in mental activity (be it perceptual, emotive, or intellectual). Unlike a patient (defined as undergoing an internal change of state), a *mover* changes position with respect to its surroundings. The term *zero* is employed for an entity that merely occurs in some location or exhibits a certain property. These role archetypes naturally give rise to metaphorical extensions. There are also hybrid roles, intermediate cases, and other role conceptions that may achieve some salience. One should therefore not expect linguistic theory to provide a brief and exhaustive list of the roles with potential grammatical significance.

Role archetypes can be grouped in various ways reflecting either abstract commonalities or the structure of more inclusive archetypal conceptions. One such group comprises patient, experiencer, mover, and zero, all of which instantiate a more schematic notion for which I use the term *theme*. The roles in question are those characteristic of the single participant in a minimal, conceptually autonomous *thematic process*, as in *They melted* (PAT), *I itch* (EXPER), *It rose* (MVR), and *She is tall* (ZERO). These processes are autonomous in the sense that we can conceive of them in isolation, independently of causation or the transmission of energy from another participant. To the extent that we conceptualize a process without reference to causation or energy transfer, I say that it receives an *absolute construal*.[34] Of course, a thematic process does not have to be construed in absolute fashion. When portrayed as being instigated or executed by some kind of force or energy input, it is said to have an *energetic construal*: *We melted it*; *She tickled me*; *He threw it*. A series of energetic interactions, each inducing the next, is called an *action chain*.[35] The notion of agency implies at least a minimal action chain, wherein the agent induces a thematic process by exerting some force on the theme (AG $\Rightarrow$ TH). The archetypal conception of using an instrument to affect another entity comprises a longer action chain, in which the instrument is an intermediary in the flow of energy (AG $\Rightarrow$ INSTR $\Rightarrow$ TH).

Observe that the agent and instrument roles are inherently nonthematic. A thematic process is potentially absolute, and if it is construed energetically, it constitutes the action chain's terminus (the ultimate *energy sink*). By definition, however, an agent or instrument is a *source* of energy transmitted farther downstream along an action chain, hence its construal is necessarily energetic. On this basis we can distinguish between the *source domain* of an interaction, comprising those elements which lie upstream in the flow of energy with respect to others (X $\Rightarrow$ ...), and the *target domain*, which lies exclusively downstream (... $\Rightarrow$ X). Within each domain, a further distinction can be drawn between an *active participant* and a *passive* one, depending on whether its role is in some sense *initiative*. The active source-domain participant is clearly the agent, whereas an instrument is merely a passive conduit in the flow of energy. The grounds for the contrast are less evident in the target domain, since any kind of theme — *qua* theme — is purely passive.

The key to the matter resides in the dual nature of the experiencer role. In its thematic capacity, an experiencer does nothing more than passively register sensations (*She's happy*; *I ache*; *That pleased me*). Yet we also find expressions where a person engaged exclusively in mental activity can nonetheless be attributed some kind of initiative role. The activity may be quasi-agentive, in the sense of being volitional and effortful (*He meditated*; *I figured it out*). But even in expressions such as *She likes it* or *I see them*, where force-dynamic notions are either negligible or absent altogether, the experiencer subject may reasonably be considered initiative in certain respects: it is the only participant portrayed as being active in any way (the object's role is zero); it generates (or at least entertains) a mental representation of the object; and it is thought of as the source of a mental or perceptual path that extends to the object. Of course, an experiencer that is active and initiative will tend to be construed as a source-domain participant and coded as the clausal subject. In *She likes it*, for example, the profiled mental interaction (of the form EXPER ----> ZERO) is construed as an abstract analog of the energetic interaction (AG $\Rightarrow$ PAT) that is prototypical for transitivity, so it is coded linguistically as a transitive clause. There are however situations in which an active experiencer is relegated to the target domain. Consider *I showed him the picture*. Here the agentive subject initiates the overall event, which terminates in the experiential relationship between *him* and *the picture*. Because this relation (EXPER ---> ZERO) lies downstream in the flow of energy, and is not itself energetic, it comprises the target domain, which thus has both an active and a passive participant.[36]

We can now describe the more schematic values assumed by the subject and object relations as they undergo extension from their prototypes to accommodate progressively wider arrays of data. Sentences like the following, cited by Fillmore (1968) to motivate his subject-choice hierarchy, show that the subject in English may be an instrument (in the absence of an agent), or even a theme (in the absence of an agent and instrument):

(4) a. *Leona opened the door with this key.*
     $$(\mathbf{AG} \Rightarrow \mathbf{INSTR} \Rightarrow \mathbf{MVR})$$
     b. *This key opened the door.*
     $$(\mathrm{AG} \Rightarrow \mathbf{INSTR} \Rightarrow \mathbf{MVR})$$
     c. *The door opened.*
     $$(\mathrm{AG} \Rightarrow \mathrm{INSTR} \Rightarrow \mathbf{MVR})$$

(5) a. *My daughter woke me up with an explosion.*
     $$(\mathbf{AG} \Rightarrow \mathbf{INSTR} \Rightarrow \mathbf{EXPER})$$
     b. *An explosion woke me up.*
     $$(\mathrm{AG} \Rightarrow \mathbf{INSTR} \Rightarrow \mathbf{EXPER})$$
     c. *I woke up.*
     $$(\mathrm{AG} \Rightarrow \mathrm{INSTR} \Rightarrow \mathbf{EXPER})$$

As shown by the formulas, I analyze these sentences as profiling action chains of different lengths. Examples (4)a and (5)a profile the entire action chain leading from agent (ultimate energy source) to theme (energy sink). Examples (4)b and (5)b evoke that same action chain as their base, but they profile only the instrument-theme interaction. Finally, examples (4)c and (5)c designate only the thematic process.[37] It is evident that the subject-choice hierarchy (AG > INSTR > TH) recapitulates the order of participant involvement in the flow of energy along an action chain, various segments of which may stand in profile. It should also be evident that the choice of subject follows a consistent principle in such data: the subject is always the *head* (i.e. the initial element) in the *profiled* portion of the action chain. The rule is valid even for examples (4)c and (5)c, where the profile comprises only the thematic process (a degenerate action chain).

We can accommodate further ranges of data in terms of the metaphorical extension of these notions to the domains of mental experience and social interaction. For instance, the events described in (6) and (7) do not imply any physical contact or energy, yet we construe the subject metaphorically as exerting or transmitting an abstract force that induces the thematic process.

(6) a. *The shaman frightened the children with his mask.*
     b. *His mask frightened the children.*

(7) a. *He persuaded me with his lucrative offer.*
     b. *His lucrative offer persuaded me.*

There are, however, many transitive clauses which seem not to involve, even metaphorically, the conception of an action chain or the
transfer of energy. Prime examples are relationships of mental or
perceptual contact where the object is totally unaffected (EXPER ---->
ZERO):

(8) a. *She barely remembers her childhood.*
     b. *I can see the mountains in the distance.*

Such cases would appear to demand a still more schematic characterization, by which a subject is simply the more active participant in
an asymmetrical interaction.
    Starting from the prototype, we have now considered several
values of the subject relation, each more schematic and broadly applicable than its predecessor: agent; head of a profiled (physical) action
chain; head of any action chain (physical or metaphorical); active participant in an asymmetrical interaction. Even so, we have not yet
accounted for all the data. There are, for example, clauses which profile relationships that are perfectly symmetrical in terms of their conceptual content but nevertheless distinguish between a subject and an
object:

(9) a. *Line A intersects line B.*
     b. *Janet resembles Margo.*

I suggest that there is a subject-object asymmetry here, but one that
the speaker imposes in construing the situation for linguistic purposes. The subject is in each case the entity that the speaker is concerned with situating or assessing, the object serving as a landmark
for that purpose. It is reasonable, then, to describe the subject as the
primary figure with respect to the profiled relationship (or the primary
clausal topic, in the local sense of the term). I believe this highly schematic characterization, invoking the basic cognitive ability of figure/
ground organization, to be valid for all subjects. In most instances, a
clause's conceptual content affords some basis for the choice—the
most active participant stands out as the natural focus of attention. But
even in canonical agent-patient interactions we have the capacity to
override such motivation and make an alternative choice (as we do in

passive clauses). In the last analysis, subject choice is always a matter of construal.

Precisely analogous comments apply to the direct object category. If the role archetype patient defines the category prototype, we must nevertheless acknowledge the centrality of a slightly more schematic characterization, namely as the *tail* of a profiled action chain. By this definition, a direct object lies downstream from the subject in the flow of energy, but might instantiate any thematic role; the object is, for example, a patient in (3), a mover in (4)a-b, and an experiencer in (5)a-b. The analogy continues in (6) and (7), which show that the action chain in question can also reside in non-physical, metaphorically structured domains. Expressions like those in (8) motivate a further abstraction, whereby a direct object is characterized schematically as the passive participant in an asymmetrical interaction. Finally, the examples in (9) point out the need for a value based on construal alone. At the most schematic level, I suggest that a direct object is properly described as the secondary figure with respect to the profiled relationship.

Various threads can now be gathered together. As an inherent aspect of its internal structure, virtually every relational expression — even a simple adjective or preposition — accords special prominence to one or more focal elements. Recall that a trajector is defined as the primary figure within a profiled relationship, and a landmark (should there be one) as the secondary figure. One kind of relationship is a process, which functions as the profile of a verb and its higher-level "projections", including a finite clause. A verb stem thus imposes a particular trajector/landmark (figure/ground) organization on the process it designates. The same is true of a finite clause, whose own processual profile and trajector/landmark alignment is often inherited from the verb stem, but may diverge owing to passivization, aspectual modification, or other phenomena involved in assembling a full clause from the stem. Although the terms subject and object are used in multiple ways pertaining to different levels of structure, in their central use — the one that concerns us here — they refer to overt nominals (i.e. full noun phrases) at the clausal level of organization. A subject, then, is characterized schematically as a nominal that elaborates the clausal trajector; more precisely, its profile corresponds to the primary figure within the process profiled at the clausal level. Analogously, a direct object is defined schematically as a nominal that elaborates the clausal landmark, its profile corresponding to the secondary figure within the designated process.[38]

2.3. Case marking

In the last analysis, subject and object status reduces to the focal prominence of relational elements. While this prominence has a natural tendency to correlate with certain semantic roles, the extent to which it does so is variable, and ultimately it represents a distinct dimension of conceptual and linguistic organization. This brings us to the topic of case markers, which are often thought of as semantically empty morphological devices used mechanically to signal grammatical relations. In CG, they are necessarily analyzed as symbolic in nature, hence as meaningful elements. I suggest, moreover, that their semantic value pertains for the most part to semantic roles. It is true that some languages have case markings, usually called *nominative* and *accusative*, that consistently mark subjects and direct objects (though they may have other uses as well). This does not render them meaningless, since the subject and object relations are themselves attributed conceptual import. To the extent that nominative and accusative case are specifically identified with these relations, they assume and symbolize the same conceptual value. And since subject and object are themselves correlated with semantic roles, having agent and patient as their prototypes, the two cases are also role-related.

For cases other than nominative and accusative, the function of marking semantic roles is more evident. Case categories generally coalesce around particular role archetypes, which constitute their prototypical values. Perhaps most obviously, the archetypal conception of an instrument provides the central value for the *instrumental* case. Likewise, the experiencer role is prototypical for *dative* case. One should not be misled by the frequent use of the dative to mark indirect objects: it is not always limited to indirect objects,[39] which I analyze in any event as representing a semantic role rather than a grammatical relation (fn. 36). The meaningfulness and role-based nature of locational cases (*locative, ablative, allative*, etc.) should be readily apparent. Furthermore, I will argue below that *ergative* and *absolutive* case, which take agent and theme as their respective prototypes, are only incidentally associated with grammatical relations.

Whereas prepositions (more generally, adpositions) profile atemporal relations, the elements that I would identify as case markers in the strictest sense do not affect the nominal status of the structures they combine with. They can thus themselves be analyzed as nominal in character, on the assumption that a derivational element is generally a schematic representative of the class it derives.[40] From an unmarked nominal, a true case marker derives a higher-order nominal which incorporates a specification concerning the semantic role of its profile (a thing) in some relationship (typically a process). Consider a marker of instrumental case, for example. As its base, it evokes the schematic conception of a process comprising an action chain that includes an instrumental participant. That instrument (a schematically specified thing) functions as its profile. The case marker combines with a nominal by virtue of a correspondence that equates their two profiles. Hence the composite expression designates a specific thing which is further characterized as having the role of instrument in some process. Subsequently, in the assembly of a clause, the schematic process evoked by the case-marked nominal is identified with the specified process profiled by the verb.

It is usual to describe ergative as a case which marks a transitive subject, whereas absolutive case marks both transitive objects and intransitive subjects. I doubt, however, that the signaling of these grammatical relations represents their actual function (although it may be a subsidiary effect). Considered as markers of subject vs. object status, ergative and absolutive case are auspiciously ill-designed, since absolutive marks both subjects and objects, while subjects are marked by both ergative and absolutive. Moreover, case marking is just one manifestation of ergative/absolutive organization, which appears to be a recurrent aspect of language design; it is probably true that every language contains phenomena that treat intransitive subjects and transitive objects alike to the exclusion of transitive subjects.[41] The same can be said for nominative/accusative organization, whereby transitive and intransitive subjects group together in opposition to transitive objects. Though languages mix these two strategies in varying proportions, each is a universal feature of linguistic structure and must therefore have some natural cognitive basis.

In the case of nominative/accusative organization, which pivots on the notion subject (corresponding to nominative), we find this basis in the natural correlation between figure/ground alignment and the flow of energy along an action chain. For each parameter it is clearly reasonable to speak of a *natural path*, i.e. a cognitively natural ordering: defining these respective paths are the level of participant prominence (*primary figure* > *secondary figure* > *ground*) and the direction of flow (from energy source to energy sink). Observe, now, that as both the primary figure and the action-chain head a subject is the *starting point*—the initial element—with respect to each of these paths. It is symptomatic of the subject's starting-point status that, in a nominative/accusative system, nominative case is typically marked by zero.[42]

What might be suggested as the natural cognitive basis for ergative/absolutive organization? My proposal is that it reflects a natural path based on *conceptual autonomy*.[43] Recall that a thematic process is conceptually autonomous in the sense of having the potential to be construed in absolute fashion, i.e. independently of causation or the energy that drives it. By contrast, the notion of causation or energy input is *conceptually dependent* in the sense of being incoherent without some conception (however nebulous) of its downstream consequences. Thus, whereas *The door opened* is quite acceptable because it describes a conceptually autonomous thematic process, we cannot (except perhaps elliptically) say either **Bill caused* or **Bill opened* (with Bill construed as an agent). Starting from a conceptually autonomous process, however, we can add the dependent notion of causation to form a complex event conception that is itself conceptually autonomous: *Bill opened the door*. In fact, any number of "layers" of causation can be successively added, each deriving an autonomous conception of greater complexity. The sentences in (10) exemplify the progressive, layer-by-layer expansion of a thematic process to yield a highly complex event conception comprising an action chain with numerous links.

(10) a. *The ice melted.*
b. *A torch melted the ice.*
c. *She melted the ice with a torch.*
d. *I made her melt the ice with a torch.*
e. *He had me make her melt the ice with a torch.*
f. *They induced him to have me make her melt the ice
    with a torch.*

I suggest that a set of expressions of this sort reflects a natural path based on conceptual autonomy. Its starting point is the thematic process (T), the conceptually autonomous core of the overall event. Every step along the way consists in adding a dependent element (D) to the autonomous structure (A) already assembled. The result is a higher-order autonomous structure, which can in turn combine with another dependent element, and so on:[44]

(11) $(T)_A \; > \; (D\,(T)_A)_A \; > \; (D\,(D\,(T)_A)_A)_A \; > \; ...$

If one now considers the processual participants successively encountered along this path, it is evident that their ordering is precisely the inverse of the one observed in tracing along an action chain. With respect to participants, the theme is thus the starting point, and the ultimate energy source (the action-chain head) lies at the endpoint of the path.

This dimension of conceptual structure constitutes the natural cognitive basis for ergative/absolutive organization. Since a dependent structure presupposes an autonomous structure for its full implementation, a path of assembly consisting exclusively of autonomous, independently manipulable structures has a legitimate claim to being cognitively natural. A thematic process is one that lies at the origin of such a path, so it has the potential to occur without the support of other structures (absolute construal).[45] Observe, now, that the participant in this core process—the theme—is generally the one that is coded by a transitive object or an intransitive subject. When ergative/absolutive organization takes the form of case marking, it is that participant which bears absolutive case. The fact that absolutive case is virtually always marked by zero corroborates the claim that the theme represents the starting point of a natural path.

Consider, then, a canonical transitive clause that profiles a full action chain (e.g. **AG ⇒ INSTR ⇒ TH**). I assume that, regardless of case marking, the spotlights of focal prominence are directed at the endpoints of this chain: the brighter spotlight is directed at the agent (which is thus the trajector, or primary figure), and a lesser one at the theme (the landmark, or secondary figure). This differential focal prominence is definitional of subject and object status, to which a variety of grammatical phenomena are sensitive. One such phenomenon is nominative/accusative case marking, which signals and effectively reinforces this focal status. Because nominative case marks the action chain head, the starting point with respect to energy flow, its form is very often zero. Accusative case then attaches to the other focal participant (the theme), which lies at the opposite extremity of that natural path. On the other hand, ergative/absolutive case marking reflects a different aspect of conceptual organization, based on autonomy, whose alignment runs counter to the flow of energy. Here the absolutive case is usually zero in form, since it marks the theme, the starting point of the natural path in question. Ergative case then attaches to the focal participant (the agent) which lies at the opposite extremity.

2.4. *Marked coding*

Although we have concentrated on expressions in which canonical events are coded linguistically in the most natural (unmarked) fashion, every language also displays a diverse assortment of constructions to accommodate other kinds of situations and special discourse objectives (cf. van Oosten 1986). The basic effect of many such constructions is to confer focal prominence on a participant that would not ordinarily receive it. This may result from a change in profiling, as in (12).

(12) a. *The mud scraped off his boots quite easily.*
     b. *The ice cream scooped out only with great difficulty.*

Semantically, these sentences evoke an agent who carried out the activity and experienced either ease or difficulty in doing so. Yet the agent is unmentioned and unspecified. Even though a verb like *scrape* or *scoop out* normally profiles an entire action chain, in this construction the agent and its exertions remain unprofiled within the base, as does any instrument. The profile is restricted to those portions of the action chain that are directly centered on the theme: the thematic process itself (motion in these examples), and the theme's contribution (by virtue of its constitution) to either facilitating or hindering the execution of the overall action (van Oosten 1977). As the only participant within the profiled segment of the action chain, the theme counts as the action-chain head. It is consequently the clausal trajector and is coded by the subject nominal.

A comparable shift in focal prominence can also be effected without a change in profiling. The most obvious kind of example is a passive construction, like that of English:

(13) a. *The mud was scraped off his boots (by his butler).*
     b. *The ice cream was scooped out (by a waiter).*

The primary difference between the constructions in (12) and (13) is that, in the latter, the entire action chain profiled by the verb (*scrape*; *scoop out*) is also profiled by the passive clausal head (*be scraped*; *be scooped out*) and by the clause as a whole.[46] The constructions are alike—and different from an unmarked active clause (e.g. *His butler scraped the mud off his boots*)—in that trajector status is conferred on the theme. In passives, therefore, it is not the head but the tail of the profiled action chain that receives trajector status and is coded by the clausal subject. As such, a passive subject is an atypical and rather peripheral member of the subject category, but it does still conform to the most schematic characterization, namely primary figure within the profiled relationship.

Various other phenomena affecting the status of clausal participants can be briefly mentioned. We may first note a certain amount of flexibility in the selection of direct objects. A well-known example is the "dative-shift" construction, which permits an alternate choice of landmark (secondary figure) in much the same way that passives allow an alternate choice of trajector (primary figure):

(14) a. *He sent a lot of postcards to his friends.*
      b. *He sent his friends a lot of postcards.*

A ditransitive verb like *send* has two downstream participants that compete for focal prominence: the theme (*a lot of postcards*), a canonical direct object by dint of being the action-chain tail (at least in the physical realm); and the recipient (*his friends*), which tends to be salient as the active (initiative) participant in the target domain, and may also be conceived as the endpoint of an action chain in the more abstract, experiential sense of being affected by the transfer. Languages differ as to which motivation they seize upon as the basis for choosing the direct object, and some—like English—allow either option (cf. Dryer 1986).

In passives, as well as the pattern exemplified in (12), the overall action-chain head is generally left unspecified. These constructions are among the considerable variety of devices by which languages accommodate situations of reduced participant distinctness and identifiability. Common, of course, is the avoidance of individual specification made possible by using an indefinite pronoun like French *on* or German *man*, or else a personal pronoun with generic or uncertain reference (*They say you can't be too thin or too rich*). Some languages have verbal affixes whose precise function is to indicate that the trajector or the landmark is unspecified and will remain unelaborated.[47] A reflexive marker signals that there is no need for elaboration because a single participant fills two roles that are normally played by distinct participants. Closely related to reflexives (from which its marking usually derives) is *middle voice*, insightfully surveyed and analyzed by Kemmer (1993). Kemmer has shown that middle marking typically occurs with processes characterized by a diminished level of internal differentiation, in terms of either participants or component subprocesses.

Finally but importantly, I note that processual participants are not the only clausal elements capable of attracting focal prominence. Recall that the canonical event model draws a distinction between the global setting in which an event unfolds, on the one hand, and the participants whose interaction constitutes the event, on the other. I believe the setting/participant contrast to be a fundamental aspect of conceptual structure, not only in the realm of physical and perceptual experience but in abstract domains as well. Moreover, the distinction is closely tied up with force dynamics: whereas participants are conceived as *interacting* with one another, they merely *occupy* a setting or location.[48] Interaction is first and foremost a force-dynamic notion, a pivotal component of the archetypal billiard-ball model. By contrast, mere location—even change of location—lends itself to absolute construal.[49]

The setting/participant distinction proves to have many grammatical ramifications (Langacker 1987b). As exemplified in (15), settings tend to be coded by clause-level adverbs of time and place, and participants by subject, object, and oblique nominals.

(15) *Last night at the stadium, I paid $30 to the vendors for*
        hot dogs and beer.

This correlation is not exceptionless, however, and sometimes the contrast is entirely covert: there need not be anything that explicitly indicates whether a given nominal element is construed as a participant or as a setting/location. But even when covert, the distinction may well have linguistic consequences, particularly in regard to transitivity. The reason is that the archetypal basis for transitivity is an *energetic interaction*, and an interaction only holds between participants. If a relation holds instead between a participant and a setting or location, it is not in any narrow sense a transitive one. To be sure, we are dealing with a subtle aspect of construal that may be flexible and a matter of degree. It can nonetheless have observable, even striking effects.

Let me note just one recurrent phenomenon: the conferral of trajector status on the setting, rather than on a participant. That this should happen is not surprising, since focal prominence is simply a matter of figure/ground organization, at which we demonstrate considerable flexibility. Shown a display with several objects portrayed against a larger background, we are not only able to shift our focus from object to object, but can also focus on the background per se, which then becomes a kind of foreground.[50] In terms of the stage model, we often look at the stage itself, as a whole, before "zooming in" to focus on specific actors and props. Suppose, then, that the global setting should be put in focus as the trajector (primary clausal figure). In lieu of the canonical arrangement depicted in (16), we thus have (17), where the inner brackets represent the setting (X and Y being participants):

(16) $[\quad V \text{----}> [\quad ... \; X_{tr} \Rightarrow Y_{lm} \; ... \;] \;]$

(17) $[\quad V \text{----}> [_{tr} \; ... \; X_{lm} \; ... \;] \;]$

The primary focus is now on the setting itself, with secondary focal prominence (landmark status) falling on the most salient participant (which would otherwise be the trajector). Moreover, because the trajector and landmark are the focal points of a profiled relationship, the difference in focal prominence entails a concomitant difference in profiling: whereas in (16) the profiled relation resides in the interaction of participants, the profile in (17) centers instead on the locational, "container-content" relation that the setting bears to a participant therein (or a relationship involving that participant).

It follows that a clause of this sort ought to be intransitive, and that is indeed the case. A *setting-subject construction* may appear to be transitive, since the nominals that elaborate the trajector and landmark occur in the normal subject and object positions. An example is (18)a, where the subject *November* designates the temporal setting.

(18) a. *November witnessed a series of surprising events.*
      b. **A series of surprising events was witnessed by November.*

Observe that the landmark nominal *a series of surprising events* comes immediately after the verb, the usual position of a direct object. Yet, if passivizability is symptomatic of transitivity, the construction is non-transitive, since its passive counterpart (18)b is decidedly ungrammatical. This pattern recurs across a variety of setting-subject constructions. I would argue, for instance, that the so-called "dummy" or "expletive" *it* represents an abstract, maximally schematic setting (FCG2: 8.3). Even when the clause contains a nominal in object position, it does not passivize:

(19) a. *It is snowing big flakes.*
    b. **Big flakes are being snowed by it.*

(20) a. *It appeared that they had won.*
    b. **That they had won was appeared by it.*

I would also analyze the "dummy" or "existential" *there* as a kind of abstract setting:

(21) a. *There was an eagle on the roof.*
    b. **An eagle was been on the roof by there.*

These sentences do not profile participant interactions. Because they first evoke the global setting, and then zoom in to focus on a specific element, they are better described as having a "framing" or "presentative" function.[51]

3. Conclusion

This chapter has provided a general introduction to CG illustrated by its application to a major domain of linguistic investigation, namely clause structure. The next two chapters further illustrate its potential for revealing description. Chapter 2 discusses a basic working strategy followed in proposing and justifying descriptive constructs. Ideally a construct is motivated by converging evidence from three sources: in addition to having a plausible psychological basis, it is shown to be necessary on purely semantic grounds, and turns out to be needed as well for the explicit characterization of diverse grammatical phenomena. Chapter 3 describes in some detail the preposition *of* and certain grammatical constructions in which it participates. As a grammatical morpheme whose meaning is tenuous and has often been ignored, *of* represents an important test case for the claim that grammar comprises only meaningful elements.

Chapter 2
Evidence for descriptive constructs

Despite their intuitive naturalness, the descriptive constructs adopted in CG are proposed and justified on the basis of specific evidence.* A variety of considerations can in principle be brought to bear in assessing their validity. A primary consideration is their efficacy in the revealing description of both semantic and grammatical structure. Another is generality, achieved by positing a limited set of constructs that prove systematically applicable to a broad array of diverse phenomena. In CG it is further required that they be psychologically plausible and consistent with what we know about cognitive processing.

These principles will be illustrated through their application in justifying several basic constructs: *scope*, *search domain*, *active zone*, and the *setting/participant* distinction. Each construct is psychologically natural, with clearly evident non-linguistic manifestations. Each has been posited to accommodate varied phenomena in multiple languages. Moreover, each has both semantic and grammatical motivation. Semantically, they afford principled descriptions capturing subtle differences among sets of expressions with similar conceptual content. In grammar they allow the explicit characterization of constructions, as well as predictions about distribution and well-formedness. Demanding that all these conditions be satisfied constitutes a powerful method based on converging evidence.

As a preliminary example, consider profiling (discussed in Chapter 1). An expression's profile is the entity it designates, or refers to, and as such is a focus of attention within the overall conception evoked. Its attentional nature makes profiling quite reasonable from the psychological standpoint. Linguistically it is fully general: within broad limits (perhaps up through the sentence level), essentially every expression is characterized as imposing a profile on its conceptual base. Moreover, this construct is demonstrably necessary for viable semantic description. One can hardly describe a *knuckle*, for example, without both presupposing the conception of a finger and further indicating that a particular subpart is being referred to (Figure 1.1(a)). Also, by positing alternate profiles we can readily describe the semantic differences between pairs of expressions that evoke the same conceptual content: *cry* vs. *tear*, *husband* vs. *wife*, *dance* vs. *dancer*, *break* vs. *broken*, etc. Lastly, profiling proves essential for grammar. An expression's profile—rather than its overall conceptual content—is what determines its grammatical class. *Dance* is thus a verb, since it designates a process, while *dancer* is a noun because it profiles a thing (namely a participant in that process). Profiling is also the basis for characterizing the grammatical notions *head* (a component structure whose profile is inherited at the composite structure level) and *subordinate clause* (one whose profile is overridden at a higher level of organization (FCG2: 10.1)).

Of prime concern here is the relation between semantic and grammatical investigation. CG recognizes an inherent dialectic between them. Since grammar is largely a matter of imposing and symbolizing particular ways of construing conceptual content, it cannot be effectively studied without the appropriate semantic tools. At the same time, we tend not to be aware of construal until particular grammatical phenomena make apparent the need to posit it. The study of grammar is thus an important stimulus and source of evidence for semantic investigation. It is therefore most productive for semantic and grammatical investigation to proceed in parallel as simultaneous, mutually dependent facets of a single overall enterprise.

1. "Invisible" semantic constructs

The conceptual nature of meaning does not make it subject to analysis by mere introspection. In particular, the various dimensions of construal tend to be "invisible" to the conceptualizer, crucial though they are to linguistic semantics. This is only natural: we are more concerned with *what* we are conceiving than that we are conceiving it in a particular way. In uttering a sentence like *The cat is on the mat*, I am quite aware of the conceptual content it evokes—especially the notions 'cat', 'mat', and 'on'—but at the level of conscious attention I am quite unaware (*qua* naive speaker) of the fact that I am profiling a temporally-extended relationship ('be on the mat') and imposing a specific figure/ground organization on the scene (choosing the cat as clause-level figure). The situation is analogous to that of a person wearing glasses. The glasses are in large measure responsible for shaping the wearer's perceptual experience, determining what is seen and how it appears. Yet ordinarily the wearer is not even conscious of them. When attention is strongly focused on the external situation, the glasses themselves become almost literally "invisible".

The identification of meaning with mental experience therefore does not provide us with direct access to the factors that shape it, any more than wearing glasses makes us knowledgeable about optics. Inaccessible to simple introspection, the construal inherent in expressions can only be ascertained by careful linguistic analysis subject to normal standards of justification and descriptive adequacy. The focus here will be on grammatical motivation. Discussed are several constructs pertaining to construal that, while neither intuitively obvious nor recognized in semantic tradition, are nonetheless essential to both meaning and grammar. It is in fact grammatical structure that makes these notions visible to the analyst: they leave their traces in grammar in much the same way that atomic particles leave tracks in a bubble chamber.

A prime example of "invisible" semantic constructs is *mental space organization* (Fauconnier 1985, 1997; Cutrer 1994; Fauconnier and Sweetser 1996). Fauconnier first demonstrated the critical importance, to both semantics and grammar, of an elaborate, dynamic process of "meaning construction" intervening between the situation being described and the linguistic structures employed in describing it. He showed that many classic problems of reference, logic, and formal semantics find natural solutions if mental spaces are posited as a basic feature of conceptual organization at this level. Abstractly, a mental space is just a set of elements and a set of relations holding between them. A typical conception comprises multiple spaces linked in particular ways defining natural paths of access. Elements in different mental spaces can be identified by means of correspondences ("connectors").

For instance, sentence (1) exhibits the well-known ambiguity between the specific and non-specific interpretations of the indefinite nominal:

(1) *Xavier wants to marry a Norwegian.*

Relevant aspects of the two meanings are sketched in Figure 2.1. Circles represent the crucial mental spaces: reality, and the world of Xavier's desire. Xavier (X) is an element of both spaces, and his two instantiations correspond. Moreover, on either interpretation a Norwegian (N) inhabits the space representing Xavier's desire, as does the relationship of marriage (m) between X and N. The difference between the two readings resides in whether N is confined to that space or is also an element of reality. On the non-specific interpretation, diagrammed in Figure 2.1(a), the Norwegian is merely a figment of Xavier's desire; she is "conjured up" just as part of this mental space and has no status outside it (FCG2: ch. 3). What distinguishes the specific reading is that N does exist outside this space, as shown in 2.1(b). The Norwegian that figures in Xavier's desires is equated with one established outside that context by other means, hence independently accessible.

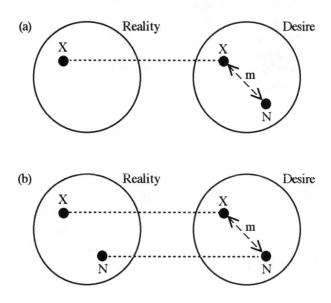

Figure 2.1

As a descriptive consequence, there is no need to posit two distinct senses for the indefinite article. The contrast in specificity derives from a single meaning given the inherent flexibility of mental space construction, together with a general principle allowing a description to be transferred to a counterpart in another, accessible space.[1] This brief example offers just a glimpse of the advantages and insights achieved by positing mental spaces. While the notion may seem obvious in retrospect, it does not specifically represent the meaning of any linguistic element and is not part of the apparatus of traditional semantics—only through painstaking analysis, extensive description, and explicit theoretical formulation was it rendered "visible". The same is true for the other constructs to be examined.

2. Scope

As the term is used in CG, an expression's *scope* is the array of conceptual content that it specifically evokes and relies upon for its characterization. It thus pertains to the extensiveness of the content directly invoked: which conceptions are activated, and which portions of them actually come into play. Any aspect of our mental experience can be called upon as the basis for an expression's meaning.

We can usefully start with a perceptual analogy (cf. Chapter 7). Consider a person seated in the audience watching a play. With respect to this familiar viewing arrangement, a number of constructs might be characterized: (i) the *viewer*, who has the perceptual experience; (ii) the *perceptual relationship* between the viewer and what is perceived; (iii) the *maximal field of view*, subsuming everything that falls within the visual field (the stage, surrounding portions of the theater, part of the audience); (iv) the *general locus of viewing attention*, namely the stage; and (v) within that area, the specific *focus of attention* (usually one of the actors).

Now I do not claim that all conceptualization is modeled on visual perception—despite its privileged status, vision is only one type of mental experience. I do however suggest that the constructs just described for perceptual experience represent specific instantiations of more abstract notions applicable to any kind of conception. Respectively, these are: (i) the *conceptualizer*, who for our purposes can be identified as the speaker (and secondarily the addressee); (ii) the *construal relationship*, which holds between a conceptualizer and the conceptualization entertained (in particular, the meaning of a linguistic expression); (iii) an expression's *maximal scope*, i.e. the full array of content it evokes; (iv) the *immediate scope*, comprising those facets of the maximal scope that figure most directly in the characterization of the profiled entity; and (v) the expression's *profile* (the entity it designates), which serves as a kind of focal point within its immediate scope.

Every expression has a scope, however vaguely it might be delimited. At the very least, the conception evoked must be extensive enough to encompass the profile together with any unprofiled entities crucial to its characterization. The preposition *above*, for instance, requires for its scope at least enough spatial expanse to include its two participants and their divergent locations along the vertical axis. Similarly, the scope of *aunt* subsumes enough of a kinship network to incorporate the profiled individual, the reference individual (ego), and the linking relative (Figure 1.1(b)). A subtler example is *island*, whose scope includes more than just a land mass wholly surrounded by water. If that were sufficient, we could say that a castle protected by a moat occupies an *island*, yet this usage is not really felicitous. An island is *insular*, i.e. separated from other land by a fairly substantial expanse of water (at least on most sides). Though it cannot be precisely specified or delimited, *island*'s scope must be broad enough for this notion of insularity to be manifested.

The notion of immediate scope can be illustrated by the prepositional phrase in a sentence like (2):

(2) *There's a mailbox **across the street**.*

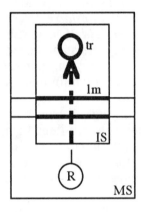

Figure 2.2

As shown in Figure 2.2, *across the street* profiles a locative relationship wherein the trajector (which the full sentence specifies to be a mailbox) lies at the endpoint of a path leading from one side of the landmark (the street) to the other. The path's source is a reference point (R) that usually remains implicit, being identified with the location of the speech event. The trajector and landmark are central participants—they stand out as focal points within the profiled relationship, and are rendered salient by being mentioned explicitly. They are "onstage", as it were, in contrast to the "offstage" reference point, which anchors the path but is not itself a focus of attention (Langacker 1985, 1990c). Within the expression's maximal scope (MS) we can thus distinguish a restricted immediate scope (IS) comprising the "onstage region" (the general locus of attention). Whereas the maximal scope includes the reference point as well as the knowledge that the street extends indefinitely far in either direction, the immediate scope is limited to the profiled trajector/landmark configuration and subsumes just enough of the street to support this conception.

We will see that there is good reason for considering an expression's scope to constitute a bounded region having some kind of cognitive reality, even when the boundary imposed is not inspired by any objective factors and we are unable to pin it down to any specific location. In many cases the distinction between maximal and immediate scope is also more apparent than in the foregoing example. Consider body-part terms, such as *knuckle, finger, hand,* and *arm.* Clearly, *knuckle* evokes as one facet of its base the conception of a finger, since the joint it designates is identified primarily by its position within the finger as a whole (Figure 1.1(a)). Likewise, *finger* invokes the conception of a hand as an essential aspect of its characterization, while *hand* in turn calls forth the notion of an arm, and *arm* makes crucial reference to the body overall. There is consequently a sense in which *knuckle* takes the entire body as its scope (since *knuckle* presupposes *finger,* which calls up *hand,* and so on). Still, it is obvious that a finger figures directly and saliently in the meaning of *knuckle,* whereas the more inclusive body parts are subsidiary, being related to *knuckle* only through a chain of intermediaries. We can say, then, that the conception of a finger provides the immediate scope for *knuckle,* and that larger portions of the body—or the body as a whole—can serve as its maximal scope. With respect to the sequence *body > arm > hand > finger > knuckle* (and many comparable hierarchies), we can observe that each noun's profile constitutes the immediate scope for the noun that follows.

If this quantization is not sufficiently evident on semantic grounds, grammatical phenomena make it so. One trace is found in sentences with *have* (cf. Bever and Rosenbaum 1970; Cruse 1979; CIS: 8):

(3) a. *This house has 7 doors. Each door has 3 hinges. Each hinge has 6 screws.*
     b. *??This house has {21 hinges/126 screws}. ??This door has 18 screws.*

A *have*-sentence describing a partonymy is most felicitous (other things being equal) when the subject's profile constitutes the object's immediate scope. The constructs profile and immediate scope must therefore be invoked for an explicit characterization of the construction's prototype. We find another trace in partonymic noun-noun compounds, where N_1's profile is the immediate scope for N_2, as in *house door* (possible though not usual), *door hinge*, and *hinge screw*. Here an expression directly relating non-adjacent levels seems not just marginal but deviant: **house hinge, *house screw, *door screw*.

These examples indicate that some grammatical constructions make specific reference to immediate scope. Partonymic compounds, for instance, instantiate the constructional schema sketched in Figure 2.3 (a special case of Figure 1.6). The crucial feature of this subschema is a correspondence between N_1's profile and N_2's immediate scope, which is also the immediate scope at the composite structure level. Note that N_2's profile also prevails at that level.

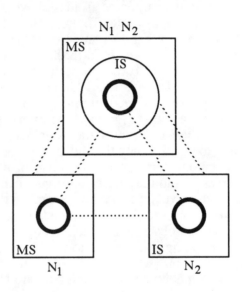

Figure 2.3

The distinction between maximal and immediate scope is crucial as well to the characterization of progressive constructions (e.g. *They were eating*). In this case the domain is time. The maximal scope is a span of time sufficient for the occurrence of the full, bounded event profiled by the verb stem (*eat*). The progressive *be...-ing* construction imposes on it an immediate temporal scope which is internal to the event and excludes its endpoints. By definition, an expression's profile is the focus within its immediate scope. A progressive verb (*be eating*) therefore profiles a process comprising an arbitrary internal portion of the bounded event designated by the verb stem on which it is formed. The usual informal description of a progressive as taking an "internal perspective" on an event can thus be handled by means of a specific construct strongly justified on independent grounds. Additional evidence for this construct is provided in the following section.[2]

3. Search domain

Adapted from Miller and Johnson-Laird (1976: 384), the term *search domain* is used by Hawkins (1984) for a construct that pertains to locative expressions. It reflects a basic aspect of an everyday experience, namely that of finding things in space. We frequently search for something by physically moving or perceptually scanning through an extensive yet limited region, typically identified with reference to a salient landmark. For example, I might systematically walk the streets around my hotel in order to find a certain restaurant that I know is located in its vicinity. Or, after reading this book, you might look for a particularly memorable statement by scanning through the text that immediately follows a certain diagram it pertains to. The conception of a limited domain of search, specified in relation to a landmark, is thus an independently attested mental phenomenon.

Hawkins defines a locative expression's search domain—shaded in Figure 2.4—as the region to which it confines its trajector, i.e. the set of trajector locations that will satisfy its specifications.

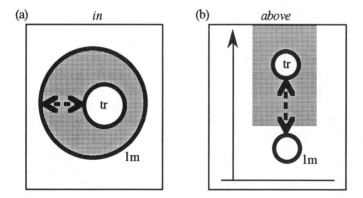

Figure 2.4

Seldom does a locative situate its trajector with absolute precision; usually it indicates only that the trajector is somewhere within a certain region characterized with reference to the landmark. In the case of *in*, for example, the search domain is the landmark's interior, as seen in Figure 2.4(a). More commonly the search domain is external to the landmark, as shown for *above* in 2.4(b).

Like scope, this notion is a theoretical construct devised and adopted for specific descriptive purposes in the context of CG, being unrecognized in traditional semantics. Search domains are neither precisely bounded nor explicitly mentioned. In *the table beside his bed*, for instance, *the table* and *his bed* respectively specify the preposition's trajector and landmark, while the vaguely delimited search domain is left implicit. Yet there is strong linguistic evidence for attributing to search domains the status of psychologically real entities. A number of phenomena can only be revealingly described by directly referring to this construct.

Consider first the sentences in (4):

(4) a. *?Near the fire is warmer.*
     b. *?Under the bed is all dusty.*

Though marginal for some, expressions like these do occur and are readily accepted by many speakers. It is in any case not their degree of conventionality that is relevant here, but rather their meaning, as well as the seeming peculiarity of a prepositional phrase appearing in subject position. The crucial observation about their meaning is that the prepositional phrase is construed as naming a spatial *region*, not a locative *relationship*. It is incoherent, for example, to speak of a relationship as being dusty—that is a property of physical *things* (objects and places). *Near the fire* and *under the bed* are therefore best analyzed as designating regions in space, to which warmth and dustiness are straightforwardly ascribable. In accordance with basic principles and definitions of CG, the very fact that *near the fire* or *under the bed* profiles a type of thing is sufficient to effect its categorization as a noun, which makes it eligible to function as a clausal subject.

Thus *near the fire* and *under the bed* qualify as nouns because of their meaning. That they assume the form of a prepositional phrase is not, in this framework, considered problematic for the categorization. The form reflects their source: they instantiate a pattern of semantic extension (or zero derivation) whereby a prepositional phrase, which profiles a locative relationship, gives rise to a nominal expression that evokes the same conceptual content but profiles instead a spatial region. As shown by comparison of Figures 2.5(a) and 2.5(b), the profiled region is none other than the prepositional phrase's search domain. The effect of this zero nominalization is to make the search domain—only latent in the expression's basic relational meaning—a focus of explicit concern and maximal prominence. Let me note that every facet of this analysis represents an independently attested linguistic phenomenon.[3]

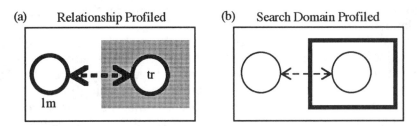

Figure 2.5

The notion search domain is also pivotal to the analysis of dative and accusative case in German. Smith (1987) has offered a convincing account of these cases which treats them as consistently meaningful elements in both the clausal and prepositional realms. Their values are best understood with respect to one of the cognitively fundamental *image schemas* proposed by Johnson (1987) and Lakoff (1987), namely source-path-goal. Accusative case takes as its central value the path-goal portion of this schema, whereas dative indicates certain kinds of departures from this configuration. At the clausal level, the path-goal schema is typically manifested in the transmission of energy from an agent to a patient. With prepositions, on the other hand, its usual interpretation pertains to spatial motion.

Our interest lies with the prepositional uses. A distinction is made between "1-way" prepositions, which consistently govern a single case, and "2-way" prepositions, which take either a dative or an accusative object depending on the circumstances. For the most part the 1-way accusative prepositions saliently invoke either the path-goal schema (e.g. *bis* 'until', *gegen* 'against', *für* 'for') or else a configuration plausibly analyzed as an extension from this prototype (e.g. *durch* 'through', *um* 'around'[4]). Likewise, the 1-way dative prepositions have values that diverge from the path-goal schema in fundamental ways. *Aus* 'out of', *von* 'from', and *seit* 'since' evoke instead the source-path portion of source-path-goal. *Mit* 'with' and *bei* 'by' lack the notion of a path and also involve mere proximity instead of the contact inherent in path-goal. *Nach* 'after, toward' does invoke a goal-directed path, but one that is only partial (so that contact is not achieved). Although it is less obvious why *zu* should govern dative, Smith observes that 'at' is often the proper gloss, and that when 'to' is more appropriate the goal tends to be a general location rather than a specific, focused target. In any event, it is not denied that the choice of case with the 1-way prepositions is a matter of convention that has to be specifically learned—it has clear semantic motivation but is not claimed to be strictly predictable apriori.

The 2-way prepositions include *an* 'at', *auf* 'on', *hinter* 'behind', *in* 'in', *neben* 'beside', *über* 'over', *unter* 'under', *vor* 'in front of', and *zwischen* 'between'. Here it is generally recognized that the contrast between dative and accusative is meaningful, or at least that it correlates with a semantic opposition for which it is sometimes the only overt signal. In basic spatial uses, dative case indicates either the absence of motion or else motion that takes place within a particular location; movement from one location to another is signaled by accusative case. Hence the contrasts in (5) and (6):

(5) a. *Wir wanderten in den* (DAT) *Bergen.*
        'We wandered (around) in the mountains.'
    b. *Wir wanderten in die* (ACC) *Berge.*
        'We wandered into the mountains.'

(6) a. *Das Auto steht hinter dem* (DAT) *Baum.*
        'The car is standing behind the tree.'
    b. *Er stellt das Auto hinter den* (ACC) *Baum.*
        'He parks the car behind the tree.'

It will now be shown that the notion search domain allows us to characterize explicitly and precisely the nature of the dative/accusative opposition, as well as an interesting semantic difference between the 1-way and the 2-way prepositions.

With the 1-way prepositions, the choice between dative and accusative hinges on whether the preposition invokes the path-goal schema (or a related configuration), where the goal is specifically identified as the preposition's landmark, i.e. the entity profiled by the prepositional object. Consider *gegen den* (ACC) *Baum* 'against the tree', for example. As shown in Figure 2.6(a), the trajector (or some associated entity, such as the force it exerts) makes contact with the landmark itself (the tree). For 1-way prepositions either accusative or dative case is motivated by a configuration involving the landmark object per se. This is not so with the 2-way prepositions. Observe that in (6)b, for instance, there is no contact between the preposition's trajector (the car) and its landmark (the tree), yet the object is marked accusative. For the 2-way prepositions, case choice is determined by a configuration that does not involve the preposition's landmark, but rather its search domain.[5] Figure 2.6(b) sketches the accusative configuration: the trajector's path reaches and traverses the boundaries of the search domain (wherever that might be in relation to the landmark). By contrast, dative case signals that the trajector's path (or static location) is confined to the search domain's interior, as seen in 2.6(c). Dative is chosen because the path-goal schema required for accusative case fails to be instantiated.

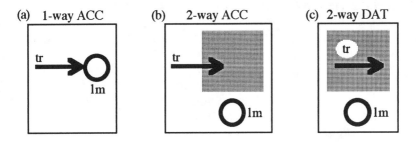

Figure 2.6

Also best described with reference to search domains is a grammatical peculiarity of the preposition *bis* 'until'. Consider these examples:

(7) a. *Ich fahre nur bis Hamburg.*
     'I'm travelling only as far as Hamburg.'
  b. *Wir bleiben bis {Weihnachten/zehn Uhr}.*
     'We're staying until {Christmas/ten o'clock}.'
  c. *Er begleitete mich bis {an/*Ø} die Tür.*
     'He accompanied me to the door.'

It appears that in some cases *bis* combines directly with an object nominal, whereas in others it takes a prepositional phrase as its complement. Let me suggest, however, that its behavior conforms to a single, unifying generalization: *bis* always takes as its complement a noun phrase construed as designating a *location* (as opposed to a *participant*). The nouns that combine directly with *bis* are limited to those whose locational status is hardly disputable. If locations and participants need to be distinguished (as argued in section 5), then a city like Hamburg represents a canonical instance of the former category. Similarly, Christmas and ten o'clock are reasonably considered to be locations in time. But to the extent that construal as a participant becomes feasible, direct combination with *bis* is precluded. Even a nominal such as *die Tür* 'the door', which is plausibly construed in either fashion, requires the interpolation of another preposition.

To maintain the generalization, we must analyze the complement of *bis* as a locational noun even when it has the form of a prepositional phrase. In (7)c, for example, *an die Tür* 'at the door' does not designate a relationship but must instead be analyzed as a complex noun that profiles a location (a type of thing). The nature of the requisite analysis should by now be quite apparent—it is the same analysis proposed earlier for expressions like *near the fire* and *under the bed* in their role as subjects (see (4)). In its basic use as a prepositional phrase, *an die Tür* profiles a locative relationship that places its trajector within an implicit search domain. Zero derivation yields a nominal meaning by shifting the profile to the search domain, which is clearly a location (not a participant), as demanded by *bis*. With respect to their profiling and trajector/landmark organization, phrases like *bis Hamburg* and *bis an die Tür* are therefore exactly parallel, as shown in Figure 2.7: each profiles a complex relationship in which the trajector traces a path whose goal (the landmark) is construed as a location (LOC). The only difference is that *Hamburg* names a location directly, as its primary value, whereas *an die Tür* does so only derivatively, evoking as its base the prepositional relationship whose search domain it designates.

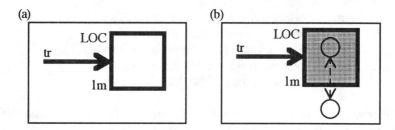

Figure 2.7

We have now seen examples from both English and German in which a locative expression is nominalized by a shift in profile to its search domain, which is thereby rendered more prominent. The opposite is also encountered: cases where the profile is lowered to the status of a search domain, implicit and non-salient. We find this in the well-attested path of grammaticization whereby body-part nouns evolve into prepositions (see Rubba 1994 for analysis and exemplification drawn from modern Aramaic). A noun meaning 'belly', for instance, is a common source of a preposition meaning 'in'; 'head' yields 'above'; and so on (cf. *beside*; *behind*). Let us focus on the essential aspects of 'belly' > 'in', abstracting away from various details that would have to be treated in a full account of any particular occurrence.

As a body-part noun, 'belly' profiles a specific bounded region within the body. This is diagrammed in Figure 2.8(a), where the outer circle represents the body as a whole. Though it is not essential to the account, I suggest that one step in the N > P evolution consists in the noun being construed as a location rather than a participant (as body-part terms often are). Inherent in the notion location is the conception of some entity being located. So to the extent that a locational construal prevails, schematic reference to such an entity becomes at least a latent aspect of the conceptualization N invokes; it is represented by the dashed circle in Figure 2.8(b). Another factor is metonymy, whereby N comes to designate not the body part per se but rather an associated or more inclusive area (cf. Brugman 1983). Via such metonymy N's profile expands from the belly in particular to encompass the body's full interior.

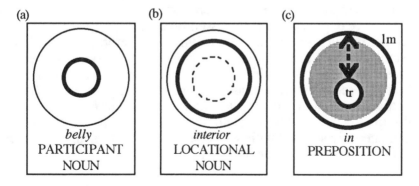

Figure 2.8

  The resulting configuration has all the elements of a preposition—it differs from a true preposition only by virtue of profiling the *interior region* as opposed to the *locative relationship*. The prepositional meaning is thus obtained by shifting the profile to that relationship, as shown in Figure 2.8(c). The change in grammatical category (N > P) does not necessarily reflect any change in conceptual content, but only in the prominence accorded its substructures. In particular, the body's interior becomes less prominent: it is no longer profiled, nor does it function as P's landmark or trajector. It does however retain a covert presence as the preposition's search domain.

  A final example makes reference to the notion scope as well as to search domain. The sentences in (8) illustrate the "nested locative" construction:

(8) a. *Your camera is upstairs, in the bedroom, in the closet, on the top shelf, behind the binoculars.*
  b. *The pet food is in the back, in aisle 6, near the center, next to the disposable diapers.*

This is one of several constructions that permit an indefinitely long chain of locative expressions, all of which locate the same trajector. Distinguishing the nested locative variant is a kind of "zooming in" effect: as we move through the chain, the component locatives successively direct our attention to smaller and smaller areas, each nested inside the one that precedes. How can this phenomenon be characterized? Given the constructs at our disposal, its description turns out to be perfectly straightforward.

  Figure 2.9 represents the addition of a single link to the chain, i.e. the integration of one component locative (LOC_2) to the composite locative expression already assembled (LOC_1). Each component structure profiles a relationship involving a trajector, a landmark, and a search domain. The two trajectors have to correspond, as indicated by the dotted line connecting them. Responsible for the "zooming in" effect is a second correspondence: the *search domain* of LOC_1 is identified with the *scope* of LOC_2, and is thus the immediate scope of the more specific locative relationship. As a result, the trajector is simultaneously situated with respect to two landmarks and two search domains, one nested inside the other.

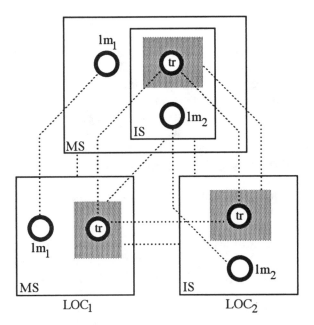

Figure 2.9

For our purposes here, the essential observation is that an explicit characterization of the construction hinges on a correspondence between two "invisible" semantic constructs, each established on independent grounds. Let me note in passing, however, that these notions also figure in the conditions determining use of the definite article. Sentence (8)a, for example, is fully appropriate even when the house in question has numerous bedrooms, provided that only one of them is upstairs. Because the search domain of the first locative (*upstairs*) constitutes a restricted immediate scope for purposes of construing the second (*in the bedroom*), there is only a single bedroom to consider, which makes it contextually unique. Similarly, *the* occurs in the third locative (*in the closet*) no matter how many closets the house might have, assuming that there is only one in the upstairs bedroom.

4. Active zone

This construct has been discussed in detail elsewhere (CIS: ch. 7) and also figures importantly in Chapter 11. We will thus consider it fairly briefly here, with emphasis on the dialectic between semantic and grammatical investigation.

The entities conceived as participating in a relationship seldom do so as undifferentiated wholes. That is, relatively few expressions resemble (9)a, in which every part of the subject participates equally in the profiled relationship, as does every part of the object.

(9) a. *The spacecraft is now approaching Venus.*
     b. *Your dog bit my cat.*

More typical are examples like (9)b, where certain portions of the dog (notably the teeth and jaws) are directly and crucially involved in the biting, and others (e.g. the tail and pancreas) hardly at all. By the same token, only some (unspecified) portion of the cat enjoys the privilege of directly participating in the action. Those portions of an entity which participate most directly and crucially in a relationship are said to constitute its *active zone* with respect to that relationship. As in the case of scope and search domain, the active zone is not necessarily either salient or precisely delimited, yet for many descriptive purposes we need to adopt this construct and treat it as a bounded region.

Expressions like (9)b display a kind of *metonymy*, wherein a pivotal entity (here a part) is referenced only indirectly, via the term for another, associated entity (the whole). They represent one way of resolving a tension inherent in the choice of central clausal participants. Determining which entities are to be made explicit and prominent as a subject or object usually involves a conflict between two competing desiderata: that of being precise and accurate in regard to which entities actually participate in the profiled interaction; and that of focusing attention on entities that are inherently salient or of primary interest. Since we normally conceive of dogs and cats as integral wholes, being only secondarily concerned with their individual subparts, it is cognitively natural to select the former as focal participants, as in (9)b. This is generally sufficient to override the desideratum of accuracy. Note the infelicity of (10): .

(10) **Your dog's teeth (and jaws, etc.) bit my cat's tail.*

The result is a discrepancy between, on the one hand, the entities that are profiled by the subject and direct object nominals and serve as focal participants (clause-level trajector and primary landmark), and on the other hand, those entities which constitute their active zones with respect to the profiled relationship.

Such discrepancies represent the *normal situation* and hence should not be regarded as either special or pathological. This typical situation is depicted abstractly in Figure 2.10(a). The entities profiled as central relational participants are whole individuals (e.g. the dog (tr) and the cat (lm) in (9)b). However, only selected portions of these individuals figure directly in the profiled relationship (indicated by a heavy line) and thus comprise their active zones (shaded). Diagrammed in 2.10(b) is the less usual situation exemplified in (9)a, where the focal participants interact as undifferentiated wholes. In this case there is no discrepancy—the active zones and profiles coincide. Figure 2.10(c) shows the other way to avoid a profile/active-zone discrepancy, namely by selecting the active zones to be the profiled participants. The result is often infelicitous, as we saw in (10). *Bite* imposes a discrepancy as an intrinsic aspect of how it construes the scene: its trajector can only be the agent as a whole, not the teeth or any other part(s) of the body (cf. *His head bit me*).

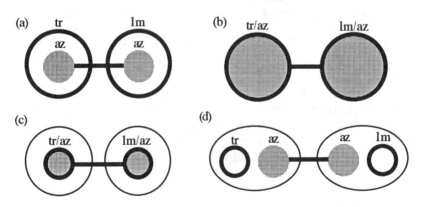

Figure 2.10

Active zones are not limited to subparts of the profiled entity. More generally, they need only be *associated* with that entity:

(11) a. *I'm in the phone book.*
     b. *The kettle is boiling.*
     c. *That car doesn't know where he's going.*

Thus it is only a representation of the speaker's name and phone number that appears in the phone book, not the actual individual. Similarly, it is not really the kettle that is boiling, but the water it contains, and it is not the car *per se* but rather its driver who needs directions. This type of situation is shown in Figure 2.10(d), with respect to which diagrams 2.10(a)-(c) can be seen as special cases.

    Such discrepancies are unproblematic in CG. The meaning of a sentence is not taken to be a "logical representation" in any standard sense, but is rather an integrated conceptualization some facets of which are rendered more salient than others. Nor are the notions subject and direct object characterized on apriori "logical" grounds, or even in terms of semantic roles. Though agent and patient represent their prototypical values, the schematic characterizations suggested for subjects and objects in general are based on prominence: in the relationship profiled at the clausal level of organization, the subject stands out as primary figure within the scene, and an object as secondary figure. The choice of subject and object can therefore vary (i.e. the spotlights of focal prominence can be directed at different participants) without necessarily affecting the array of conceptual content evoked as the basis for a clause's meaning. For instance, even though *bite* confers trajector status on the agent as a whole, its meaning still subsumes the full conception of biting, including the central role of the teeth and jaws.

    Although profile/active-zone discrepancies are natural (and even expected) from the standpoint of CG, there is often some communicative need or purpose for being specific in regard to the active zone. A variety of devices are potentially available to make this possible. One option, exemplified in (12), is to add another argument to the verb.

(12) a. *She blinked.*
     b. *?She blinked her eyes.*
     c. *She blinked her big blue eyes.*

Blink manifests a striking discrepancy between profile and active zone: only the eyes are involved, yet the person as a whole is chosen as trajector. There is usually not much reason to make the active zone explicit—seldom does one have occasion to blink anything other than one's own eyes—so a sentence like (12)b is marginal by virtue of pointless redundancy. But when there is some point to it, as in (12)c, where explicit mention of the eyes allows the specification of their properties, an object nominal referring to the active zone can be added quite felicitously. I would analyze *blink* as having two semantic variants: one in which the person as a whole is the only salient participant (the trajector, or primary figure); and another variant in which the active zone is also rendered prominent (as a landmark, or secondary figure).

An active zone is more commonly specified periphrastically by means of a prepositional phrase (or some comparable device). In (13)a, *on the tail* and *with its sharp teeth* respectively serve this function for the direct object and the subject.

(13) a. *Your dog bit my cat on the tail with its sharp teeth.*
b. *?Your dog bit my cat somewhere with its teeth.*

But as shown once more by the marginality of (13)b, resorting to such periphrasis is otiose unless it provides information not otherwise available. For our purposes here, the important feature of these prepositional-phrase constructions is a correspondence between the phrasal landmark (or equivalently, the profile of the prepositional object) and the subject's or direct object's active zone with respect to *bite*.

A frequent option in some languages is for the active zone to be specified by an incorporated noun. The following example is from Tetelcingo Nahuatl (see Tuggy 1986 for further data and discussion):

(14) *ni-k-[kama-teriksa]ᵥ*   'I kick him in the mouth.'
I-him-mouth-kick

The prefixes *ni-* 'I' and *k-* 'him' refer to the clausal subject and object, each of which manifests a profile/active-zone discrepancy motivated by the salience of a whole relative to its parts. The subject's active zone is apparent from the meaning of *teriksa* 'kick'. Serving this function for the object is the incorporated noun, whose profile corresponds to the active zone of the verb's primary landmark. I should note in passing that there is no need to posit a rule of "Possessor Ascension"; 'him' (rather than 'mouth') is the "true" direct object of 'kick'. The main reason for thinking otherwise has been the gratuitous assumption that the notions subject and object are somehow based on "logic", and that certain kinds of relationships (such as possession) have to be represented syntactically in underlying structure. By contrast, CG claims that subject- and objecthood are primarily matters of prominence. Moreover, it allows that essential relationships like possession might simply be inherent in the complex conception evoked by an expression or a construction—they do not have to receive individual syntactic representation in order to figure importantly in an expression's meaning.

We have seen that profile/active-zone discrepancy need not be based on a whole/part relationship, but merely requires some evident association. One kind of entity a thing can be associated with is a relation in which it participates. We might therefore anticipate the possibility of a relation serving as the active zone through which one of its participants takes part in another relationship, as shown abstractly in Figure 2.11. In fact, because a relation is intrinsically associated with its participants, which usually have greater cognitive salience (owing to concreteness or to their nominal character), the occurrence of profile/active-zone discrepancies of this sort can actually be predicted.

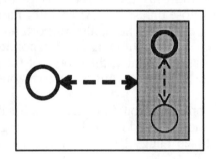

Figure 2.11

Examples are readily found:

(15) a. *Fred is really slow at paying his debts.*
      b. *When it comes to paying his debts, Fred is really slow.*
      c. *I started my dissertation—planning it, that is.*
      d. *Goldfish are easy to swallow.*

In (15)a, *at paying his debts* specifies Fred's active zone with respect to the profiled relationship of being slow; it is only by engaging in some process, in this case *pay his debts*, that an individual can be located on a scale of relative speed. The same active zone is specified in 15(b) by another grammatical device, namely a *when*-clause. In

(15)c, the afterthought *planning it, that is* identifies the actual process the speaker has initiated; this process is the active zone of *my dissertation* with respect to *start*. And in (15)d, the infinitival complement *to swallow* describes the relationship enabling *goldfish* to be situated on a scale of difficulty.

Profile/active-zone discrepancy is a special case of metonymy. More precisely, it represents the metonymic choice of focal participants in a profiled relationship. Though usually regarded as a semantic phenomenon, metonymy turns out to be central and essential to grammar. We have seen it to be a pivotal factor in determining the subject and object of relational expressions. Moreover, a variety of grammatical constructions function to identify an active zone when there is reason to make it explicit. Grammar is thus a rich source of data for the investigation of metonymy. At the same time, a recognition of its prevalence and centrality is critical not just for describing grammar but for a realistic assessment of its basic nature.[6]

5. Setting vs. participant

As physical creatures, we exist in space. At any given moment, we find ourselves in a global spatial setting (e.g. a room, a street, or a valley), within which we occupy a particular location. Whenever we open our eyes, a broad expanse fills our visual field, but we normally focus our attention on the occupants of a limited area within it. The domain of time is comparably organized. Within its vast extension, our immediate experience is always confined to a small portion of it, and we typically direct our attention to events and situations of limited duration.

These fundamental aspects of our moment-to-moment experience give rise to a number of conceptual archetypes. A *setting* is a global expanse of space or time. A *location* is some "fragment" of a spatial or temporal setting, e.g. the portion containing a certain thing or event. The entity found at a given location can be called its *occupant*: a person or physical object in the case of spatial locations, an event or situation for temporal ones. Whereas people and objects merely *occupy* locations, they are thought of as *interacting* with one another, most often force-dynamically. They are *participants* by virtue of engaging in relationships that constitute events or situations. A canonical event consists of the energetic interaction between two participants.[7]

A common type of situation consists of a participant occupying a particular location.

The conceptual opposition between a setting or location on the one hand, and a participant on the other, has considerable grammatical import. We saw previously, for example, that German *bis* 'until' requires its object to be a location (cf. (7) and Figure 2.7). A shift from participant status to a locational construal may also figure in the evolution of body-part nouns into prepositions (Figure 2.8). It is usual for participants to be coded by subject and object nominals, locations by clause-internal complements, and settings by clause-external modifiers, as in (16)a.

(16) a. *In the auditorium, Gerald placed the package under a seat.*
      b. *At the very top of the tree, she could see a bluejay.*

There are however many departures from this prototypical arrangement. For instance, the clause-external adverb in (16)b specifies the location of the object rather than the setting for the overall event. There are also many constructions in which the referent of a subject or object nominal is construed as a setting or location rather than a participant.[8]

People and smallish physical objects are ideally suited to function as participants, and large spatial or temporal regions as settings. Status as a participant, setting, or location is not, however, intrinsic to an entity, but depends on how it is construed in the context of the overall situation. Thus *the park* functions as a setting in (17)a, as the object's location in (17)b, and as a participant in (17)c.

(17) a. *In the park last Sunday, Janet saw a friend.*
      b. *From the top of the building, Janet saw a friend in the park.*
      c. *The bulldozers destroyed the park.*

Not only is the distinction a matter of construal, but it can also remain covert: whether an entity is conceived as a setting, a location, or a participant cannot invariably be ascertained on the basis of its form, its position, or even the grammatical relation it bears in a clause. The distinction may nevertheless have grammatical consequences which make it visible to the analyst.

Consider the following examples (Rice 1987a):

(18) a. *Fred rushed to Marsha, because he needed advice.*
     b. *Fred rushed to the countryside, because he needed a rest.*

The position and grammatical role of *Marsha* in (18)a would appear to be precisely analogous to that of *the countryside* in (18)b. Yet, since people are usually participants, and the countryside is a canonical setting or location, they tend strongly to be so construed unless there are contrary indications. A consequence of these alternate construals is observed in the fact that the first sentence passivizes far more easily than the second:

(19) a. *Marsha was rushed to by Fred, because he needed advice.*
     b. **The countryside was rushed to by Fred, because he needed a rest.*

    At issue is whether the verb-preposition sequence *rush to* is capable of being analyzed as a complex transitive verb taking the following nominal as its object. Only to the extent that it can does passivization become an option, since passives in English are sensitive to transitivity. Rice (1987a, 1987b) has demonstrated that transitivity is a global semantic property which cannot be localized in any particular clausal element.[9] An essential component of transitivity is the *interaction of participants*. The contrast in (19) is thus ascribable to the requirement that a transitive object (and hence a passive subject) have participant status. In (19)a Fred and Marsha are readily construed as participating in an interaction. By contrast, the relationship Fred bears to the countryside in (19)b is simply one of occupying a certain location.

    If transitivity presupposes interacting participants, then it should also be diminished or absent in a *setting-subject construction*, where the status of subject (clause-level trajector) is conferred on the global setting. Consider first Figure 2.12(a), which represents the usual situation of a clause profiling the interaction between two participants and putting them in focus as trajector and landmark. The relation these bear to the setting is indicated by a two-headed arrow, but it has no particular salience and need not even be expressed. Figure 2.12(b) depicts the contrasting situation, not at all uncommon, in which the setting is chosen as trajector (hence subject). The setting's prominence enhances that of any relationship involving it, notably the one it bears to its occupants, consisting of participants and their interaction. In fact, this "container-content" relation becomes the primary segment of the clausal profile (thus the two-headed arrow is given in bold). Because it holds between a setting and its occupants, rather between than interacting participants, the profiled relationship is non-transitive. In English the resulting clauses should therefore fail to passivize.

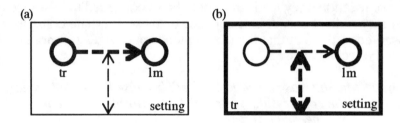

Figure 2.12

The sentences in (20) exemplify the contrast between partici-pant-subject and setting-subject constructions.[10] The verb *feature* allows as its subject either the creator of a depictive work (in this case a novel) or the work itself, as respectively shown in (20)a-b.

(20) a. *Hillerman features Jim Chee in his latest novel.*
      b. *Hillerman's latest novel features Jim Chee.*

Whereas an author is clearly a participant who interacts with charac-ters when creating them, portraying them, or deciding their role in a novel, this latter is more readily construed as a setting for them. It is therefore correctly predicted that only (20)a should passivize:

(21) a. *Jim Chee is featured by Hillerman in his latest novel.*
      b. **Jim Chee is featured by Hillerman's latest novel.*

Though it is not overtly marked, the semantic distinction between a participant and a setting proves to be grammatically significant.

6. Semantics and grammar

Numerous other "invisible" semantic constructs can be posited and justified. They represent facets of conceptual structure that are crucial to both meaning and grammar even though they are not per se either noticed or signaled explicitly. They do however leave grammatical tracks that linguists can learn to recognize and interpret. Such constructs are strongly motivated on grounds of descriptive utility: they enable one to account for subtle semantic contrasts and differences in grammatical behavior, and to properly characterize grammatical constructions.

Linguistic theorists commonly pose the question of whether grammar is predictable on the basis of meaning. The question is misguided, for it presupposes prior and independent knowledge of what an expression means. Perhaps ironically, a conceptualist semantics implies the absence of such knowledge, the reason being that meaning is largely a matter of construal, and construal is largely invisible. Before conducting sophisticated analysis, therefore, we know very little about an expression's actual semantic value. Usually, in fact, grammatical structure provides the best clues in this regard: through its grammar, a language is trying to tell us something about how it structures meanings, and it is our task as linguists to learn to interpret these signs. To ask whether meaning affords a basis for predicting grammar is consequently to misconceive the basic logic of the situation. The problem is rather to formulate—simultaneously—a characterization of semantic structure that accommodates construal, as well as a characterization of grammar that elucidates its role in the structuring and symbolization of conceptual content. Ideally, the two facets of this endeavor should be mutually revelatory and mutually supportive, their success judged in terms of the coherence and insight of the overall description.

Chapter 3
The meaning of *of*

The preposition *of* poses an important challenge to the CG doctrine that all elements validly posited in grammar have a meaning.* In the generative tradition, it has a long history of being analyzed as a meaningless element manipulated by syntactic rules for purely grammatical purposes. I will argue, however, that even *of*—the English preposition for which such an analysis seems most plausible—can in fact be ascribed a semantic value that motivates its grammatical behavior.

1. The question of meaningfulness

The analysis of *of* as a meaningless syntactic element was already manifest in one of the earliest classic works of transformational grammar. In *The Grammar of English Nominalizations*, R. B. Lees (1960: 65-70, 104-105) posited derivations like the following:

(1) a. *the machine's humming* ==> *the humming of the machine*
     b. *He's selling the car.* ==> *He's the seller of the car.*
     c. *He drew the picture rapidly.* ==>
          his rapid drawing of the picture
     d. *the appointment of John by the committee* ==>
          John's appointment by the committee

In the spirit of the times, I myself felt no compunction about hypothesizing, for French, a rule that (in effect) changed *à* to *de* (Langacker 1968: 69):

(2) *la porte qui est à la cathédrale* ==> *la porte à la cathédrale* ==>
          la porte de la cathédrale 'the door of the cathedral'

The tradition of treating *of* as a semantically empty element, with the sole purpose of being kicked around by syntactic rules, was continued by Chomsky (1970: 202, 211), who proposed the derivations in (3).

(3) a. *John's picture ==> the picture of John's*
   b. *the picture of John ==> John's picture*
   c. [*[several [John]*$_{N''}$ *]*$_{Spec}$ [*[proofs]*$_N$ *[the theorem]*$_{N''}$ *]*$_{N'}$ *]*$_{N''}$
      ==> several of John's proofs of the theorem

This pattern of *of*-abuse has persisted. For instance, Hudson (1984: 136, 143, 147) has stated that *of* is a word "without any independent semantic structure", that it does "not contribute any distinct meaning of its own", that it is "an empty word".

By contrast, central claims of CG lead directly to the expectation that *of* will prove meaningful. In an earlier work (1982), I suggested a meaning that *of* exhibits in a number of its basic uses: it profiles a relationship between two entities such that one of them (the trajector) constitutes an *inherent and restricted subpart* of the other (the landmark).[1] Straightforwardly accommodated by this characterization are expressions like *the bottom of the jar*, *a kernel of corn*, and *some of the peas*. The bottom of a jar, for instance, is clearly an inherent and restricted subpart of it. Similarly, a single kernel represents an intrinsic but quite limited portion of the mass referred to by *corn*. As for the third example, I analyze certain quantifiers (notably *some*, *most*, and *all*) as nouns that profile a mass characterized as constituting some proportion of a larger, reference mass (FCG2: ch. 3). Hence *some of the peas* portrays the mass designated by *some* as a limited but non-zero portion of the larger mass identified as *the peas*.

Two considerations supporting the proposed characterization were advanced in the earlier paper. First, in conjunction with appropri-ate descriptions of *on* and *to*, it accounts for judgments like these:

(4) a. *the {bottom/?label/?lid} of the jar*
   b. *the{?bottom/label/lid} on the jar*
   c. *the {??bottom/?label/lid} to the jar*

Whereas *of* profiles an inherent-and-restricted-subpart relationship, *on* designates a relationship of contact and support involving two distinct objects, and *to* a relationship between separate (or separable) objects that belong together in an integrated assembly. Thus with *of*, in (4)a, *bottom* is more felicitous than *label* or *lid*, since a jar's bottom is intrinsic to it, the label and lid being more extrinsic. Conversely, *label* and *lid* go better with *on*, as seen in (4)b, provided that they are actually attached to the jar; *bottom* is problematic because a jar and its bottom are not distinct objects. In (4)c, *lid* fully satisfies *to*'s requirement of separability, while *label* does so only partially and *bottom* not at all. It seems to me that there is nothing mysterious or implausible about the meaning ascribed to *of*, which if anything is less abstract and more easily grasped than that of *to*.

The second consideration pertained to constructions involving quantifiers, as exemplified in (5).

(5) a. *{all/most/some/many/seven} of the peas*
     b. *{all/*most/*some/*many/*seven} the peas*

Note that *all* contrasts with most other quantifiers by participating in the construction of (5)b, in which it combines directly with a full noun phrase, without *of* intervening. If *of* does indeed profile the relationship that an inherent, restricted subpart bears to a whole, this distribution can be seen as quite natural. Unlike the other quantifiers, *all* profiles a mass whose relation to the reference mass is one of coincidence, i.e. it exhausts the reference mass. Thus for *all*, but not for the other quantifiers, the subpart relation between the two masses fails to qualify as a proper one—the degree to which the profiled mass is restricted vis-à-vis the reference mass is zero. It is hardly surprising, then, that for this quantifier in particular the language might evolve an alternative construction lacking *of*, for which the notion of restrictiveness constitutes a salient specification. Confirming this analysis is the alternation between *both of the peas* and *both the peas*, since *both* is essentially the dual counterpart of *all* (it profiles a mass that coincides with a reference mass comprising just two members).

Further support was offered in FCG1 (227):

(6) a. *the tip {of/*in} my finger*
     b. *the splinter {*of/in} my finger*

(7) a. *the {color/center/edge/growth} of the lawn*
     b. *that brown spot {in/*of} the lawn*

In (6), the tip is an inherent part of a finger, whereas a splinter is considered extrinsic to it, even though spatially it may be wholly included. Likewise in (7), facets of a lawn such as its color, center, edge, and growth are all in some sense intrinsic to it, whereas a brown spot is regarded as an unwanted intrusion. But if these examples support the contention that *of* is meaningful, they also suggest that the proffered definition, as it stands, is valid only in certain uses.

Observe that while the center and edge of a lawn can be considered intrinsic and restricted subparts of it, the same cannot be said for its color or its growth (without doing violence to the notion part).

Additional non-conforming data is easily found:

(8) a. *the chirping of birds; the consumption of alcohol;*
            the destruction of the Iraqi army
    b. *a ring of gold; a book of matches; a man of integrity*
    c. *the state of California; the crime of shoplifting;*
            a distance of 10 miles
    d. *an acquaintance of Bill; the chief of this tribe;*
            the father of the bride

In (8)a, *of* introduces periphrastically the argument of a nominalized verb. Now even if we stretch the notion of a part/whole relationship to encompass the relation between an event and its participants, nominal periphrasis still contravenes the previous definition with respect to trajector/landmark alignment: the participant, corresponding to *of*'s object, has to be identified as the part, and the event as the whole, yet the definition specifies that the subject (trajector) is an inherent, restricted subpart of the object (landmark). Moreover, characterization in terms of a part/whole relationship is rather dubious for the expressions in (8)b and clearly inappropriate in (8)c-d. In (8)b, *of*'s landmark is better described as the source material or an essential quality of its trajector than as a whole which has it as a subpart. In (8)c, *of*'s trajector and landmark are conceived as being the same entity, characterized schematically by the head noun (e.g. *state*) and in more specific terms by the prepositional object (*California*). And in (8)d it is evident that the trajector is merely associated with the landmark, not a subpart of it in any narrow sense.

Like most other expressions, *of* must therefore be regarded as polysemous. The value described previously, wherein *of* profiles an inherent-and-restricted-subpart relationship between its trajector and landmark, holds for only some of its uses, though it is reasonably considered prototypical. This sense is sketched in Figure 3.1(a), where the double line represents an *intrinsic* relationship. A variety of other senses can be posited to accommodate the kinds of uses exemplified in (8). Is there some schematic value that all these more specific senses can plausibly be said to share? I believe so. It seems quite accurate to describe them all as designating an intrinsic relationship of some kind between the two participants, as diagrammed in Figure

3.1(b). A part/whole relation is just one type of intrinsic relationship, albeit one with special cognitive salience. Though participants may not, strictly speaking, be subparts of an event, they are clearly intrinsic to it. Obviously intrinsic to an entity is the material from which it is made, as are essential (as opposed to accidental) qualities. The examples in (8)c are similarly unproblematic, for an entity could hardly not be intrinsic to itself. As for (8)d, observe that the head noun is in each case *relational* (though it profiles a thing): an *acquaintance*, *chief*, or *father* can only qualify as such by virtue of a particular kind of relationship it bears to another entity (specified by the prepositional object). This relationship is thus intrinsic to the head's characterization.

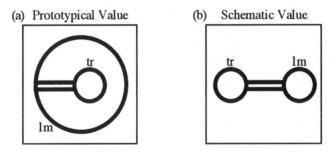

Figure 3.1

2. Complement vs. modifier

At this juncture, it is worth noting an iconicity between *of*'s phonological value and the meaning ascribed to it (cf. Haiman 1983). Of all the English prepositions, *of* is phonologically the weakest by any reasonable criterion. Note that it usually reduces and cliticizes, often being virtually inaudible. Now as one facet of its iconicity, *of* is arguably the most tenuous of the English prepositions from the semantic standpoint as well, if only by virtue of being abstract and lacking a basic spatial value. Its phonological minimality is further iconic with respect to its meaning in that the notion of intrinsicness implies a minimal conceptual distance between the relational participants. To see this clearly, we might compare the normal use of a locative preposition, for instance *the bench under the tree*, with a typical use of *of*, e.g. *the father of the bride*. When *under the tree* combines with the head noun *bench*, it introduces a relationship and a participant that the head itself does not invoke; it expands the scene to encompass new elements not prefigured by the head. When *of the bride* combines with *father*, on the other hand, the relationship and participant it specifies serve merely to characterize in more precise detail notions that the head itself introduces in schematic terms. A *father* is necessarily a father with respect to some other individual, which the prepositional phrase identifies as *the bride*. The scene evoked by the head is rendered more specific but is not expanded (except insofar as *bride* itself implies other elements).

Diagrammatically, this contrast can be observed by comparing the difference between *bench* and *the bench under the tree* in Figure 3.2, below, with that between *father* and *the father of the bride* in Figure 3.3. These diagrams show in explicit detail relevant aspects of the semantic and grammatical organization of the two complex expressions, as analyzed in CG.[2] The theory holds that grammar reduces to patterns for the successive integration of simpler symbolic structures to form progressively larger ones. At each level of organization (or constituency), two or more component structures are integrated to form a composite structure (which can in turn function as a component structure at the next higher level). Such integration takes place at both the semantic and the phonological pole, the phonological integration serving to symbolize the semantic integration. Only the semantic pole is represented in these diagrams (the orthographic labels merely identify the structures).

Sketched in Figure 3.2 is the semantic pole of *the bench under the tree*. At the first (or lower) level of constituency, *under* combines with *the tree* to form the prepositional phrase *under the tree*. *Under* profiles a relation between two things at different locations along the vertical axis, construing the higher of these entities as a landmark for purposes of situating the other, the trajector. Being a nominal expression, *the tree* profiles a thing; for diagrammatic convenience, its complex semantic specifications are abbreviated by a mnemonic indication of its shape. Integration is always effected by correspondences established between subparts of the component structures; these are indicated by dotted lines. In a prepositional phrase, the landmark of the preposition corresponds to the profile of the object nominal. Thus, when corresponding entities are superimposed and their specifications merged to form the composite structure, *under the tree* inherits the specifications of *the tree* for the characterization of its landmark. *Under the tree* is then left with a specified landmark but a highly schematic trajector. This is rectified at the second level of constituency, where *under the tree* combines with *bench*. As is typical in a modifying construction, their integration is effected by a correspondence between the modifier's schematic trajector and the profile of the modified element. By superimposing corresponding entities, one obtains the overall composite structure for *the bench under the tree*, shown at the top.

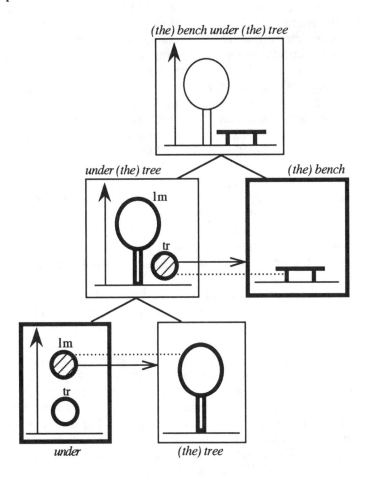

Figure 3.2

Two other aspects of this diagram need to be explained. First, it is usual for the composite structure at a given level of organization to inherit its profiling from one of the component structures. Thus *under the tree* retains the relational profile of *under*, whereas *the bench under the tree*, being nominal in character, retains the nominal profile of *bench* (i.e. it profiles a thing). The component that lends its profile to the composite structure is termed the *profile determinant* and indicated diagrammatically by means of the heavy-line box enclosing it. The profile determinant at a particular level of constituency is what is traditionally known as the *head*—thus *under* is the head of the prepositional phrase, and *bench* the head noun of the full noun phrase. Second, it is usual for one component structure to elaborate a schematic substructure of the other component. In the present example, *the tree* elaborates the schematic landmark of *under*, whereas *bench* elaborates the schematic trajector of *under the tree*. Elaboration is represented by a solid arrow, and the elaborated substructure (termed an *elaboration site*, or *e-site* for short) is marked by hatching. These notions enable us to characterize the traditional distinction between complements and modifiers. A *complement* can be defined as a component structure that *elaborates* a salient substructure of the head; hence *the tree* is a complement (or *argument*) of *under*. Conversely, a *modifier* is a component structure a salient substructure of which is *elaborated by* the head. *Under the tree* is thus a modifier with respect to *bench*.

Analogous relationships can be observed in *the father of the bride*, diagrammed in Figure 3.3. *Of* profiles an intrinsic relationship and serves as head (profile determinant) at the first level of constituency, where its landmark is elaborated by a noun phrase complement, namely *the bride* (whose complex semantic specifications are abbreviated as B). At the second level of constituency, *of the bride* counts as a modifier because its schematic trajector is elaborated by the head, *father*, which profiles a thing characterized by the parent-offspring relationship it bears to a reference individual. There is however an important grammatical difference between the two complex expressions, as previously noted: whereas *under the tree* introduces a relationship that *bench* itself does not invoke, *of the bride* reinforces and renders more precise a relationship that is fully prefigured by its head. This contrast is reflected diagrammatically in the multiple correspondence lines linking *father* with *of the bride*. In addition to the trajector-profile correspondence typical of a modifier construction, we observe two others. First, the intrinsic relationship profiled by the prepositional phrase is equated with the parent-offspring relationship evoked

by *father* as part of its inherent characterization. And within these relationships, the reference individual (offspring) implied by *father* is
identified with the landmark of the prepositional phrase (i.e. the
profile of the prepositional object). Hence these two relationships are
superimposed and merge into one at the composite structure level.

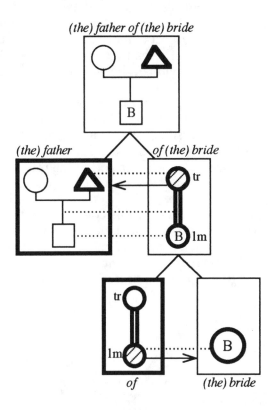

Figure 3.3

We thus begin to see the grammatical consequences entailed
by *of*'s semantic value. The fact that it designates an intrinsic relationship facilitates a tighter grammatical bond wherein that relationship is
equated with a central and salient facet of the head. This in turn affects
complement/modifier organization, since CG defines these notions in
terms of the extent to which one component structure elaborates a
salient substructure of the other. So defined, complement status and
modifier status are matters of degree. Moreover, they need not be
incompatible with one another. We have just noted that an *of*-phrase

counts as a modifier in expressions like *the father of the bride*: the head, *father*, elaborates a highly salient substructure of it, namely the trajector (figure within the profiled relationship). By virtue of its meaning, however, the *of*-phrase can also—to a somewhat lesser extent —be regarded as a complement of its head. This is so because *of the bride* elaborates the parent-offspring relationship that is pivotal to the head's semantic structure. To be sure, it does not elaborate all aspects of that relationship: with respect to the nature of the relation itself, the head is actually more specific than the prepositional phrase. Yet in regard to the reference individual, the head is wholly schematic and the *of*-phrase quite specific.

The valence link between *father* and *of the bride* is depicted more fully in Figure 3.4. As before, the prepositional-phrase trajector constitutes an elaboration site spelled out in finer detail by the head noun. What is added to the diagram is an elaborative relation going in the other direction, wherein the parent-offspring relationship inherent in *father* functions as an e-site rendered more specific by *of the bride* (at least in regard to the reference individual). The head/modifier configuration is better instantiated by this construction than is the head-complement configuration, for the latter involves a less salient e-site only a portion of which is actually elaborated by the other component structure. The expression nonetheless manifests head/complement organization to a substantial degree.

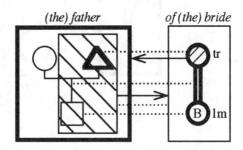

Figure 3.4

We can expect this partial complement status to have grammatical ramifications, provided that the traditional complement/modifier distinction is indeed linguistically significant. One grammatical consequence cited by Hudson (1984: 79-81), who does not himself make that distinction, is the contrast in (9). Hudson took the example from

Jackendoff (1977: 60), who in turn cited Lakoff, who noted (1970b: 405) that *many* can have "wide scope" in (10)a but not in (10)b.

(9) a. *Fathers of few children have any fun.*
    b. **Fathers with few children have any fun.*

(10) a. *Fathers of many children read few books.*
     b. *Fathers with many children read few books.*

This is not the place for a detailed examination of quantifiers or quantifier scope (see FCG2: 3.3). Here we can simply note that a quantifier contained in an *of*-phrase is more "accessible" than one in a *with*-phrase for purposes of sanctioning a negative-polarity item (*few* sanctions *any*) or being interpreted as having broad scope with respect to another quantifier. We can attribute this greater accessibility to the *of*-phrase's semi-complement status, whereby it elaborates a relationship that is salient and fully prefigured within the head noun itself. By contrast, *with* encodes a contingent, hence extrinsic relationship.[3] A *with*-phrase thus partakes of complement status to a lesser degree if at all, and the participant it introduces is less accessible because the head does not prefigure it.

3. Nominal periphrasis

We are now ready to address *of*'s use in specifying periphrastically the argument of a nominalized verb, as exemplified earlier in (8)a. This use follows naturally from the proposed semantic characterization, since an event's participants are inherent to its conception. In the terminology of CG, participants are *conceptually autonomous* in the sense that it is possible to conceive of them independently of any event conception. On the other hand, an event is *conceptually dependent* in that one cannot conceptualize the event without in some way invoking the conception of its participants (if only in vague, schematic terms). Further supporting the conceptual dependence of an event vis-à-vis its participants (and hence their intrinsicness to an event conception) are several observations: that an event's location cannot be distinguished from that of its participants; that participants are easy to localize (or "point to") within a scene, whereas an event per se is more abstract and diffuse; and consequently, that participants are natural *reference points* for purposes of conceiving and distinguishing events (Chapter 6).

It is well known that *of*-periphrasis follows an ergative pattern, being used to specify transitive objects and intransitive subjects. If only one participant is specified periphrastically, *of* can introduce it regardless of whether it corresponds to a clausal subject or object (i.e. to the trajector or landmark of the verb stem). We see this in (11)a, where *the demonstrators* specifies *chant*'s trajector (on an intransitive construal), and (11)b, where *the slogans* spells out its landmark (on a transitive construal).

(11) a. *the chanting {of/by} the demonstrators*
      b. *the chanting of the slogans*
      c. *the chanting of the slogans by the demonstrators*

When both participants are specified periphrastically, *of* can only introduce the landmark, as in (11)c. The periphrastic role of *by*, on the other hand, is limited to a trajector ascribed some measure of control or initiative capacity.

This alignment is no accident, for ergativity reflects an aspect of the structure of event conceptions whereby a transitive object or an intransitive subject has a greater degree of intrinsicness than do other participants.[4] What an intransitive subject has in common with a transitive object is that they both encode the theme, i.e. the single participant in a thematic relationship that functions as an event conception's conceptually autonomous "core". Thematic relationships include the simple conception of a change of state (e.g. *melt*), a change of position (*rise*), having an experience (*itch*), or merely occupying a location or exhibiting a static property (*exist, be tall*). To varying degrees, thematic relationships are conceptually autonomous in that we are able to conceptualize them independently of any agent or initiative force that might be responsible for them. A relationship so conceived is said to receive an *absolute construal*. To the extent that a thematic relationship is conceived as the endpoint of an action chain, being induced by the transmission of energy from an external source (whose action may in turn result from external forces), it is said to receive an *energetic construal*. An action chain with three participants (e.g. an agent, instrument, and patient) is sketched in Figure 3.5, where circles stand for participants, a double arrow for the transmission of energy, and the arrow inside the circle for an internal change of state.

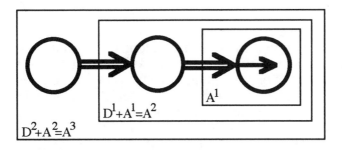

Figure 3.5

     The essential point is that a complex event conception generally has a *layered* structure: the thematic relationship constitutes its conceptually autonomous core, and each successive causal link (working backwards along the action chain) is conceptually dependent on the event it induces and thus comprises an "outer" layer with respect to it. This layered organization is motivated not only on semantic grounds but also by overt grammatical evidence. If we assume (quite plausibly) that a conceptually autonomous structure is more likely than a conceptually dependent one to be coded by a linguistic expression felt to be non-elliptic, complete, and self-contained, the following judgments are predicted:

(12) a. *The glass broke.* $[= A^1]$
       b. *A hammer broke the glass.* $[= A^2]$
       c. *Floyd broke the glass (with a hammer).* $[= A^3]$
       d. **Floyd {broke/caused}.* [*Floyd* = agent]
       e. **The hammer {broke/caused}.* [*hammer* = instrument]
       f. **Floyd {broke/caused} the hammer.* [*hammer* = instrument]

That is, only a thematic relationship, or a higher-order autonomous structure formed by augmenting a thematic relationship with one or more layers of energy input, should in general be codable by a sentence judged well-formed and natural. The notion of causation or energy transmission is conceptually dependent—it necessarily invokes some conception of the event induced—so a causative expression that makes no mention of the thematic relationship will usually be considered infelicitous.

     There is reason, then, to regard the thematic relationship as the conceptually autonomous core—and hence the most intrinsic component—of a complex event conception (cf. Keenan 1984). It follows that the theme is more intrinsic to the overall event conception than other participants, which makes it natural that a preposition profiling an intrinsic relationship should be adopted to specify themes peri-phrastically. How does this work, exactly? It is actually quite straight-forward. We need only adapt the semantic value and grammatical con-structions previously examined to the special case in which a nomi-nalized verb functions as the head noun.

For our purposes, we can simply assume that a nominalized verb like *chirping, consumption, destruction, chanting*, or *breaking* represents the *conceptual reification* of an event conception.[5] Let us adopt the abbreviatory notation in Figure 3.6(a) for an event, or more generally a process, the kind of complex relationship claimed to be characteristic of verbs. A processual expression profiles a relationship (shown here as a line connecting the circles representing two partici-pants) followed sequentially in its evolution through conceived time (as indicated by the heavy-line segment of the time arrow). The ef-fect of conceptual reification can then be diagrammed as in Figure 3.6(b): the heavy-line circle signifies that the event or process as a whole is construed as an abstract thing and is profiled by the nominal expression. The meaning of a nominalized verb will thus be depicted in this fashion.

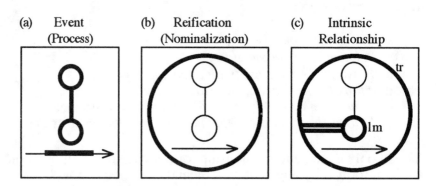

Figure 3.6

Schematically, *of* profiles an intrinsic relationship between two entities (Figure 3.1(b)). We have seen, moreover, that an event's participants are intrinsic to its conception. That *of* should be used to code the relationship between an event overall and one of its partici-pants is therefore quite natural. The particular sense assumed by *of* in this use is sketched in Figure 3.6(c): it is just a matter of applying the schematic value (Figure 3.1(b)) to the special situation where the trajector is a reified process and the landmark is a participant in that process (specifically the theme, the most intrinsic participant). Observe that the trajector/landmark alignment depicted in the diagram pertains to *of*, not to the reified process. Indeed, the reified process as a whole is one participant in the relationship of intrinsicness that *of* profiles.

Let us now examine in detail a particular periphrastic expression, namely *the breaking of the glass* (again ignoring definite articles). Its semantic pole is diagrammed in Figure 3.7. At the lower level of constituency, *of* combines with *the glass* to form the prepositional phrase *of the glass*. Their integration follows the usual pattern for prepositional-object constructions: the preposition's landmark corresponds to the nominal profile, and the nominal's semantic specifications (abbreviated as G) elaborate this schematic landmark. Superimposing the specifications of these corresponding entities yields the composite structure *of the glass*, which inherits its relational profile from *of*. Observe that the line connecting the two event participants is dashed at both levels, to indicate that the nature of the reified event is characterized only schematically by either the preposition or the prepositional phrase itself. It is the head noun (*breaking* in this example) that identifies the specific event type in question.

At the higher level of constituency, the schematic reified event functioning as trajector of the prepositional phrase is elaborated by the head noun and is thus identified as the specific event of breaking. Observe that the lowest correspondence line equates the prepositional trajector and the nominal profile, as in most modifier constructions; this entails the other correspondences, which hold between the reified events' participants and component relations. The composite structure is formed, as usual, by superimposing corresponding entities and adopting the head's profile. Hence the overall expression designates the reified conception of an act of breaking, in which the theme is characterized as a specific glass.

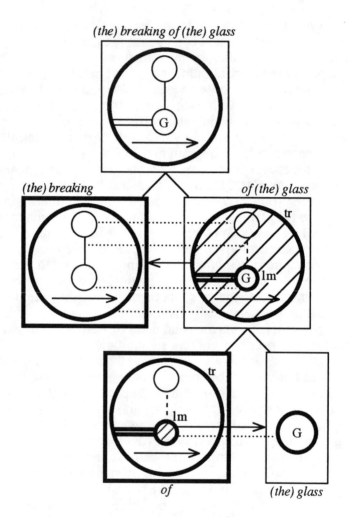

Figure 3.7

For sake of comparison, let us briefly consider a case of *by*-periphrasis, e.g. *the breaking of the glass by Floyd*, whose semantic pole is diagrammed in Figure 3.8. Like the relevant sense of *of*, the periphrastic *by* profiles the relationship between a reified event as a whole and one of its participants. What distinguishes *by* from *of* is that the participant in question initiates the event or is in some way responsible for it, as indicated diagrammatically by the double-line arrow. Otherwise, the two periphrastic constructions are quite parallel, as comparison of Figures 3.7 and 3.8 readily shows. Notice that the composite structure of Figure 3.7, *breaking of the glass*, functions as a component structure in Figure 3.8: it elaborates the schematic trajector of the prepositional phrase *by Floyd*, which in turn specifies the initiator of the reified event. Hence the full nominal profiles an act of breaking in which the theme is identified as a specific glass, and the actor as Floyd.

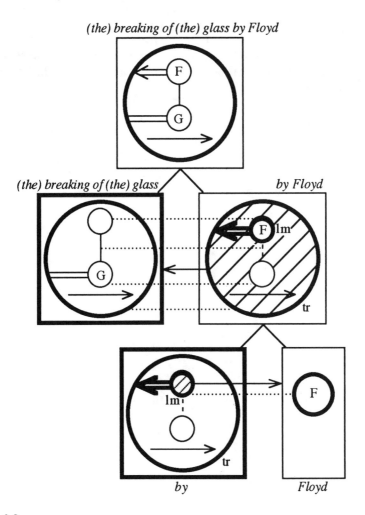

Figure 3.8

4. Conclusion

I conclude that *of* is a consistently meaningful element whose grammatical behavior reflects its semantic value. Since *of* has long been a prime example of a semantically empty grammatical marker, and since complex nominals like *the breaking of the glass* have typified the apparent influence of purely formal factors in the shaping of linguistic expressions, it is a matter of some significance that a coherent account is possible in which each component element has a meaning (in fact, a meaning related to those it displays in other uses), and each grammatical construction reduces to a configuration of symbolic structures. All facets of grammatical structure are claimed to be describable in symbolic terms.

Chapter 4
A dynamic usage-based model

This chapter and the next will address some foundational theoretical issues.* The present chapter focuses on the very nature of linguistic structure. It shows how a small set of basic psychological phenomena operate in all domains, giving rise to patterns exhibiting any degree of regularity. Chapter 5 will then address constituency, considering both its cognitive status and its role in grammar.

1. The usage-based conception

In a *usage-based model*, "substantial importance is given to the actual use of the linguistic system and a speaker's knowledge of this use; the grammar is held responsible for a speaker's knowledge of the full range of linguistic conventions, regardless of whether these conventions can be subsumed under more general statements. [It is a] nonreductive approach to linguistic structure that employs fully articulated schematic networks and emphasizes the importance of low-level schemas" (FCG1: 494). The "maximalist", "non-reductive", "bottom-up" nature of CG contrasts with the "minimalist", "reductive", "top-down" spirit of generative theory, at least in its original (archetypal) formulation. Let me start by briefly describing each property.

Generative theory has always tried to minimize what a speaker has to learn and mentally represent in acquiring a language. Its minimalism was originally based on economy: the best grammar was the one that did the job with the fewest symbols. In recent years, the emphasis has shifted to positing a richly specified universal grammar, so that the role of experience in learning a language involves little more than the setting of parameters. By contrast, CG accepts that becoming a fluent speaker involves a prodigious amount of actual learning, and tries to minimize the postulation of innate structures specific to language. I consider these to be empirical issues. If one aims for psychological reality, it cannot be maintained on purely methodological grounds that the most parsimonious grammar is the best one. Should it prove that the cognitive representation of language is in fact massive and highly redundant, the most accurate description of it (as a psychological entity) will reflect that size and redundancy.[1]

The issue of reductionism pertains to the relation between general statements and more specific statements that amount to special cases of them. Suppose a speaker has learned both a general "rule" (such as the pattern for combining prepositions with their objects) and certain specific expressions which instantiate the pattern (e.g. *for me*, *on the floor, in the garage*). Traditionally, in generative accounts, the instantiating expressions would be excluded from the grammar on grounds of economy. Since they are regularly derivable by rule, to list them individually would be to miss a generalization. This reasoning however rests on the spurious assumption that rules and lists are mutually exclusive (the *rule/list fallacy*). There is a viable alternative: to include in the grammar both rules and instantiating expressions. This option allows any valid generalizations to be captured (by means of rules), and while the descriptions it affords may not be maximally economical, they have to be preferred on grounds of psychological accuracy to the extent that specific expressions do in fact become established as well-rehearsed units. Such units are cognitive entities in their own right whose existence is not reducible to that of the general patterns they instantiate.

The "top-down" spirit of generative grammar is evident in its emphasis on general rules and universal principles, as well as its historical neglect of lexicon, low-level subpatterns, and the patient enumeration of idiosyncrasies. Less-than-fully-general phenomena were in fact embarrassing and problematic from the outset, handled by a series of ad hoc devices (e.g. the "rule features" proposed in Lakoff 1970a) appended to the rule-based system. Now certainly an objective in CG is to capture whatever generalizations the data will support. There are nonetheless several respects in which the framework manifests a "bottom-up" orientation. For one thing, it recognizes that linguistic patterns occupy the entire spectrum ranging from the wholly idiosyncratic to the maximally general. In a complete account of language structure, fully general rules stand out as being atypical rather than paradigmatic. Another facet of CG's bottom-up orientation is the claim that "rules" can only arise as schematizations of overtly occurring expressions. However far this abstraction may proceed, the schemas that emerge spring from the soil of actual usage. Finally, there is reason to believe that lower-level schemas, expressing regularities of only limited scope, may on balance be more essential to language structure than high-level schemas representing the broadest generalizations.

The assumptions made about mental abilities and cognitive processing are both minimal and relatively non-controversial. A few basic mechanisms are operative in all domains of language structure and afford a unified account of phenomena traditionally handled separately and in very different ways. Together with the austerity they entail in the positing of both psychological and linguistic entities, these factors render a usage-based framework intrinsically desirable.

2. Psychological phenomena

I start by recognizing a number of basic and very general psychological phenomena that are essential to language but certainly not limited to it. The first of these, which I refer to as *entrenchment*, has also borne such labels as "routinization", "automatization", and "habit formation". The occurrence of psychological events leaves some kind of trace that facilitates their re-occurrence. Through repetition, even a highly complex event can coalesce into a well-rehearsed routine that is easily elicited and reliably executed. When a complex structure comes to be manipulable as a "pre-packaged" assembly, no longer requiring conscious attention to its parts or their arrangement, I say that it has the status of a *unit*. It is convenient notationally to indicate unit status by means of boxes or square brackets, enclosing non-unit structures with closed curves or parentheses: [A] vs. (A).

A second basic phenomenon, *abstraction*, is the emergence of a structure through reinforcement of the commonality inherent in multiple experiences. By its very nature, this abstractive process "filters out" those facets of the individual experiences which do not recur. We will mostly be concerned with a special case of abstraction, namely *schematization*, involving our capacity to operate at varying levels of "granularity" (or "resolution"). Structures that appear very different when examined in fine-grained detail may nonetheless be quite comparable in a coarse-grained view. A *schema* is the commonality that emerges from distinct structures when one abstracts away from their points of difference by portraying them with lesser precision and specificity. I use a solid arrow for the relationship between a schema and a more specific structure that *instantiates* or *elaborates* it: A→B. The formula indicates that B conforms to the specifications of A but is characterized in finer-grained detail.

Also fundamental to cognition is the ability to *compare* two structures and detect any discrepancy between them. This operation involves an inherent asymmetry, whereby one structure functions as a *standard* of comparison, the other as its *target*. We can reasonably consider *categorization* to be a special case of comparison, obtaining when the standard represents an established unit and the target (at least originally) is novel. Categorization is most straightforward when there is no discrepancy, i.e. when the standard can be recognized in the target because the latter fully satisfies its specifications. In this case the two structures stand in an elaborative relationship: [A]→(B). An act of categorization may also register some disparity between the categorizing structure and the target. In this case I speak of *extension*, indicated with a dashed arrow: [A]--->(B).

Yet another basic phenomenon is the combination of simpler structures to yield a more complex structure. Let us call this *composition*. It involves the *integration* of two or more *component* structures to form a *composite* structure. If [A] and [B] are units, not previously combined, their integration to produce the novel composite structure (C) can be given as follows: ([A][B])$_C$. The formula should not however be taken as implying that (C) is merely the union of [A] and [B], nor that [A] and [B] occur unmodified in (C). When motor routines are chained together into a complex action, their coordination entails that no component routine is manifested in precisely the form it would have in isolation; typing *kl*, for instance, is not just the same as typing *k* then typing *l*. The same is clearly true of speech sounds, and (I would argue) of most any kind of conceptual integration. A composite structure has to be regarded as an entity in its own right, not strictly reducible to it components. For this reason I speak of *partial compositionality*.

Let us mention, finally, the well-known phenomenon of *association*, in which one kind of experience is able to evoke another. The particular kind of association that concerns us is *symbolization*: the association of conceptualizations with the mental representations of observable entities such as sounds, gestures, and written marks. An established symbolic relationship—a *symbolic unit*—is conveniently given as [[A]/[a]], where upper and lower case stand respectively for a conceptualization and a symbolizing structure. A symbolic structure is said to be *bipolar*: [A] is the *semantic pole*, and [a] the *phonological pole* (in the case of sounds).

While there may be differences in approach and terminology, I consider it self-evident that something akin to each phenomenon has to be ascribed to cognition generally and to language in particular. It should also be evident that these operations occur in various combinations, some applying to the results of others. Composition, for example, is applicable to its own output—composite structures can in turn function as components integrated to form a more elaborate composite structure. Repeated episodes of composition yield constituency hierarchies having indefinitely many levels of organization. Here is another plausible sequence of operations: (A_1), (A_2), (A_3) > [A] > $([A] \rightarrow (A_4))$ > $[[A] \rightarrow [A_4]]$. From a series of similar experiences, represented as (A_1), (A_2), and (A_3), a schema emerges that embodies their commonality and achieves the status of a unit, [A]. This structure is subsequently used to categorize a new experience, (A_4), which instantiates it. If (A_4) recurs and continues to be recognized as an instance of [A], both it and the categorizing relationship undergo entrenchment and gain unit status. $[[A] \rightarrow [A_4]]$ then constitutes an established categorization.

I suggest that repeated applications of such processes, occurring in different combinations at many levels of organization, result in cognitive assemblies of enormous complexity. The vision that emerges is one of massive networks in which structures with varying degrees of entrenchment, and representing different levels of abstraction, are linked together in relationships of categorization, composition, and symbolization. I believe that all facets of linguistic structure can be reasonably described in these terms.

3. Processing interpretation

The network model just presented deserves to be handled with caution, for like any metaphor it has the potential to mislead. In particular, the network metaphor encourages us to think of linguistic structures as discrete, object-like entities forming a static assembly observable as a simultaneously available whole. All of these features are problematic in regard to the neural implementation of language. From the processing standpoint, language must ultimately reside in patterns of neurological activity. It does not consist of discrete objects lodged in the brain, and it cannot all be manifested at any one time. An important question, then, is whether and how these two perspectives can be reconciled.

As a general orientation, I incline to the *connectionist* style of computation based on *parallel distributed processing* (McClelland and Rumelhart 1986; Rumelhart and McClelland 1986). This mode of processing has the advantage of resembling what the brain actually does, at least at a basic level, and I believe it to be both realistic and revelatory with respect to language. I realize how enormous the gap is between existing PDP models and a system that would approximate the actual complexity of linguistic structure, even in limited domains. This huge discrepancy reflects the fact that the PDP-style processing constitutive of human language occurs in the context of a highly-structured brain of unfathomable complexity, and draws upon the structures that progressively emerge over the course of many years through continuous and multifaceted interaction with a rich environment. Since actual connectionist systems are not embedded in such a matrix, there are severe limitations on how close they can come to realistically modeling linguistic structure. That is not per se an argument against connectionist-type processing, however.

Here I will merely try to indicate that the psychological phenomena discussed in the previous section can all be given a connectionist interpretation. For analytical purposes, it is helpful (if not necessary) to think in terms of discrete structures represented by distinct symbols enclosed in brackets or boxes. Such reifications are not too harmful so long as we do not lose sight of the dynamic reality they conceal. In the final analysis, linguistic structures and relationships reside in cognitive processing, identified as neurological activity.

Entrenchment is straightforwardly identifiable as an adjustment in connection weights, brought about by the occurrence of a pattern of activation, which renders more likely the re-occurrence of the same or a comparable pattern. With respect to the system's movement through state space, entrenchment amounts to the emergence of an attractor. The term fits quite well with the topographical conception of state space, where attractors of different strength are thought of as wells or valleys of varying depth that the system tends to settle into as it relaxes into a state of minimum energy.

Connectionist systems are well known for their ability to extract whatever regularities are inherent in their input. I have previously discussed the extraction of schemas in connectionist terms (1990b; FCG2: 12.3). Let me first reiterate that discrete representations such as A→B are not to be taken as implying that a schema and its instantiation are wholly distinct and separately stored. Rather, I think of schemas as being *immanent* in their instantiations, and while a schema may in some cases be independently accessible (e.g. the schematic notion common to *apple, orange, banana*, etc. is individually symbolized by *fruit*), there is no supposition that this is true in general. In saying that a schema is extracted, what is necessarily being claimed is actually fairly minimal: that the commonality inherent in multiple experiences is reinforced and attains some kind of cognitive status, so that it has the potential to influence further processing.[2]

In offering a connectionist interpretation of schema extraction, we can first equate a particular experience (or "structure") with either a point in state space or a trajectory through it (cf. Elman 1990). To the extent that two experiences are similar, their constitutive patterns of neural activation will be neighbors in state space: either points in close proximity, or trajectories following roughly parallel courses. We can focus on the simpler case of points, since a trajectory reduces to a series of points ordered in processing time. Suppose, then, that the patterns representing a number of similar structures all cluster in the same general region of state space. Call this region R. The occurrence of a given pattern will impact connection weights in such a way that the occurrence of any pattern close to it in state space will tend to be facilitated. The repeated use of similar structures will thus facilitate the occurrence of any pattern within the general region R. This amounts to the extraction of a schema. With reference to state space, a schema is describable as a basin of attraction (R) which subsumes a number of more point-like locations corresponding to its instantiations. A schema is immanent in its instantiations in the sense that being located in a point-like region of state space entails being located in a broader region that encompasses it.

Categorization is then interpretable as capture by an attractor. Presenting the system with a certain input tends to activate a variety of previously established patterns, some of which may be mutually inhibitory. When an input (B) results in the full activation of pattern [A]—which may have won out over numerous competitors—we can reasonably say that [A] is used to categorize (B). Of course, if the input is only fragmentary, categorization via the activation of [A] may serve to reconstitute the full, familiar experience it represents. The categorizing experience will also be qualitatively different depending on whether (B) is compatible with [A] or succeeds in eliciting [A] despite some discrepancy between them. We will return to these matters in the following section.

With respect to composition, it can plausibly be suggested that component structures are to some degree activated in the process of carrying out the more elaborate pattern of activation constitutive of the composite conception. Ultimately I would like to argue that composition reduces to categorization (FCG1: 12.2). I have already noted that component structures are not appropriately conceived as "building blocks" stacked together to form the composite structure. The latter is an entity in its own right, facets of which correspond to the components but either elaborate or diverge from their specifications. I believe the component structures are properly thought of as categorizing those facets of the composite structure to which they correspond. Like a categorizing structure, the components are in some sense prior, most obviously in cases where they represent established units while the composite structure is novel. Moreover, a composite structure resembles the target of categorization in being the structure of concern, the one being assessed in relation to others having some kind of prior standing. Yet another resemblance between composition and categorization is that in each case the quality of the target experience is partially shaped and (re)constituted by the structures activated for its assessment.

Finally, symbolization is readily interpretable as one pattern of activation reliably serving to elicit another. If semantic structures are represented as patterns occurring in one bank of processing units, and phonological structures in another, a connectionist system can easily be trained to establish the proper correlations.

4. Basic linguistic problems

In CG, a language is described as a *structured inventory of conventional linguistic units*. The units (cognitive "routines") comprising a speaker's linguistic knowledge are limited (by a restriction called the *content requirement*) to semantic, phonological, and symbolic structures which are either directly manifested as parts of actual expressions, or else emerge from such structures by the processes of abstraction (schematization) and categorization. In describing these units as an inventory, I am indicating the non-generative and non-constructive nature of a linguistic system. Linguistic knowledge is not conceived or modeled as an algorithmic device enumerating a well-defined set of formal objects, but simply as an extensive collection of semantic, phonological, and symbolic resources that can be brought to bear in language processing. This inventory of resources is structured in the sense that some units are incorporated as parts of larger units, specifically in relationships of categorization, composition, and symbolization: [[A]--->[B]]; [[A][B]]$_C$; [[A]/[a]]. For some purposes it may be helpful to reify linguistic knowledge or ability as something called the "grammar" of a language. We must however resist the temptation to think of it as a separate or sharply bounded cognitive entity, if only because a structure's characterization as being conventional, linguistic, or a unit is inherently a matter of degree (FCG1: 2.1).

Can a grammar of this sort actually do the job? We somehow have to deal with a number of basic problems: the creation and understanding of novel expressions; the ascription of particular structures to such expressions; judgments of well- and ill-formedness; distributional restrictions; and the varying degrees of compositionality, productivity, and generality exhibited by linguistic structures and patterns.

4.1. Categorization of usage events

It is not the linguistic system per se that constructs and understands novel expressions, but rather the language user, who marshals for this purpose the full panoply of available resources. In addition to linguistic units, these resources include such factors as memory, planning, problem-solving ability, general knowledge, short- and longer-term goals, as well as full apprehension of the physical, social, cultural, and linguistic context. An actual instance of language use, resulting from all these factors, constitutes what I call a *usage event*: the pairing of a vocalization, in all its specificity, with a conceptualization representing its full contextual understanding. A usage event is thus an utterance characterized in all the phonetic and conceptual detail a language user is capable of apprehending. For immediate purposes it makes no difference whether we consider the speaker or the addressee, since each has to establish some connection between the linguistic system and a usage event that supposedly manifests it. In comprehension, the hearer has to interpret the event as the intended realization of particular linguistic structures. In production, the speaker has to select linguistic structures capable of evoking the desired contextual understanding, and has to then ensure that the event can indeed be so interpreted.

In both production and comprehension, therefore, facets of a usage event must somehow be assessed in relation to linguistic units. I take this to be a matter of categorization. Let us consider the minimal case, in which a single linguistic unit, [A], is used to categorize a particular facet, (B), of a usage event. There are two basic possibilities, depicted in Figure 4.1, where the box labeled L represents the linguistic system (i.e. the inventory of conventional units), and the overall usage event is given as the circle labeled U. On the one hand, [A] can be recognized in (B), which thus instantiates [A], as seen in

Figure 4.1(a). This amounts to the judgment that (B) is *well-formed* with respect to [A]. We can also describe it as being *conventional*, in the sense of conforming to the linguistic convention embodied in [A]. On the other hand, there may be some discrepancy between the two structures. In this case (B) is not perceived as an elaboration of [A], but rather as an extension from it, as shown in Figure 4.1(b). This amounts to the judgment that (B) is *ill-formed*, or *non-conventional*, with respect to [A].

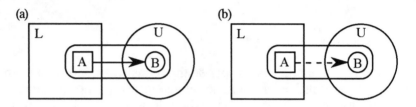

(a)   (b)

Figure 4.1

We have already noted the oversimplification inherent in representing the linguistic system, L, as a discrete box. For example, since entrenchment is a matter of degree, there is no clear line of demarcation between novel structures and those with the status of units. Moreover, a boundary imposed at any particular threshold will continually fluctuate, since every use of a structure reinforces it and entrenches it more deeply, whereas non-use has the opposite effect. Even the first occurrence of a novel structure constitutes an initial step along the path of progressive entrenchment and conventionalization, for it must leave some kind of trace in at least one member of the speech community. Suppose, then, that structure (B) begins to occur with some frequency in a speech community, and that speakers consistently invoke unit [A] to categorize it. For example, [A] might be the basic meaning of a lexical item, and (B) a semantic extension, as when *mouse* first started being applied to a piece of computer equipment. With frequent recurrence, both (B) and ([A]--->(B)), i.e. (B)'s categorization as an extension from [A], will become progressively entrenched and eventually achieve the status of units. To the extent that this happens, both [B] and the categorizing relationship [[A]--->[B]] become members of L as a matter of definition. Figure 4.2 diagrams the expansion of L to incorporate these new conventional units.

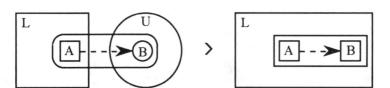

Figure 4.2

Actually, a slight refinement of Figure 4.2 should be noted. Since (B) is part of a usage event, it represents a conceptual or phonetic structure in the full detail of its contextual apprehension. Numerous fine-grained details, as well as contingent features of the context, are bound to vary from one usage event to the next. On successive occasions, for example, the referents of *mouse* may be slightly different shades of gray and occupy different positions vis-à-vis the computer. Failing to recur consistently, such details will not be reinforced and hence will not be included in the new conventional unit that emerges. The categorizing judgments that occur on particular occasions can thus be given as $([A]\text{--->}(B_1))$, $([A]\text{--->}(B_2))$, $([A]\text{--->}(B_3))$, etc., where the subscripts indicate divergence in the targets. The structures that undergo entrenchment and achieve the status of conventional units are schematic relative to those which figure in any actual usage event: [B] is schematic with respect to (B_1), (B_2), and (B_3), and $[[A]\text{--->}[B]]$ with respect to $([A]\text{--->}(B_1))$, $([A]\text{--->}(B_2))$, and $([A]\text{--->}(B_3))$. The point is a general one — linguistic units are always schematic in relation to their instantiations in actual usage events.

Repeated occurrences of the processes sketched in Figures 4.1 and 4.2 can naturally be expected, and a unit added to L at any point is then eligible to serve as a categorizing structure in subsequent occurrences. Thus, from a single structure [A], there may eventually develop an elaborate *network* comprising any number of conventional units linked by categorizing relationships. These structures and relationships are said to form a *complex category*. To the extent that the network consists of chains of extensions radiating outward from [A] (thereby identifiable as the prototype), it constitutes a "radial category" (Lakoff 1987).

While accepting the insight and basic validity of the radial model based on extension (i.e. A--->B), I also emphasize schematization and relationships of instantiation (A→B), if only because the latter correspond to essential linguistic phenomena: the extraction of generalizations, and judgments of well-formedness (conventionality).

The two kinds of categorization are in any case very intimately related (and may in practice be hard to distinguish). Both involve an act of comparison in which a standard (S) is matched against a target (T). Instantiation can then be regarded as the special, limiting case of extension that arises when the discrepancy registered between S and T happens to be zero. Conversely, if categorization is interpreted as the attempt to "recognize" S in T, instantiation represents the privileged case where this happens unproblematically, and extension constitutes recognition accomplished only with a certain amount of "strain". The source of the strain is that, for S to be recognized in a target which does not fully conform to its specifications, the conflicting features of S somehow have to be suppressed or abstracted away from.

Extension can thus be thought of as recognition achieved at the cost of invoking a schematized version of the categorizing structure, one whose coarser-grained specifications are satisfied by the target. For this reason I suggest that extension tends to be accompanied by schematization, that the "outward" growth of a network by extensions from a prototype tends to induce its "upward" growth via the extraction of higher-level schemas. The general mechanism is diagrammed in Figure 4.3.

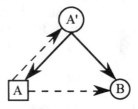

Figure 4.3

I presume that extension does not occur at random; there is always some basis for it. The categorization of (B) as an extension from [A] implies some abstract commonality—however limited or tenuous—which enables [A] to be evoked for that purpose in the first place and to successfully categorize (B) despite a conflict in their properties. By definition, that commonality amounts to a schema, labeled (A') in the diagram, having both [A] and (B) as instantiations. It is not necessary that (A') be salient or separately apprehended, or that it endure beyond its fleeting occurrence as an implicit facet of the categorizing event ([A]--->(B)). Still, the very fact that [A] and (B) occur together tends to reinforce their commonality and thus facilitates (A')'s emergence as an established cognitive entity. Should (A') attain the status of a unit, it is validly describable as both a schema instantiated by [A] and (since the latter is prior) as an extension from it: $[[A'] \rightarrow [A]]; [[A]\text{--->}[A']]$.

I assume, then, that linguistic categories are usually complex, developing from prototypical structures via such processes as extension, the extraction of schemas, and the articulation of coarse-grained units into more specific ones (as finer discriminations are made and particular instantiations gain unit status). Bearing in mind the limitations of the metaphor, we can view complex categories as *networks* in which linguistic structures of any kind and any size are linked in pairwise fashion by categorizing relationships (FCG1: ch. 10). These structures—the "nodes" or vertices of the network—might consist, for example, of the allophones of a phoneme, the alternate senses of a lexical item, a family of related metaphors, or variant forms of an elaborate grammatical construction. There is more to such a network, however, than just a set of nodes and a set of arcs connecting them. Additionally, each structure and each categorizing relationship has some degree of entrenchment and ease of activation. Moreover, the target of categorization in each case lies at a certain "distance" from the standard, depending on how far T elaborates S or how many features of S it violates. Entrenchment and distance are respectively indicated in Figure 4.4 by the thickness of boxes and the length of arrows. In general, though, my diagrams will not attempt to represent these parameters.

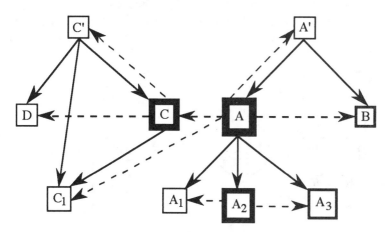

Figure 4.4

4.2. Selection of categorizing structures

At this juncture a basic problem arises. I have suggested that the units constitutive of linguistic knowledge are related to actual expressions by means of categorization, as shown in Figure 4.1. Yet even a single category may well contain a large number of units all of which are in principle available to categorize some particular facet of a usage event. They cannot all do so at once, for chaos would then ensue. A given target is well-formed with respect to certain potential categorizing units and ill-formed with respect to others. Unless these units are recruited in some specific way to assess the target (on any one occasion), there will be no basis for the clear judgments of well- and ill-formedness that commonly occur. I assume, in fact, that primary categorization is effected by just one unit at any given moment. How, then, does a particular target manage to be categorized by a single unit selected from a large network of potential categorizing structures?

Let me first point out that this is a general problem in cognition, not specifically a linguistic one. Consider the recognition of a familiar face. Among others, I possess schematized representations of both Suzanne Kemmer's face and Sydney Lamb's. When Suzanne walks into the room, I usually manage to correctly recognize her as Suzanne and not confuse her with Syd. To do so, I have to activate the Kemmer schema for the categorization of my visual experience, not the Lamb schema—otherwise I would see her as Sydney Lamb and marvel at how much he had changed. Suzanne is, after all, a very good instance of Suzanne, but a rather poor instance of Syd. Depending on which schema I activate, therefore, the episode of facial recognition will yield a judgment of either well-formedness or deviance, as sketched in Figure 4.5.

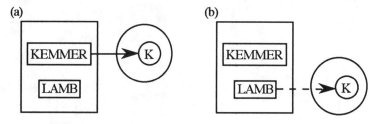

Figure 4.5

For both linguistic and non-linguistic input, I assume we have to tell a certain kind of story. It has no claim to novelty, being basically what is envisaged in the interactive activation model (Elman and McClelland 1984; McClelland and Elman 1986a; McClelland and Elman 1986b), the competition model (MacWhinney 1987), and for that matter in connectionist processing generally. The story runs more or less as follows. A particular target of categorization tends to activate a variety of established units, any one of which could in principle serve to categorize it. Let us call this set of units (which may belong to a single complex category or to multiple categories) the *activation set* of the target. Initially, as shown in Figure 4.6(a), the members of the activation set are all activated by T to some degree.[3] Only one member can actually categorize T, however, so in effect they compete for this privilege; some are no doubt mutually inhibitory and tend to suppress one another. One member of the activation set eventually wins the competition in the sense of becoming highly active relative to all the others. It is this unit—termed the *active structure*—which serves to categorize the target, as seen in 4.6(b).

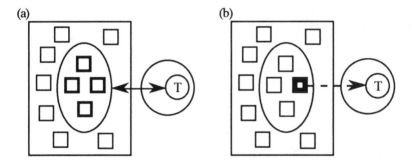

Figure 4.6

Several factors interact to determine which particular member of the activation set wins the competition and emerges as the active structure evoked to categorize the target. The first is level of entrenchment, or inherent likelihood of activation. In a neutral context, for example, *Bali* would more easily be misheard as *belly* than conversely. A second factor is contextual priming, which can override the effects of familiarity. Suppose we are discussing our upcoming trip to Bali and (my mind wandering) I happen to say—out of the blue—that I would like to see some *belly dancers*. The context might well lead you to misinterpret me as saying that I want to see some *Bali dancers*.

A third factor is the amount of overlap between the target and a potential categorizing structure. We can reasonably assume that the sharing of features is what enables the target to stimulate members of the activation set in the first place, and that the degree of stimulation is roughly proportional to the number of features shared. This has the important consequence that lower-level schemas, i.e. structures with greater specificity, have a built-in advantage in the competition with respect to higher-level schemas. Other things being equal, the finer-grained detail of a low-level schema affords it a larger number of features potentially shared by the target.

We can now describe, in very general terms, how expressions are evaluated with respect to the linguistic system. A usage event has many facets susceptible to categorization by conventional linguistic units, which in CG are limited to semantic, phonological, and symbolic structures. The potential categorizing units are entrenched to varying degrees and form a vast, structured inventory through relationships of symbolization, composition, and categorization. These units can be of any size, represent any dimension of linguistic structure, and are characterized at all levels of specificity. By virtue of overlapping content, each facet of the usage event serves to activate a set of potential categorizing structures—its activation set—which then compete for the right to categorize it. The winner of each competition is determined by a dynamic interactive process on the basis of degree of overlap, inherent ease of activation (correlated with entrenchment), contextual priming, and mutual inhibition.

The resulting set of categorizations, in which the winners (the active structures) categorize the facets of the usage event which elicit them, constitute the expression's *structural description* (i.e. its interpretation with respect to the linguistic system). The expression is fully well-formed (conventional) provided that all of these categorizations are elaborative in nature. It is ill-formed (non-conventional) to the extent that any of them involve extension rather than elaboration. We can expect many extensions to pass unnoticed in normal language use. It is only when a conflict is egregious, or when small conflicts have a cumulative effect, that the strain they produce rises to the level of conscious awareness (cf. Ross 1987).

In principle, then, a linguistic system conceived as being non-generative and non-constructive can nonetheless support the ascription of structural descriptions to expressions and provide the basis for judgments of well- and ill-formedness. One need only envisage this inventory of semantic, phonological, and symbolic resources as being embedded in a dynamic processing system which operates in accordance with minimal and highly plausible assumptions.

4.3. Categorization vs. construction

I have posed the question of whether the linguistic system per se specifies in full detail how expressions are constructed (thus characterizing a well-defined set of expressions as its "output"), or whether it is merely an inventory of units invoked for the categorization of usage events. Should responsibility for constructing expressions be assigned to the "grammar", or to the language user drawing upon a full range of psychological and contextual resources? Though it may seem slight, this distinction has important consequences for how we think about linguistic problems. At stake are basic questions such as the scope of linguistic meaning, how rules are related to instantiating expressions, and whether the linguistic system constitutes a discrete, well-delimited cognitive entity.

The difference between construction and categorization can first be illustrated by a simple case of semantic extension, e.g. the aforementioned extension of *mouse* to indicate a piece of computer equipment. Prior to the first occurrence of this usage, the linguistic system (for a representative speaker of English) contained the symbolic unit [[MOUSE]/[mouse]], where the semantic structure given as [MOUSE] designates a type of rodent, and [mouse] stands for the phonological structure that symbolizes it. Consider now a speaker who—for the very first time—faced a usage event in which the same term was used in reference to a computer device. We can represent this novel expression as ((MOUSE')/[mouse]), where (MOUSE') is the conception of the new referent. Now, in either producing or comprehending this novel usage, the speaker must somehow relate it to the conventional unit [[MOUSE]/[mouse]], from which it derives via the metaphorical extension ([MOUSE]--->(MOUSE')). It is evident that the linguistic system per se cannot be responsible for constructing the new expression ((MOUSE')/[mouse]), if only because the concept (MOUSE') is (by assumption) a novel one. It is clearly the speaker who, from the context (e.g. seeing the device on a desk) and by means of abilities that are not specifically linguistic, entertains the new conception and apprehends the resemblance that motivates the extension. The role of the conventional unit [[MOUSE]/[mouse]] is not to construct but simply to categorize the new expression, which it motivates by serving as the basis for metaphorical extension. Of course, once the usage becomes familiar and conventionalized, it is incorporated in the language as the new symbolic unit [[MOUSE']/ [mouse]], in the manner of Figure 4.2.

In terms of this scenario, what can we identify as the meaning of *mouse* at different stages? According to standard doctrine, its linguistic meaning was simply [MOUSE] when first applied to the novel conception (MOUSE'), since the latter was not yet a conventional semantic value; its metaphorical understanding in the context of the initial usage event lies beyond the scope of linguistic semantics. Yet standard practice would accept [MOUSE'] as a conventional meaning of *mouse* at the present time. When did this change in status occur? When did (MOUSE') go from being an extra-linguistic understanding of *mouse* to being one of its linguistic semantic values? Does such a transition occur after one usage event? After seven? After *m* usage events involving each of *n* speakers? We could certainly adopt a threshold number to determine when new senses will be described as "linguistic" and admitted to the mental lexicon. This would allow us to maintain a strict dichotomy between linguistic and non-linguistic meanings, consistent with the notion that a language is a discrete and well-delimited cognitive entity. I submit, however, that any particular threshold would be arbitrary, in which case the claim that linguistic meanings are clearly distinguishable from contextual understandings is vacuous, rendered true just as a matter of definition.

I prefer to view things in a rather different manner. The very first time the term *mouse* is used in regard to a piece of computer equipment, it is contextually understood by the interlocutors as referring to that device. It is also so understood (in appropriate contexts) once the new sense is fully established as a conventional semantic value. Since *mouse* is understood with the value (MOUSE') from the very outset, and winds up having [MOUSE'] as an indisputably linguistic meaning, it seems pointless to say that (MOUSE') was ever non-linguistic (though it did start out being non-conventional). Stated more precisely, and in positive terms, I would want to say the following. On the occasion of the initial usage event, *mouse* has the meaning ([MOUSE]--->(MOUSE')), i.e. the conception of the computer device construed metaphorically as a kind of rodent. Through continued usage, this complex meaning undergoes progressive entrenchment and conventionalization, and eventually the metaphorical value [[MOUSE]--->[MOUSE']] emerges as a fully conventional meaning of *mouse* with unit status. The only thing special about the initial usage event is that the linguistic meaning's prior entrenchment and conventionality lie at the zero end of the scale. However, the very first use starts to move it away from the endpoint, and to the extent this happens it becomes part of the linguistic system.

The same holds for complex expressions involving grammatical composition. Consider the use of *printer* to indicate a computer output device. Its *compositional meaning*, i.e. the one predictable on the basis of the *V-er* morphological pattern, is simply 'something that prints'. Its conventional semantic value is far more elaborate: *printer* designates an electronic device, of a certain approximate size, run by a computer to record its output on paper, etc. These extra-compositional specifications correspond to facets of its *contextual meaning* that were no doubt present from the outset, eventually becoming entrenched and conventional through their recurrence in usage events. They are unproblematic because the *V-er* compositional pattern is not at any stage responsible for constructing the semantically enriched expression, but merely for its categorization. In this way an expression analyzed as belonging to a particular grammatical construction can nonetheless diverge from its specifications, by either elaboration or extension. Let me note just in passing that the point is equally valid for syntax. What we intuitively accept as the meaning of a clause or a sentence is usually more elaborate than its compositional value, if not in conflict with it. The contrast with morphology is simply that syntactic expressions are less likely than single words to recur with non-compositional meanings and establish themselves as conventional units.

4.4. Composition

Let us take a closer look at how a non-constructive model deals with complex novel expressions and their relation to established grammatical patterns. In CG, complex expressions are described as *assemblies of symbolic structures*. These assemblies consist primarily of compositional relationships, wherein two or more component symbolic structures are integrated—semantically and phonologically—to form a composite symbolic structure. For example, the component symbolic units [[JAR]/[jar]] and [[LID]/[lid]] are integrated to form the composite symbolic structure [[JAR LID]/[jar lid]]. An assembly of this kind, involving composition at one level of organization, is a *minimal construction*. Larger assemblies arise when the composite structure of one minimal construction functions in turn as a component structure in another, representing a higher level of organization (e.g. *jar lid* might be pluralized to form *jar lids*). Naturally this can happen repeatedly, at progressively higher levels, yielding composite symbolic structures of ever greater semantic and phonological complexity. Expressions of any size can thus be assembled.

Grammar consists of patterns for creating symbolic assemblies. In accordance with basic principles of CG (in particular the content requirement), these patterns can only assume the form of *schematized expressions*: templates abstracted from a set of complex expressions to embody whatever commonality is inherent in them. Hence grammatical patterns are themselves assemblies of symbolic structures comprising compositional relationships at various levels of organization. These assemblies are directly analogous to their instantiating expressions, except that the symbolic structures which form them are more schematic. In particular, the schematic template corresponding to a construction—a *constructional schema*—itself resides in component symbolic structures integrated to form a composite symbolic structure. For example, the compositional pattern instantiated by *jar lid*, *garage door*, and countless other noun-noun compounds is merely a symbolic assembly in which two schematic nouns, [[A]/[a]] and [[B]/[b]], are integrated in a certain manner to yield the composite symbolic structure [[AB]/[ab]] (Figures 1.5-6). This entire symbolic assembly serves to categorize either a fixed or a novel expression that instantiates it. Moreover, the global categorizing relationship is resolvable into local categorizing relationships between particular substructures. The categorization of *jar lid* as an instance of the noun-noun compounding pattern therefore subsumes the local categorizations [[[A]/[a]]→[[JAR]/[jar]]], [[[B]/[b]]→[[LID]/[lid]]], and [[[AB]/[ab]]→[[JAR LID]/[jar lid]]].

Consider, then, the construction of a novel expression in accordance with an established grammatical pattern. We may suppose that at the time of the utterance the linguistic system L contains the various conventional units indicated in Figure 4.7(a). One such unit is a constructional schema comprising two component symbolic structures, [A] and [B], as well as the composite symbolic structure, [C]. We can further suppose the existence of two lexical items, [A'] and [B'], which respectively instantiate the schematic units [A] and [B]. Assuming that these instantiating relationships represent established categorizations, they constitute the categorizing units [[A]→[A']] and [[B]→[B']].

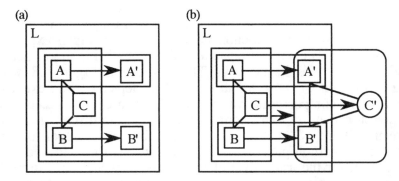

Figure 4.7

Together, these units implicitly define a complex expression, assumed to be novel, which in Figure 4.7(b) is thus surrounded by a closed curve (rather than a box) to indicate its non-unit status. The latent composite structure, (C'), represents the expression's *compositional value*: the structure that emerges if [A'] and [B'] are integrated precisely as the constructional schema specifies, at both the semantic and the phonological poles. In this case (C') elaborates [C], and the complex expression ([A'][B'])$_{C'}$ elaborates the constructional schema [[A][B]]$_C$.

In referring to (C') as merely "latent", and saying that the conventional units "implicitly" define the complex expression, I am once more emphasizing the non-constructive nature of a grammar. Novel expressions are not created by the linguistic system per se, but rather by the speaker, drawing on all available resources. Of course, the distinction is of little moment provided that we confine our attention to the (possibly hypothetical) situation of full compositionality. On the assumption of full compositionality, both (C') and the entire assembly ([A'][B'])$_{C'}$ are wholly prefigured by conventional units of L: [A'] and [B'] are established units, in which the schematic units [A] and [B] are respectively immanent; the constructional schema [[A][B]]$_C$ represents an established pattern for integrating [A] and [B] to form [C]; therefore, constructing ([A'][B'])$_{C'}$—with composite structure (C')—is simply a matter of carrying out the established pattern of integration when [A] and [B] are embedded in the more elaborate structures [A'] and [B']. In effect, the potential structure ([A'][B'])$_{C'}$ is rendered actual just by coactivating the conventional units in question. I call this *actualization* (FCG1: 11.3).

I have argued, however, that full compositionality is unchar-
acteristic of normal language use. In a typical usage event, the contextual understanding and phonetic rendition of a complex expression
diverge from its compositional value if only by being more specific,
and often in more drastic ways. This is shown in Figure 4.8, where
the expression's *contextual value*, (C''), is depicted as an extension
vis-à-vis its compositional value, (C'). To be sure, those facets of the
expression that are extra-compositional (i.e. the discrepancies between (C') and (C'')) start out as being non-conventional, but it is
only by terminological fiat that they are also considered non-
linguistic, for the usage event begins their conventionalization. Indeed, prior to actualization in a usage event, (C') itself lies beyond the
scope of established convention, a non-unit prefigured by L but
unexploited and unfamiliar to speakers.

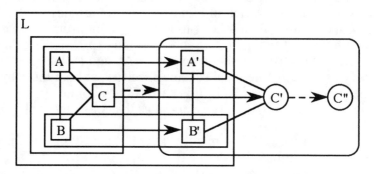

Figure 4.8

Because (C'') represents the way the expression is actually
understood (and may eventually become its conventional meaning, as
we saw in the case of *printer*), it is only (C') whose status is reasonably called into question. I believe it does have both linguistic status
and some kind of cognitive presence. Since it represents the latent
potential inherent in an assembly of conventional units, we can
reasonably suppose that (C') is activated when those units are
invoked in a usage event. It thus embodies whatever motivation
conventional units provide for (C'') and serves as a kind of stepping-
stone on the way to it. The expression's actual value, then, is neither
(C') alone nor (C''), but (C'') construed in relation to (C'), which
categorizes it: ((C')--->(C'')). I would say, for example, that the
compositional value 'something that prints' does figure in the meaning of *printer* as a computer term. More obviously, a metaphorical

expression like *chopper* (for 'helicopter') retains the compositional value 'something that chops' as a secondary facet of its meaning; an expression is metaphorical just by virtue of construing the target domain against the background of the source domain. If (C') and the categorizing relationship ((C')--->(C")) do indeed have some cognitive presence, they might well retain it as the expression coalesces into an established unit, as shown in Figure 4.9.

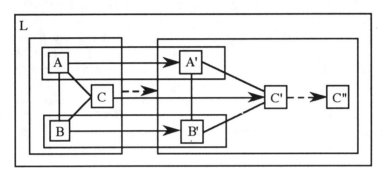

Figure 4.9

4.5. Degrees of regularity

If all grammatical patterns reside in constructional schemas, they nonetheless vary considerably in the nature and extent of their regularity. At least three parameters need to be distinguished: compositionality, generality, and productivity. While there is some tendency for these properties to be associated with syntactic patterns, and their opposites with morphological ones, I see no empirical grounds for believing that position along these scales correlates in any absolute way with whether a pattern obtains above or below the word level. The lack of absolute correlations is one reason for a basic claim of cognitive grammar, namely that morphology and syntax form a continuum (fully describable as assemblies of symbolic structures). Nor is grammar distinct from lexicon, defined in the theory as the set of "fixed" expressions in a language (i.e. expressions with unit status), regardless of size or type.

    Compositionality pertains to how closely an expression approximates the result predicted for the integration of particular component structures in the manner specified by a constructional schema. To be completely compositional, therefore, an expression can exhibit no discrepancy between its predicted value and its actual composite structure. In terms of Figures 4.7-9, the complex expression $([A'][B'])_{C'}$ is compositional with respect to pattern $[[A][B]]_C$ just in case the predicted value (C') and the contextual value (C") precisely coincide; their identity entails that the composite structure $((C') \text{---} >(C''))$ collapses onto (C'). Previous discussion raises the question of whether an expression is ever completely compositional. One can plausibly argue that an expression's contextual understanding always diverges to some extent (however minimally) from its predicted value, and that a residue of such divergence is retained even when the expression coalesces into an established lexical unit. However, in this non-constructive framework nothing much hinges on whether the limiting case of zero divergence is ever actually attained.

As defined, degree of compositionality is not a property of grammatical patterns per se, but rather of particular expressions that they categorize. The other two parameters do pertain to the patterns themselves and are thus reflected in the constructional schemas which embody them. *Generality* relates to the level of specificity at which such schemas are characterized. A given pattern has greater or lesser generality depending on whether it is potentially applicable to a wider or a narrower range of elements. In English, for example, tense marking is applicable to essentially any verb, whereas only "perfective" verbs enter into the progressive construction (Langacker 1987c). Constructions can also be limited to smaller classes that I likewise consider to be semantically definable, e.g. change-of-state verbs, verbs of transfer, "unaccusative" verbs, etc. Limitations of this sort are readily accommodated by the proper formulation of constructional schemas. Thus, whereas the schemas describing tense marking identify one component structure just as a verb, the progressive schema is more specific by requiring a perfective verb in particular. There is no inherent limit to the level of specificity at which a constructional schema can characterize its components. Indeed, a schema can incorporate a particular lexical item, even a specific variant of a lexical item, as one of its component structures.

Productivity is a matter of how available a pattern is for the sanction of novel expressions. Though productivity tends to correlate with generality, they are often dissociated and have to be distinguished. Patterns of comparable generality can easily differ in their degree of productivity. For example, a causative construction applicable (say) to intransitive verbs might be fully productive, applying to any such verb if the result is semantically coherent, or it might be limited to particular lexical combinations and unavailable for the creation of new expressions. Conversely, a pattern representing any level of generality has the potential to be fully productive. For instance, a certain plural marker might be restricted to a small class of nouns (such as animal names) but be freely applicable to any noun in that class.

In a usage-based model with dynamic processing (of the sort described previously), productivity amounts to likelihood of being selected as the active structure used to categorize a novel expression. The constructional schema representing a highly productive pattern must be well-entrenched and easily activated for this purpose. The schema representing a non-productive pattern presumably expresses a valid generalization, but if it cannot compete successfully for selection as an active structure, this pattern cannot extend beyond the range of data from which it is extracted. For example, English past-tense formation subsumes both the productive, default-case pattern with the conditioned variants [-d], [-t], and [-əd] (as in *rowed*, *kicked*, and *goaded*), and also a variety of largely non-productive patterns restricted to fixed sets of verbs, such as the ablaut pattern which changes everything after the initial consonant cluster to [ɔt] (as in *bought*, *brought*, *caught*, and a number of others). We must therefore posit a deeply entrenched, easily elicited past-tense schema that we can abbreviate as [[V/...][PAST/-D]], whose phonological pole specifies the suffixation of an alveolar stop, as well as various non-salient schemas, among them [[V/C(C)...][PAST/C(C)ɔt]]. We must further assume their difference in salience to be such that, even though they are both quite non-specific in their characterization of the verb stem, the former will virtually always win the competition for the privilege of categorizing a novel form.

Suppose, then, that *leached* is offered as the past-tense form of *leach*. Its interpretation as a past-tense form tends to activate both [[V/...][PAST/-D]] and [[V/C(C)...][PAST/C(C)ɔt]] as possible categorizing schemas. By assumption, [[V/...][PAST/-D]] will win the competition and be selected as the active structure, so the expression is judged well-formed (since *leached* conforms to its specifications). On the other hand, suppose that *lought* is offered as the past-tense form. While this does conform to a pattern in the language, namely [[V/C(C)...][PAST/C(C)ɔt]], that alone is not sufficient to guarantee its well-formedness. A judgment of well-formedness additionally requires that the schema an expression instantiates be in fact selected as the active structure with respect to which the assessment is made. The situation in English is such that usually the default-case pattern suppresses less salient patterns even when the latter have a greater degree of overlap with the target.[4] As a consequence, *lought* will not be categorized by [[V/C(C)...][PAST/C(C)ɔt]], but rather by [[V/...]] [PAST/-D]], whose specifications it violates. Only established past-tense forms like *bought, brought, caught*, etc. are accepted as well-formed. Since they are themselves entrenched conventional units, they require no sanction from constructional schemas.

I conclude that a usage-based model with dynamic processing is able in principle to accommodate the full range of regularity encountered in natural language. Degree of compositionality is free to vary owing to the non-constructive nature of constructional schemas (whose role is merely to categorize target expressions), while generality and productivity are respectively determined by the level of specificity at which such schemas are characterized and their ease of selection as an active (categorizing) structure. It should be emphasized that nothing precludes the emergence of patterns that are highly general and fully productive. For example, a schema that we can abbreviate as [[V][NP]] might describe the semantic integration of a verb with an object noun phrase and specify phonologically that this NP immediately follows V in the temporal sequence. The pattern has full generality: since V and NP are schematic characterizations, it refers to the combination of any verb with any noun phrase. The pattern is productive to the extent that entrenchment assures its activation in preference to any lower-level constructional schemas making conflicting specifications. A dynamic usage-based model is therefore perfectly capable of handling productive general rules whose application is exceptionless for all intents and purposes.

At the same time, CG agrees with construction grammar (e.g. Fillmore, Kay, and O'Connor 1988; Goldberg 1995) in viewing such rules as special and actually rather atypical cases in the overall spectrum of linguistic patterns, most of which exhibit some lesser degree of generality and/or productivity. Even with respect to word order, there will usually be alternatives to the basic pattern that are able to preempt it in specific circumstances. A language might have, for example, both the general constructional schema [[V][NP]] and also the more specific schema [[PRON][V]], which describes the verb's semantic integration with an object pronoun and specifies phonologically that a pronominal NP precedes V in the temporal sequence rather than following it. Assuming that [[V][NP]] and [[PRON][V]] are comparable in their degree of entrenchment, it is [[PRON][V]] that will be elicited to categorize an expression with a verb and an object pronoun, by virtue of its greater overlap with the target. The sequence *PRON V* will thus be judged grammatical, and *V PRON* ill-formed, despite the fact that the latter conforms to the higher-level schema [[V][NP]]. The pattern described by this high-level schema is rendered less productive by the existence of a more specific pattern that preempts it.

4.6. Distribution

Like most linguistic phenomena, grammatical patterns usually arrange themselves in complex categories comprising numerous related variants (see, for example, Lakoff 1987: case study 3). Such families of patterns are describable as networks, as in Figure 4.4, where each node in a network consists of an entire constructional schema. The patterns are thus characterized at different levels of specificity, some are special cases of others (constructional subschemas), some constitute extensions relative to more prototypical variants, and so on. At the extreme, the lowest-level subschemas in such a network incorporate particular lexical items (even lexical variants) as component structures. If, for example, the schema [[V][NP][NP]] describes the English ditransitive pattern in general terms, the constructional subschema [[SEND/send][NP][NP]] represents the lower-level generalization that *send* in particular conventionally occurs in this construction (e.g. *I sent my mother a birthday card*).

It is perhaps more obvious that particular instantiations of morphological patterns have the status of conventional units. The English past tense, for instance, requires a family of constructional schemas including the category prototype, [[V/...][PAST/-D]], as well as various schemas representing minor patterns, e.g. [[V/C(C)...][PAST/C(C)ɔt]], which can be regarded as extensions from the prototype. Clearly, it is part of a speaker's conventional knowledge of the language that particular verbs like *buy*, *bring*, and *catch* occur in this latter pattern. This knowledge takes the form of lower-level subschemas in which these specific stems function as component structures: [[BUY/buy][PAST/C(C)ɔt]]; [[BRING/bring][PAST/C(C)ɔt]]; [[CATCH/catch][PAST/C(C)ɔt]]. In fact, although it might not be apparent from this notation (which omits the composite structures), these subschemas are nothing other than the specific forms *bought*, *brought*, and *caught*. Experimental evidence suggests that instantiations of even productive morphological patterns are stored as units provided that they occur with sufficient frequency (Stemberger and MacWhinney 1988).

It is in this manner that a usage-based framework accommodates distributional restrictions. The fact that *send* participates in the ditransitive construction is not indicated by means of an arbitrary device such as a "rule feature" or a diacritic, but merely by the inclusion of the constructional subschema [[SEND/send][NP][NP]] in the conventional units comprising the linguistic system. The fact that *buy* occurs in the morphological pattern [[V/C(C)...] [PAST/C(C)ɔt]] is likewise given by the inclusion in L of the instantiating subschema [[BUY/buy][PAST/C(C)ɔt]] (i.e. *bought*). I conclude that idiosyncrasies such as these are readily described in a theory that posits only assemblies of symbolic structures for the characterization of lexical and grammatical structure.[5]

Moreover, the examples illustrate the "bottom-up" orientation of CG and the observation that lower-level schemas, expressing regularities of only limited scope, may on balance be more essential to language structure than high-level schemas representing the broadest generalizations. A higher-level schema implicitly defines a large "space" of potential instantiations. Often, however, its actual instantiations cluster in certain regions of that space, leaving other regions sparsely inhabited or uninhabited altogether. An adequate description of linguistic convention must therefore provide the details of how the space has actually been colonized. Providing this information is an elaborate network of conventional units including both constructional subschemas at various levels and instantiating expressions with unit status. For many constructions, the essential distributional information is supplied by lower-level schemas and specific instantiations. High-level schemas may either not exist or not be accessible for the sanction of novel expressions.

A simple example is provided by postpositional phrases in Luiseño (a Uto-Aztecan language of southern California). In this language postpositions occur suffixed to either inanimate nouns or pronouns, as in *ki-yk* 'to the house' and *po-yk* 'to him', but not to animate nouns: **hunwu-yk* 'to the bear'. For the latter we instead find expressions like *hunwut po-yk* (bear it-to), where the postposition attaches to a coreferential pronoun. Forms like *ki-yk* 'to the house' give rise to the constructional schema [N_{inan}-P], and those like *po-yk* 'to him', to the schema [PRON-P]. From these two patterns, moreover, the higher-level schema [N-P] is presumably capable of emerging to embody the generalization that postpositions attach to nouns of any sort: they occur on both pronouns and non-pronouns, and they are not limited to inanimates (since the pronouns are usually animate in reference). [N-P] is thus an expected outcome of the usual process of abstraction, whereby commonalities are reinforced and points of divergence effectively cancel out. Additionally, forms like *hunwut po-yk* 'to the bear' permit the extraction of the more complex constructional schema [N_{an} [PRON-P]], which incorporates [PRON-P] as a component structure.

It is readily seen that the crucial distributional information resides in the lower-level schemas [N_{inan}-P], [PRON-P], and [N_{an} [PRON-P]]. If the high-level schema [N-P] were accessible for the categorization of novel forms, expressions like **hunwu-yk* 'to the bear', which conform to its abstract specifications, would be accepted as conventional. We must therefore suppose that [N-P] always loses the competition to be selected as the active structure; it is consistently superseded by the lower-level schemas as a function of its own non-salience and the inherent advantage accruing to more specific structures through their greater overlap with the target. Hence a form like *hunwu-yk* 'to the bear' would not be categorized by [N-P], but rather by either [N_{inan}-P], [PRON-P], or [N_{an} [PRON-P]], all of whose specifications it violates.

We can say that the space of potential structures defined by the high-level generalization [N-P] is only partially inhabited. In particular, the region corresponding to expressions with non-pronominal animate nouns is completely unoccupied; the notions potentially coded by forms in this region are instead handled by another, more complex construction, namely [N_{an} [PRON-P]]. A constructive model might account for this unexpected "gap" in the general pattern by positing a rule which transforms the non-occurring "underlying" forms into those which actually surface in their stead: [N_{an}-P]==>[N_{an} [PRON-P]]. Alternatively, one could remove the non-occurrent forms from the grammar's output by means of a filter: *[N_{an}-P].[6] We have just seen, however, that a dynamic usage-based model straightforwardly accommodates the data without resorting to either filters or underlying structures. The distributional gap simply results from the existence of [N_{an} [PRON-P]] as a possible sanctioning unit, and the non-existence of [N_{an}-P]. That in turn reflects the respective occurrence and non-occurrence in the input data of expressions like *hunwut po-yk* and **hunwu-yk*. The schemas speakers extract are those supported by the expressions they are exposed to.

If it is workable, a theory that does not posit filters or derivations from underlying structures should definitely be preferred. Their avoidance simplifies the problem of language acquisition, which in essence then reduces to reinforcement of the commonality inherent in expressions that actually occur. I emphasize in particular that descriptions comprising only positive statements of what does occur are in principle able to account for distributional gaps. To be sure, a systematic attempt has not yet been made in CG to show in precise detail how every known type of distributional restriction could be dealt with, and every proposed filter eliminated. The working hypothesis that only positive specifications are needed could be weakened if necessary without undermining the essential claims of the theory. Yet I see little reason to doubt that appropriate arrays of constructional schemas, varying in their degree of specificity and ease of activation, are capable of handling actual distributional phenomena.

This expectation extends to general constraints, such as those advanced for movement rules (Ross 1967b [1986]; Chomsky 1973) and pronoun-antecedent relationships.[7] Such constraints pertain to constructions in which corresponding entities lie at some distance, so that in their most general form the patterns describe the intervening material only in schematic terms. When the corresponding entities occur in certain "structural" configurations—e.g. when one occurs inside a tensed clause, or when they are separated by more than one boundary of a certain kind—deviance ensues, the details being in some measure language-specific. It is reasonably supposed that the restrictions partially reflect processing difficulties associated with simultaneously activating particular sorts of complex structures and selectively accessing their substructures (Deane 1991; Kluender 1992). Still, the processing limitations are not absolute, and a given language manifests them in conventionally determined ways.

In CG, the constructions in question are described by families of constructional schemas characterized at varying levels of specificity. A relative clause construction, for example, will have multiple variants differing as to whether the argument corresponding to the head noun is a subject, an object, or has some other grammatical relation within its clause, whether that clause combines directly with the head or is part of a larger clause which does so, whether the clause is finite or non-finite, and so on. The highest-level constructional schema may define a vast space of structural possibilities, but occurring expressions will not be distributed evenly within it. As with the other kinds of patterns described above, constructional subschemas specify which regions of that space are actually used, and with what degree of likelihood. If well-entrenched subschemas sanction particular configurational relationships between the corresponding entities, they can consistently win out over higher-level schemas for the privilege of categorizing novel expressions. Configurations not covered by the subschemas will consequently result in judgments of ill-formedness.

It can even happen that comparable sets of configurational relationships become conventionally established for multiple constructions (e.g. for multiple "extraction rules"). If, in one construction, speakers learn to effect a dependency between two elements in a particular kind of structural configuration, that itself constitutes a pattern which might be extended to other constructions. For instance, once a speaker learns to make a correspondence between the object argument in a finite clause and a nominal in the clause containing it (say for relative clauses), it might subsequently be easier to make an analogous correspondence in another type of construction (e.g. in clefting). Conventionalized dependencies of this sort can themselves be represented as constructional schemas which abstract away from the differences between the types of constructions involved. Thus, although a detailed study has not yet been undertaken, I believe that even such "parameter setting" is susceptible to characterization in a dynamic usage-based model.

5. Structural applications

The usage-based model described above is applicable to all domains of language structure: semantics, phonology, lexicon, morphology, syntax. A linguistic system comprises large numbers of conventional units in each domain, and a target expression is simultaneously categorized by numerous active units, each assessing a particular facet of its structure. A few basic psychological phenomena (listed in section 2), applying repeatedly in all domains and at many levels of organization, give rise to structures of indefinite complexity, which categorizing relationships—each pertaining to a particular structural dimension—link into cross-cutting networks. A description of this sort is further unified in that seemingly diverse phenomena are seen as residing in different aspects of the same or comparable structural assemblies, or the same aspects "viewed" in alternate ways.

5.1. Lexicon and grammar

CG itself offers conceptual unification. It posits only semantic, phonological, and symbolic structures. Lexicon, morphology, and syntax form a gradation claimed to be fully describable as assemblies of symbolic structures. The distinction between grammatical rules and symbolically complex expressions is only a matter of whether (or the degree to which) the symbolic assemblies constituting them are schematic rather than specific. While there is some tendency for morphological and syntactic rules to differ in terms of generality and productivity, the only consistent basis for distinguishing them is whether the phonological composition they specify takes place within a word or involves word sequences. Expressions constructed in accordance with grammatical schemas can also be of any size. With repeated use, an expression of any size or degree of compositionality can be entrenched and conventionalized. The lexicon of a language is then definable as the set of expressions with the status of conventional units.

Constructional schemas and complex lexical items both consist of symbolic assemblies with unit status, often comprising component and composite symbolic structures at multiple levels of organization. The reason for referring to such an assembly as a rule or constructional schema, rather than as a lexical item, is the incorporation of one or more symbolic components too schematic—especially phonologically—to actually be expressed as such. There are however degrees of schematicity, even at the phonological pole, and in a complex structure different numbers of components can be characterized schematically. The fixed expression *crane one's neck* would generally be considered a lexical item, yet the possessive element is actually schematic: *one's* is just a placeholder for *my*, *your*, *his*, etc., all of which are monosyllabic. Does *crane one's neck* count as a grammatical pattern instead of a lexical item by virtue of this schematic component? What about *X take Y over X's knee and spank Y*, which is schematic in several positions? If these are still considered lexical rather than grammatical, there is no evident reason why a constructional schema that incorporates a specific element, e.g. [[send][NP][NP]], should not also be a lexical item. That in turn is only one step away from according lexical status to assemblies like [[V][NP][NP]], all of whose components are schematic. My point, of course, is that lexicon and grammar grade into one another so that any specific line of demarcation would be arbitrary.

To make the same point in another way, let us consider more carefully the status of the ditransitive pattern [[send][NP][NP]], i.e. the commonality inherent in complex expressions like *send me a package, send your mother an eviction notice, send Washington a message*, etc. On the left in Figure 4.10, enclosed in an ellipse, is a fragment of the network of constructional schemas and subschemas constituting conventional knowledge of the English ditransitive construction. Verbs of transfer function as a prototype giving rise to various extensions (Goldberg 1992). Subschemas specify the occurrence of particular verbs in this pattern, *give* and *send* of course being common and well-entrenched. Special cases of these subpatterns may themselves be established as familiar units, e.g. [[give][me][NP]] (note the contraction *gimme*).

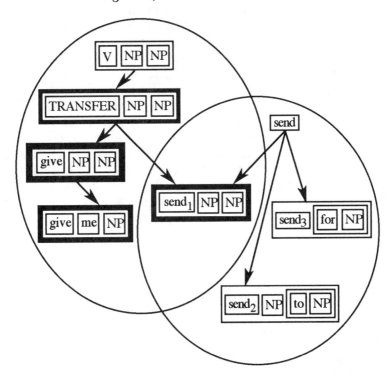

Figure 4.10

At the same time, however, the subschema [[send][NP][NP]] represents a lexical property of *send* and belongs to a network of constructional schemas describing its grammatical behavior. Some of these are shown in the ellipse on the right in Figure 4.10. In both construction grammar and CG, a lexical item's characterization includes a set of "structural frames" in which it conventionally occurs. While comparable in function to the "syntactic features" used in generative theory to specify the permitted contexts of lexical insertion, these frames are actually just partially schematic symbolic assemblies representing the commonality of certain complex expressions. They are, moreover, inherent and essential to a lexeme's value. Lexical items arise through a process of progressive decontextualization, where non-recurring aspects of usage events are filtered out through lack of reinforcement. Part of the relevant context is their occurrence in larger symbolic assemblies. To the extent that a form like *send* has any cognitive status independently of the structural frames in which it appears, it emerges by abstraction from these larger assemblies. Figure 4.10 should not be read as indicating that *send* is a distinct element which merely happens to be incorporated in a set of constructional subschemas. Rather, it is immanent in these assemblies and apprehended as a separate entity only by suppressing them.

What, then, is the status of [[send][NP][NP]]? Does it belong to the ditransitive construction or to the lexical item *send*? The answer, of course, is that the question is wrong: it is simultaneously part of both. Viewed in relation to the construction, it constitutes a subschema helping to specify the conventional distribution of a more general grammatical pattern. Viewed in relation to the lexical item, it specifies one grammatical environment in which the form occurs. In the present model, it is unproblematic (and certainly usual) for the same element to participate in multiple networks, which thereby intersect.

5.2. Lexical semantics

A lexeme is not precisely the same in all its environments. Since elements are always shaped by the contexts in which they occur, it is only by abstracting away from contextual variation that a constant representation emerges. *Send* is thus shown in Figure 4.10 as having the contextual variants [send$_1$], [send$_2$], and [send$_3$]. In particular, [send$_1$] chooses the recipient as its direct object—defined in CG as a participant receiving a secondary degree of "focal prominence"—and further highlights the resultant possessive relationship. On the other hand, [send$_2$] confers object status on the mover and highlights the path it follows, whereas [send$_3$] downplays both the mover and the recipient, focusing instead on the entity the sender hopes to obtain. It is I think pointless to ask whether these differences in relative prominence are responsible for the variants occurring in distinct structural frames, or whether the frames themselves induce the differences by virtue of what they explicitly encode. In any case a variant enters into a kind of "ecological system" with its structural context and does not necessarily exist outside that habitat. I am suggesting that these context-dependent variants may be more fundamental than the context-neutral schematization we tend to regard as primary.

In a "bottom up" account of this sort, the polysemy of lexical items should be expected as the normal state of affairs. Whether the contexts are structural, collocational, or pragmatic, they inevitably shape the construal of symbolic structures and thus give rise to semantic variants. Polysemy results when multiple variants become entrenched as units, provided of course that some connection is established between them (otherwise we speak of homonymy). Often a particular variant is both prior and sufficiently salient to serve as the basis for extension to other contexts, in which case we anoint it as the lexical item's prototypical semantic value. Through the reinforcement of common features, schemas emerge at different levels of abstraction to represent the commonality inherent in sets of variants. These alternate semantic values constitute a complex category describable as a network (as in Figure 4.4).

A classic problem of lexical semantics is whether an expression is truly "ambiguous", so that we must indeed posit two senses, or whether it is only "vague", in which case there may be just one. In practice the line is often hard to draw, with standard tests (Zwicky and Sadock 1975) failing to produce a clear-cut distinction. Consider the question of whether the verb *paint* is ambiguous between designating an artistic endeavor and a utilitarian one, or whether it is merely vague in this regard. One way to test this is by ascertaining whether a sentence like *Bill has been painting and so has Jane* is semantically coherent or anomalous when the two clauses are construed as differing on this point. Thus, if Bill is painting a portrait while Jane is putting lines on a highway, the sentence feels zeugmatic. This suggests two distinct meanings, whereas the anaphoric expression *so has* requires that the two clauses be semantically parallel. However, Tuggy (1993) has argued convincingly that judgments like these are often graded, making the test results indeterminate. The above example is less zeugmatic if Jane is instead painting a wall, and virtually normal if Bill is covering a wall for artistic purposes (say with a mural) and Jane for purely utilitarian purposes.

Tuggy shows that graded judgments like these, as well as clear-cut assessments of vagueness or ambiguity, are expected and readily accommodated in a dynamic usage-based model using networks for the description of complex categories. The nodes in such a network vary in their entrenchment and ease of activation, hence in the extent of their accessibility for specific grammatical purposes. The issue of vagueness vs. ambiguity hinges on the relative status of three structures: the putative specific senses (e.g. 'paint for artistic purposes' and 'paint for utilitarian purposes'), and also the schematic meaning representing their commonality ('paint'). Each structure is established to some degree as a conventional meaning of the lexical item in question. The possibilities range from being relatively unfamiliar and lacking unit status, at one extreme, to being very well-entrenched and easily elicited, at the other.

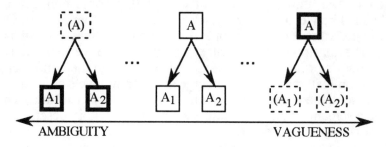

Figure 4.11

As shown in Figure 4.11, clear-cut cases of ambiguity are those where only the specific senses are entrenched and accessible. If *paint* were like this, a neutral sense would be unavailable for anaphora, and one could not say *Bill has been painting and so has Jane* in mixed circumstances comparing artistic and utilitarian intent. Conversely, definite cases of vagueness are those where only the schematic meaning is entrenched and accessible. If this were true of *paint*, it should always be felicitous to use the sentence in mixed circumstances (even with portraits and lines on a highway). The actual situation appears to fall somewhere in between. When the two instances of painting are similar enough, the neutral value is able to emerge for anaphoric purposes. However, egregious differences call attention to themselves and make it harder to suppress the specific senses in favor of the neutral one. Thus, if Bill has been painting a portrait, Jane's having done so with lines on a highway can only be zeugmatic.

Comparable differences in salience and likelihood of activation are responsible for another important dimension of lexical semantics, namely degree of *analyzability*. By analyzability I mean the extent to which speakers are cognizant of the presence and the semantic contribution of component symbolic elements. A novel combination is by definition fully analyzable, since a speaker has to actively manipulate the components in constructing it. Its meaning then is not just the novel composite conception (C), but (C) construed in relation to the component meanings [A] and [B], which categorize different facets of it. If I coin the term *flinger* to describe a new device, I necessarily recognize the contribution of *fling* and *-er*, thereby understanding it to mean 'something that flings'. That is the situation shown on the left in Figure 4.12.

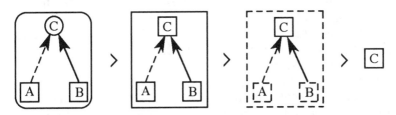

Figure 4.12

A composite expression's entrenchment as a conventional unit does not entail any immediate loss of analyzability. The composite meaning [C] will then have unit status, but it is still construed against the background of the component meanings [A] and [B], as depicted in the second panel of Figure 4.12. Thus a *printer* is still understood as 'something that prints', and a *scanner* as 'something that scans'. Once [C] is established as a unit, however, it has at least the potential to be activated independently of [A] and [B]. There is an overall long-term tendency for the analyzability of composite lexical units to gradually decline: I do not always think of a *computer* as 'something that computes', I am less likely to think of a *freezer* as 'something that freezes', and a *propeller* is hardly ever thought of as 'something that propels'. We can interpret this lessening analyzability as a reduction in the likelihood of [A] and [B] being activated along with [C] and/or as a decrease in their level of activation. This is shown in the third panel of the diagram. The final step is for [A] and [B] to remain completely inert when [C] is activated. Linguistically we can then describe the expression as having lost its original symbolic complexity via reanalysis.

One factor facilitating a decline in analyzability is the usual discrepancy between an expression's expected compositional meaning and the actual contextual meaning that eventually becomes its conventional value. In accordance with the discussion of Figures 4.7-9, the structure given as [C] in Figure 4.12 is resolvable into [[C']--->[C"]], in which the compositional value [C'] is merely a stepping-stone for arriving at the contextual value [C"]. Thus a *printer* is not just 'something that prints' but a specific kind of computer equipment. More drastically, a *ruler* is less commonly understood as a device used for ruling lines than as an instrument of measurement. The more [C"] diverges from [C'], the less it is motivated by [C'], and the easier it becomes for [C"] to be activated autonomously. Hence a decline in analyzability involves [C'] gradually fading out the picture along with [A] and [B].

Because mainstream theories have little to say about analyzability, it has largely been ignored by linguistic theorists despite its omnipresence as a significant dimension of meaning and a recurring problem in lexical and grammatical description. The one situation where degrees of analyzability are often noted is in the discussion of "fading" metaphors. In yachting, for example, there is a crew member who turns a crank in a manner resembling that involved in grinding meat. This person is metaphorically called a *grinder*, but for those immersed in the sport the term's familiarity has no doubt substantially reduced the salience of its metaphorical basis. We can describe this fading of the metaphor as a gradual decrease in the likelihood of the "literal" meaning [C'] being activated along with the "figurative" meaning [C"], as well as in its level of activation.

5.3. Phonology

Let us now turn to phonology and to the phonological aspects of morphology. Phonological structures are one of the three kinds of units permitted by the content requirement, the others being semantic and symbolic units. The difference between phonology and morphology resides in whether we consider phonological organization in its own terms or with respect to its role in symbolic structures.[8]

Purely phonological structures include such elements as segments, syllables, words, feet, and intonation groups. These can all be represented at various levels of specificity. A form like *pot*, for example, can be characterized phonologically in precise phonetic detail as a sequence of "phones" ([pʰát]), more abstractly as a series of phonemes (/pat/), or schematically as a syllabic template ([CVC]). From the usage-based perspective, we can reasonably anticipate that structures of any size and any level of abstraction are capable of being learned and represented as conventional units. A schema that describes a general pattern, thus defining a space of possible structures, coexists with instantiating units that specify which regions of the space are actually used. For instance, the syllable schema [CVC] might coexist with subschemas such as [SVC] (where S=STOP), [NVC] (N=NASAL), [SVN], [SVS], [pVC], [NVt], etc. (but not— for English—either [CVh] or [ŋVC]).

Phonological units are also organized into complex categories describable as networks. A phoneme, for example, is a complex category whose prototype corresponds to what was traditionally regarded as its basic allophone, the one occurring in the greatest variety of contexts. Since every context induces some phonetic adjustment (if only very minor), the prototype must in some measure be schematic. Its manifestations in particular contexts constitute either instantiations of the schema, which may themselves have unit status, or extensions recognized as secondary allophones owing to their divergent specifications. Higher-level schemas may also be abstracted to represent what is common to the prototype and different sets of extensions.

A variety of basic phonological entities can be seen as naturally arising via the same process of abstraction that we have been discussing throughout. Consider sound segments. At the phonetic level, segments have no independent existence. To the extent that we need to posit them, we can regard them as being abstracted from syllables—perhaps to be modeled as constellations of articulatory gestures, as proposed by Browman and Goldstein (e.g. 1992)— which have some claim to being the minimal units of speech. It is only through phonological decontextualization that a segmental phoneme like /p/ emerges as a distinct cognitive entity. From actual syllables, an array of schemas are presumably extracted representing a *p*-like sound in various syllabic contexts: syllable initial, syllable final, before or after particular vowels, as part of certain consonant clusters, etc. We can identify these *p*-like sounds with phones or allophones of the complex category defining /p/, and the syllabic schemas as their conditioning environments. If these phonological variants have enough in common, and occur in enough distinct environments, a schematized segment arises which embodies their commonality but makes no specific reference to syllabic position or the surrounding context.

Likewise, classificatory phonological features constitute abstractions from sounds (or sound sequences). To the extent that we need to posit them, they are merely the schematic characterizations of "natural classes" of sounds. Representing the feature [STOP], for example, would be a stop consonant schematic in regard to such properties as voicing and place of articulation. Of course, sounds vary in the nature and the degree of their commonality, so alternate sets give rise to schemas with different numbers and combinations of specific properties: [STOP], [ALVEOLAR STOP], [HIGH FRONT VOWEL], [CONSONANT], [NASAL], etc. Standard features can then be described as schemas that are specific in regard to just a single phonological parameter. In the same vein, the "tiers" employed in contemporary phonological description amount to sequences of seg-mental schemas all of which are specific in regard to certain para-meters while abstracting away from the others.

What about phonological rules? As in grammar, rules are limited to schemas abstracted from actual expressions. This concep-tion of phonological rules is quite straightforward in the case of phonotactics. Consider the constraints a language imposes on the form of permitted syllables. An array of syllable schemas—[nVt], [NVt], [NVS], [CVS], [CVC], etc.—represent the patterns inherent in occurring syllables, described at various levels of generality. When embedded in a dynamic processing model based on interactive activation, these schemas specify the actual syllabic distribution of segments, certain combinations being assessed as non-conventional. For example, we can posit for English the low-level schemas [mVC] and [nVC], as well as the higher-level generalization [NVC], but not the non-occurring pattern [ŋVC]. To account for the judgment that a syllable like (ŋæk) is un-English, we need only assume that a lower-level schema wins out over [NVC] for the privilege of categorizing it, e.g. ([nVC]--->(ŋæk)).

Less obvious is the treatment of phonological rules tradition-ally formulated in process terms as derivations from underlying representations. Although the content requirement proscribes deriva-tions from underlying structures, it does permit relationships of cate-gorization, including extension.[9] Moreover, from other domains of linguistic structure we know that chains of extensions often occur, that extensions are sometimes limited to particular contexts, and that analogous categorizing relationships can themselves give rise to schemas describing their abstract commonality. These properties suggest an analysis of derivational phonological rules as *patterns of phonological extension.*[10]

Consider, for example, a rule voicing [t] to [d] intervocali-cally. We can posit such a rule when there is evidence that speakers pronounce certain forms with a [d] which they nonetheless categorize as instantiating /t/. For instance, variants with [t] and [d] might co-exist as the careful and fast-speech pronunciations of numerous lexical items: [fita]~[fida], [oti]~[odi], [ketul]~[kedul], etc. I follow Bybee (1994) in supposing that each habitual pronunciation is mentally represented in considerable phonetic detail. Assuming, then, that [t] is felt to be "basic", phonological characterizations of the lexical items in question include categorizing relationships between their prototypical and extended phonetic variants: [[fita]--->[fida]], [[oti]--->[odi]], and [[ketul]--->[kedul]]. Like any other regularity, the commonality inherent in these alternations can be extracted as a schema: [[...VtV...]--->[...VdV...]]. We can describe this schema in a number of mutually consistent ways. First, it is immanent in the networks describing the phonological variants of individual lexical items. Second, it is part of the complex category representing the phoneme /t/. It specifies that the basic allophone [t] is extended to [d] in the context [...V_V...]. Finally, the schema can be regarded as a phonological rule (which may or may not be productive, i.e. accessible for the sanction of new instances). These are not competing analyses, but a matter of the same cognitive entity being considered from alternate perspectives.

5.4. Morphology

Let us turn now to morphology.[11] A number of classic problems pertain to the notion "morpheme". We present the concept to students by means of data sets like {*fast, faster, fastest, cool, cooler, coolest, red, redder, reddest*}, where words are exhaustively decomposable into discrete chunks from which they derive in a transparently regular way. However, linguists are well aware that this archetypal concep-tion of morphemes as building blocks has severe limitations—with any representative array of data, the metaphor breaks down immediately. The difficulties lie with the metaphor itself. When the same phenomena are examined from the usage-based perspective, the problems simply fail to arise.

Just as segments are abstracted from syllables, morphemes are abstracted from words. Though some stand alone (just as vowels can stand alone as syllables), there are many morphemes—in some languages the vast majority—which only occur as part of larger words. By and large, it seems fair to say that speakers are more intuitively aware of words than of their parts, and that large numbers of complex forms are initially learned as wholes and analyzed only subsequently (if at all). Words, then, have some claim to primacy.

In the usage-based perspective, morphemes are naturally seen as arising by the usual process of abstraction. The interpretation of abstraction as the reinforcement of recurring commonalities echoes the basic technique of classic morphemic analysis, where the objective is to identify recurrent pairings between particular conceptual and phonological structures. The pairing observed in *fast* is also inherent in *faster* and *fastest*. Analysts therefore posit the symbolic unit [FAST/fast], just as speakers abstract it from usage events. From forms like *fastest, coolest,* and *reddest,* both linguists and speakers extract the morpheme [MOST/-est] to represent the systematic co-occurrence of the concept 'most' (with respect to a property) and the phonological sequence *-est.* In straightforward cases like *fastest,* the symbolic units thus extracted are exhaustive of the word and readily taken as yielding it compositionally.

We have seen, however, that complex words are not in general fully compositional, whether we look at their initial use or their established conventional value. The morphemic analysis of *printer* into [PRINT/print] and [ER/-er] does not (in conjunction with compositional patterns) provide a full characterization of its linguistic meaning (where it specifically indicates a piece of computer equipment). We saw earlier how this is a natural consequence of learning via schematization based on contextual understanding (Figures 4.7-9). From the standpoint of morphemic analysis, this typical situation is nonetheless problematic if one thinks of words as being built out of morphemes (where does the extra material come from?). On the other hand, it is unproblematic if words have a status of their own and morphemes are abstracted from them. While [PRINT] and [ER] do not exhaust the specialized meaning of *printer,* they are discernible in that meaning. [PRINT/print] can thus be extracted from *printer, printing, printed,* etc. by reinforcing their commonality, and [ER/-er] from *printer, freezer, eraser,* etc., regardless of whether any particular word is fully compositional. This is the morphemic consequence of the distinction previously discussed between construction and categorization.

Once the abstractive nature of morphemes is recognized, a raft of other classic problems evaporate. Degrees of analyzability are readily accommodated. If forms like *propeller*, *ruler*, and *stretcher* are originally learned as unanalyzed wholes, it makes little difference to their efficacious use whether speakers ever make a connection with *propel*, *rule*, and *stretch*, acquired from other contexts. If they do establish a connection, the extent to which the composite expressions activate these components is likewise inessential and no doubt variable. Should we then say that words like *propeller*, *ruler*, and *stretcher* are polymorphemic? Either a positive or a negative answer would, I think, be simplistic. In the present framework it is both reasonable and coherent to say instead that their analyzability into component morphemes is a matter of degree.

The extraction of morphemic components need not be uniform for all portions of a word. For example, since *-er* occurs in so many nouns, particularly those indicating agentive or instrumental participants in actions, it is sufficiently entrenched and salient that appropriate forms strongly tend to be analyzed in terms of it. Intuitively, I would judge that *-er* is more clearly apparent in *propeller*, *ruler*, and *stretcher* than are *propel*, *rule*, and *stretch*. The disparity is even more evident in *pliers* and *plumber*, where *ply* and *plumb* cast a faint shadow at best. The limiting case of such disparity is when morphemic analysis touches only part of a word, leaving the remainder as an unanalyzed residue. There are of course numerous examples involving *-er*: *father*, *mother*, *brother*, *sister*, *hammer*, *roster*, *sliver*, *master*, *geyser*, *crater*, *miser*, and so on. Bybee (1988: 128) notes the residues *Mon*, *Tues*, *Wednes*, etc. left when an obvious commonality is observed in the names for days of the week. An account of morphemes based on the reinforcing of common features renders it unproblematic for only portions of words to participate in such associations.

Bybee correctly notes that this account extends to phonaesthemes, e.g. the *str* of *strip*, *stripe*, *strap*, *strop*, *street*, *stretch*, *strand*, *string*, etc., which indicates length and thinness. Whether it has iconic motivation or comes about merely by historical accident, a recurring sound/meaning association of this kind allows the extraction of a schema with the potential to be used in coining or analyzing other expressions. Elaborate systems of sound symbolism might arise in this fashion (cf. FCG1: 399-401). On the other hand, the schema may have little salience if only because so many forms containing the phonological sequence lack the meaning component, and conversely. Still, the basic process is the same one operative in canonical morphemic analysis. What varies is how far the intrinsic organization of the data allows this process to proceed—how close it comes to the "ideal" situation where the morphemic components are salient and exhaust the content of the words from which they are extracted.

In her description of modern Aramaic verb morphology, Rubba (1993) shows that with this kind of approach no special problems are posed by non-concatenative morphology. A simple illustration is given in Figure 4.13.

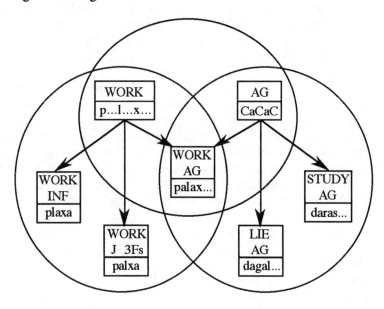

Figure 4.13

The symbolic units shown at the bottom are specific words and stems: the infinitival, third feminine singular jussive, and agentive forms of 'work', and the agentive forms of 'lie' and 'study' (the agentive stems are further inflected for gender and number). If morphemes are abstracted from words by a process of schematization, the data straightforwardly yields the symbolic units shown at the top. The stem [WORK/p...l...x...] comprises the consonants [p], [l], and [x], occurring in a particular linear sequence, but abstracts away from the placement (and also the identity) of vowels—since the vocalism is variable, it is filtered out as common features are reinforced. Conversely, the agentive morpheme [AG/CaCaC] is specific in regard to vocalism but schematic with respect to the surrounding consonants. Such morphemes are non-prototypical in the sense that their specified segments are not all contiguous in the temporal sequence. However, the process of schematization does not itself require any particular distribution of shared and canceled properties. While there is often a partitioning between specific and schematic substructures, their interdigitation is not at all unusual (cf. *X take Y over X's knee and spank Y*).

Figure 4.13 further illustrates the point that the same network of structures can be viewed in different ways, corresponding to different linguistic constructs. I noted earlier that part of the overall characterization of a lexical item is a set of structural frames in which it conventionally occurs. While these frames were identified earlier as constructional subschemas (as in Figure 4.10), they also include specific complex expressions with unit status (constructional subschemas and complex expressions form a gradation in any case). Hence the structures in the ellipse on the left are part of the overall characterization of the lexical item [WORK/p...l...x...], and those in the ellipse on the right help define the agentive morpheme. At the same time, many specific forms like *palax-* 'worker' have the status of conventional units and thus constitute lexical items (fixed expressions). A form like *palax-* is of course polymorphemic, comprising the two morphemes under discussion. The structures in the middle ellipse are thus interpretable as a construction, in which two component structures categorize and motivate the composite expression. These in turn instantiate (or have immanent in them) a constructional schema describing the formation of agentive noun stems.

5.5. Morphophonemics

Rubba (1993) has also examined in preliminary terms the treatment of phonological rules in a network account of morphology. Recall that phonotactic rules are simply schematized representations of occurring phonological sequences, whereas "derivational" rules are schemas representing patterns of phonological extension. The examples given previously were purely phonological in the sense that the schemas made no reference to any particular morphological context. Sometimes patterns of extension are however limited to certain morphological contexts, in which case the rules are considered "morphophonemic". Their description in CG remains the same except that appropriate reference to the context is incorporated in the schema characterizing the extension (for illustration, see Langacker 1988: 143-145). The example to be considered here involves a phonotactic constraint and a rule that is morphophonemic in the sense that extension affects a segment's phonemic categorization.

Rubba documents for modern Aramaic a phonotactic constraint to the effect that obstruent clusters agree in voicing. For our purposes, it is sufficient to posit the cluster template [TT], reflecting the frequent co-occurrence of voiceless obstruents, as well as the absence of the schema [DT], which speakers do not extract since clusters consisting of a voiced and a voiceless obstruent do not occur. There are however verb roots, such as [HEAL/b...s...m...], where voiced and voiceless obstruents occur in consecutive consonantal slots. These are abstracted from specific occurrent forms in which a vowel appears between the two obstruents, so that the phonotactic constraint is not violated. Now certain stem forms, including the infinitive, involve patterns of vocalization that leave the first two root consonants adjacent to one another. The composite expression is then pronounced with a voiceless initial obstruent, e.g. *psama* 'to heal' (not *bsama*). In process terms, one could say that a rule changes /b/ to /p/ to agree in voicing with the following consonant. Of course, it has sometimes been taken as problematic that the assimilation rule effectively duplicates the phonotactic constraint, which has to be posited for independent reasons. Much has also been made of the fact that such a rule can either be phonological or morphophonemic depending on whether the phoneme it applies to happens to have a counterpart with the opposite voicing (Halle 1959).

A partial description of the situation is given in Figure 4.14, adapted from Rubba (1993: 499). At the top in this diagram are three symbolic structures: the root [HEAL/b...s...m...], the infinitival morpheme [INF/CCaCa], and the composite infinitival expression [HEAL INF/psama]. Collectively these make up a construction, in which the two component morphemes categorize the composite structure. The box labeled (i) is part of the overall characterization of the lexeme *b-s-m* 'heal'. Its full description comprises not only the root morpheme, but also an array of structural frames, including various specific composite expressions in which it conventionally appears. One of these is the infinitive *psama* 'to heal'. At the phonological pole, the relation between [b...s...m...] and [ps...m...] (inherent in [psama]) is a fragment of the complex category representing the variant phonological shapes of the root morpheme. It is in particular a relationship of extension from the presumed prototype [b...s...m...] to the variant that appears in the context of the infinitival construction.

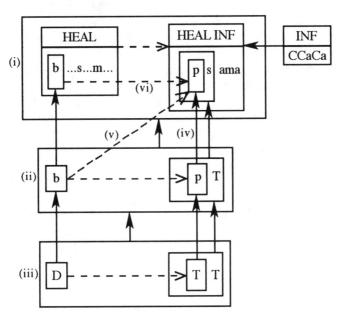

Figure 4.14

Also apparent in the diagram is the schema [TT], which specifies the conventionality of a cluster of voiceless obstruents. This is instantiated by [pT], representing a special case of the general pattern, in turn elaborated by the specific cluster [ps] (as part of [psama]). These units and categorizing relationships are a fragment of the network describing permissible consonant clusters in the language. Moreover, these elements also function as components of the structures in boxes (ii) and (iii), which belong to another network describing a family of phonological extensions. Extracted from numerous specific extensions like [[b...s...m...]--->[ps...m...]], schema (ii) represents the pattern of [b] extending to [p] before a voiceless obstruent. Since the analogous extension occurs with other voiced obstruents, the higher-level schema (iii) is extracted to embody the generalization that any such obstruent devoices in this context. Observe that (ii) is a subschema with respect to (iii), and that the relevant portions of (i) are a specific instantiation of (ii).

Yet other facets of the diagram pertain to the phonemes /b/ and /p/. The elements [b] and [p] in (ii) are more or less identifiable with the basic allophones of these respective categories. The relationship [[D]→[b]] shows [b] as a member of the more inclusive class of voiced obstruents, while [[T]→[p]] relates [p] to the class of voiceless obstruents. The existence of both voiced and voiceless obstruent phonemes entails that the systematic extension [[b]--->[p]] (before T) effects a change in category membership: one variant of /b/ coincides with the basic (or at least a central) allophone of /p/. That, however, is a contingent matter which depends on the specific inventory of phonemes the language happens to have—the extension in (ii), and its generalized version in (iii), are not intrinsically either phonological or morphophonemic. Another instantiation of (iii) in the same language could perfectly well be purely phonological (this is in fact the case in Aramaic).

How, then, do we characterize the [p] or [psama]? It is shown in Figure 4.14 as both an instantiation of the phoneme /p/ (note the arrow labeled (iv)) and also an extension vis-à-vis the phoneme /b/ (arrow (v)). The former categorization has a phonetic basis, and the latter a morphological one, [psama] being understood as a manifestation of [b...s...m...] (arrow (vi)). While phonologists will have to determine the relative salience and the consequences of the alternate categorizations, it seems to me that the framework portrays the complex situation in a realistic way.

5.6. Larger assemblies

Diagrams like Figures 4.13-14 are initially rather forbidding. To be sure, they are no more so than a set of algebraic rules or formulas providing comparable information, and probably less so once certain notational conventions become familiar. Complex representations such as these can only be avoided at the price of failing to be even minimally explicit about essential aspects of linguistic organization. These diagrams are in any case drastically oversimplified relative to the actual complexity of the linguistic reality they seek to model. At best they depict only small fragments of pertinent structures and networks, selected for minimal illustration of some particular point.

These fragmentary representations afford at least a hint of the large coalitions of structures and relationships that are brought to bear in shaping even the smallest portions of expressions and determining their linguistic interpretation. Coalitions of diverse character and indefinite complexity have the potential to coalesce into higher-order structures having some kind of cognitive status in their own right. The most obvious examples are lexical items (fixed expressions), which in principle have no upper bound on their possible size. While *X take Y over X's knee and spank Y* is longer than lexical items are traditionally thought of as being, it is certainly a conventionally established unit, and by no means the largest conventional expression to be found. Complex expressions can also give rise to constructional schemas spanning multiple levels of organization, i.e. not just a single pattern for integrating two component structures to form a composite structure, but multi-level assemblies of such patterns defining constituency hierarchies.

For example, English has both a morphological pattern deriving adjectives from nouns by means of *-ful*, and one deriving adverbs from adjectives by means of *-ly*. We can represent the two constructional schemas as $[[...]_{N}\text{-ful}]_{ADJ}$ and $[[...]_{ADJ}\text{-ly}]_{ADV}$. On the basis of a large set of well-established forms—*artfully, carefully, hopefully, sinfully, dutifully, shamefully, deceitfully, beautifully, playfully, cheerfully, successfully, lawfully, scornfully, zestfully*, etc.—it is evident that the combination of these two patterns in successive layers of morphological organization also represents a conventional pattern. We can therefore posit the higher-order constructional schema $[[[...]_{N}\text{-ful}]_{ADJ}\text{-ly}]_{ADV}$ to capture the generalization. Immanent in particular forms like those cited, this structure is both a complex pattern in its own right and a subschema of $[[...]_{ADJ}\text{-ly}]_{ADV}$ in the network spelling out its conventional exploitation. Even a morphologically impoverished language like English has still more elaborate assemblies of this kind, e.g. $[[[[...]\text{-al}]_{ADJ}\text{-iz}]_{V}\text{-ation}]_{N}$, from *centralization, normalization, nationalization, radicalization, marginalization, lexicalization, grammaticalization*, and so on (cf. Chapin 1967). Without going into any detail, let me suggest that comparable assemblies of constructional schemas correspond to such traditional descriptive devices as morpheme-order charts and templates specifying permitted clitic sequences.

I should also mention higher-order coalitions such as paradigms and conjugation classes. I make no apriori claims about the proportion of specific inflected forms that are learned and stored as units, nor about the nature and extent of their organization into psychological assemblies analogous to the paradigms described by grammarians. However, as Bybee has long maintained, we can reasonably suppose that speakers learn and store large numbers of specific forms, especially those that are idiosyncratic or represent minor patterns, but no doubt also including high-frequency forms instantiating major patterns. A particular stem is abstracted from an array of inflected forms, many of which may have unit status, as shown in Figure 4.13 for Aramaic *p...l...x...* 'work'. Through the categorizing relationships thus established, a stem provides access to a set of inflected forms which—if complete enough in relation to the structural patterns of the language—we can recognize as a paradigm. Like a grammarian's paradigm, moreover, it is a structured set in which forms are connected to one another in myriad ways. Schematized forms capture similarities observable with respect to various parameters at different levels of abstraction. With a verb, for instance, schemas might be extracted to represent the commonalities of singular forms, non-future forms, third-person plurals, etc.

At the same time, other schemas are extracted to capture what is shared by analogous forms in the paradigms of different lexemes. These amount to constructional schemas and subschemas. Consider Figure 4.15.

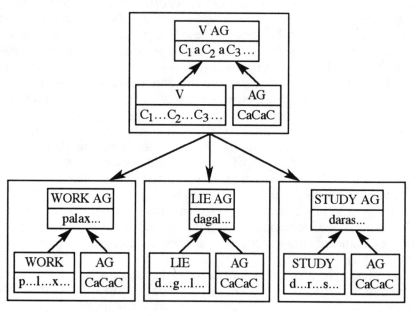

Figure 4.15

The diagram depicts a constructional subschema describing one pattern of agentive-noun formation in modern Aramaic. It specifies how a root is integrated with the agentive morpheme to yield the

composite agentive expression which interdigitates the root consonants with the agentive morpheme's vocalism. Three instantiations are
shown, the same ones as in Figure 4.13, which however did not give
the constructional schema or the component structures for *dagal...*
'liar' or *daras...* 'studier'. Hence the two diagrams offer different
partial views of the same elaborate web of structures and relationships.

　　Figure 4.15 is a fragment of the network of constructional
schemas, subschemas, and specific instantiations describing agentive-
noun formation in Aramaic. Comparable networks describe the patterns for other forms appearing in verbal paradigms (see Rubba 1993
for details). Consider now a particular verb root, e.g. *p...l...x...*
'work'. A given root functions as a component structure in numerous
constructions, corresponding to the different inflected forms in its
paradigm. Just two of these are shown (enclosed in ellipses) in Figure
4.16: *p...l...x...* 'work' is a component of both the agentive *palax...*
and the infinitival form *plaxa*. We can think of this diagram as abbre-
viating a much larger array of constructions in which the root occurs.
This larger collection of symbolic assemblies constitutes a higher-
order coalition of the sort whose cognitive status is under discussion.

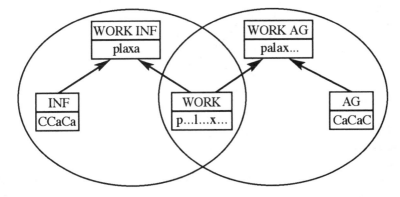

Figure 4.16

　　Let me now suggest that the entire complex configuration in
Figure 4.16 (and even the larger configuration that it abbreviates) may
have the status of a conventional linguistic unit. It may in any case
provide a basis for schematization. Suppose a number of other verb
roots participate in precisely the same inflectional patterns. For each
of them a higher-level symbolic assembly directly analogous to Figure

4.16 can thus be posited. The usual process of abstraction could then apply, resulting in the schematized higher-order assembly depicted in Figure 4.17. This is a coalition of particular constructional subschemas, describing inflectional patterns all of which are conventionally applicable to the same root. In other words, this higher-order schema defines a *conjugation class*. It is a set of associated inflectional patterns, which certain verbs plug into, and which might have sufficient entrenchment and salience to exert an influence on others. If accessible for the sanction of novel expressions, it can simultaneously specify all the inflected forms of a newly minted root.

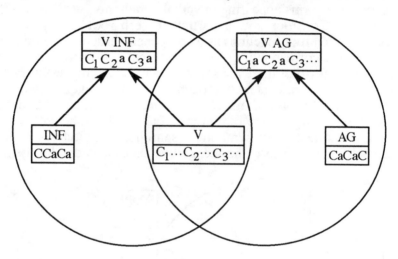

Figure 4.17

6. A final issue

I would like to conclude by comparing this model to two alternate proposals with respect to the nature of linguistic "rules". One proposal, recently advanced by Pinker and Prince (1991: 230-233), is that regular and irregular expressions are handled by distinct systems very different in nature:

> *Regular inflection* (e.g., *walk-walked*) is perfectly rule-governed, and thus looks like a paradigm case of a grammatical rule implemented in human brains. Irregular inflection (e.g., *sing-sang*) shows varying degrees of unpredictability and thus would seem to involve brute-force memory...The regular process seems to be

the very essence of the symbol-manipulating, algorithmic approach to language underlying most theories of grammar, whereas the irregular process seems to involve a quite different kind of memory-driven processing...The conclusion we draw is that generative theories are fundamentally correct in their characterization of productive rules and structures, but deficient in the way they characterize memory of less predictable material, which must be associative and dynamic, somewhat as connectionism portrays it. It is necessary, then, to develop a new theory...which explicitly acknowledges the roles of rules on the one hand and of associative memory on the other. From such a theory, it follows that regular and irregular inflection must be computed by two different systems. Regulars are computed by an implementation of a classic symbolic rule of grammar, which concatenates an affix with a variable that stands for the stem. Irregulars are memorized pairs of words, but the linkages between the pair members are stored in an associative memory structure with certain connectionist-like properties.

Thus, something akin to a dynamic usage-based model is accepted for the kinds of examples—involving less than full compositionality, generality, and productivity—that have always been problematic in generative grammar. At the same time, rules in the classic constructive sense (algorithmic operations on strings of discrete symbols) are held necessary for truly systematic phenomena.

In one respect Pinker and Prince are no doubt correct: there is a difference in processing between regular and irregular forms. The latter are indeed stored and retrieved from memory, whereas the former are assembled in accordance with productive patterns (an option available even for high-frequency forms also learned as units). The two modes of processing are qualitatively distinct in ways that might very well explain the psycholinguistic and neurological evidence the authors advance to support their dichotomous view. Still, I am mystified by their apparent inclination to seek a dichotomous account in preference to a unified one. This inverts the usual scientific practice of seeking a unified account for seemingly diverse phenomena. I should think that positing two distinct cognitive systems would be done only reluctantly and as a last resort, after all other options have been thoroughly explored.

The linguistic facts do not suggest a strictly dichotomous organization, since sporadic exceptions are possible even for highly productive general rules, and since minor patterns often show a certain measure of productivity (Bybee and Slobin 1982). Research from the usage-based perspective consistently reinforces the idea that linguistic patterns run the full gamut in terms of systematicity, that rules approximate full generality and productivity more commonly than they actually reach it, and that such rules are at best a small minority in any case. The question, then, is whether a unified account can be given for the entire spectrum of patterns, including those which approach full systematicity. I have tried to show that a dynamic usage-based model offers a realistic prospect of achieving this. Under the right circumstances, a dynamic system of the sort envisaged is capable of crisp, reliable behavior representing any desired approximation to categorical rules. I see no reason to doubt that the observed degrees and kinds of systematicity can all be accommodated by positing appropriately configured networks in which conventional units vary in their specificity and inherent ease of activation.

The other alternate proposal is for linguistic regularities and the creation of novel expressions to be described in terms of "analogy" rather than "rules". This is, of course, a classic issue (see, for example, Bloomfield 1933: 16.6; Householder 1971: ch. 5), which appears to be reviving as alternatives to the generative paradigm are increasingly being sought (e.g. Itkonen and Haukioja 1996). What the issue amounts to naturally depends on how the key terms are defined. For example, if "rules" are equated with constructive statements and "analogy" with schemas or templates, then the model proposed here is purely analogical. My own practice, however, is to use the term "rule" for extracted regularities with some kind of enduring cognitive presence, regardless of their specific nature. I will understand "analogy" as referring to expressions being directly formed on the model of others, not on the basis of stored abstracted patterns. By these definitions, the dynamic usage-based model I propose is rule-based rather than analogical. The rules, though, are templatic schemas (as opposed to constructive statements), and are immanent in their instantiations (as opposed to being represented as distinct cognitive entities).

The question, then, is whether rules (schemas) can be wholly dispensed with in favor of the direct modeling of novel expressions on the basis of familiar ones. I think the answer is clearly negative. An exclusively analogical account—one that posits no abstraction or schematization—runs directly counter to the usage-based notion that language exhibits patterns at all levels of generality. It is also internally inconsistent, since even the learning of specific expressions (required as the basis for analogy) involves abstraction and schematization from actual usage events. Moreover, the standard argument against analogy is still a forceful one: if only analogy is posited, how is the distinction drawn between those analogical formations we find acceptable and those we do not? If the past tense of *swim* is *swam*, why can I not analogize and use *tram* as the past tense of *trim*? One cannot merely say that there are relatively few pairs like *swim/swam* to analogize from, and many more like *film/filmed*, since nothing would ensure that only the latter would be chosen as the model. If one were to claim that the much more numerous pairs like *film/filmed* reinforce one another and thus offer an irresistible model for analogy, the analogical position becomes indistinguishable from one which posits schemas. As I have characterized them, schemas are simply reinforced commonalities with the potential to influence subsequent processing.

　　As this example shows, the distinction between an analogical and a schema-based account is not necessarily a drastic one (FCG1: 11.3.4). For one thing, schemas can represent any level of abstraction, and low-level schemas are preferentially invoked (other things being equal) for the categorization of novel expressions. An expression sanctioned by a low-level schema rather than a higher-level generalization is likely to be considered "analogical", but a schema abstracted from just a handful of forms is a schema nonetheless. Moreover, analogy itself presupposes structural parallelism. In solving a proportion—e.g. in computing *trimmed* as the value of X in the formula *film/filmed* = *trim*/X—one must first determine that *film* and *filmed* are related in a specific way, and then find an X such that *trim* and X are related in the same way. But what is "the same way"? It is an abstract commonality, which the two pairs share. It is therefore a schema which they both instantiate, and if made explicit it would actually constitute a constructional schema of the sort proposed in CG. I have no doubt that true analogies do occur, where new expressions are modeled on others without the prior extraction and enduring cognitive presence of any schema. However, the very process of analogizing induces the apprehension of an abstract commonality, at least as a fleeting occurrence. The distinction between rule and analogy then reduces to whether the operative schema has already achieved the status of a unit. This is at most a matter of timing and may well be one of degree.

Chapter 5
Conceptual grouping and constituency

Constituency—hierarchies of part/whole relationships between smaller and more inclusive structures—is a foundational notion of modern grammatical theory.* "Trees" showing constituency groupings are commonly adopted as the primary representations for analyzing and describing syntactic structure. By contrast, CG does not take constituency per se to be fundamental or even essential.

In the generative tradition, constituency trees have long been used for the characterization of "grammatical relations" (notably subject and object). Other frameworks, broadly known as "dependency" theories (e.g. Tesnière 1965; Robinson 1970; Anderson 1971; Perlmutter 1983; Hudson 1984), do essentially the opposite: grammatical relations are directly represented by the branches of dependency trees, whereas the grouping of elements into structures of progressively larger size is left implicit. CG agrees with such approaches in recognizing the primacy of dependencies and showing them explicitly (in the form of correspondence lines). Although constituency is acknowledged in CG and represented with tree-like diagrams (cf. Deane 1992), it is seen as emergent rather than basic, hence flexible and often variable.

1. Constituency and grammatical relations

As traditionally conceived in generative grammar, constituency is represented by syntactic tree structures, as exemplified in Figure 5.1. Such trees are regarded as formal objects comprising a separate, purely grammatical dimension of representation. Although they are referred to by rules of semantic and phonological "interpretation", the trees and their nodes (NP, VP, etc.) are not themselves thought of as having any kind of meaning or phonological value. Instead, interpretation rules operate on the semantic and phonological substance of inserted lexical items. In the main generative tradition, moreover, syntactic tree structures provide the basis for "configurational" definitions of grammatical relations. A *subject*, for example, was defined in Chomsky 1965 as an NP directly dominated by S, and an *object* as an NP directly dominated by VP.

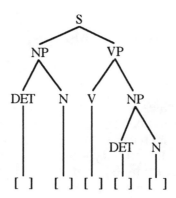

Figure 5.1

Of course, there is reason to speak of subject and object relationships even in sentences where the defining configurations cannot be observed. This problem was dealt with by positing a level of "deep" or "underlying" structure at which tree structure is fixed and invariant. Grammatical relations can then be specified at this level despite the "transformations" that deform it to yield the ultimate "surface" form. Thus, *This pear nobody ate* has the same grammatical relations as *Nobody ate this pear* because it has the same deep structure, from which it derives by a rule that fronts the direct-object NP.

CG, on the other hand, posits neither deep structures nor anything analogous to transformational derivations. From the grammatical standpoint, an expression is merely an assembly of symbolic structures, comprising any number of constructions. A typical construction is a symbolic assembly in which two component structures are integrated—both semantically and phonologically—to form a composite structure. Integration depends on correspondences between subparts of the two components. The overlap thus established allows the component structures to merge and form a coherent composite notion. Of course, the composite structure created at one level of organization can in turn function as one component of a higher-level construction, and so on. Symbolic assemblies of indefinite size and complexity can arise in this fashion.[1]

An example is given in Figure 5.2 (only the semantic pole is shown). At the lower level, the verb *saw* combines with *Bill* to form the composite expression *saw Bill*. (The dashed arrow represents a perceptual relationship, in this case one of seeing.) This composite structure in turn functions as one component structure at a higher level of organization, in which *Alice* is integrated with *saw Bill* to form the full clause *Alice saw Bill.*

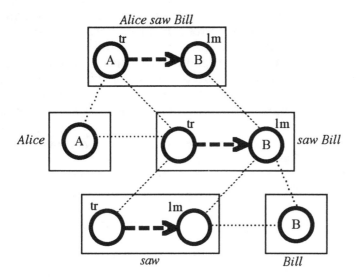

Figure 5.2

It should be evident that the order in which a complex symbolic expression is assembled corresponds to the traditional notion of constituency. In the clause *Alice saw Bill*, for example, the formation of the intermediate-level composite structure *saw Bill* reflects the grouping implied by the statement that *saw* and *Bill* together make up a grammatical constituent. Observe, however, that the notion of constituency that emerges in this framework is quite different from the one embodied in syntactic tree structures as normally conceived in the generative tradition. Constituency hierarchies do not amount to a separate, purely grammatical dimension of representation: they merely reflect the order in which simpler symbolic structures are successively integrated to form progressively more elaborate ones. In contrast to the nodes of a syntactic tree structure, which are attributed neither semantic nor phonological content, each node in an assembly like Figure 5.2 resides precisely in the symbolic association between a semantic and a phonological structure. Thus, rather than being *distinct* from semantic and phonological structures, a constituency hierarchy *reduces* to such structures together with their symbolic linkages.

A second way in which constituency hierarchies differ from generative phrase trees is that they are not invoked for the definition of grammatical relations like subject and object. Rather than being defined configurationally, such relations are characterized in terms of semantic notions as well as correspondences between subparts of semantic structures. At a given level of organization, an *object* is a noun phrase whose profile corresponds to the landmark of the relation profiled by the composite structure. A *direct object* is an object at the clausal level of organization: a noun phrase whose profile corresponds to the landmark of the process profiled by the clause as a whole.[2] *Bill* is consequently the direct object of *saw* in Figure 5.2, since its profile corresponds to the landmark of *saw*, whose own profile is inherited as the clausal profile. A *subject* is a noun phrase whose profile corresponds to the trajector of the process profiled at the clausal level of organization. By this definition, *Alice* is the subject in Figure 5.2.

It may be evident that these conceptual relationships are independent of any particular order of symbolic assembly. The same connections can often be established even when symbolic structures combine in alternate sequences, resulting in different constituency hierarchies. Note Figure 5.3:

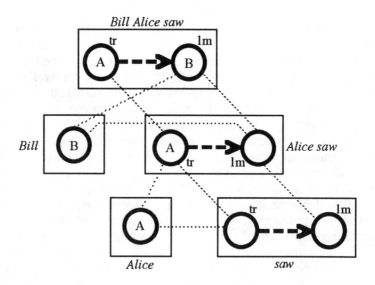

Figure 5.3

Here *Alice* first combines with *saw* to form the intermediate-level composite structure *Alice saw*, whose landmark is then elaborated by *Bill* at a higher level of organization. This alternative order of integration entails a difference in constituency—*Alice saw* forms a constituent, while *saw Bill* does not—but has no effect on grammatical relations, as just characterized. *Bill* is still the direct object because its profile corresponds to the clausal landmark, and *Alice* the subject because it elaborates the processual trajector.[3]

There is consequently no reason in this framework to hypothesize a level of representation (distinct from surface structure) at which constituency is fixed and invariant. Even if we recognize canonical patterns of integration (described by constructional schemas) that yield the familiar *(Subject (Verb + Object))* constituency, we can also posit alternative, secondary patterns for those expressions in which the subject and verb form an overt constituent that excludes the object. Several constructions that manifest *((Subject + Verb) Object)* constituency are exemplified in (1).

(1) a. *Potatoes **she dislikes** (but squash she really loves)*.
    b. *The potatoes **I bought** were rotten*.
    c. ***Joe peeled** and **Bill cooked** the potatoes*.

2. Assemblies vs. building blocks

The way linguists tend to think about both morphological and syntactic composition is strongly influenced by a metaphorically structured *idealized cognitive model* (Lakoff 1987), in which smaller constituents are seen as building blocks out of which larger constituents are constructed. The building-block metaphor portrays a complex structure as being put together in a single, strictly compositional fashion out of smaller parts which have a predetermined shape, are unaffected by the combinatory process, and are fully discernible within the composite whole. Although this metaphor is powerful, unavoidable, and useful to a certain extent, I believe that—pushed too far—it is inappropriate for natural language in every respect. We have already seen, in Figures 5.2-3, that there may be distinct ways (*compositional paths*) to arrive at the same composite structure. I further suggest that components are neither fixed nor predetermined in their semantic or phonological shape, but are flexibly construed to *accommodate* adjacent elements and the overall context; hence they may never have exactly the same value on any two occasions.

Moreover, it is inappropriate and quite misleading to think of component structures as providing the actual material out of which a composite structure is built. In CG, components are seen instead as *categorizing* certain facets of the composite structure, and thus as *motivating* it to a certain degree. Together with compositional patterns (embodied in constructional schemas), the components provide a kind of "scaffolding" that helps one "reach" the composite structure, but they do not in general serve to predict it in its entirety. I therefore speak of language as exhibiting *partial* (rather than full) *compositionality*. This alternative view avoids a number of classic conceptual problems that prove in retrospect not to be linguistic problems at all but merely artifacts of the misleading building-block metaphor. These include various kinds of discrepancies between component and composite structures, and cases where components are only partially discernible (or even indiscernible) within the composite whole.

For one thing, the classical conception of constituency based on the building-block metaphor has no way to deal with the problem of partial analyzability. *Analyzability* (discussed in Chapter 4, section 5.2) is the extent to which speakers are cognizant of the components within a complex expression. Intuitively, such expressions run the gamut from full analyzability (characteristic of novel expressions) to virtual opacity, as exemplified in (2):

(2) *squealer* > *complainer* > *computer* > *propeller* > *drawer*

Thinking in terms of building blocks makes it difficult even to recognize the phenomenon: either something is built out of smaller pieces or it isn't. By contrast, the phenomenon is predicted and straightforwardly accommodated in CG, which views constructions as assemblies of symbolic structures linked by correspondences and categorizing relationships (recall that composition reduces to categorization). On this account, analyzability resides in *coactivation* of component and composite structures, with the former thus serving to categorize and motivate the latter. For fixed expressions — where the composite structure already has the status of a learned, established unit (so that no computation is required to arrive at it) — one naturally expects the component structures to vary in their likelihood or level of activation (and hence in their cognitive salience).

Illustration is provided in Figure 5.4(a). Though a *computer* is indeed 'something that computes', we are, I think, less frequently or less saliently aware of its derivation from a verb stem than we are with other examples, e.g. *complainer*. This partial or optional activation of the component structures is represented diagrammatically by enclosing them in dashed-line boxes. Observe that the component and composite structures are connected by dashed arrows, which indicate a relationship of partial compositionality (i.e. categorization and motivation).

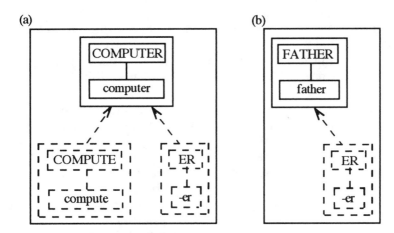

Figure 5.4

Degrees of analyzability are thus recognized and easily accommodated. Equally unproblematic is the discrepancy usually observed between component and composite structures: the fact that a composite structure is either more specific than anything which could be computed from its components by means of regular compositional rules, or else conflicts in some fashion with the expected compositional value. For instance, a *computer* is not just 'something that computes' — the term's conventional meaning is far more specific and finely specified. Likewise, a *professor* would not necessarily profess to anything at all. Such discrepancies are unproblematic because the component structures merely categorize and motivate the composite structure, as opposed to providing the actual "substance" out of which it is "built".

Other classic problems also fail to even arise in this framework. One is the problem of *residues*: expressions in which there are reasonable grounds for isolating a subpart and according it morphemic status, but where the remainder cannot be recognized as a "building block" that occurs in any other forms. For example, there are countless nouns in English that end in *-er/-or*, many of which clearly instantiate some variant of the derivational pattern illustrated by the nouns in (2). There are many others, however, that are compatible with the semantics of this pattern (in one or another of its variants), but where the residue—the part that remains when *-er/-or* is sub-tracted—has no independent existence. A case in point is the set of terms *father*, *mother*, *brother*, and *sister*, whose related meanings suggest that the "recurrent partial" *-er* ought to be isolated as a morpheme. Linguists resist this analysis because it leaves the other-wise unattested residues *fath*, *moth*, *broth*, and *sist* (cf. Hockett 1958: 124-5). But in CG there is no problem in simply saying, for instance, that certain aspects of *father* are categorized and partially motivated by *-er*, even though the remainder lack such support. To the extent that it is analyzable, *father* is a composite expression that happens to have only one component structure, as sketched in Figure 5.4(b).

A word like *father* represents a *defective construction*— defective in the sense that it lacks certain of the elements that figure in canonical constructions like those in Figures 5.2-3. Canonically, a construction comprises a composite symbolic structure and two com-ponent symbolic structures, all linked by correspondences and cate-gorizing relationships. Moveover, the composite structure is a regular compositional function of its components (full compositionality), both of which are quite salient (full analyzability). I have intimated that this ideal situation seldom if ever actually obtains, since fixed expressions tend not to be fully analyzable, and full compositionality is character-istic of neither fixed nor novel expressions in actual usage. A defec-tive construction in which one component is wholly lacking can thus be seen as a rather more drastic departure from the canon, but one that simply carries to the extreme certain tendencies observable in virtually any fixed expression. Defective constructions are not a problem for CG, for it merely claims that grammar reduces to assemblies of sym-bolic structures (comprising semantic structures, phonological struc-tures, and symbolic linkages). A construction like Figure 5.4(b) satisfies these conditions. There is no claim or expectation that every assembly of symbolic structures will be canonical.

Other kinds of defective constructions are illustrated in Figure 5.5. The past-tense verb *went* exemplifies *suppletion*, describable as *phonological opacity*: whereas *went* is recognized semantically as the past-tense form of *go*, there is no comparable phonological recogni-tion of the verb stem *go* as being part of *went*, and probably not of the past-tense morpheme. Phonologically, *went* is usually regarded as unanalyzable and *sui generis*, being unrelated to the forms that the component elements assume in other contexts. This is shown in Figure 5.5(a), where the usual symbolizations of the component structures fall outside the expression's scope (indicated by the outer rectangle). That is, *went* is defective in the sense that—for all intents and purposes—its components consist of semantic structures alone, not the full, symbolic structures characteristic of canonical constructions. A verb like *prefer* represents the converse situation of *semantic opacity*, as shown in Figure 5.5.(b). In view of forms like *pretend, predict, prevail, prevent, precede, preclude, preempt*, etc., and also those like *confer, defer, refer, transfer*, and *infer*, both *pre* and *fer* are usually considered morphemes, even though their meanings are vague if not tenuous and problematic. To the extent that it remains semantically unanalyzed, an expression like *prefer* constitutes a defective construction—defective in the sense that its components consist of phonological structures alone, not the full, symbolic structures of the canon.

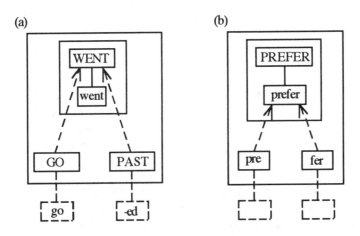

Figure 5.5

Let us now pause and take stock. The syntactic phrase trees of generative grammar reflect a "classical" notion of constituency that strongly influences how linguists think about grammatical structure. According to this archetypal conception, constituents are basic and essential to linguistic structure. A phrase tree comprises a single, strictly hierarchical organization that represents important grammatical relationships in a regular, consistent manner. Moreover, "classical constituency" incorporates the building-block metaphor, and assumes that a construction (i.e. the relationship between a structure and its immediate constituents) exhibits full analyzability and full compositionality. There is probably no linguistic theorist who believes that this classical view holds without qualification or elaboration for all aspects of grammatical organization. It serves instead as a tacit default, exerting a subtle but constant pressure to focus on data that appears to be compatible with it, and to set aside as "secondary" or "problematic" the myriad phenomena that are not. I have argued, however, that this classical view is itself highly problematic. The building-block metaphor is inappropriate, and full compositionality cannot in general be assumed. A consistent representation of basic grammatical relationships is achieved only at the cost of positing an unobserved level of "deep" or "underlying" structure. On the surface constituency is variable, and while it tends to correlate with grammatical relations, it does not offer a reliable basis for their characterization. Nor a necessary basis: I have sketched an alternative account in which grammatical relations are semantically defined and independent of any particular constituency hierarchy.

3. Conceptual groupings

There are further problems with the classical view. One motivation for positing constituents in the first place (especially deep structure constituents) is that they supposedly capture certain kinds of semantic relationships or *conceptual groupings*.[4] However, a standard constituency tree captures only some of the conceptual groupings that would have to figure in a complete account of linguistic structure. For instance, lexical items are not confined to single "slots" at the bottom of a tree, as indicated by the brackets in Figure 5.1, but often subsume larger portions of syntactic tree structures that are not necessarily either continuous or coincident with grammatical constituents. Some well-known examples are given in (3). Although the idiom *take the bull by the horns* may well be a constituent in (3)a, the same can obviously not be said for *the cat is out of the bag* in (3)b, or for *make headway* in (3)c.

(3) a. *You should **take the bull by the horns**.*
     b. ***The** damn **cat is** already **out of the bag**.*
     c. *The **headway** that we managed to **make** was quite limited.*

Fauconnier (1985) has shown that certain kinds of conceptual groupings, which he calls *mental spaces*, play an important role in semantic and grammatical structure. Consider, for example, the mental space representing a person's desire or belief. This space will often correspond to the content of a subordinate clause, as in (4)a. The two need not be coextensive, however. On the natural interpretation of (4)b—the one that does not portray Alice as believing a contradiction—the mental space representing her belief fails to coincide with the subordinate clause describing it. That clause also incorporates the speaker's assessment of Bill's intelligence, as well as a comparison of this assessment and the one made by Alice.

(4) a. *Jill hopes [**her daughter will find a good job**].*
     b. *Alice thinks [that **Bill is smarter** than he is].*

Another kind of mental space is a *type description*. It can be shown that type descriptions are essential to grammar, although they often cross-cut grammatical constituents (FCG2). Consider (5)a, which can perfectly well mean that each trainer put his own head in the mouth of a different lion. Three heads, three lions, and three mouths are thus involved, but *head, lion,* and *mouth* all occur in the singular. The sentence specifies a *process type*—that of *putting one's head in a lion's mouth*—and indicates that three trainers each participate in an *instance* (or *token*) of that type. Although portions of the sentence (including the subject and the possessive) directly encode the overall complex event, other portions (in bold) reflect instead the abstract type description common to the three process instances.

(5) a. *Only three trainers dared put their **head in a lion's mouth**.*
     b. *[[**Everyone here**] [**speaks** [two languages]]].*

Type descriptions also figure in "quantifier scope". An example is (5)b, on the (marked) reading in which *two* has "wide scope". I would say that each of the languages in question is portrayed as participating in an instance of the same process type, namely the type *everyone here speaks* X. Yet the type description is not reflected in grammatical constituency, which remains the same whether *two* or *every* is given wide scope.

Conceptual groupings can also be established by discourse factors. A well-known case is *focus* (the locus of "new information", signaled by unreduced stress), which often but does not invariably coincide with grammatical constituents (for a survey of analyses, see Culicover and Rochemont 1983). For example, the focus is a constituent in the second clause of (6)a, but not in (6)b.

(6) a. *He wanted a large house, but what he wound up getting was* ***that small condominium.***
   b. *He wanted a large brick house, but a **small** brick **cottage** was all he could afford.*

Previous discourse may also induce a constituency grouping that might not otherwise occur. In the first clause of (7), there is no particular reason to think that *fluffy* and *towel* form a constituent; the "comma intonation" suggests that *large* and *fluffy* are simultaneous, co-equal modifiers of *towel*. The second occurrence of *fluffy towel* does however appear to form a constituent, being the antecedent of *one*.

(7) *A large, fluffy towel was just what she needed for the beach, but a small **fluffy towel** was the only sized **one** she could find.*

Now it might be argued that these various sorts of conceptual groupings are purely semantic in nature and thus should not necessarily be expected to coincide with the constituency established on syntactic grounds. Of course, so-called "grammatical" constituents also represent conceptual groupings, but let us put that aside momentarily to point out other kinds of phenomena—which are not so easily dismissed—that the classical notion of constituency leaves us ill-equipped to deal with.

The first kind of problem is posed by *discontinuous constituents*. I cannot explore this complex issue here (see Huck and Ojeda 1987), and will limit myself to the single example cited in (8)a. The apparent difficulty is that the relative clause (*that you were expecting*) "belongs" to the subject noun phrase (*the package*) yet is not adjacent to it in the phonological sequence. This could of course be handled by a transformational rule that "extraposes" the relative clause, but only at the expense of positing derivations from underlying structures. The same holds for *parenthetical insertions*, as exemplified in (8)b. The problem here is that what appears to be the main clause—namely *I think*—does not show up in main-clause position, but rather in the middle of its complement. While a rule that lowers it into the subordinate clause might be considered, it is not (on the traditional view) a constituent, and it is not obvious where to attach it (cf. McCawley 1982). Finally, (8)c is problematic because one instance of the noun phrase *a lie* functions *simultaneously* as the predicate nominative in the first clause and as the subject of the second clause. For two clauses to share a nominal in this fashion is decidedly contrary to the classical notion of constituency.

(8) a. **The package** *arrived* **that you were expecting.**
     b. *Your wallet was, **I think**, on the desk.*
     c. *A lie is **a lie** is a lie.*

There are, then, ample grounds for suspecting that the classical view may be fundamentally misconceived. One can perfectly well accept the existence of constituency without committing oneself to either the classical conception of it, the autonomy of grammar, or the formal devices of generative syntax. I have argued that grammar reduces to assemblies of symbolic structures. Rather than comprising a separate, purely "syntactic" level of representation, constituency is merely the order in which simpler symbolic structures combine to form progressively larger ones. Although some of the information they encode is valid (and is readily accommodated in CG), syntactic tree structures—viewed as autonomous formal objects—are descriptive artifacts which substantially distort the nature of linguistic reality.

4. Constituents as emergent entities

The phenomena we have briefly surveyed suggest an even more radical view of constituency, one that is fully consistent with the spirit and principles of CG. According to this radical alternative, the kinds of constituents reflected in syntactic phrase trees are neither essential nor fundamental to linguistic structure. They are instead interpreted as being *emergent* in nature, as arising in language processing just in special (though not untypical) circumstances. A capacity for *grouping* —guided by such factors as contiguity and similarity—must clearly be recognized as a basic psychological ability. Both semantic and phonological elements are grouped in multiple, often inconsistent ways, each pertaining to a distinct conceptual or phonetic parameter. Conceptual groupings of any size suggest themselves for potential symbolization (as *signifiés*), while phonological groupings offer themselves as potential symbolizing structures (*signifiants*). A "classical constituent" emerges when a particular kind of conceptual grouping happens to coincide with a particular kind of phonological grouping, and a well-behaved constituency hierarchy (tree structure) arises when classical constituents happen to emerge at every level of organization. However, the coherence of a complex expression does not depend on the emergence of a classical constituency hierarchy, nor does such a hierarchy necessarily exhaust the symbolic relationships that figure in its characterization.

Of the factors that encourage phonological grouping, only *temporal contiguity* is generally taken into account. In syntactic phrase trees, as in Figure 5.1, left-to-right order on the page represents temporal order in the speech stream, which is properly regarded as one dimension of phonological space. For elements to comprise a constituent, it is generally required that they be directly adjacent along this dimension: given the sequence *A B C*, either *A B* or *B C* might be a constituent, but not *A C*. The result is that constituents subsume temporally continuous portions of the speech stream, and the branches of a phrase tree can never cross. Time, however, is not the only phonetic parameter capable of being exploited as a basis for grouping. Another possibility is *accent*. In (6)b, for instance, the higher level of stress on *small* and *cottage* (relative to their immediate surroundings) sets them apart as a phonological group, one which simply happens not to be temporally contiguous. *Pitch* can also be used for grouping. In (8)b, it is natural for the parenthetical insertion *I think* to be lower in pitch than its complement. Conversely, the complement—*your wallet was on the desk*—forms a group on the basis of its higher pitch level even though it is discontinuous along the time axis. Nor is segmental content irrelevant for grouping purposes. Agreement, for example, often involves a common phonological property, as in Spanish noun phrases like *la gata blanca* 'the white female cat', where each word ends in *a*. Though hardly an infallible signal, such a property has the potential to be seized upon as one basis for the grouping of grammatically related elements.

Important though it is, to single out temporal contiguity as the only grouping factor of possible grammatical significance would clearly be both arbitrary and factually incorrect. Indeed, recognizing other kinds of groupings has immediate advantages for the explication of grammatical structure. Consider once again an expression like (8)b, involving a parenthetical insertion. If only linear order is taken into account, usual assumptions prevent us from representing the complement (*your wallet was on the desk*) as a constituent, even though we need to do this for semantic and syntactic reasons. The situation is shown abstractly in Figure 5.6(a), where T stands for speech time, and lower-case letters for words. Suppose, however, that we accept both time and pitch level (P) as phonetic parameters allowing groupings with the potential to be exploited for grammatical purposes. Then, as seen in Figure 5.6(b), both the main clause (*I think*) and its complement are grouped phonologically on the basis of pitch.

(a)   (b)

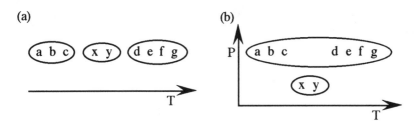

Figure 5.6

Conceptual grouping is likewise encouraged by a variety of factors, some of which have already been mentioned. A distinct *mental space* represents a natural conceptual group; examples include the world of a dream, a type description (as in (5)), or a person's belief or desire (e.g. (4)). In the context of a discourse, certain portions of an expression stand out as being "new" or "noteworthy" in some respect; collectively, these constitute the *focus*, whose conceptual grouping on the basis of "noteworthiness" is comparable to their phonological grouping on the basis of unreduced stress (as in (6)). *Topic/comment* organization, exemplified in (9), reflects another kind of discourse-based grouping.

(9) *As for the students here, we never have any discipline problems.*

Less often discussed is the type of arrangement observed in (8)b, where one clause—*your wallet was on the desk*—occupies the *foreground* in the sense of providing the main content the speaker wishes to convey, while the other clause—*I think*—remains in the *background* as a secondary qualification.

What appears to be the strongest grouping factor is a kind of *conceptual overlap* involving the component symbolic elements of a complex expression. In CG this overlap is explicitly recognized and described in terms of *semantic correspondences*, which figure in the characterization of every construction (note the dotted lines in Figures 5.2-3). More implicit reference to conceptual overlap is found in the traditional observation that elements which "belong together semantically" tend to occur together syntactically (Behaghel's law); it is only by positing specific conceptual correspondences that one can explicate the notion "belong together semantically" and render it precise. I further suggest that tacit recognition of semantic overlap is part of the motivation for syntactic tree structures (Figure 5.1), especially for the postulation of "deep" or "underlying" structures at variance with surface constituency.

Taken as a whole, a complex expression evokes and symbolizes a coherent, integrated conceptualization: its *composite semantic structure*. To one degree or another, a complex expression is analyzable into simpler symbolic elements, each of which reflects and categorizes some facet of the composite conceptualization. I have emphasized that the component symbolic elements should not be thought of as building blocks. That metaphor is inappropriate for various reasons, one being that building blocks do not overlap, but are separate and discrete even when stacked together to form a larger structure. Symbolic components do however show substantial conceptual overlap; it is in fact precisely this overlap which permits their integration to form a coherent composite conceptualization. If we change metaphors and think of the component elements as "covering" the composite semantic structure (for purposes of linguistic coding), the picture that emerges does not resemble a *mosaic* so much as it does a *collage*.

Thus, to encode an elaborate conceptualization we must usually resort to a symbolically complex expression, whose component elements map onto selected facets of the overall conception, facets that are generally different but nevertheless overlap in myriad ways. It is not the case, however, that every component overlaps with all the others, or that the nature and extent of their intersection is always comparable. Indeed, variation in this regard—the fact that particular components overlap with certain others in particular ways—constitutes the very foundation of grammatical structure. It is a certain kind of conceptual overlap between symbolic components that is ultimately at issue when linguists speak of "grammatical relations" or of elements "belonging together semantically".

Recall that every expression (whatever its size) evokes a conceptual base, within which it profiles some substructure (its conceptual referent). As the focus of conception, an expression's profile is maximally salient. When a relationship is profiled, its primary participants are also highly prominent, the trajector and landmark being the focal points of the relational profile. Consider now a grammatical construction, as exemplified in Figures 5.2-3. Constructions are typically based on correspondences between entities that are salient within the component structures. In particular, it is usual for the profile of one component structure to correspond to an entity that has privileged status within the other: either its profile, part of its profile, or its entire base. The constructions in Figures 5.2-3 are canonical in this respect. Observe from the dotted lines that the profile of *Bill* corresponds to one of the focal participants in the process profiled by *saw* (the landmark), while the profile of *Alice* corresponds to the other focal participant (the trajector). However, there is no *direct* linguistic association between *Bill* and *Alice*: neither one figures centrally or prominently in the meaning of the other. They are connected only indirectly, via the verb, whose two participants correspond to their respective profiles.

By its very nature, direct conceptual overlap provides a strong impetus for conceptual grouping. Each symbolic component evokes and categorizes some fragment of a coherent overall conceptualization (the composite semantic structure). When two such fragments overlap, it is natural to conceive of them together—as forming a single, larger fragment—and the tendency to merge them in this fashion is stronger to the extent that the shared element is central and salient within the two components. Continuing with the same example, the composite semantic structure of *Alice saw Bill* is represented at the top in Figure 5.7, and three semantic components (the fragments coded by *Alice*, *saw*, and *Bill* individually) are depicted at the bottom. The two ellipses indicate natural conceptual groupings based on the direct overlap of prominent substructures, as shown by correspondence lines. Clearly, more than one set of components may be susceptible to grouping on this basis, whereas other sets (e.g. *Alice* and *Bill*) may not be. It should be apparent that the alternate groupings in Figure 5.7 are reflected in the two intermediate-level composite structures shown in Figures 5.2-3. That is, either *saw Bill* or *Alice saw* is capable of emerging as a coherent conceptual fragment intermediate in size between the overall composite semantic structure and the ultimate semantic components.

Composite Semantic Structure

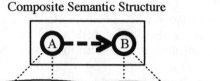

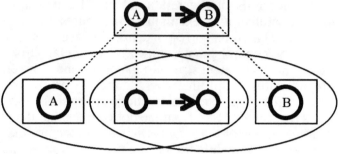

Component Semantic Structures

Figure 5.7

When two semantic components combine in this fashion, I will speak of a *valence link* between them and say that they form a *conceptual constituent*. This is, I believe, the kind of conceptual grouping that linguists have in mind when they speak of elements "belonging together semantically", and also when they posit underlying tree structures to represent "grammatical relations". Valence links thus provide the semantic basis for classical constituents. We can likewise define a *phonological constituent* as arising when two phonological structures form a group on the basis of temporal contiguity. This is what linguists have in mind when they speak of elements "occurring together syntactically"; it provides the phonological basis for classical constituents. A classical constituent can now be characterized as emerging when a conceptual constituent is symbolized by a phonological constituent. Moreover, a *well-behaved constituency hierarchy* (as reflected in a syntactic tree structure) arises when classical constituents emerge at every level of organization, exhausting the symbolic elements that comprise a complex expression.

5. Groupings and symbolic linkages

A well-behaved constituency hierarchy comprises an assembly of symbolic structures, each residing in the symbolic linkage of a particular kind of conceptual grouping (the kind I have called a conceptual constituent) with a particular kind of phonological grouping (the kind I have called a phonological constituent). Syntactic tree structures were specifically devised to accommodate classical constituents and well-behaved constituency hierarchies, as were CG diagrams like those in Figures 5.2-3. However, my central point is that classical constituents and well-behaved hierarchies represent just a special case in the spectrum of possible symbolic assemblies. Not every linguistic expression manifests such a hierarchy, nor do such hierarchies reflect all the conceptual groupings, phonological groupings, and symbolic linkages that must figure in a full characterization of grammatical structure. To begin thinking about symbolic assemblies in all their actual variety and complexity, we need an appropriate notation, one in which the notion of a single hierarchy is emergent rather than fundamental.

By way of initial illustration, the structures in Figures 5.2-3 are reformulated in Figure 5.8:

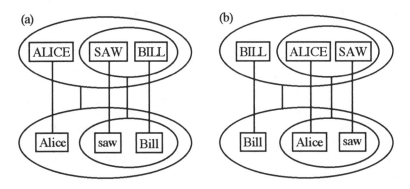

Figure 5.8

Observe that conceptual and phonological groupings are indicated by ellipses, and that only the component structures and their groupings are shown explicitly. Left implicit are the composite structures obtained—at every level of organization—by the integration of grouped elements. They are however essential and must be understood as present though not separately shown. Every ellipse in the diagram can thus be taken as representing not only a grouping but also a composite semantic or phonological structure various fragments of which are categorized by the components it subsumes. Additionally, I have simplified the diagrams by using words in capital letters to abbreviate semantic structures.

So far as they go, the diagrams in Figure 5.8 are equivalent to those in Figures 5.2-3. Each represents a well-behaved constituency hierarchy in which every conceptual constituent is symbolized by a phonological constituent. Although the diagrams in Figure 5.8 involve different hierarchies, with distinct intermediate-level composite structures (*saw Bill* vs. *Alice saw*), they yield the same overall composite semantic structure (as shown in Figures 5.2-3 and 5.7). We have seen, moreover, that—regardless of constituency—basic grammatical relations are captured by means of valence links (i.e. correspondences between salient substructures), as indicated by the correspondence lines in Figure 5.7. These valence links are present regardless of which intermediate-level grouping happens to emerge.

I am suggesting, then, that a *potential* conceptual grouping does not invariably have to emerge in every expression in which that potential is manifest. In our simple example, either *saw Bill* or *Alice saw* has the potential—by virtue of a valence link—to emerge as a conceptual constituent (a "larger fragment" of the composite semantic structure), yet presumably only one of them actually does so in a given expression.[5]

The notation adopted in Figure 5.8 is designed for maximal flexibility. It is meant to accommodate the many cases where conceptual or phonological groupings cross-cut, as well as the varied instances where conceptual and phonological groupings fail to exhibit a one-to-one correspondence in regard to symbolic relationships. The key, once again, is to abandon the building-block metaphor and to think in terms of assemblies of semantic and phonological structures connected by symbolic linkages. Since there are many possible bases for both conceptual and phonological grouping, we have no inherent reason to expect that all groupings—either semantic or phonological—will invariably stack together neatly; that is, the ellipses representing such groupings need not always be properly nested, but may sometimes intersect. Nor is it necessary that every semantic grouping be linked symbolically to a unique phonological grouping. With respect to the idealized situation of a perfect one-to-one correspondence between semantic and phonological groups, certain constructions may well be *defective*.

For concrete illustration, let us return to the three examples in (8), all of which are problematic from the standpoint of classical constituency. The problem posed by (8)a, *The package arrived that you were expecting*, is that a relative clause which modifies the subject does not occur adjacent to it in the phonological sequence; hence the subject and its modifier do not form a classical constituent even though they "belong together semantically". A simplified diagram of this expression is offered in Figure 5.9.

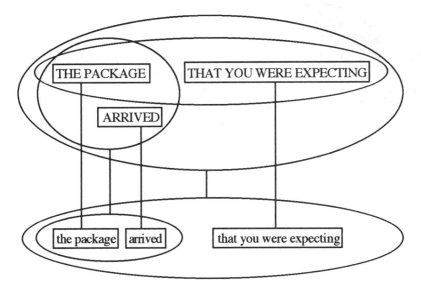

Figure 5.9

The special feature of this construction, the one that renders it problematic in classical terms, is that the subject participates simultaneously in two conceptual constituents (each based on a canonical valence link), whereas only one such grouping is capable of being symbolized by a phonological constituent. *The package* and *arrived* form a conceptual constituent because the former's profile corresponds to the latter's trajector. They also make up a *presentational* unit, *arrived* serving to "introduce" *the package* and "put it on stage". This doubly-motivated conceptual group is of course symbolized by the phonological sequence *the package arrived*, which forms a phonological constituent on the basis of temporal contiguity and rhythmic cohesiveness. However, the subject also combines semantically with the relative clause, forming a conceptual constituent by virtue of a correspondence between the subject's profile and the clausal landmark. In this case there happens not to be any phonological grouping capable of symbolizing the conceptual constituent. Phonologically, *the package* and *that you were expecting* are not temporally adjacent, nor do they exhibit any common phonological trait (e.g. a distinctive level of stress or pitch) that would set them apart as a group. I therefore analyze the construction as being defective in the sense that one conceptual constituent (*the package that you were expecting*) simply remains unsymbolized.

   Let us next consider (8)c, *A lie is a lie is a lie.* This sentence displays an unusual but clearly possible sort of clause chaining, wherein a single overtly manifested noun phrase functions simultaneously as the predicate nominative in one clause and as the subject of the following clause.[6] Impressionistically, I would say that the clausal repetition renders the expression emphatic, and that the compactness achieved by this special phonological overlap reinforces its emphatic character. The constituency hierarchy for a single component clause (*a lie is a lie*) is shown at the left in Figure 5.10:

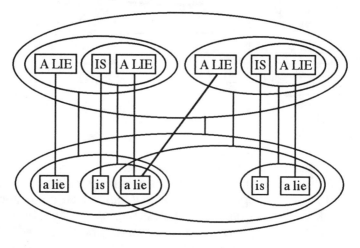

Figure 5.10

Semantically, the sentence comprises two assertions of that proposition, as indicated at the top. It also comprises two phonological symbolizations of the proposition, with the qualification that these symbolizations are not entirely disjoint: a single occurrence of the phonological sequence *a lie* participates in two symbolic linkages involving distinct clauses. This phonological intersection entails the absence of the usual one-to-one correspondence between phonological and semantic groupings.

Our final example is (8)b: *Your wallet was, I think, on the desk.* We used this sentence previously to illustrate the grammatical significance of phonological grouping factors other than temporal adjacency. In particular, the subordinate clause *your wallet was on the desk* does not form a group on the basis of temporal contiguity (i.e. it is not a phonological constituent), but does on the basis of pitch level (P). We see this grouping at the bottom in Figure 5.11.

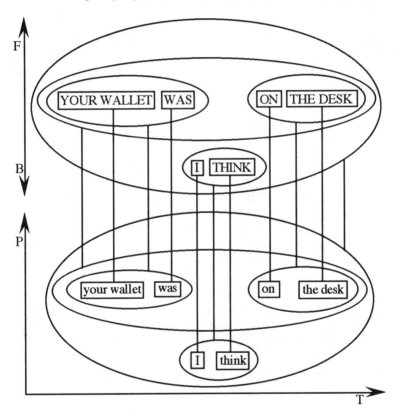

Figure 5.11

Semantically, of course, there is no question that the subordinate clause comprises a conceptual constituent, and that it functions as a complement of *think* (i.e. its profile corresponds to the landmark of *think*). There is however another aspect to the semantic organization of this sentence. I have suggested that—despite the nature of their valence link—the complement clause is *foregrounded*, in the sense of providing the main content the speaker wishes to convey, whereas *I think* remains in the *background* as a secondary qualification. We can observe a kind of iconicity, wherein the discourse-semantic contrast of foreground (F) vs. background (B) is signaled phonologically by a difference in pitch level that can also be described as one of foreground vs. background. But for our purposes, the essential point is that multiple grouping factors need to be recognized for both semantic and phonological structure. Though not shown explicitly, the valence link between *think* and the complement clause is present in this symbolic configuration, in addition to the grouping based on foregrounding. Expressions like (8)b are thus described straightforwardly, despite the problem they pose for classical constituency.

6. Conclusion

In this chapter, I have outlined a radical view of constituency that differs from the classical view in regard to both the nature of constituents and their status in linguistic structure. I have argued that classical constituents are neither autonomous, nor fundamental, nor essential to grammatical structure. Though natural and even prototypical, they are nonetheless *emergent*, arising (under the proper circumstances) from the broader, more basic processes of conceptual grouping, phonological grouping, and symbolization. This view of constituency renders unproblematic various phenomena that have long resisted analysis in other theories of grammar and have thus tended to remain at the periphery of linguists' attention and interest. With the prospect of incorporating them straightforwardly in a more general account of grammatical relationships, it is now time to start seriously investigating the entire spectrum of grouping phenomena, in order to better appreciate the special place of classical constituency within it.

Chapter 6
Reference point constructions

As one of its organizing principles, cognitive linguistics asserts the non-autonomy of linguistic structure.* It claims, in particular, that fundamental cognitive abilities and experientially derived cognitive models have direct and pervasive linguistic manifestations, and conversely, that language structure furnishes important clues concerning basic mental phenomena. This chapter explores the linguistic ramifications of one such phenomenon: the use of cognitive *reference points*. The importance of reference points will first be made apparent in regard to possessive constructions. The notion's applicability to a broad variety of other linguistic phenomena will then be demonstrated. It appears, in fact, that reference points are fundamental to both linguistic and cognitive organization.

1. Basic cognitive assumptions

What can we reasonably posit as basic elements of conceptual structure? The answer need not be unique, as there are different ways of being "basic". I have suggested, for example, that certain cognitive *domains* (such as space, time, and the sensory domains) are basic by virtue of constituting irreducible realms of conceptual potential (FCG1: 4.1.1). Fundamental in other ways are certain cognitive *abilities*, as well as various *concepts* plausibly accorded the status of "archetypes". Examples of basic abilities are the directing and focusing of attention, the imposition of figure/ground organization, the capacity for mental scanning, and the creation of abstract "things" by conceptual reification. Presumably these are innate.[1]

By contrast, the notions I refer to as *conceptual archetypes* clearly have a strong experiential basis. Examples of such concepts are the human body, the human face, a discrete physical object, an object moving through space, an agent, a canonical transitive event (agent-patient interaction), a face-to-face verbal exchange, and using an instrument to affect another entity. Although these too are abstract, they incorporate substantial conceptual content representing the commonality inherent in countless everyday experiences. They are complex notions, intermediate in level of specificity, that are so ubiquitous in our experience that they are in some sense cognitively fundamental despite their complexity.

Of special interest here is the relationship between particular abilities and particular conceptual archetypes, e.g. between reification and the concept of a physical object, or between mental scanning and the concept of an object moving through space. The ability is *immanent* in the corresponding archetype, i.e. inherent in its conception. For example, conceiving of an object moving through space necessarily involves mental scanning through the spatial domain. We are usually not aware of the mental scanning—it does not constitute a separate mental experience—precisely because it is immanent in (or manifested through) the richer, more contentful conception of spatial motion by a physical object. Developmentally, I think it likely that the innate abilities are responsible for the emergence of coherent experience, initially in the physical realm. They are subsequently applied in other, more abstract domains.

The linguistic import of these pairings pertains to basic and universal linguistic categories such as noun, verb, subject, and object. Why do these categories have their privileged status? I suggest that they are basic and universal precisely because they represent the natural pairing of essential cognitive abilities and fundamental conceptual archetypes; the ability supports a schematic characterization valid for all category members, whereas the conceptual archetype defines the category prototype. I claim, for example, that every noun designates a product of conceptual reification, which is intrinsic to the conception of physical objects—the category prototype—but less automatic (hence more "visible" and striking) when applied to such entities as events and properties. I likewise characterize a subject in schematic terms as the clause-level figure (invoking our capacity for imposing figure/ground organization on a scene), while the archetypal conception of an agent defines the category prototype.

Basic and universal to a comparable degree is the linguistic category of *possession*, particularly as manifested in determiner constructions (e.g. *my shoulder*; *Sally's dog*). For possessives also I posit the pairing of an essential cognitive ability with a fundamental conceptual archetype (in this case, multiple archetypes). The ability, that of invoking a *reference point*, accounts very nicely for various well-known properties of possessive expressions.

2. Reference points

The reference point phenomenon is so fundamental and ubiquitous in our moment-to-moment experience that we are largely oblivious to it. For the analysis of possessives, it is best described as the ability to invoke the conception of one entity for purposes of establishing *mental contact* with another, i.e. to single it out for individual conscious awareness. Sometimes, of course, we realize full well that this is what we are doing. For example, I deliberately use a perceptual reference point when I locate the North Star by mentally tracing a path along the end of the Big Dipper. The invocation of a reference point is also quite apparent in expressions like (1).

(1) *You know that hunk who works in the bank? Well, the woman he's living with just got an abortion.*

For the most part, however, our reference point ability remains below the threshold of explicit attention; we simply use it without realizing that we are doing anything of the kind. As I recite the alphabet, for instance, each letter calls the next one to mind, but I do not think of the letters as reference points—I merely recite the alphabet. For another example, think of your computer's on-switch. If you are like me, you can hardly locate the on-switch, or even imagine its existence, without first envisaging the computer as a whole. Finally, observe that one can only conceive of a *dent* with reference to the expected shape from which it departs. The two conceptualizations are not necessarily distinct or temporally sequenced at the level of conscious experience, but in functional terms, at least, invoking the expected shape is a precondition for the conception of a dent (*qua* dent) to emerge. To be sure, these examples are quite diverse, but my purpose here is precisely to take a very broad perspective and elucidate the commonality I feel is lurking in numerous phenomena that also have to be treated in their own terms.

Essential aspects of the reference point ability are sketched in Figure 6.1. The circle labeled C represents the conceptualizer, R is the reference point, and T the *target,* i.e. the entity that the conceptualizer uses the reference point to establish mental contact with. The dashed arrows indicate the mental path the conceptualizer follows in reaching the target. Finally, the ellipse labeled D represents an abstract entity that I refer to as the *dominion,* which can be defined as the conceptual region (or the set of entities) to which a particular reference point affords direct access (i.e. the class of potential targets).

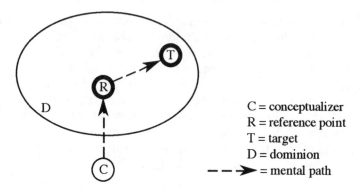

C = conceptualizer
R = reference point
T = target
D = dominion
— — ➤ = mental path

Figure 6.1

Heavy-line circles indicate the successive salience, through processing time, of the reference point and the target. Initially the reference point has a certain cognitive salience, either intrinsic or contextually determined. It is, of course, owing to some kind of salience that an entity comes to be chosen as a reference point in the first place. To function as a reference point, a notion must first be activated and thus established as an entity currently capable of serving in that capacity. In this initial phase, corresponding to the arrow between C and R in Figure 6.1, R becomes prominent as the focus of C's conception, thus creating the potential for the activation of any element in R's dominion. However, when this potential is exploited—when R is actually used as a reference point—it is the target thereby reached that now becomes prominent in the sense of being the focus of C's conception. Even as it fulfills its reference point function, R recedes into the background in favor of T, which may itself then be invoked as a reference point for reaching another target. In this way the reference point phenomenon is inherently dynamic.[2]

3. Possessives

When I speak of possessives as a basic and universal linguistic category, I am referring most specifically to determiner constructions, as in (2).

(2) *my watch; her cousin ; your foot; the baby's bib; his rook;*
     our host; their group; Sara's office; the book's weight;
     your anxiety; our neighborhood; its location; my
     quandary; Lincoln's assassination; Booth's assassination;
     their candidate; my bus; the cat's fleas

Other kinds of possessive expressions, like possessive verbs and prepositional-phrase modifiers, show more language-specific variation and tend to be colored to a greater degree by semantic nuances overlaid on their reference point function.[3]

3.1. Characterization

The analytical challenge is to account in a unified way for the extraordinary variety of relationships coded by possessive determiners. One approach would be to say that all of the uses in (2) represent metaphorical extensions from the prototypical sense, presumably that of 'ownership', as in *my watch.* Now this may well prove correct, and a description based on metaphor would not be incompatible with the schematic characterization I will offer. Still, a metaphorical account is problematic in certain respects and does not itself tell the whole story. First, it is not clear what the basic, non-metaphorical sense would be. Merely to speak of 'possession' would be circular. A more precise term like 'ownership' conveys a notion that is, I suspect, too sophisticated and culture-specific to account for the universality of possessives and their early appearance in child speech. Moreover, it is not obvious to me that all the uses in (2) are in fact reasonably considered metaphorical with respect to the basic value, if the term metaphor is used in any restrictive way (e.g. to indicate that the target domain is understood in terms of the source domain). Also, senses other than 'ownership' have a strong claim to prototype status: possessives occur with kinship and body-part terms in every language, and in many languages such nouns are obligatorily possessed. Finally, we must account for the widespread incidence of possessives for nominal periphrasis, even with non-agents (e.g. *Lincoln's assassination*).

     Another approach would be to say that any kind of association between two entities can be coded by a possessive. This too has something very right about it, and it obviously accommodates all the examples in (2). But it is not enough to speak of mere association—

i.e. conceptual co-occurrence—and let it go at that. Simple association does not explain the striking asymmetries observable in possessive expressions, e.g. the naturalness of the locutions in (3)a in contrast to those of (3)b.

(3) a. *the boy's watch; the girl's uncle; the dog's tail; the cat's*
       fleas; Lincoln's assassination
     b. **the watch's boy; *the uncle's girl* [i.e. 'his niece']; **the*
       tail's dog; *the fleas' cat; *the assassination's Lincoln

In particular, an owner is virtually always coded as the possessor, even though the relationship of association per se is symmetrical. Likewise, kinship terms and body parts almost always function as the possessed element.

The characterization I will offer constitutes a refinement of these approaches and accounts straightforwardly for the observed properties of possessives. As noted previously, I ascribe the basic and universal nature of possessives to the pairing of an essential cognitive ability with a fundamental conceptual archetype, in fact with several such archetypes. The ability is not that of mere association (conceptual co-occurrence), but rather the intrinsically asymmetrical reference point relationship. What all possessive locutions have in common, I suggest, is that one entity (the one we call the possessor) is invoked as a reference point for purposes of establishing mental contact with another (the possessed), as sketched in Figure 6.1. And instead of assuming that any one concept (like ownership) necessarily constitutes a unique, clear-cut prototype and basis for metaphorical extension, I propose that the category clusters around several conceptual archetypes, each of which saliently incorporates a reference point relationship: these archetypes include ownership, kinship, and part/whole relations involving physical objects (the body in particular).

Let us contemplate the virtues of this analysis. First, the schematic characterization is sufficiently abstract and flexible to cover the entire broad range of possessive use, as exemplified in (2). At the same time, it accounts for the asymmetries noted in (3), as well as the centrality to the category of ownership, kinship, and physical part/whole relations. Obviously, these notions represent basic and salient aspects of our quotidian experience and thus qualify as conceptual archetypes. Crucially, moreover, each involves a clear and clearly asymmetrical reference point relationship. The very purpose of a kinship term is to situate people—socially and genealogically—with respect to a reference individual ("ego"). Only in relation to a particular "ego" does it make sense to call someone a *cousin*, an *uncle*, a *sister*, or a *stepson*; a person is not a *cousin* or an *uncle* autonomously, nor does one bear the same kin relation to every individual. There are of course elements of symmetry and reciprocity: anyone can function as "ego", and every kinship relation has an inverse. It is nonetheless true that a kin term imposes an asymmetric construal in which the target is identified solely and specifically via its connection to a genealogical reference point. It is hardly surprising, then, that kinship relations are central to the possessive category and that kin terms are often obligatorily possessed.

Similar observations can be made concerning the other two central notions. I would argue that a part—as such—can only be conceived in relation to the whole, which functions as a natural reference point for its conception and characterization. A part term, like *elbow*, *tail*, *roof*, or *on-switch*, evokes as its base the conception of a whole, with respect to which it serves to profile an entity whose nature and subpart status depend on its function within the overall configuration. Furthermore, it is not the case that we think of the world as being populated by entities like elbows, tails, roofs, and on-switches, that we know and recognize autonomously and individually. Rather, we think of the world as being populated by people, animals, houses, and computers, and only with reference to a particular individual of this sort do we normally identify a subpart. The exceptions only prove the rule. Suppose I find a detached tail lying in the road. In that (fortunately somewhat unusual) circumstance, I might well ask *Where is the tail's dog?* The utterance is contextually appropriate, since the tail's solo presence and visibility lend it sufficient cognitive salience to serve as a reference point. It is only because I see the tail—and thus have mental contact with it—that I am led to think about—and thus establish mental contact with—(the remainder of) the dog as a (near) whole.

I am open to the possibility that ownership has some degree of primacy with respect to the three basic values of possessives (cf. Taylor 1989). Or if not 'ownership', perhaps a slightly more general (less culture-laden) notion like 'having something at one's exclusive and permanent disposal'. A notion of that sort is clearly asymmetrical and lends itself very naturally to reference point function. We know and recognize people as individuals, but for the most part we do not have comparable individual familiarity with their possessions (except our own). Moreover, a given person has numerous possessions, each of which he uniquely controls (according to our idealized cognitive model), and for any general type of object (e.g. watches) there are many exemplars that we know nothing about except that each belongs to a particular individual. Hence a person is naturally invoked as a "mental address" providing access to the cluster of items he possesses. The opposite arrangement—organizing our cognitive "map" of entities around individual owned items, many providing mental access to the same person—would be far less natural or efficient.

The reference point analysis thus has the virtue of accounting for the asymmetries observed in possessive relationships, both in prototypical uses and more generally. Consider the expression *the cat's fleas*. It is natural that the cat, and not the fleas, should be construed as the reference point and coded as the possessor: there is one cat, but almost certainly many fleas; we are more likely to be individually familiar with the cat than with its fleas; we can see the cat more readily than its fleas; and in most circumstances we have greater empathy for the cat. But suppose we construct a special context in which the fleas attract our attention and empathy. Imagine, for instance, a cartoon featuring a flea family that gets lost on its way back home to its host. In that situation we might very well find ourselves talking about *the fleas' cat*.

A particular advantage of the present analysis is that it directly and revealingly accounts for the periphrastic use of possessives with nominalizations, as in *Lincoln's assassination*. There are several respects in which an event's participants are natural reference points for it. Participants are usually concrete and easily pointed to, while events are by nature more abstract and not so readily localized. In fact, an event's location cannot be distinguished from that of its participants. Moreover, whereas participants can normally be conceptualized autonomously, the converse is not true: we cannot conceive of an event without in some way (if only schematically) conceptualizing its participants. Finally, instances of the same event type can be distinguished by the identity of their participants (e.g. *Lincoln's assassination* vs. *Kennedy's assassination*). Thus, in multiple ways participants anchor the conception of a process and serve as reference points for establishing mental contact with it. Observe that either major participant should be able to serve this function (e.g. *Booth's assassination* vs. *Lincoln's assassination*), although the subject (or trajector) of the nominalized verb does so preferentially by virtue of its greater prominence (as primary figure within the profiled relationship).

The analysis has the further advantage of correctly predicting that a possessed noun ought to be definite (provided that the possessor noun phrase is itself definite). This prediction follows from the proposed schematic description, together with a characterization of definiteness justified on independent grounds (FCG1: ch. 3). In fact, I devised the notion "mental contact" for the specific purpose of characterizing the definite article, which—very roughly—indicates that the speaker and addressee have each established mental contact with the same instance of the relevant nominal class (which is specified by the remainder of the noun phrase). When the possessor is definite, therefore, the speaker and hearer already have mental contact with the reference point. From there, the possessive construction as defined suffices to put them in mental contact with the target (the referent of the head noun), which makes the target definite as well. In short, the definiteness of a possessed noun (when it has a definite possessor) is an automatic consequence of both possession and definiteness being characterized in terms of mental contact.

3.2. *Possessive elements*

We can now attempt the characterization of basic possessive elements. At the most schematic level, the possessive morpheme (i.e. the ending on *Sally's*, or the possessive component of *my*) invokes as its base nothing more than the reference point relationship, as abbreviated in Figure 6.1. My working assumption is that, within this base, the possessive morpheme profiles the reference point relationship itself, as shown in Figure 6.2. I further assume, in accordance with the usual pattern of modifying expressions, that the trajector is to be identified with the element designated by the modified noun. By this criterion it is the target that functions as trajector, with the reference point then having the status of a landmark (or secondary figure).[4] In a modifying construction (i.e. in an expression like *Sally's dog*), the possessive morpheme's landmark is put in correspondence with the entity profiled by the possessor nominal (*Sally*), and its trajector with the profile of the head noun (*dog*). The entities that the possessive morpheme itself evokes only schematically are thereby characterized in more specific terms at the level of the full noun phrase.

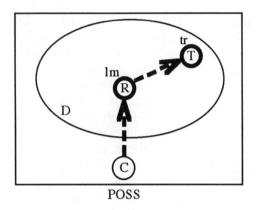

POSS

Figure 6.2

It is well known that possession can often be coded by locative expressions, e.g. Russian *U menja kniga* 'I have a book' or French *Ce livre est à moi* 'That book is mine'. The obvious difference between a simple possessive morpheme and a locative preposition with possessive use is that the latter construes the basic reference point relationship in terms of spatial metaphor. We can thus posit for such a preposition the structure sketched in Figure 6.3, where the source domain configuration profiles the relationship between the trajector and a spatial landmark.

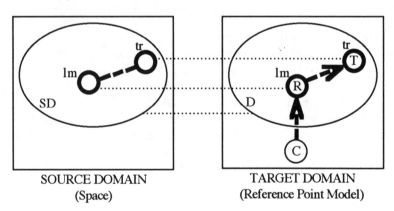

SOURCE DOMAIN   TARGET DOMAIN
(Space)   (Reference Point Model)

Figure 6.3

Observe that the ellipse labeled SD—which corresponds to the possessive dominion—represents the locative *search domain* (a construct motivated in Chapter 2). The search domain is defined as the region to which a locative expression confines its trajector, i.e. the set of trajector locations that satisfy its specifications. With the kinds of spatial prepositions used for possessive function, the search domain encompasses the location of the landmark itself and its immediate vicinity. A dominion can thus be thought of as a possessive search domain. We will see that both notions have considerable semantic and grammatical significance.

The preposition used for possession in English is of course *of*, which is not primarily spatial (at least synchronically). I argued in Chapter 3 that *of* designates an *intrinsic relationship* between two entities. As exemplified in (4), intrinsicness can be interpreted in various ways: it may pertain to part/whole organization; to the material or constitutive entities an object is made of; to the characterization of one entity by the relation it bears to another; or to the relationship between an event and its central participants.

(4) a. *the back of the bus; the tip of my finger; most of the guests*
     b. *a bracelet of pure gold; a lump of coal; a row of trees*
     c. *a friend of Sheila; the mayor of San Diego; the mother of Saddam Hussein*
     d. *the assassination of Lincoln; the howling of wolves; the chanting of slogans*

Many of these uses are commonly considered possessive, others perhaps not. For our purposes, however, the essential point is simply this: the more intrinsically one entity figures in the characterization of another, the more likely it is to be used as a reference point for it. Thus a preposition expressing an intrinsic relationship is naturally employed for many relationships usually thought of as possessive—the two notions have broadly overlapping applicability and are readily combined.

With all the possessive elements examined so far, the target has been the trajector, with the reference point serving as landmark. This correlation might seem obvious, if not inescapable, but in fact the two sets of notions—target vs. reference point and trajector vs. landmark—pertain to very different levels of organization and need not be associated in this fashion. Reference point relationships manifest a fundamental cognitive ability that is claimed to inhere universally in possessive constructions, providing their minimal content and most abstract description. By contrast, trajector/landmark alignment reflects the packaging of experience in one particular way for specific expressive purposes. It is basically a matter of figure/ ground organization—trajector and landmark being characterized respectively as primary and secondary figure within a profiled relationship—and is thus peculiar to individual elements and constructions, whose richer conceptual content may motivate a certain choice. In construing a given scene, we obviously have some flexibility as to where we direct the spotlights of primary and secondary focal prominence. So depending on what kind of conceptual content is invoked to embody and manifest the basic reference point relationship, alternate selections of trajector and landmark are not only possible but ought to be expected.

There are two main diachronic sources of possessive elements, namely locatives (such as spatial prepositions) and verbs of control (with meanings like 'grasp', 'hold', and 'keep'). Their original content involves two experientially basic ways in which we locate objects physically: we can either find them because we know their spatial location, i.e. their position within a spatial frame or in relation to some reference object; or else because we actively control them and determine their position. When the source expressions are extended to possessive use, and thus from physical to mental contact, some vestige of their original value remains and motivates a particular trajector/ landmark alignment. Consequently, even a fairly bleached-out verb like English *have* assigns trajector (hence subject) status to the reference point, reflecting its vestigial role as controller, and landmark (or object) status to the target, as befits the controllee. These assignments are shown in Figure 6.4. Since *have* is a verb, the profiled relationship is followed in its evolution through conceived time, as indicated by the heavy-line portion of the time arrow (cf. Langacker 1987c). It is, more specifically, an imperfective verb, which means that the profiled configuration is construed as being stable through time with no intrinsic temporal bounding (this is the import of the ellipses in the diagram).

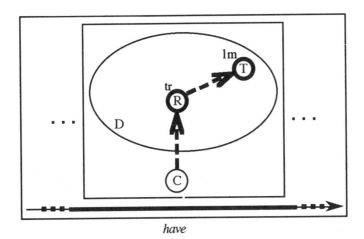

Figure 6.4

The diagram shows just the reference point function of *have*, which I take to be its only constant import. Of course, *have* also displays a variety of more specific senses in which some vestigial notion of control or access is overlaid on this schematic value. Its uses thus cover the spectrum illustrated in (5): they range from immediate physical control; to ownership, implying the possibility of physical access whenever desired; to more abstract kinds of ownership and access; to situations where the subject interacts with the object without in any way controlling it; to instances where the subject's role is essentially limited to its reference point function. As we move from (5)a to (5)e, properties characteristic of immediate physical control are successively stripped away until the reference point function stands alone.

(5) a. *Watch out—he has a gun!*
    b. *I have an electric drill, though I never use it.*
    c. *They have a good income from judicious investments.*
    d. *She often has migraine headaches.*
    e. *He has a lot of freckles.*

3.3. Further uses

Additional support for the reference point characterization emerges when we turn to other uses of possessive elements. Consider first the expressions in (6):

(6) a. *Sheila's student*
     b. *That student is Sheila's.*
     c. *a student of Sheila's*

Examples (6)a and (6)b employ the possessive morpheme in its basic, relational sense, which was diagrammed in Figure 6.2. *Sheila's* is thus analogous to a prepositional phrase, and *Sheila* to a prepositional object, for it elaborates the relational landmark (the reference point). In (6)c, however, *Sheila's* is itself the object of a preposition, and thus—in view of how English works in general—appears to be nominal in character rather than relational. What should we make of this?

    The most straightforward approach is to assume that *Sheila's* is in fact a noun-phrase prepositional object in this construction. What, then, does this noun phrase profile? Clearly, it does not designate either the reference point or the target: the entity labeled *Sheila's*, which the student is evidently a part of, cannot be either the student (who functions as the target) or Sheila herself (the reference point). I would instead analyze it as profiling the reference point's dominion, as shown in Figure 6.5. In the phenomena thus far examined, this notion has not been of much importance; here we have the first specific indication that linguistic phenomena actually hinge on it. Normally latent, in this construction the dominion is explicitly invoked and rendered salient as the entity profiled by the possessive morpheme and by expressions like *Sheila's*, derived by elaborating the reference point.[5] *Of* can then be interpreted as describing the part/whole relation that a target bears to the dominion overall.

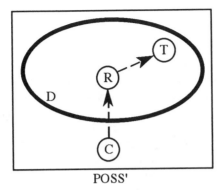

POSS'

Figure 6.5

I noted previously that a possessive dominion is analogous to a locative search domain. It is therefore of interest that a search domain can also be conceptually reified and put in profile. Recall examples like *Under the bed is all dusty*, where the subject derives from a prepositional phrase in precisely this fashion (Figure 2.5). Our ability to conceptually reify and refer to the search domain argues strongly for the psychological validity of this notion, and by implication the parallel notion of a possessive dominion.

Let us return now to possessive verbs like *have*. Though it often expresses prototypical varieties of possession such as ownership, part/whole, and kinship relations, *have*'s value is sometimes essentially limited to its reference point function, as we saw in (5)e. That function is also quite apparent in the construction illustrated in (7).

(7) a. *We have a lot of skunks around here.*
    b. *They have armadillos in Texas.*

The only vestige of the original sense of physical control is that the subject and object have some vague potential to interact (e.g. one might occasionally encounter a skunk or smell one at night). Primarily, however, the subject serves as a locative reference point, defining a spatial region—its dominion—within which the target can be found. By way of corroboration, observe that the subject *we* or *they* does not refer to specific people, but to all the people in some geographical area, and that the locative complement is virtually obligatory.

(By itself, *We have a lot of skunks* would suggest that specific people own them.)

Essential aspects of this construction are diagrammed in Figure 6.6, representing the integration of *have* and its object with the locative complement. Basically, as indicated by the correspondence lines, the target's inclusion in the possessive dominion is equated with the locative trajector's inclusion in the spatial search domain. Another feature of the diagram is the dashed, two-headed arrow between the possessive trajector and landmark; this represents their potential for interaction, the last remnant of the notion of physical control. Finally, the heavy-line box enclosing *have* + *X* identifies it as the profile determinant, or head, i.e. the component structure whose profile is inherited by the composite structure (not shown).

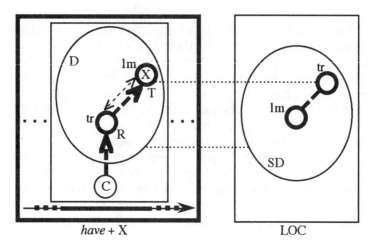

Figure 6.6

I will mention only in passing *have*'s grammaticization to form a perfect auxiliary, in English and analogously in other European languages. What is important here is that the perfect construction—exemplified in (8)a—is widely recognized as having a reference point function: an event is situated with respect to a "reference time", which need not be equated with the time of speaking.

(8) a. *They had been there several times.*
     b. *Elle a fini.* 'She has finished.'/'She finished.'

Hence the reference point characterization of possessives accounts very naturally for the evolution of *have* into a marker of perfect aspect. This evolution involves: (i) extension of reference point organization to the temporal domain; (ii) changing the target from a thing to a relationship (coded by the perfect participle); and (iii) the process of *subjectification*, which I have described in detail elsewhere (1990c; FCG2: ch. 5). Observe that the nuance of "current relevance" that is commonly ascribed to the perfect construction is once more the last vestige of *have*'s original sense of physical control (as was the notion of "potential interaction" in (7)). Eventually that too can fade away, as it is doing in French, so that only the temporal reference point function is left. Note the alternate glosses in (8)b.

Also nicely accommodated by the reference point analysis is the locative/existential use of possessive verbs. Consider, for instance, the Mandarin expressions in (9) (from Lyons 1967):

(9) a. *Wǒ yǒu shū.* 'I have a book.'
   b. *Zhūo-shàng yǒu shū.* 'The table has a book [on it].'/'There is a book on the table.'

Despite the contrasting English translations, I analyze the two sentences as being quite parallel, both grammatically and semantically. The apparent contrast stems from the fact that the possessive verb *yǒu* allows as its subject an entity construed as either a participant or else a setting or location (Chapter 2). In the case at hand, the effect of choosing a participant subject, like *wǒ* 'I', versus a locational subject, such as *zhūo-shàng* 'table', comes down to whether the reference point and dominion remain distinct. With a participant subject, as in (9)a, they do remain distinct—the possessor subject anchors a dominion that encompasses entities which need not be spatially coextensive with it. On the other hand, with a subject that is itself construed as naming a location, as in (9)b, there is a natural tendency for this spatially extended reference point to serve as its own dominion, as sketched in Figure 6.7. This represents a special case of the reference point model, obtained by equating the dominion with the reference point, so that the target has to be located somewhere within the reference point's own spatial expanse.[6]

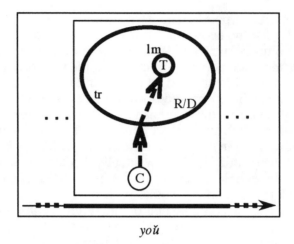

yŏu

Figure 6.7

4. Additional reference point phenomena

There are many other grammatical constructions that the reference point model enables one to understand and explicitly describe. Some of these constructions are traditionally regarded as possessive, despite the absence of any overt possessive element. Others, I suggest, reflect the same cognitive ability, which I take to be quite general. Though it bears a natural affinity to the possessive conceptual archetypes, I consider this cognitive ability to be a fundamental one having numerous and varied linguistic manifestations.

4.1. Quasi-possessive constructions

Reference point relationships are ubiquitous and basic to our mental experience. Readily available, they do not require explicit lexical or morphological coding to be incorporated as part of a construction's conventional semantic value. The reference point function may thus be pivotal to an expression's semantic and grammatical structure irrespective of how saliently (if at all) it is normally invoked by the elements overtly present. At one extreme lies an overt element, like the possessive morpheme, that actually profiles a reference point relationship and thus renders it maximally prominent. Intermediate cases are those in which an element that does not designate a reference point relationship nevertheless has some tendency—stronger or weaker—to evoke one. Toward the other extreme we find expressions which manifest a reference point interpretation that would not normally be elicited by any of the component elements taken individually.

To start with the simplest case, some languages encode possession by mere juxtaposition of the possessor noun phrase and the possessed head noun. This is one option in Papago (Uto-Aztecan), as exemplified in (10)b (Saxton 1982).[7]

(10) a. *g kii-j̃ g huan* (ART house-his ART Juan) 'Juan's house'
       b. *g huan kii* (ART Juan house) 'Juan's house'

Now either a person or a house can certainly be conceived of autonomously—we do not invariably think of a person as an owner or a house as a possession. These roles are nonetheless reasonably salient aspects of the encyclopedic characterization of the two notions, so that a reference point relationship is latent within them and easily activated. As shown in Figure 6.8, it is through the implicit reference point function that the two component expressions are grammatically linked by correspondences (typically grammatical integration is effected by correspondences between profiled entities). The evocation of this function represents an obviously crucial aspect of the construction's conventionalized semantic value.

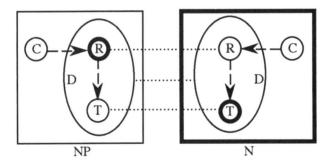

Figure 6.8

In many constructions, comparable links are superimposed on other, more explicit relationships. A case in point is the construction of French illustrated in (11).

(11) a. *Il lève la main.* 'He raises his hand.'
     b. *Elle ferme les yeux.* 'She closes her eyes.'
     c. *J'ouvre la bouche.* 'I open my mouth.'

On the normal interpretation of these sentences, the direct object is part of the subject's own body. But whereas a body-part relationship is usually marked by possessives (e.g. *sa main* 'his hand'; *ma bouche* 'my mouth'), here the direct object takes only the definite article; any possessive or part/whole relationship remains implicit.

These expressions represent a special case of the direct object construction, as shown in Figure 6.9. The general construction specifies the integration of two component structures: a transitive verb, which designates the temporal evolution of a relationship between two things (its trajector and landmark); and a noun phrase, which profiles a thing (indicated by the heavy-line circle). Their integration hinges on a correspondence between the verb's landmark and the direct object's profile, whose specifications are merged to form the composite structure. The constructional variant in Figure 6.9 is special because it further incorporates the reference point function. The direct object specifically designates a body part, which inherently invokes the conception of its natural reference point, namely the body as a whole.[8] A distinctive property of this subconstruction is a second correspondence, which equates that reference point with the verb's trajector. The result, at the composite structure level, is that the trajector's exertion is directed at a portion of its own body. (More precisely, the import is that the trajector induces the part to move, and controls its motion, via the internal transmission of energy.)

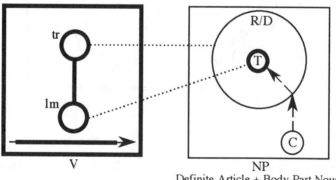

Definite Article + Body-Part Noun

Figure 6.9

Without going into any details, let me suggest that the constructions in (12) and (13) also involve a superimposed reference point relationship.

(12) a. *Je lui ai coupé le doigt.* 'I cut his finger.'
    b. *Henri a cassé le bras à Pierre.* 'Henry broke Peter's arm.'
    c. *Hélène s'est frotté l'oreille.* 'Helen rubbed her ear.'

(13) a. *I tapped her on the shoulder.*
    b. *André kicked his opponent in the stomach.*

In (12), the direct object is once again a body-part expression, so that the person as a whole—its natural reference point—is saliently evoked. A correspondence specifically identifies that reference point with the indirect object, semantically an experiencer, which is thus portrayed as undergoing an experience affecting a portion of its own body.[9] In (13), we observe a comparable reference point relationship between the direct object and the prepositional object.

The examples in (14) illustrate the so-called "dative-shift" construction.

(14) a. *She gave me a watch.*
    b. *Jill baked Helen some bread.*

A well-known property of this construction is that the profiled event results in the first post-verbal element coming into possession of the second. There is no explicit marker of possession—the two noun phrases are simply juxtaposed, as in (10)b. And as in Figure 6.8, we can analyze the two post-verbal nominals as being linked by correspondences involving an implicit reference point relationship. Usually, of course, the verb itself implies the existence of a resultant possessive relation, *give* being prototypical in this regard. The extent to which it does so is however variable, and in cases like (14)b neither the verb nor either post-verbal complement invokes possession as a central and consistent aspect of its meaning. To be sure, we know that baking creates a product intended for someone's use, that bread is such a product, and that people are controllers and consumers. Still, the reference point relationship in (14)b is contributed more by the construction itself than by any component element (cf. Goldberg 1995).

Finally, I propose that reference point relationships are pivotal to a common yet problematic type of construction in which two noun phrases appear to have equal claim to subject status. Consider the Luiseño examples in (15) (from Steele 1977).

(15) a. *noo=p* *no-te'* *tiiwu-q* 'I have a stomach ache.'
I=3s my-stomach hurt-TNS

b. *noo=n* *no-puuš* *konokniš* 'I have green eyes.'
I=1s my-eye green

c. *noo=n* *no-toonav* *qala* 'I have a basket.'
I=1s my-basket is

Although these sentences translate with *have*, no possessive verb is actually present. Moreover, while the initial NP acts in some respects like a subject (e.g. the pronoun occurs in its subject form, and the subject clitic often agrees with it, as in examples b and c), it is also true that the remainder of the sentence constitutes a well-formed clause having the second NP (the one referring to the body part or possession) for its subject. The issue of subjecthood is not our concern here (though I do analyze the first NP as the sentential subject— cf. Steele 1977; Langacker To appear-b). The essential point is that an implicit reference point relationship is once more the vehicle for integrating sentential elements.

This construction evidently involves the juxtaposition of a noun phrase and a clause-like component. Their integration is diagrammed in Figure 6.10. The noun phrase profiles a thing, and the clause an imperfective process, in which a stable situation (e.g. the eyes being green, or a basket existing) is followed in its temporal evolution. My principal semantic claim about these sentences is that the entity designated by the initial NP is construed as a reference point in whose dominion the clausal process is situated. The essential correspondence is thus the lower one shown, which specifies that the target mentally accessed via the reference point is to be identified with the clausal process in its entirety. Now it happens that this particular construction in Luiseño also incorporates a second reference point relationship, coded explicitly by the possessor prefix on the second NP. For that reason the clausal trajector is itself the target with respect to a reference point. The construction also specifies that the two reference points coincide (i.e. the initial NP and the possessor of the second NP are coreferential); hence the upper correspondence line. But although the construction is to some degree redundant, it is definitely coherent: a person is naturally taken as the reference point for a process whose focal participant is something he possesses (especially when it is part of his own body).

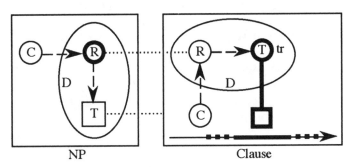

NP   Clause

Figure 6.10

This reference point characterization explains the English translations with *have*. I must reiterate, however, that the translations are misleading, for the primary import of the Luiseño sentences is not to describe a possessive relationship between two things (i.e. that the speaker possesses a basket, green eyes, or a stomach ache). Their main value is rather to specify that a particular individual (in this case the speaker) functions as a conceptual reference point with respect to which a process (e.g. that of a basket existing, eyes being green, or a stomach hurting) can be situated. The reference individual is not (in any narrow sense) the possessor of that process (though he is the possessor of its trajector) but serves instead as a "mental address" providing the conceptualizer with the context needed to locate and properly interpret it. It is therefore a kind of topic (in addition to being the subject).[10]

4.2. Non-possessive constructions

Although 'possession' is a very broad notion, it manifests a phenomenon of far greater generality. As traditionally conceived, the possessive category centers on values evoking particular conceptual archetypes, such as ownership, kinship, and part/whole relations. From there it is widely extended, and if there is anything common to all uses of possessive elements, it must be highly abstract; I have identified this abstract commonality with our cognitive ability to invoke one conceived entity for purposes of establishing mental contact with another. Yet, what would appear to be the same ability can also be observed in linguistic phenomena that are neither intrinsically related to the possessive conceptual archetypes nor traditionally regarded as possessive. We have seen, for example, that the not uncommon construction type exemplified in (15) is best analyzed as having topic-like function, and while this particular construction type is closely associated with possessive relationships, the same is not true for topic constructions in general. I thus propose to treat topics and possessives as overlapping but distinguishable manifestations of the reference point ability.

The very definition of a reference point recalls the notion topic: a salient entity evoked for purposes of mentally accessing another can also be thought of as providing a mental "address" to which some notion is "delivered" (i.e. as being what an expression "is about"). Or to put it another way, a reference point's dominion—the range of conceptions that it itself tends to evoke—can equally well be thought of as providing a context with respect to which an expression is interpreted (or into which its content is integrated). The dynamic aspect of the reference point model is also highly reminiscent of topics. A topic has a life history: it must first be established as such, often by a device that makes it salient as the explicit focus of attention. Once established, on the other hand, it may well remain implicit as subsequent expressions, themselves now in focus, are integrated into the context it provides. Though implicit, a topic may continue to hold sway through a substantial stretch of discourse, until some other topic is established to supplant it. A sequence of this kind is exemplified in (16).

(16) *Our vacation may be a problem. There won't be anyone to feed the cats. The lawn has to be mowed. The mail and newspapers have to be stopped. But as for the trip itself...*

If the reference point ability figures in both topics and possessives, how, then, do these notions differ? We are most inclined to speak of a possessive relationship when the target and reference point are both things (i.e. when they are nominal in character), and when they are both elements within the scene that is being described. The conceptual archetypes that anchor the possessive category are clearly of this sort; e.g. *Sally's dog* describes a scene (or scene fragment) involving an objectively construed relationship between two physical entities coded by nouns. By contrast, the clearest cases of topics are those in which the target is not a thing, but is rather clausal or processual in nature, and where neither the reference point nor the relation it bears to the target is part of the objective scene being portrayed. A Japanese example (from Li and Thompson 1976) is given in (17).

(17) *sakana wa tai ga oisii*
    fish   TOP red:snapper SUBJ delicious
    '(As for) fish, red snapper is delicious.'

The topic *sakana* 'fish' is not a participant in the (generic) scene described by the target clause (*tai ga oisii* 'red snapper is delicious'), but rather names a superordinate category to be used as a conceptual reference point for discourse purposes. The reference-point/target relationship is not part of the objective situation, nor does it hold between two things. Instead, the topic has the subjective function of specifying which domain of speaker/hearer knowledge should be accessed in order to properly interpret the processual target.

    Of course, the extension of terms like possessive and topic is neither pre-ordained nor definitively circumscribed in traditional usage. The terms can be used in either a broad or a narrow sense, thus determining the extent to which these descriptive categories overlap. The important point is that the categories have different prototypes or centers of gravity. Thus, if *Sally* is considered a local topic in a phrase like *Sally's dog*, it is nonetheless peripheral to the topic category. Likewise, if we extend the notion of possession to encompass (17), *sakana* 'fish' is still at best a marginal possessor.[11]

    If the reference point function is in fact fundamental and pervasive in our mental experience, we ought not be surprised to find it manifested at multiple levels of conceptual and grammatical organization, even within a single expression. The cases just examined— prototypical possessive and prototypical topic—lie toward opposite extremes of the spectrum. A possessive relationship is typically manifested internally to a single noun phrase; the possessor is just a local reference point allowing the conceptualizer to establish mental contact with another element within the objective scene being described. At a higher level of organization, we have examples like those in (15), where one element within the objective scene serves as a reference point for the entire event or situation profiled by a clausal component. We saw in Figure 6.10 that these two levels of reference point function are capable of coexisting, even when the same reference point is invoked for both targets. At a higher level still, as in (17), the reference point may specify a domain of speaker/hearer knowledge and be external to the objective scene represented by its clausal target. Finally, there are global reference points that serve as topics over a longer stretch of discourse, as in (16).

In addition to topic constructions, certain presentational constructions that serve to introduce an element into the scene are reasonably attributed reference point function.[12] One such construction is illustrated in (18).

(18) a. *On the table sat a nervous calico cat.*
      b. *Beside the pond stood an enormous marble sculpture.*
      c. *In her room were many exquisite paintings.*

Intuitively, the initial prepositional phrase directs our attention to a particular location, in which the new element is then established. This shift in focus from the locative frame to the element established therein recalls the dynamic aspect of the reference point model. Moreover, the construction is topic-like in the sense that it first provides a spatial context in which the new element is subsequently integrated. One difference from a topic construction (as normally conceived) is that the initial constituent is relational rather than nominal in character, i.e. it profiles a relationship instead of a thing. Now it is not, I think, the profiled relationship per se that functions as the reference point, but rather the locative expression's *search domain*, i.e. the set of trajector locations that satisfy its specifications (Chapter 2). Although the locative does not specifically designate this spatial region (as in *Under the bed is all dusty*), it nevertheless evokes it directly as the range of possible locations for its schematic trajector, which is then elaborated by the clausal subject (the target). This construction thus has a property previously observed in Figures 6.7 and 6.9, namely that the reference point and the dominion (or search domain) coincide.

I would also ascribe reference point function to the "nested locative" construction of (19)a, as well as the "chained locative" construction of (19)b.

(19) a. *Your copy of **Women, Fire, and Dangerous Things** is in the study, in the bookcase, on the bottom shelf, next to the **Illustrated Encyclopedia of Glottochronology**.*
      b. *The Lexicostatistics Museum is across the plaza, through that alley, and over the bridge.*

In either construction, the successive locative constituents lead one along a mental path, from reference point to reference point, in order to find the clausal subject (which is also the trajector of each individual locative). There are actually two levels of reference point organization in these expressions. On the one hand, objects (such as the bookcase) or spatial landmarks (e.g. the plaza) are being used as reference points to situate the subject/trajector. At this level the subject is the target, and it is located somewhere within each reference point's dominion (i.e. the search domain of the locative for which it serves as landmark). A second level of reference point organization pertains to the spatial path per se. At this level, each reference point and each target is itself a spatial location. It is by scanning mentally from one such location to the next that the conceptualizer traces a mental path.

In the nesting construction of (19)a, the reference points and targets are the search domains of the individual locative expressions, and the target is in each case construed as being somewhere inside its reference point, hence the nesting effect. Thus, in moving from locative to locative we initially focus our attention on the study; we then use that region as a reference point for directing our attention to the interior of the bookcase; taking that interior region as a point of reference we can then establish mental contact with the surface of the appropriate shelf; and with that as reference point, we can easily zoom in on the final spatial target (the area adjacent to the encyclopedia). Observe that each target, once reached, functions in turn as reference point for purposes of reaching the next target (the search domain of the following locative). This chaining, in combination with the common pattern of a reference point including its target (a whole being a natural point of access to its parts), yields the nested structure of (19)a (see Figure 2.9).

In this respect, the nested locative construction is analogous to the possessive expressions in (20)a, where each possessor (reference point) in the sequence is a whole that includes its target as a subpart.

(20) a. *my ring finger's middle knuckle; the book's title's
          second word*
      b. *Tom's girlfriend's cousin's mother; my computer's
          warantee's expiration date*

Likewise, the chained locative construction of (19)b is parallel to the possessive expressions in (20)b, where the target is in each case external to the reference point. The resulting mental path leads in chain-like fashion from one distinct entity to the next, where these entities may be people, physical objects, points in space, or something more abstract. In the chained locative construction, the reference points and targets are points in space. Each locative in the series describes a spatial path along which the conceptualizer scans mentally to its endpoint, which is thus a target of scanning. This target is then the reference point for the next spatial path in the chain, specified by the following locative, which takes it as its point of departure. The set of possible paths departing from a particular reference point constitute its dominion in regard to this kind of scanning operation.

Let me also mention a reference point analysis of pronominal anaphora worked out in careful detail by Karen van Hoek (1995; 1997a). The central idea is that an antecedent functions as a reference point, its dominion providing the context in which a pronoun is interpreted. Depending on their salience, as well as the conceptual/ grammatical connections they have with other elements, potential antecedents establish local or global dominions over which they exercise their interpretive influence. This reference point/dominion organization remains implicit (as in (11) and Figure 6.9), being superimposed on the kinds of grammatical structures that are traditionally recognized.[13] These notions allow van Hoek to achieve a natural, insightful, and unified account of the data treated in both syntactic and discourse-based approaches to anaphora, including much that was previously problematic.

4.3. Metonymy

Up to this point, we have concentrated on grammatical constructions, i.e. on syntagmatic relationships among sentential elements. In view of their supposed generality, however, we can also predict the occurrence of reference point phenomena in the paradigmatic plane. They do in fact have paradigmatic manifestation, a primary one being *metonymy*. We can define metonymy as occurring when an expression that normally designates one entity is used instead to designate another, associated entity. The requisite association is quite variable in nature. Often the term for a part is used for the whole, as in (21):

(21) a. *The coach is going to put some fresh legs in the game.*
   b. *I need some wheels so I can go to the drive-in.*
   c. *By various off-season trades, the Padres acquired
        several strong young arms.*

Conversely, the name for a whole can be extended to a part:

(22) a. *Yorick is slightly larger than Polonius.* [gravediggers comparing two skulls]
   b. *My pencil broke.* [when actually only the lead point did]
   c. *That car doesn't know where he's going.*

The examples in (23) involve associations other than part/whole relationships:

(23) a. *She bought Lakoff and Johnson, used and in paper, for just $1.50.*
   b. *I see Rommel now.* [looking through binoculars in North Africa during World War II, and actually seeing only a cloud of dust]
   c. *The {vasectomy/herniated disk} in room 304 needs a sleeping pill.* [one nurse to another in a hospital]

Why are we not confused by these changes in reference? Why is metonymy so prevalent? Why, indeed, does it occur at all? The answers become apparent as soon as we recognize that metonymy is basically a reference point phenomenon. More precisely, the entity that is normally designated by a metonymic expression serves as a reference point affording mental access to the desired target (i.e. the entity actually being referred to). We are not confused by the change in designation precisely because the reference point adopted is deemed capable of evoking that target. Metonymy is prevalent because our reference point ability is fundamental and ubiquitous, and it occurs in the first place because it serves a useful cognitive and communicative function. What is this function? Metonymy allows an efficient reconciliation of two conflicting factors: the need to be accurate, i.e. of being sure that the addressee's attention is directed to the intended target; and our natural inclination to think and talk explicitly about those entities that have the greatest cognitive salience for us. By virtue of our reference point ability, a well-chosen metonymic expression lets us mention one entity that is salient and easily coded, and thereby evoke—essentially automatically—a target that is either of lesser interest or harder to name.

   Various kinds of factors can make an entity sufficiently salient to serve as a metonymic reference point. Unless overridden by other considerations, certain principles of cognitive salience generally hold, among them *human > non-human, whole > part, concrete > abstract,* and *visible* > *non-visible*. People make especially good reference points, as seen in (22)a and (23)a-b. Indeed, these expressions indicate that a person is often selected even when absent, non-visible, or no longer in existence (as an integral whole). The salience of a whole relative to its parts is exemplified in (22), with (22)c also showing the importance of visibility: the car's greater visibility in the car-driver assembly evidently overrides the humanness factor. These general tendencies can of course all be overridden given enough motivation. In (21), we see a part adopted as reference point in preference to the whole, to some extent for expressive purposes, but also because the part in question has special salience with respect to a particular contextually important function. And (23)c illustrates the skewing of salience relationships that specific circumstances often induce. In a hospital setting, nurses may well know virtually nothing about their individual patients except the nature of their malady or medical procedure; this is what they are primarily responsible for dealing with. Consequently, when they have to mention a particular patient (whose name they may not even recall), the malady or procedure suggests itself as an obvious reference point.

A special case of metonymy is the phenomenon of *active zones*, involving the connection between relational expressions and their nominal arguments.[14] Active zones prove pivotal to the analysis of "raising" constructions, to be presented in Chapter 11. In a sentence like (24)a, for instance, the "raised" nominal (*Jones*) stands metonymically for the clausal event (*Jones sue us*) that participates directly in the main-clause relationship (*be unlikely*). Its referent is a kind of local topic for purposes of construing the infinitival complement—a status it does not necessarily have in the non-raising counterpart expression, in this case (24)b.

(24) a. *Jones would be unlikely to sue us.*
  b. *For Jones to sue us would be unlikely.*

We can extend this kind of analysis to relative clause constructions. It is sometimes claimed that the noun modified by a relative clause functions as a topic with respect to it (or that the relativized noun undergoes topicalization). We can interpret this as saying that the head noun serves as a reference point and thus defines a dominion in which the content of the relative clause must be integrated. The most obvious kind of integration involves construing the head noun's profile as a central participant in the subordinate-clause relationship.

Sometimes, however, the nature of the integration is less obvious. For instance, Matsumoto (1988) cites relative clauses in Japanese whose integration with the head depends on "pragmatic" (as opposed to "syntactic") relationships. An example is given in (25).

(25) *toire-ni   ike-nai   komaasyaru*
      bathroom-to go-cannot commercial
      'commercials [because of which one] cannot go to the bathroom'

The likely interpretation, based on cultural knowledge (Japanese culture, obviously), is that the commercials are so well made that one cannot go to the bathroom for fear of missing them. Matsumoto correctly regards these cases and more traditional relative-clause constructions as forming a gradation. I would simply say that examples like (25) depend more crucially than certain others on the reference point's dominion, i.e. on knowledge that the reference point itself makes accessible for purposes of interpreting the subordinate clause.

5. Conclusion

It is legitimate to ask whether we might not have cast our nets too broadly, bringing together—on the basis of the most tenuous fancied similarity—linguistic phenomena that really have very little to do with one another. Are these phenomena really all basically alike? What about the obvious differences among them? Is there anything that does *not* involve reference points? I would not, of course, claim that the phenomena are all alike, only that they resemble one another in a certain respect. Merely imputing reference point organization to them does not constitute a complete analysis of any, nor does it absolve us of the responsibility to describe each in its own terms with full appreciation of its complexity and the motivating factors peculiar to it.

As I am presently conceiving of it, reference point organization represents so basic a cognitive ability that there may indeed be no linguistic phenomenon that does not involve it in some way. I realize full well that any such notion runs the risk of being vacuous, yet I feel that something very general and important is going on that we need to explore and come to terms with. I sense an abstract commonality uniting multitudinous aspects of language and cognition that are normally studied separately, discussed using unrelated terminology, or simply ignored because they are difficult to study and talk about. There is something tantalizingly similar, for example, among such linguistic constructs as subject, topic, possessor, and relative clause head, and linguists have found a variety of reasons for relating them in some fashion. Working in CG, I have been struck by the number of clearly essential notions involving an entity that is somehow "prominent" or "focused" within a more inclusive "dominion". This is evident in such opposing pairs as profile vs. base, trajector vs. landmark, participant vs. setting, immediate scope vs. overall scope, objective vs. subjective, autonomous vs. dependent, and thing vs. relation. In general cognition, we can cite such phenomena as attention, figure/ground organization, prototypes (sometimes characterized as "cognitive reference points"), comparison (which clearly involves a "point of reference" and a "target"), metaphor (where we speak of a "target domain"), and most broadly, the interpretation of novel experience with reference to previous experience.

I cannot help but suspect, therefore, that linguistic and cognitive processing rely fundamentally on an ability manifested in all domains and at all levels of organization: the dynamic exploitation of asymmetrically prominent entities to structure the experience that falls within their province. We will explore this notion further in the final chapter.

Chapter 7
Viewing in cognition and grammar

In attempting to formulate a conceptualist semantics, one is soon led to ponder the role of spatial and visual experience in shaping other aspects of cognition.* Undoubtedly its role is both pervasive and highly important—we are first and foremost spatial and visual creatures. The problem is however quite complex and far from resolution, as numerous distinct issues need to be disentangled, clarified, and carefully investigated. Though often misinterpreted, my own stance has been quite conservative in this regard. I have never claimed, for example, that all conceptual or semantic structures are visuo-spatial in nature, nor should my frequent use of spatial diagrams be so construed (cf. Friedrich 1985: 184). Moreover, while it is evident that space and vision play a major role in the metaphorical structuring of other domains, I make no specific claim concerning the nature or the extent of their primacy.

      This chapter examines a range of linguistic phenomena that may ultimately bear on such issues. I will first outline a variety of ways in which *per*ception and *con*ception can be regarded as analogous. This extensive parallelism motivates using the term *viewing* ambiguously, for either visual perception or else the analogous features of a generalized conceptual capacity (of which vision constitutes a privileged special case).[1] I will then show that surprisingly many aspects of language structure are plausibly interpreted as manifestations of viewing in one or both of these senses. These findings should help to clarify the role of vision in conception, as well as the central claim of CG: that grammar reduces to the symbolization of structured conceptualization.

1. Viewing

With the possible exception of God, there is no such thing as a neutral, disembodied, omniscient, or uninvolved observer. An observer's experience is enabled, shaped, and ineluctably constrained by its biological endowment and developmental history (the products—phylogenetic and ontogenetic—of interaction with a structured environment). It is likewise determined by the observer's position with respect to the entity observed. However distinct or distant they may be, the very fact of observation establishes a link between them that inherently alters the global circumstances of the observed and brings the observer into the scope of observation (if only at the extreme periphery). In the case of language, we can equate the "observer" with a speaker, whose "observational" experience resides in apprehending the meaning of a linguistic expression.[2]

Is it in fact legitimate to characterize the apprehension of linguistic meaning as a kind of "observation"? It may be relevant that our language itself encourages us to do so. The word *observe* and its derivatives are conventionally used not only in regard to vision but for perception in any modality as well as certain kinds of conceptualization not driven by immediate sensory input. Likewise, *see* is used for both vision and comprehension, and *view* for judgment and opinion. There can be little doubt that certain aspects of conceptualization are understood metaphorically in terms of visual perception (Sweetser 1990). Of course, there is no guarantee that our metaphors are scientifically accurate. That we think and talk of conception in terms of vision does not entail, for example, that conception in general actually derives from vision by abstraction or metaphorical extension, in either the individual or the species.

My working assumptions in this regard are quite minimal. I assume, first, that we have a basic mental capacity for dealing with *extensionality*, of which spatial extensionality is the primary manifestation. Moreover, vision constitutes a central (though not exclusive) means of apprehending space and spatial configurations. Other assumptions pertain to the relation between *con*ception and *percep*tion. From the broad definition of *conceptualization*, whereby it encompasses any kind of mental experience, it follows that perceptual experience represents a special case. Less obvious is my hypothesis that conception in general has various properties that are most evident and clearly discernible in perception, vision in particular. Leaving aside the question of primacy, I suggest that certain aspects of visual perception instantiate more general features of cognition, so that we can validly posit abstract analogs for numerous constructs useful in describing vision.

Some constructs that apply to visual perception are presented in Figure 7.1(a). First is the *viewer* (V), also describable as the *subject* of perception. At a given moment, the viewer faces in a particular direction, thus determining the *maximal field of view* (MF), i.e. everything observable given this orientation. This overall field of view has both a dimly perceived periphery, where the viewer is situated, and a center characterized by greater perceptual acuity. Using a theater metaphor, I refer to the center as the *onstage region* (OS); this is the general locus of viewing attention and constitutes the area in which acuity renders focused observation possible. By shifting our gaze within this frame, we choose the specific target of viewing attention, the *focus* (F), also describable as the *object* of perception. The dashed arrow represents the *perceptual relationship* between the viewer and the focus (or more generally, between the viewer and everything within the maximal field of view). Additionally, any specific configuration assumed by these elements is termed a *viewing arrangement*.

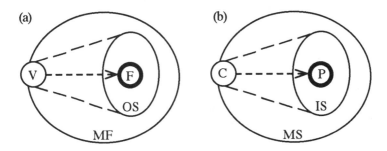

Figure 7.1

    These perceptual notions are reasonably analyzed as special, even prototypical manifestations of corresponding conceptual notions, represented in Figure 7.1(b), that are more abstract and broadly applicable. Corresponding to the viewer is the *conceptualizer* (C), or *subject* of conception. The *maximal scope* (MS) comprises the full content of a given conceptualization, not just central notions that we are specifically attending to, but also an array of more peripheral notions we may be only dimly aware of. The former constitute the *immediate scope* (IS), the conceptual analog of the onstage region.[3] The specific focus of attention, the *object* of conception, is referred to here as the *profile* (P). The dashed arrow represents the *construal relationship* wherein the conceptualizer entertains the overall conception and structures it in a certain manner. Finally, any specific configuration assumed by these elements can be called a *conceptual arrangement*.

Our concern is with conceptualizations evoked as the meanings of linguistic expressions, in which case the primary conceptualizers are the speaker and the addressee. Their conception and portrayal of a situation can never be wholly neutral, for they must always *construe* it in some specific fashion, out of the countless alternatives that are in principle available. Because linguistic elements incorporate particular construals as part of their conventional value, not even a deity is capable of assuming a neutral, "God's eye" view when using a natural language. Numerous aspects of construal that are quite important linguistically can reasonably be interpreted as general conceptual analogs of phenomena well known in visual perception. If the term *viewing* is used ambivalently for either perception in particular or conception in general (insofar as they are parallel), these aspects of construal can be characterized as *viewing effects*, which stem from the viewing arrangement.

2. Construal

One aspect of construal is the level of specificity and detail at which we conceive and portray a situation. In a series like *thing* → *object* → *vehicle* → *car* → *Dodge* → *Dodge Colt*, each expression is *schematic* for the one that follows, which *instantiates* or *elaborates* it, in the sense of providing a finer-grained characterization. The effect is quite comparable to the enhanced visual acuity we experience in approaching a distant object: the closer we get, the better we see it (the smaller the features we are able to detect and resolve).

Viewing distance correlates not only with acuity (a negative correlation) but also with scope (a positive one). If we focus our visual attention on a distant object, both the maximal field of view and the onstage region (general locus of attention) subtend large areas of the world around us. On the other hand, if we look at something quite close—e.g. a sheet of paper we are writing on—our visual horizons shrink drastically to encompass just limited portions of our immediate environment. The general conceptual analogs of the maximal field of view, the onstage region, and the focus of visual attention are, respectively, the maximal scope, the immediate scope, and the profile (i.e. the specific focus or object of conception). The imposition of maximal and immediate scopes and their interaction with distance are aspects of construal that significantly affect the behavior of linguistic expressions.

Consider a brief example from Cora, a Uto-Aztecan language of western Mexico (CIS: ch. 2). In one type of locative construction, a postpositional phrase, such as *či'i-ta* 'in [the] house', combines with an adverbial particle that comprises a deictic marker of distance (proximal, medial, or distal) as well as either *u* 'inside' or *a* 'outside'. With the medial marker *m*, for example, we thus have *mú či'i-ta* 'there inside the house', where *u* and the postpositional phrase both refer — schematically and more specifically — to the same 'inside' relationship. Another example is *ú čah-ta'a* 'off there in town', the distal marker being zero. Given this pattern, it is problematic that *čah* 'town' can only occur with the distal marking: neither **mú čah-ta'a* 'there in town' nor **íiyu čáh-ta'a* 'right here in town' proves acceptable. The apparent reason involves an incompatibility between the immediate scope imposed by the adverbial particle and the massive size of a town (as compared to a house). Other examples suggest that *u* is only used when a clear instance of an 'inside' relationship appears within the immediate scope, or "onstage". Now for such an instance to be discernible, the boundaries of the container (which delineate the 'inside' and 'outside' regions) must themselves occur onstage. We can reasonably suppose that the immediate scope for *u* is determined by the deictic element it fuses with. Thus, depending on whether the deictic specification is proximal, medial, or distal, the onstage area can be quite small or indefinitely large. We can then explain the data by observing that a container the size of a town can only fit inside the expansive immediate scope associated with a distal perspective.

The term *perspective* subsumes several aspects of construal whose characterization as viewing effects seems quite straight-forward. In actual vision, there is always a *vantage point* (or *viewpoint*), the spot at which the viewer is situated and from which the scene is viewed. A visual *reference point* is a salient entity used to locate another, less noticeable entity in relation to it (I might, for example, point out a lizard by first directing your attention to a boulder on which it is sunning itself). We also do visual *scanning* through a scene, either by turning our head or with eye movement. These perceptual notions and their abstract conceptual analogs have many linguistic manifestations. In the default interpretation of expressions like (1)a, for instance, the speaker's location functions as a spatial vantage point. More abstractly, the time of speaking is a temporal vantage point in (1)b.[4]

(1) a. *There's a video store right across the street.*
     b. *There's an election next Tuesday.*

(2) *Her father had died several years previously.*

(3) a. *The scar extends all the way from his wrist to his elbow.*
     b. *The scar extends all the way from his elbow to his wrist.*

(4) a. *As body size increases, there are fewer distinct species.*
     b. *As body size decreases, there are more distinct species.*

It is generally accepted that perfect aspect involves a temporal reference point. Sentence (2) is thus appropriate just in case the discourse has already directed attention to some earlier point in time, with respect to which the father's death was "currently relevant" despite occurring *several years previously*. The remaining examples illustrate semantic contrasts residing solely in the conceptualizer's direction of *mental scanning* through a static situation in which, objectively, nothing either moves or changes. Through mental scanning, we can impose directionality on either a visual scene, as in (3), or a more abstract conception, as in (4).

A further aspect of construal is our capacity to conceive of one situation against the *background* afforded by another. Among its varied linguistic manifestations are discourse notions, e.g. *new information*, where previous discourse functions as background to the current expression, and *metaphor*, where the *source domain* serves as a background for structuring and understanding the *target domain*. The term background is of course itself used metaphorically. It suggests that the asymmetry between the current expression and those it follows, or between the domain we are actually concerned with and the one which helps shape its conception, is somehow comparable to the visual asymmetry between the focus of attention and the background we see it against. The most evident parallelism is that the current expression is the one we are specifically attending to, as is the target domain of a metaphor. Moreover, just as the focused element is closer to the viewer than is the visual background, so the current expression is temporally immediate to the speaker and addressee, whereas previous expressions lie at some remove.[5]

I am using the term *profile* for the specific object of conception, i.e. the abstract counterpart of the visual focus. As part of its conventional meaning, every linguistic expression confers this special status on some element within the conception it evokes. We can identify this element as the one the expression designates. As shown earlier in Figure 1.1, for example, the word *knuckle* evokes as its *base* the conception of a finger, within which it profiles a particular subpart (a joint). Similarly, the term *aunt* takes as its base a certain kinship configuration, within which it profiles a female further characterized as the sibling of a parent of ego. An expression's profile is its referent, not in the traditional sense of reference "in the world", but rather the psychological sense of reference within a conceptualization. A further difference between profiling and the traditional notion of reference is that linguistic expressions can profile not only *things* (as broadly defined in CG) but also *relationships*. Whereas nouns profile things, different kinds of relations function as the profiles of verbs, adjectives, adverbs, prepositions, participles, and infinitives.

Relations do not exist independently of their participants. For instance, we cannot actually see an act of breaking if we cannot see the agent and patient, nor can we conceptualize such an act without conceiving of its participants (if only schematically). When there are multiple participants, they do not have equal status: a single participant tends to stand out in the sense that we are primarily concerned with tracking its motion, observing its interaction with other entities, or somehow assessing or characterizing it. In the perceptual realm, this asymmetry constitutes the well-known perceptual phenomenon of figure/ground organization. Note that in vision we are readily able to distinguish both a *primary figure* and a *secondary figure* within a scene. Imagine a video display in which a moon is shown rapidly circling a planet, while the planet itself is shown moving—much more slowly—against the static background of stars distributed through space. In the most natural visual construal of this scene, the moon and planet both stand out as figures, with the immobile stars and space comprising the ground. Simultaneously, the moon stands out as a local figure with respect to the larger, less mobile planet, the local ground. The moon is thus the primary figure, and the planet a secondary figure, with respect to the scene as a whole, viewed globally.

Conceptual analogs of these asymmetries are pivotal to the meanings of relational expressions. I use the term *trajector* (tr) to indicate the primary figure within a profiled relationship. When the trajector is viewed in relation to another salient entity, plausibly considered a secondary figure, the latter is called a *landmark* (lm). There are numerous cases of non-synonymous expressions that invoke the same conceptual content and profile the same relationship, the only semantic difference residing in trajector/landmark alignment. For instance, *in front of* and *in back of* can profile the same spatial configuration involving two objects lacking inherent orientation (Figure 1.2). The difference in meaning is that *in back of* construes the object closer to the viewer as a landmark for purposes of locating the more distant object (the trajector), while *in front of* imposes the opposite alignment.

In a normal viewing situation, we focus our attention on entities that are small and compact relative to the full extensionality of our surroundings. We tend, in other words, to organize scenes in terms of well-delimited *participants* who move around and interact within a stable, inclusive *setting*. In the previous example of a video display, the moon and the planet functioned as participants, the setting being the full expanse of space subsumed by the maximal field of view. Organization into setting vs. participants is a constant feature of visuo-spatial experience. It is evident, for instance, every time we open our eyes and find ourselves in a room furnished with smaller objects. Of course, we have the mental agility to focus our attention on the room as a whole, or as much of it as we can see at any one time. In this case the global setting (rather than a participant) is elevated to the status of perceptual figure. This amounts to a kind of figure/ground reversal.

The conceptual analog of the setting/participant distinction has extensive linguistic ramifications, as previously discussed.[6] Most importantly, it is reflected in basic aspects of clause structure: the prototypical arrangement is for a clausal subject and object to be participants, whereas settings are coded by clause-level adverbs. In (5), for example, the subject *Jack* and the object *several coyotes* are participants in the profiled interaction, which occurred in the temporal and spatial settings coded by the adverbs *last night* and *in the park*:

(5) *Last night in the park, Jack saw several coyotes.*

Although this arrangement is clearly prototypical, there are also many constructions in which a setting or location, rather than a participant, is chosen as clausal subject or object. The resulting expressions are non-transitive, hence they do not passivize. A case in point is the verb *contain*, which construes its subject as a location:

(6) a. *The box contained nothing of value.*
    b. **Nothing of value was contained by the box.*

Rice (1987a, 1987b) has demonstrated that transitivity (on which passivization depends) is not a matter of superficial grammatical form, but is rather a globally determined conceptual property of entire clauses. Specifically, it involves the *interaction* of participants (which merely *occupy* a setting or location).

In examining Figure 7.1(a), we see both the viewer (V) and the focus (F), linked by the dashed arrow representing the perceptual relationship. It is important to realize, however, that V does not enjoy the same bird's eye view of the situation that we do as outside observers. For us, all of Figure 7.1(a) falls within the field of view and constitutes the focus. But V is not looking at this diagram— rather, V is *in* the diagram looking at the "stage" (OS), and specifically at F, from an offstage vantage point. By directing his gaze outward in this fashion, V effectively excludes himself from OS (the locus of attention and region of visual acuity) and places himself at the extreme margin of the maximal field of view. V thus has only a vague and partial view of himself, at the periphery, if he sees himself at all. This viewing arrangement therefore maximizes the asymmetry between V's role as the *subject* of perception and F's role as the focused *object* of perception. To the extent that this asymmetry obtains, I say that V's role in the perceptual relationship is *subjective*, and that F's role is *objective*.

I have argued elsewhere (1985, 1990c, 1997a) that this perceptual asymmetry has a conceptual analog with extensive linguistic consequences. Every expression implies a construal relationship between a conceptualizer and the conception entertained. In the usual arrangement (Figure 7.1(b)), the conceptualizer (i.e. the speaker) remains offstage and unmentioned, functioning primarily as the *subject* of conception, whereas the specific *object* of conception is by definition the expression's profile (the focal point within the immediate scope). To the extent that this asymmetry obtains, I say that the conceptualizer is construed *subjectively*, and the profile *objectively*.

If this viewing arrangement is regarded as canonical, there are nonetheless other options. For example, we can lessen the subject/ object asymmetry by directing our gaze so as to put a portion of our own body onstage as the focus of attention. A conceptualizer can likewise go onstage as the profile (or focus of conception), as the speaker does in using the pronoun *I*. This yields an *egocentric* viewing arrangement in which—relative to the *optimal* arrangement of Figure 7.1—the onstage region (OS) expands to encompass all or part of the viewer.[7]

Another feature of the typical viewing situation is that V occupies a fixed location, from which he is able to observe different parts of the world around him by shifting his gaze (and hence the area subtended by the visual field). An alternative arrangement finds the viewer himself in motion, so that a continually changing segment of the world appears within the field of view even if the direction of gaze is held constant (in terms of head and eye movement). A conceptual analog of this special situation is essential to the construal of a sentence like (7) (from Talmy 1988b).

(7) *There is a house every now and then through the valley.*

Houses do not flash in and out of existence (as suggested by *every now and then*), nor do they follow a spatial path (*through the valley*). A coherent interpretation of (7) emerges only by invoking an imagined *viewer*. This viewer (not the house) is identified as the entity in motion *through the valley*, and *every now and then* pertains to the appearance of a house (a different one each time) within the moving field of view.

3. Complement vs. modifier

If every expression consisted of just a single morpheme, grammar would not exist. Grammar pertains to combinatory patterns, and thus to expressions that are *symbolically complex* in the sense of being analyzable into smaller symbolic elements. Symbolically complex expressions can be called *constructions*. A construction is thus a symbolic assembly comprising component and composite symbolic structures as well as the relationships among them. Combinatory patterns reside in *constructional schemas*, i.e. schematized representations of symbolically complex expressions. As templates reflecting what is common to a set of instantiating expressions, constructional schemas are themselves symbolic assemblies (cf. Figures 1.5 and 1.6).

Represented in Figure 7.2 (ignoring articles) is the symbolically complex expression *(the) table near (the) door*. This symbolic assembly comprises two levels of organization. At the "lower" level, the component structures *near* and *the door* are integrated to form the composite structure *near the door*. At the "higher" level, this prepositional phrase combines with *table*. Observe that *near* and *table* are enclosed in heavy-line boxes to indicate their status as *profile deter-*

minants: at their respective levels of organization, each imposes its own profile as the composite structure profile. This is the most useful way to characterize the traditional notion *head* (cf. Zwicky 1985; Hudson 1987). Note further that *the door* would traditionally be regarded as a *complement* of *near*, while *near the door* is a *modifier* of *table*.

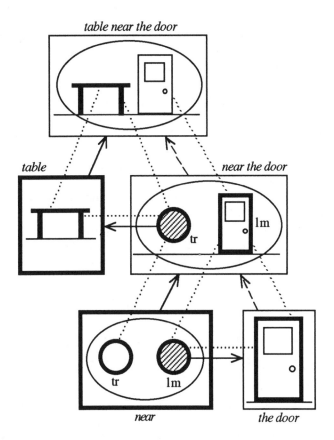

Figure 7.2

The symbolic structures forming an assembly are linked by relationships of *correspondence* (dotted lines) and *categorization* (arrows).[8] If we think in terms of composition (using the building-block metaphor), correspondences are instructions that specify which elements of the component structures are to be superimposed in deriving the composite structure. More accurately, we can think of them as records of the distortions engendered by dissociating the integrated composite conception into overlapping component conceptions for purposes of individual symbolization.

A solid arrow represents a categorizing relationship of *elaboration* (or *instantiation*). In a construction, it is typical for a substructure of one component to categorize the other component structure in this fashion. The categorizing structure (marked by hatching) is called an *elaboration site* (or *e-site*), being a schematic entity that the other component serves to specify in finer detail. In our example, the schematic landmark of *near* is elaborated by *the door*, while *table* instantiates the schematic trajector of *near the door*. Solid arrows along the vertical axis indicate that the profile determinant at a given level of organization is elaborated by its composite structure (e.g. *near* is schematic vis-à-vis *near the table*). Dashed arrows stand for categorizations based on *extension*, implying some conflict in specifications. This is characteristic of a composite structure's categorization by a non-head component. For instance, the modifer *near the door* conflicts with the composite structure *table near the door* (taken as a whole) in regard to profiling.

A *complement* is a component structure which *elaborates* a salient substructure of its head, whereas a *modifier* is a component structure a salient substructure of which is *elaborated by* the head (Chapter 3). In Figure 7.2, *the door* is a complement because it elaborates the preposition's landmark, *near* being the profile determinant at this level. At the higher level of organization, *near the door* is a modifier because the head noun *table* elaborates its trajector.

Our present concern lies with viewing, and specifically with two asymmetries between elements of typical constructions. The first asymmetry resides in the special status of the composite structure with respect to its components. The second is the status of one component as the head (profile determinant). These two asymmetries can be analyzed as viewing effects. In fact, by adopting a particular metaphor (one arguably less inappropriate than the building-block metaphor), we can see them both as consequences of a single viewing arrangement.

This metaphor involves plastic transparencies, of the sort used with overhead projectors. Imagine that each component structure is drawn on a separate transparency. Viewed individually, each has its own content, profiling, trajector/landmark alignment, etc. Next suppose that one transparency is overlaid on the other, with care taken that corresponding entities are directly superimposed. When the viewer now looks at the stack from above (or at the dual image projected on the screen), he sees a composite image which incorporates and unifies the content that the individual transparencies supply. Let us suppose, moreover, that the transparency placed on top has a greater effect in shaping the composite image—e.g. its colors show up more brightly, and the elements it contributes tend to be seen as foregrounded. The top transparency is, of course, the metaphoric analog of the profile determinant. It has a stronger effect in shaping the composite image precisely because it goes on top, so that the other transparency is only seen by looking through it. Also, the composite image is special because it constitutes what the viewer actually sees. In looking through the stack of transparencies, the viewer may find it hard to discern their individual contributions to the unified image he perceives, and when the image is projected on a screen, he is likely to be quite unaware of its composite nature.[9]

This transparency metaphor has its own limitations, one of them being its suggestion that a construction is fully compositional and that the composite structure inherits all of its content from the two component structures. Now there are indeed conventional patterns of composition (the semantic poles of constructional schemas), and some expressions are fully compositional for all practical purposes. Still, CG takes the position that semantic structure is in general characterized only by partial compositionality. The way a composite expression is actually understood usually diverges from any regularly computable value: it may more specific, it may evoke contextual factors or cognitive domains not evoked by the individual components, or it may represent an extension relative to the expected compositional value. Beyond a certain point it is therefore inappropriate to think of component structures as "building blocks" providing the material out of which the composite structure is "constructed". They are better thought of categorizing certain facets of the composite conception, as motivating its symbolization by the specific elements chosen, and as evoking enough of the envisaged situation that the addressee—by drawing on all available resources—is able to reconstruct a reasonable approximation to it.

These considerations motivate an adjustment to the transparency metaphor for the viewing of constructions. Rather than emerging from the superimposition of transparencies (i.e. component structures), the composite image exists independently and has a certain conceptual priority. It represents the integrated conception that interlocutors are actually concerned with apprehending and negotiating, whereas the components are just means to that end. The composite conception thus comprises an expression's essential meaning, and is either considered in its own right as the ultimate object of negotiation, or else is taken as a basis for further composition.[10] Our adjusted viewing metaphor should therefore be founded on the basic configuration sketched in Figure 7.3(a), where the viewer contemplates a single, elaborate image (corresponding to the construction's composite semantic structure). Within that image, the viewer's attention is focused on a specific target of conception (the composite structure profile).

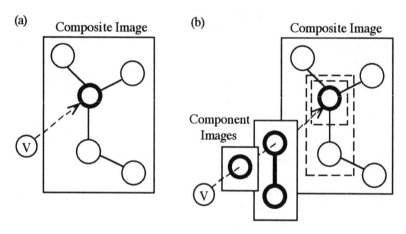

Figure 7.3

A component structure corresponds to some fragment of the integrated composite conception. When two or more components are invoked, they correspond to different fragments that typically overlap in some fashion and do not necessarily exhaust the composite image. This overlap is reflected in the "horizontal" correspondence lines of diagrams like Figure 7.2: saying that subparts of two component structures correspond is simply to indicate that they project to the same entity within the composite conception. Why, then, is this integral conception dissociated into separate fragments, when the former is what the interlocutors are actually concerned with? The reason is the unavailability of any symbolically non-complex expression capable, by itself, of symbolizing or evoking it. The fragments pulled out as semantic components are susceptible to individual symbolization. In conjunction with constructional schemas, they enable the addressee to assemble a partial conception that supposedly allows him to extrapolate to some reasonable approximation of the speaker's intent. It is nevertheless this composite conception—which the components often merely hint at—that provides their coherence and determines how the components themselves will be interpreted.

In terms of the viewing metaphor, we can still regard the component structures as being drawn on plastic transparencies. The transparencies do not create the composite image, for that exists independently, but they do bear partial images which correspond to fragments of the composite conception and approximate them within some degree of tolerance. To the extent that an expression is analyzable, the viewer can be thought of as looking through the component images in order to examine the composite image behind them, as shown in Figure 7.3(b). If the images are properly aligned—with corresponding entities directly superimposed—the components will blend into the composite structure and the viewer will tend to be unaware that he is looking at multiple images. Still, the very fact of being extracted for individual symbolization lends a certain kind of salience to the fragments in question. Viewing the composite image through the transparencies has a reinforcing or highlighting effect on their projections within it. In Figure 7.3(b), the projections of the components onto the composite conception are represented by dashed-line boxes. This projective relationship was alluded to earlier in saying that the component structures categorize certain facets of the composite structure.

The transparency metaphor allows us to describe the notions *complement* and *modifier* in terms of viewing effects. As shown in Figure 7.3(b), the component images generally project to different portions of the composite image. Yet their projections usually overlap, and if we confine our attention to the most salient entities—notably the profiles of the two components—it is common for one projection to subsume the other.[11] Recall now that the viewer's attention is focused on a specific element within the composite image (its profile), which normally coincides with the profile of one component (the head). The difference between a complement and a modifier is then a matter of whether the projection of the head includes the projection of the other component, or conversely.

These two configurations are sketched in Figures 7.4(a) and 7.4(b), respectively exemplified by the lower construction in Figure 7.2 (*near the door*) and the upper one (*table near the door*). In 7.4(a), the viewer's focus is on a relationship, the projection of a relational head, and the non-head component projects to just a portion of that relationship (one of its participants). The non-head's projection thus falls within the focused region, i.e. the region subtended by the transparency representing the head, so the viewer only sees it through that "lens". In 7.4(b), on the other hand, the focused region is confined to one participant in the relationship projected from the non-head component, so part of what the viewer sees extends beyond it. We can therefore describe a complement construction as one in which the viewer observes all major elements via the transparency representing the head, whereas certain elements of a modifier can be reached by a line of sight which does not pass through that lens.

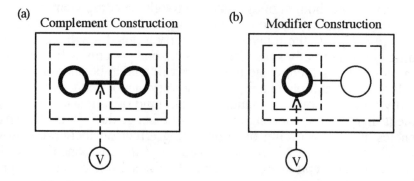

Figure 7.4

4. English tense and aspect

Viewing is especially significant in the domain of tense and aspect. We can see this by examining basic properties of the English tense-aspect system.

4.1. Grounding predications

The "viewing" we are concerned with is the apprehension of the meanings of linguistic expressions. The viewers of concern are consequently the speech event participants—primarily the speaker and secondarily the addressee—as well as any other conceptualizer whose mental experience is being described. Because of their special role in semantic structure, it is convenient to have a succinct way of referring to the speech event, its participants, and its immediate circumstances. I use the term *ground* for this purpose.

When a third party's viewing experience is invoked as part of an expression's meaning, the viewer in question is usually mentioned explicitly, as in (8)a. Naturally, the speech event participants and other ground elements can also be put onstage by explicit mention, as shown in (8)b. Their semantic role is not however limited to such examples. Even when the ground remains offstage and implicit, as in (8)c, it functions as the locus of conception and the ultimate "viewing platform". It may be invoked as a deictic reference point: thus the definite article indicates (roughly) that the nominal referent is uniquely identified to both the speaker and the addressee, and the past-tense morpheme locates a situation before the time of speaking. I suggest, however, that the ground—as locus of conception and viewing platform—figures at least marginally in the meaning of every expression, even one that contains no deictic elements. I noted at the outset that the very fact of observation brings the observer into the scope of observation, if only at the extreme periphery (Figure 7.1).

(8) a. *My daughter believes that Jerry likes her.*
    b. *I can see you better now.*
    c. *The letters were on the table near the door.*

We therefore need to distinguish at least three kinds of presence that the ground can have in semantic structures. First, with expressions like *I*, *you*, and *now* a ground element is actually profiled, i.e. it appears onstage as the specific focus of conception. It thus receives an objective construal (so far as a ground element can), being the object of conception as well as its locus. At the opposite extreme are non-deictic expressions such as *table*, *between*, and *expand*, where the ground's construal is wholly subjective. Here the ground is neither mentioned nor invoked in any capacity other than its universal role as the viewing platform. The speaker and addressee function as the subjects of conception, but that is the extent of their involvement. The ground has a third kind of presence in deictics such as articles, demonstratives, and tense markers, as well as words like *yesterday* and *tomorrow*: without being explicitly mentioned, some aspect of the ground is invoked as a point of reference serving to locate another entity. It is thus not merely the subject or platform of conception but figures at least marginally in its content. I would argue, however, that its construal is quite subjective nonetheless.

For the most part, in describing objects and situations linguistically we relate them to our own circumstances by means of expressions in which the ground has this third type of presence. In fact, the characteristic feature of a nominal (i.e. noun phrase) or a finite clause is the inclusion of what I call a *grounding predication*. The grounding predications of English are the articles, demonstratives, and certain quantifiers, for nominals, as well as tense and modals, for finite clauses. Their function is to locate the nominal or clausal profile in relation to the ground with respect to certain fundamental parameters (e.g. time, reality, identification). By invoking the ground in this fashion, each major sentential constituent makes intrinsic reference to a subjectively construed viewing platform. There is, I think, a very real sense in which the conceptualizers actually view the content of a nominal or a finite clause from that vantage point.

Grounding predications construe the ground itself quite subjectively, despite its role as a reference point.[12] Consider the past-tense inflection (*-ed* and its variants). In contrast to the periphrastic *before now*, which explicitly mentions a facet of the ground (the time of speaking), the past-tense marker leaves it implicit. Rather than being put onstage as a focused object of conception, it is offstage and subjectively construed, functioning only as the vantage point from which the speaker and hearer view the profiled entity (the process designated by the finite clause). There is a similar contrast between the definite article and a (very rough) paraphrase such as *identified to us*. Unlike the paraphrase, which makes explicit reference to the speech event participants (*us*), the definite article (*the*) leaves them offstage and unmentioned. The speaker and hearer are construed subjectively even though it is they who are viewing the profiled entity (the thing profiled by the grounded nominal) and are able to identify it uniquely in the discourse context.

The difference between periphrastic expressions like *before now* and *identified to us*, on the one hand, and the corresponding grounding elements (*-ed* and *the*), on the other hand, is shown abstractly in Figure 7.5. The former profile relationships in which some facet of the ground (G) is put onstage as a focused participant, specifically a landmark. By contrast, a grounding predication profiles only the *grounded entity*: the thing profiled by a nominal, or the process designated by a finite clause. Hence only the grounded thing or process occurs onstage, within the immediate scope (IS). The ground itself, as well as the grounding relationship (such as temporal antecedence or identification), are offstage and subjectively construed. They cannot be profiled, for by definition an expression's profile is the focus of attention within the immediate scope.

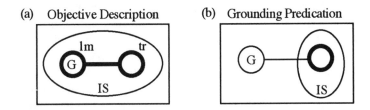

Figure 7.5

A typical grounding construction is sketched in Figure 7.6:

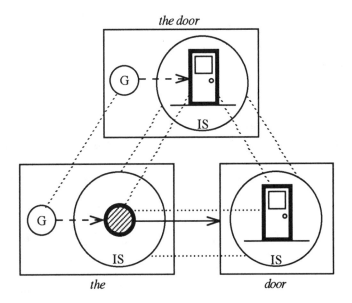

Figure 7.6

No attempt is made to indicate the precise value of the definite article (the presupposition of unique contextual identification). It is enough for our purposes to show it as profiling a schematically characterized thing viewed from the ground offstage. Its schematic nominal profile corresponds to and is elaborated by the more fully specified thing profiled by *door*. The resulting composite structure thus profiles a specific instance of the *door* category, one uniquely identified by the two offstage speech event participants.

This analysis accounts for the distinctive grammatical properties of grounding predications (see the references in fn. 12). In particular, it accounts for the ability of many grounding elements to stand alone as a full nominal or (when supplied with a subject) as a full finite clause: *this, those, all, some, each, she may, I will, they could,* etc. This comes about because an expression's grammatical class is determined by the nature of its profile (not its conceptual content overall). Since a grounding predication profiles the grounded entity (rather than the ground or the grounding relationship), it belongs to the same grammatical class as that entity. Thus a nominal grounding predication, which profiles a thing and specifies its relation to the ground, is itself a schematic nominal. Likewise, a processual grounding predication profiles and grounds a process, which makes it a schematic finite clause. Grounding elements are therefore potentially available to function as nominal or clausal pro forms.

4.2. Tense and aspect

The notion that an expression's grammatical class is determined by its profile, and the associated claim that certain basic classes have schematic conceptual characterizations valid for all members, are fundamental to CG (FCG1: part II; CIS: ch. 3). Pertinent here is how these relate to viewing. Profiling has already been described as a viewing effect: an expression's profile is the focus of attention within its immediate scope (the onstage region). The imposition of this scope is itself an important facet of viewing, as is a distinction between two basic modes of "scanning". Together these factors allow a revealing account of English tense/aspect phenomena.

A basic distinction is made between expressions that profile *things* (including nouns, pronouns, articles, demonstratives, quantifiers, and nominals) and those which profile *relationships*. A relationship is either *simple* or *complex* depending on whether it comprises a single configuration (e.g. with an adjective like *square*, or a preposition like *near*) or whether its characterization requires a series of configurations (e.g. the preposition *into*). I analyze a verb as profiling a particular kind of complex relation, in which a configuration's evolution through time is rendered salient. I call this a *process*.

Of course, since every relationship has some temporal duration (be it brief or extended), that alone does not make it a process, which further requires a certain kind of temporality in its construal. An expression may be non-processual ("atemporal") because it backgrounds the issue of temporal evolution (e.g. for *tall*, height being a non-transient property, often the result of prior growth), or else because it ignores time altogether and presents a configuration in purely static terms (*square, near, red*). Even when its temporal development does have a certain amount of salience, a relationship may still be non-processual due to its mode of scanning. We clearly have the ability to conceptualize an event in either of two ways: *sequentially*, as in watching a film clip; or in *summary* fashion, as in seeing a multiple exposure photograph, where representations of successive stages are superimposed to form a single gestalt.[13] I have suggested—speculatively, but in my own mind quite plausibly—that sequential scanning through the stages of a process predominates when a verb is used as such (e.g. when grounded and directly viewed as the head of a finite clause). On the other hand, its sequential nature may be overridden at a higher level of organization, so that the same content is viewed holistically. The summary view of a process is characteristic of infinitives and participles, and is one component of the conceptual reification involved in nominalization.

English verbs divide into two broad aspectual classes, my terms for which are *perfective* and *imperfective*.[14] The basic diagnostics for the classification are that only perfectives occur in the progressive construction, whereas only imperfectives occur in the simple, "true" present tense. By these criteria, *learn (the poem)* is perfective in (9), and *know (the poem)* imperfective:

(9) a. *He is {learning/*knowing} the poem.*
    b. *He {knows/*learns} the poem (right now).*

The perfective/imperfective contrast is precisely analogous to the count/mass distinction for nouns. More specifically, a perfective process is construed as being *bounded* within the immediate temporal scope, while an imperfective makes no intrinsic reference to bounding. A concomitant property is that a perfective process involves a change through time (if only by virtue of having an onset and an offset), while an imperfective is construed as internally homogeneous, with the consequence that any subpart, considered individually, constitutes a valid instance of the process in question. Perfectives and imperfectives are represented abstractly in Figure 7.7, where a heavy line represents the evolution through time (t) of a profiled relationship. Although the full evolution of a perfective process falls within the temporal immediate scope (the onstage region), an imperfective has indefinite temporal extension. As a matter of definition, however, the processual profile is limited to the segment of the overall relationship that occurs onstage.

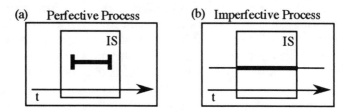

Figure 7.7

We can now explain certain interactions between English tense and aspect, notably those in (9). They interact because an immediate scope in the domain of time is crucial to both. An expression's immediate scope is the general locus of viewing attention, the default-case viewers being the speaker and addressee. As grounding predications, the tense markers specifically adopt them as viewers and construe them subjectively. From their offstage vantage point, the speaker and hearer—as implicit loci of consciousness—direct their attention to the profiled process onstage.

Iconically (for the basic forms Ø vs. *-ed*), these markers specify the grounded process as being proximal vs. distal with respect to the ground. Prototypically, proximity vs. distance is given a temporal interpretation; only the present- and past-time senses will concern us directly. The English present tense is evidently quite strict about this notion of proximity: I analyze it as imposing an immediate temporal scope that precisely coincides with the time of speaking. Similarly, the past-tense predication conveys distance by imposing an immediate scope located prior to the time of speaking.[15] In Figure 7.8, a box with squiggly lines represents the speech event, while the dashed arrow indicates the speaker's and hearer's viewing of the grounded process from this temporal vantage point.

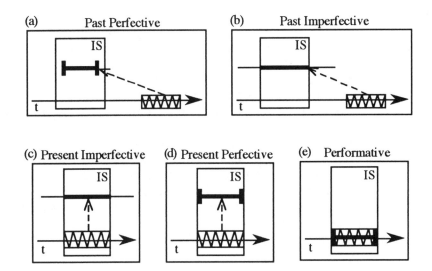

Figure 7.8

The grounded process (the one profiled by the finite verb) occupies the immediate temporal scope imposed by the tense predications. A full instance of the process type in question must occur on-stage for focused viewing by the speech event participants. In the case of perfectives, which are bounded, a full instance includes the endpoints. The usual arrangement is for the endpoints to fall inside the scope's own boundaries, in the manner of Figure 7.7(a), since the onset and offset of the process have to be observed for its identification as a valid instance of its type. By contrast, with imperfectives—which have no inherent bounding—it is usual for a process to extend beyond the immediate scope, as in Figure 7.7(b). However, since the immediate scope delimits the range of focused viewing, only the onstage portion is capable of being profiled. Still, it is characteristic of imperfectives (owing to their mass-like nature) that any portion of an overall process is itself a valid instance of the process type.

Past-tense perfectives and imperfectives (e.g. *He {learned /knew} the poem*) are both felicitous, for slightly different reasons. In the past tense, there is no inherent limit on the duration of the immediate scope. Thus in principle a perfective process can always be made to fit inside it, as sketched in Figure 7.8(a). With an imperfective, shown in 7.8(b), the size of the immediate scope makes no difference, since any portion it selects will count as a valid process instance. Moreover, imperfectives freely occur in the present for just the same reason. Here, as seen in 7.8(c), the temporal scope coincides with the time of speaking, so it is quite brief and only slightly variable (being linked to the time it takes to utter the finite clause). Yet the process segment coincident with the speech event counts as an instance of the imperfective process category.

Present-tense perfectives are another matter. Conceptually, there is nothing intrinsically anomalous about the configuration in Figure 7.8(d), where the bounded process is precisely coextensive with the speech event. The problem is rather that there is in general no correlation between how long it takes for an event to happen and how long it takes to describe it. With perfectives, moreover, a true present-tense description ('one instance, happening right now') is usually precluded, since the speaker has to start his report at the exact instant the event itself begins, before he has a chance to observe and identify it.[16] If the processual endpoints were to fall inside the scope's own boundaries, as in Figure 7.8(a), the problem would be even more acute: the speaker would have to begin describing the event even prior to its initiation.

There is however one glaring exception to the generalization that true present-tense perfectives do not occur, namely performatives (e.g. *I promise to cooperate*), which necessarily have this character. The analysis in fact predicts the exception: the defining feature of a performative is that the speech event itself is put onstage as the profiled process, as shown in 7.8(e); since they are one and the same, they must be temporally coincident. What about the other difficulty, that of the speaker having to begin describing the event before observing and identifying it? With performatives this problem simply does not arise. The speaker is a willful agent with respect to the profiled process and carries it out based on prior intent. He thus has no need to identify it through observation.

4.3. The progressive

The English *be...-ing* construction only occurs with perfective verbs. This conventional limitation has a clear functional motivation: since the progressive is an imperfectivizing construction, applying it to imperfectives would be superfluous. Each element of the construction has a meaning that it also exhibits in other uses. The effect of *-ing* is to imperfectivize the perfective process designated by the verb stem it combines with, and to impose on it the holistic, summary construal characteristic of a participle. At a higher level of organization, the participial expression *Ving* combines with the schematic verb *be*, whose sequential nature serves to retemporalize the imperfectivized relationship. The result is a complex expression *be Ving* that profiles an imperfective process and is eligible to be grounded as the head of a finite clause.

Our main concern here is with *-ing* and how it achieves its imperfectivizing function. The progressive construction is often described intuitively as taking an "internal perspective" on an event, or viewing it as an "ongoing" process. In CG, we can make this notion precise by appealing to a construct adopted for many independent reasons, namely immediate scope: *-ing* evokes as its base the schematic conception of a perfective process; it imposes on that base an immediate temporal scope from which the endpoints of the process are excluded. This basic configuration is sketched in Figure 7.9. Observe that the profile is once again restricted (as a matter of definition) to the process segment that appears onstage. Because *-ing* is not a grounding predication, it does not specifically single out the speaker and hearer as viewers. It does however specify a particular way of viewing the perfective process designated by the verb stem: besides limiting focused observation to a segment of that process, *-ing* construes this segment holistically (in summary fashion) and as being internally homogeneous, hence mass-like in nature.

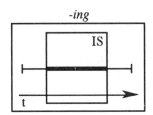

Figure 7.9

The imperfectivization effected by *-ing* resides in the exclusion of endpoints and the mass-like nature of the profiled relationship. But given that the base is perfective, and generally involves a change, how is the profiled segment rendered internally homogeneous? One answer is that *-ing* abstracts away from any distinguishing properties of the component *states* (i.e. the "time-slices" of the temporally evolving relationship) and construes them schematically as nothing more than "representative internal states" of the perfective process in question; conceived at this level of abstraction, the component states are effectively equivalent. Another answer, not at all incompatible with the first, is quite reminiscent of Lakoff's explanation for the similarities between plurals and mass nouns: "The relationship between multiplex entities and masses is a natural visual relationship. Imagine a large herd of cows up close—close enough to pick out the individual cows. Now imagine yourself moving back until you can no longer pick out the individual cows. What you perceive is a mass. There is a point at which you cease making out the individuals and start perceiving a mass. It is this perceptual experience upon which the relationship between multiplex entities and masses rests" (1987: 428).

Whereas Lakoff describes the effect of "zooming out", the homogenization effected by -*ing* is interpretable as the result of "zooming in". We can readily identify a familiar physical object when its entire contour fits within our visual field. For instance, upon perceiving a certain well-known configuration of head, legs, body, tail, and udder, we can easily recognize a cow. Imagine, however, that for some reason you decide to approach a cow, coming closer and closer until finally you touch it with the tip of your nose. At some point in your approximation, the contours of the cow overflow the limits of your visual field, so that all you can actually see is an undifferentiated mass of cowhide. You probably know that you are dealing with a cow (whether from memory, smell, or an expert's knowledge of cowhide), but since the distinguishing features and overall gestalt are now outside the field of view, you no longer have the perceptual experience of actually seeing one, *qua* cow. It is not overly fanciful to suggest that the profile of an active participle is construed as homogeneous by means of an analogous mechanism. Starting from the full, bounded event designated by a perfective verb, -*ing* confines attention to an arbitrarily chosen segment by imposing a limited immediate scope which excludes the temporal endpoints (which are analogous to the spatial outline of the cow). The event's most distinctive properties (e.g. a resultant state) are thus removed from focused observation, and without the supporting context of the overall gestalt the remaining profiled states cannot be clearly distinguished and identified.

A finite clause with progressive aspect thus incorporates a number of scopes, representing different levels of conceptual and grammatical organization, whose projections in the composite image are nested one within the other. At the lowest level of organization, the perfective verb's temporal scope has sufficient expanse to encompass the onset and offset of the designated process. At the next level,

-ing imposes a more restricted immediate scope which excludes the endpoints of that process (Figure 7.9). The subsequent addition of *be* has no effect on scope or profiling, but it does retemporalize the *Ving* participle to derive the complex imperfective verb *be Ving*, which can then be grounded as the final step in forming a finite clause. The result of adding the past- or present-tense predication to such a verb can be seen by comparing Figure 7.9 with the respective diagrams in Figure 7.10. On the imperfective process delimited by the scope of *be Ving*, the tense marker imposes its own immediate scope, which subtends some portion of it, either prior to or coincident with the time of speaking. Being imposed at the highest level of organization, the immediate scope of the grounding predication delimits the profile for the finite clause as a whole.

(a)   Past Progressive   (b) Present Progressive

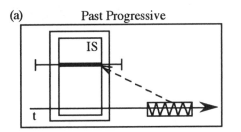 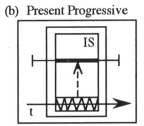

Figure 7.10

5. Subordination

The viewers invoked by a grounding predication are of course the speaker and the addressee, who view the composite image of a nominal or a finite clause. The speech event participants are not however the only viewers of linguistic consequence, since many expressions describe, adopt, or somehow take into account the viewing experience of other individuals. It is common for a main-clause verb to profile a viewing relationship, in which case the viewer is usually coded by the subject, while the subordinate clause specifies what it is that the subject views. In such instances, the relationship between the main-clause subject and the subordinate clause is analogous to that which the speech event participants bear to the grounded process profiled by a finite clause (Achard 1998). Or to put it another way, the viewing relationship inherent in a grounding predication represents a subjective counterpart to the kind of objectively construed viewing relationship that is often profiled by a complex sentence.

One ramification of this parallelism is a certain amount of overlap between the sets of elements which specify how the speaker and addressee view a finite clause, on the one hand, and how a main-clause subject views the content of a subordinate clause, on the other. In English there are two elements in particular that I would analyze as having this dual function. Formally these elements are zero and *-ing*. Except in the third-person singular, zero is the usual manifestation of the present-tense grounding predication. I will relate it to a zero subordinator that is likewise based on a notion of temporal coincidence. The subordinating use of *-ing* I have in mind is semantically and phonologically indistinguishable from the progressive *-ing*, which imposes a special way of viewing a perfective process.

Our concern is with complements to basic verbs of perception, *see* of course being the prime example.[17] Consider the data in (10):

(10) a. *He saw the ship {sink/sinking}.*
      b. *He sees the ship {*sink/sinking}.*

Intuitively, the constrast between the complements marked by zero and by *-ing* is quite apparent: if you see a ship *sink*, you observe the full, bounded event; but if you see a ship *sinking*, you observe only a portion of the overall process. I basically agree with Kirsner and Thompson (1976), who propose the abstract meanings 'bounded in time' vs. 'not bounded in time'. Let me emphasize that these values are not per se the meanings of $\emptyset$ and *-ing*. Rather, they emerge as consequences of relationships between endpoints and immediate scope in the context of the full *see [X] V* and *see [X] Ving* constructions.

I ascribe to *-ing* the same meaning it has in the progressive (Figure 7.9): on a perfective process, it imposes an immediate temporal scope that excludes the endpoints. The composite structure *Ving* thus profiles a relationship that is imperfective (as well as holistically viewed). Similarly, the zero subordinator has a meaning quite comparable to that of the present tense, in that it imposes an immediate scope precisely coincident with the duration of a perfective process (Figure 7.8(d)). This temporal scope represents the duration of viewing, but since the subordinating $\emptyset$ is not a grounding predication, it makes no inherent reference to the speaker or the speech event. In the full construction (e.g. *He saw it sink*), the viewing is that expressed by the main-clause verb, and the viewer is identified with the main-clause subject. These contrasting subordinate structures, *Ving* and *Ø*+*V*, are shown as components of their respective full constructions in Figures 7.11(a)-(b).[18]

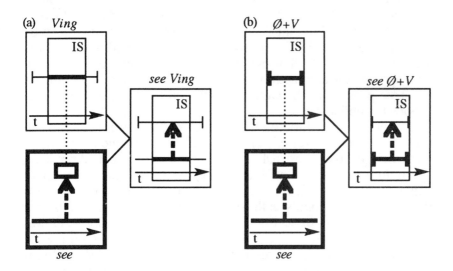

Figure 7.11

To explicate these full constructions, we must next consider the meaning of *see* (taking it as being representative of perception verbs). *See* is of course polysemous, and even in its most basic perceptual sense it can assume either a perfective or an imperfective value. The choice is largely determined by the nature of the entity perceived. In *I saw the flash*, for example, *see* is perfective because the perceptual experience it designates is necessarily brief and clearly bounded. On the other hand, *I see the moon* involves an imperfective use, which is possible because the moon has sufficient duration to support a stable perceptual experience longer than a typical viewing episode. This chameleon-like nature of *see* results from the fact that— when we are talking about actual perception—the viewing experience can only occur while the object of perception is there to be perceived. The same is true for the perception of events: if I see a ship sink, that particular visual experience ceases as soon as the event itself is over.

I will treat the relevant sense of *see* as being basically imperfective. In Figure 7.11, the horizontal line representing its temporal extension is therefore shown with no indication of inherent bounding. The dashed arrow indicates the observation by the subject, at any one instant, of the situation being viewed. That situation—the instantaneous object of viewing—is depicted as a small rectangle; a correspondence line identifies it with the situation obtaining at the same instant in the relationship expressed by the complement (*Ving* or $\emptyset + V$).[19] Through time, then, the subject sees, as it occurs, the entire relationship profiled by the complement. The profiled relationship is necessarily limited to that portion of the subordinate process (*V*) which appears onstage within the temporal immediate scope: the full perfective process in the case of $\emptyset + V$, and for *Ving* a subpart that excludes the endpoints.

Because the duration of viewing cannot be longer than the duration of what is viewed, the temporal scope of the complement affects the aspectual construal of the main-clause perceptual predicate. In particular, as shown in Figure 7.11, the immediate scope of the complement is inherited at the composite structure level and—because it determines what counts as the object of viewing—imposes itself on the profiled process of seeing. The profile of the composite expression is therefore limited to that portion of the process of seeing which occurs in this frame. In expressions of the form *see [X] Ving* (Figure 7.11(a)), the referent of *see* is therefore delimited by the immediate scope of *Ving*, even though the overall event of seeing may extend beyond its confines.[20] The referent of *see* is also delimited by the immediate scope of the complement in expressions of the form *see [X] V* (Figure 7.11(b)), but here the profile is exhaustive of the overall seeing event. With zero marking, the complement's immediate scope is precisely coincident with the duration of the subordinate process (*V*). That process is perfective, hence bounded, so its boundaries coincide with the limits of the temporal scope. And since the duration of seeing is determined by that of the observed event, the overall process of seeing is itself bounded and coincident with the immediate scope.

At the composite structure level, the profiled process is therefore imperfective in Figure 7.11(a), and perfective in 7.11(b). The former exhibits the classic imperfective configuration in which a process "overflows" the immediate temporal scope that delimits the processual profile (Figure 7.7(b)). It is thus a general property of imperfectives that they portray an overall situation as stable and segment out a portion for focused viewing. Because *see* is construed imperfectively, expressions of the form *see [X] Ving* occur unproblematically in the present tense: *He sees it sinking.* On the immediate temporal scope of *(he) see it sinking*, the present tense predication imposes a smaller immediate scope coincident with the time of speaking, as shown in Figure 7.12(a). At the highest level of organization (that of the finite clause), the processual profile is therefore limited to that time span, but this limited sample is nonetheless a valid instance of the imperfective process type.

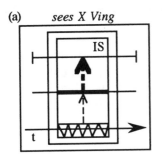 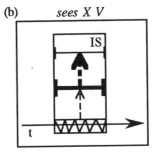

Figure 7.12

Being perfective, on the other hand, expressions of the form *see [X] V* are infelicitous in the present tense: **He sees it sink.* A present-tense perfective implies that the profiled process precisely coincides with the immediate scope defined by the speech event (Figure 7.8(d)). In the case of *see [X] V*, this is a bounded process of seeing that is itself delimited by the boundaries of the perfective subordinate verb (*V*). Thus, as shown in Figure 7.12(b), there is full temporal coincidence of all the following: the speech event, the immediate scope it imposes, the profiled perceptual process, the subordinate process, and the immediate scope associated with zero subordination. While there is nothing inherently anomalous about this configuration, the same problems arise as with other present-tense perfectives: we cannot expect an event such as *sink* or *see it sink* to take the same amount of time as its linguistic description; and in any case, by the time the speaker is able to observe and identify the process in question, it is already too late to initiate a precisely coincident description of it.

6. Anaphora

A CG description of pronominal anaphora was briefly alluded to in Chapter 6 and will be considered further in Chapter 9. Here it will be examined from the standpoint of viewing. Wholly due to van Hoek (1993, 1995, 1996, 1997a, 1997b), the analysis is based on reference point organization, whose relation to viewing should be evident: it is a matter of a conceptualizer directing attention first to one entity and then to another accessible via the first. In the case of pronominal anaphora, the antecedent sets up a reference point, thereby establishing a dominion in which the pronoun (target) is interpreted. To solve the classic problem concerning which pronoun-antecedent configurations are permissible (and which ones not), one must therefore investigate the factors that facilitate the setting up of a reference point and determine the extent of its dominion.

6.1. Pronouns and reference points

Emerging quite clearly from van Hoek's description is the importance to anaphoric relationships of *viewing*, understood as either perception or its general conceptual analog. To be sure, she is not the first to have noticed this. She has expanded the stock of examples cited by previous scholars (e.g. Cantrall 1974; Kuno 1987) which show the relevance—especially for reflexives—of the antecedent being construed as a viewer with respect to the anaphor:

(11) a. *Funny stories about **himself** won't restore **Tom** to good humor.*
      b. **Funny stories about **himself** won't restore **Tom** to life.*

(12) a. *The picture of **himself** that hangs in **Clinton**'s bedroom is quite dignified looking.*
      b. **The picture of **himself** that hangs in **Lincoln**'s bedroom is quite dignified looking.*

(13) a. *Ironically, **Joyce** owed her success partly to that scandalous rumour about **herself** that was going around.*
      b. **Ironically, **the book** owed its success partly to that scandalous rumour about **itself** that was going around.*

Furthermore, the very existence of *logophoric pronouns* should make it evident that viewing is somehow pertinent to questions of anaphora (cf. Sells 1987).

But why should this be so? If the use of pronouns in lieu of full nominal descriptions is simply a matter of avoiding excessive repetition, and if pronoun-antecedent configurations are governed by purely formal restrictions stated in terms of syntactic tree structures, then why should it matter whether the antecedent's referent is a possible viewer? In accordance with the principles and basic spirit of CG, van Hoek proposes a very different conception of pronouns and pronoun-antecedent relationships in which the relevance of viewing is natural if not predictable. Rather than treating pronouns as reduced or formally compact nominal descriptions, she ascribes to them a distinct kind of meaning. For one thing, they imply that the conceptualizers are able to establish mental contact with the intended referent in the current discourse-pragmatic context.[21] Moreover, a pronoun and its antecedent participate in a reference point relationship, the former occurring in the latter's dominion. Viewing can then be seen as relevant not only in the general sense that the use of reference points is a viewing phenomenon, but also because the likelihood of an entity being adopted as a reference point increases when it itself is a viewer. Since a viewer (V) makes mental contact with the target (T) being viewed, conceiving of a viewing relationship (V ---> T) encourages the conceptualizer (C) to follow a coaligned mental path that also leads from V to T. If C to some degree apprehends the inherent asymmetry and directionality of the viewing relationship, to that extent at least C must access T via V, which makes V a reference point.

The overall scheme of van Hoek's account is roughly as follows. Semantically, a pronoun portrays its referent as being immediately accessible in the current, shared discourse context, whereas a full nominal implies the contrary (cf. Chafe 1987). To be accessible is to be in the dominion of a currently active reference point, which—in the case of explicit pronoun-antecedent relationships—is coded by the antecedent. Every nominal offers itself as a potential reference point to be used for the construal of other nominal elements in the surrounding linguistic context. Whether a given nominal will succeed in establishing itself in this manner, and the extent of the context over which it holds sway, are determined by a multiplicity of factors, including the salience of the would-be reference point, the nature of its conceptual connections with other elements, and a large set of constructional schemas which specify conventional reference point configurations. The reference point organization which thus arises constitutes one aspect of an expression's semantic value. This aspect of an expression's meaning may either harmonize or be in conflict with the meanings of its component nominal elements (since reference points also figure in the semantic contrast between pronouns and full nominals). What linguists generally describe as "ungrammaticality" due to illicit pronoun-antecedent configurations is therefore characterized in this framework as a kind of semantic anomaly.

To be more precise about the nature of this anomaly, we must say something more about the meaning of pronouns and the reference point organization that pertains to them. The speech-event participants employ nominals (both pronouns and full nominal descriptions) to coordinate mental reference to "things" within the conceptual domains evoked in the current discourse. Every nominal designates some instance of a thing type that may have many distinct instantiations (FCG2: ch. 2). Consequently, for purposes of negotiating nominal referents and assessing pronoun-antecedent configurations, the pool of entities from which reference points and targets are drawn comprises the vast array of thing instances that—in the current situation— could reasonably be invoked as a nominal's intended profile. A nominal's *referential dominion* is then a subset of this array (a dominion being defined as the set of possible targets accessible via a given reference point).[22]

To take a brief example, suppose someone says *I finally bought a car*. The direct object nominal profiles an instance of the thing type *car*; by using the nominal, the speaker induces the addressee to establish mental contact with that instance (i.e. single it out for individual conscious awareness). Once that instance is mentally invoked, it provides immediate access to many other thing instances representing other thing types. The speaker might continue by saying *The motor has been rebuilt,* which is understood as meaning that the motor in question is the one in the car he just bought. The definite article indicates that a unique instance of the thing type *motor* is immediately accessible to both speech-event participants, and the previous reference to a car has made such an instance available given the shared world knowledge that every car has just one motor. Having mentioned the car, the speaker can likewise continue by referring to *the steering wheel, the trunk, the dealer, the warrantee, the price*, etc., whose intended referents instantiate different thing types and are singled out from other instances of those types by virtue of their association with the car already accessed. That instance of *car* thus functions as a reference point, and the associated instances of *motor, steering wheel, trunk, dealer*, etc. are among the potential nominal referents that constitute its referential dominion.

The example is not unlike (14), where *my Rolls Royce* functions as a discourse topic with respect to a series of succeeding sentences (until replaced by a new topic, *my Mercedes*):

(14) **My Rolls Royce** *is getting to be a problem. The tires are losing air. The brakes are starting to go. The radiator is leaking. One headlight is burned out. The ashtrays are full. On the other hand,* **my Mercedes** *has been no trouble at all...*

And indeed, a discourse topic defines a referential dominion for nominals appearing in these sentences: the tires, brakes, radiator, etc. referred to in (14) are interpreted as belonging to the speaker's Rolls Royce. The topic thus has a tacit possessor role, which can be made explicit by means of possessor pronouns (e.g. *Its tires are losing air*). This is an indication of the close relationship among topics, possessors, and antecedents, all of which are analyzed in CG as nominal reference points. How, then, can they be distinguished?

A possessor can be distinguished from the other two on the basis of their *structural dominion*, defined as the structural context over which they hold sway as the primary reference point. Whereas a typical possessive construction is local, holding within a single nominal, a prototypical topic has a clause, sentence, or larger stretch of discourse for its structural dominion. Antecedents are similar to topics in that their structural dominion can be of virtually any size, ranging from local configurations to substantial stretches of discourse. It is further suggestive that topics are often antecedents for pronouns occurring in the contexts they govern:

(15) *Jill just bought* **a Rolls Royce.** *She drives* **it** *everywhere.* **It** *has tinted windows and Moroccan leather seats.*

One difference pertains to the nature of their targets: a topic (in the classical sense) serves as a reference point with respect to propositions, and a pronominal antecedent with respect to things. In (15), for example, *a Rolls Royce* is a topic in relation to the clause *She drives it everywhere*, but bears a relationship of antecedence just to the object pronoun *it*.[23] Of course, the essential property that differentiates antecedence from both topic and possessive relations is that a pronoun and its antecedent are *coreferential* (i.e. they profile the same thing instance). Following van Hoek, I ascribe this to the special semantic value of pronouns, whose occurrence in the dominion of a salient reference point constitutes a central and intrinsic aspect of their meaning.

A pronoun's meaning has a number of facets, roughly sketched in Figure 7.13. It profiles a thing, whose schematic characterization is limited to person, number, and comparable specifications. It is also definite, incorporating the supposition that the speech-event participants have immediate access to the intended referent. A further property concerns the way in which access to the referent is achieved: a pronoun invokes the discourse context and equates its profile with some entity which is salient in that context. We can say that it includes, as an unprofiled portion of its base, a reference point relationship in which the schematic reference point, R, is portrayed as being salient in the discourse context, hence available to serve in that capacity. It is further specified that the pronoun's referent falls within R's dominion, which implies its immediate accessibility to C in the current discourse state. Finally, the profiled target bears another relation to R that sets it apart from other elements in R's dominion: R and T are equated, as indicated by the dotted correspondence line. More precisely, they are construed as two representations of the same thing instance.

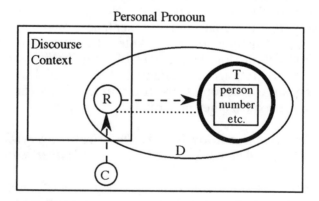

Personal Pronoun

Figure 7.13

A pronoun thus incorporates a *degenerate* reference point relationship in which R and T—normally distinct—collapse on a single entity. This limiting case can be seen as privileged if not expected, for of all the entities potentially accessible from R, the most easily accessible is R itself, which is already focused and lies at zero distance. Internally, however, a pronoun's characterization of R and the discourse context is quite schematic; it is only in particular expressions and usage events that they assume specific values. By itself a pronoun merely contributes the notion of a salient reference point and thereby creates the expectation that the context will provide one. With first- and second-person pronouns, which identify R with speech-event participants, the latter's omnipresence as primary conceptualizers and default-case reference points ensures that this expectation will be satisfied under normal circumstances of language use. Hence the degeneracy of the reference point relationship is carried even further: not only is R equated with T, but R and T are further identified with C.

With third-person pronouns, the availability of a salient discourse referent is more contingent. An appropriate reference point is sometimes provided by the non-linguistic context. If we are walking down the street, for example, and see a man running after a departing bus, I can felicitously utter *He'll never catch it*, even though neither the man nor the bus has been mentioned in the previous discourse (cf. Hankamer and Sag 1976). When the reference point is specified linguistically, the nominal seized upon for this purpose is the one we recognize as the pronoun's antecedent. The pronoun-antecedent relationship resides in a correspondence established between the profile of the nominal and the pronoun's schematic reference point.

6.2. Pronoun-antecedent configurations

As noted, every nominal offers itself as a potential reference point available for the construal of other elements. Various factors — including its salience, how it is connected to other elements, and linguistic convention as embodied in constructional schemas — determine whether a given nominal succeeds in establishing itself as a reference point, and if so, the extent of its structural dominion (the structural context in which it prevails over other candidates and exerts its influence). An antecedent can now be described as a nominal whose structural dominion contains a pronoun whose reference point is put in correspondence with its profile. Thus the nominal holds sway over the pronoun in the specific sense of imposing its own reference on it.

Suppose, then, that one nominal succeeds in establishing itself as a reference point, and is thus available for purposes of determining

reference. Suppose further that another nominal, understood as designating the same thing instance, occurs in its structural dominion. This
is the kind of configuration that supports a felicitous pronoun-antecedent relationship, but whether the resulting expression will actually
be judged well-formed depends on the nominals chosen in the two
positions and how well their intrinsic semantics matches this reference
point organization. Consider the topic construction in (16). A topic is
by definition a reference point, and the sentences instantiate a constructional schema which specifically indicates that the following
clause is in the structural dominion of the topic nominal. This struc-
turally correlated reference point alignment virtually demands the
kinds of lexical choices made in (16)a, where the topic is a full
nominal and a pronoun occurs in its structural dominion, as the
clausal subject. The topic specifies the intended pronominal reference
by means of a correspondence between its profile and the pronoun's
reference point.

(16) a. *My new Rolls, it always breaks down.*
     b. **?My new Rolls, my new Rolls always breaks down.*
     c. **?It, it always breaks down.*
     d. **It, my new Rolls always breaks down.*

   Any other combination of lexical choices produces some measure of incompatibility between their own semantic values and the
ones imposed by the structural frame. Recall that a full nominal
presents its referent as *not* being immediately accessible in the current
discourse context. Hence the unreduced subject in (16)b implies that
the Rolls needs to be rendered accessible, whereas the topic has
already established it as such. The opposite problem arises in (16)c.
Here the subject pronoun portrays its referent as accessible by virtue
of being identified with a contextually salient reference point, and the
construction indicates that the preceding topic functions in that capacity. However, the topic nominal is itself a pronoun and fails to
supply an appropriate referent; like the subject, it invokes the notion
of a salient reference point but is too schematic to direct attention to
any particular thing instance.[24] Finally, the semantic values of the
topic and subject nominals in (16)d are precisely the opposite of what
the construction demands. The topic is supposed to specify the intended referent, but the nominal chosen (the pronoun *it*) asks for one
instead. Conversely, while the construction implies that the subject
should not have to introduce the referent, its unreduced form (*my new*

Rolls) indicates that it does. The expression's ill-formedness—a standard case of "ungrammaticality" deriving from an illicit pronoun-antecedent configuration—is thus in the final analysis a matter of semantic anomaly.

Obviously, the crucial problem is to elucidate the specific factors whose interaction determines the rise and fall of reference points and the extent of their structural dominions. This is the primary focus of van Hoek's analysis, of which the remainder of this section constitutes a brief summary of just a few central points; the intent is merely to show its relevance to certain notions presented earlier.[25] Perhaps the most general statement to be made is that an element tends to establish itself as a reference point with respect to others that it precedes along some *natural path* (i.e. a cognitively natural ordering). Alternatively, we can say that an element tends to establish itself as a reference point to the extent that it is salient with respect to others. These two formulations are, I think, ultimately equivalent, since precedence along a natural path amounts to a kind of salience, and since any dimension of salience defines a natural path reflecting the ranking of elements along it. The problem is thus to ascertain which particular natural paths (or salience rankings) contribute to establishing reference points for purposes of pronominal anaphora, as well as the relative strength of their contributions.

We have already noted the advantage that being a viewer confers on a potential reference point. The effect of linear (temporal) order is well known, though less powerful than one might think and usually outweighed by other factors. One such factor is profiling, whose manifestations include the asymmetry between a main clause (a profile determinant) and a subordinate clause (whose profile is overridden at a higher level of organization). Both sentences in (17) are thus acceptable, for in each case the antecedent is able to establish itself as a reference point by preceding the pronoun along a natural path: the path based on linear order in (17)a, and the asymmetry between main and subordinate clause in (17)b.

(17) a. *If Jack has any sense, he won't go out in this rain.*
      b. *If he has any sense, Jack won't go out in this rain.*

In both examples the antecedent's salience is further enhanced by its status as clausal subject. The natural path *subject > object > oblique* reflects the salience of clausal participants with respect to figure/ground alignment (*primary figure > secondary figure >*

ground) and proves to be a factor of considerable strength. Hence the subject readily serves as a reference point for a direct object or an oblique nominal, and a direct object for an oblique, as in (18).

(18) a. ***The kitten** always follows **its** mother.*
      b. *I brought **the kitten** back to **its** mother.*

(19) a. **It* always follows **the kitten's** mother.*
      b. **I brought **it** back to **the kitten's** mother.*

The effect is strong enough that an inappropriate choice of nominals, as in (19), results in a judgment of anomaly under most circumstances.

An especially strong effect is associated with what van Hoek calls a *complement chain*: an ordered set of structures {A > B > C > D > ...}, where B is a complement of A, C a complement of B, and so on. A complement chain is a natural path whose biasing influence on the choice of reference point is hard to override. If A and B are clauses, then a nominal in the main clause is readily chosen as a reference point whose structural dominion encompasses the complement clause, but not conversely; hence the judgments in (20). On the other hand, if B is not a complement of A but rather a modifier, as in (21), it becomes at least marginally possible to establish the subordinate-clause nominal as the reference point. A sentence like (21)b might therefore be acceptable in an appropriate discourse context.[26]

(20) a. ***Bill** just wouldn't believe that **he** was confused.*
      b. **He* just wouldn't believe that **Bill** was confused.*

(21) a. ***Bill** just wouldn't leave, because **he** was confused.*
      b. **?He* just wouldn't leave, because **Bill** was confused.*

The contrast is much more evident for complements and modifiers that are preposed to the main clause; van Hoek argues that in this position they more easily escape the dominion of a main-clause nominal. Thus (22)b, where the antecedent is in a preposed complement, is noticeably better than (20)b. The essential point, however, is that (23)b is completely unproblematic.

(22) a. *That **he** was confused **Bill** just wouldn't believe.*
      b. **?That **Bill** was confused **he** just wouldn't believe.*

(23) a. *Because **he** was confused, **Bill** just wouldn't leave.*
     b. *Because **Bill** was confused, **he** just wouldn't leave.*

Unlike a complement, a preposed modifier is roughly comparable to the main clause in its likelihood of hosting a nominal reference point.

But why should complement status have the strong effect it does in determining reference point organization? The answer resides in the conceptual characterization of complement and modifier constructions as involving different kinds of viewing relationships. We described these earlier by invoking the transparency metaphor, sketched in Figure 7.3(b): the viewer observes the composite image through the stacked transparencies representing the component structures. Corresponding entities are aligned,[27] and the viewer's attention is focused on the composite structure profile; this usually coincides with the profile of one component, which is thus the head. The component images project to overlapping portions of the composite image. The distinction between a complement and a modifier can then be described in terms of whether the projection of the head subsumes that of the non-head component, or conversely, as shown in Figure 7.4. In a complement construction, the viewer observes the entire non-head component through the transparency representing the head (i.e. a complement elaborates a salient substructure of the head). On the other hand, in a modifier construction (where the head elaborates a salient structure of the modifier) major elements of the non-head component are accessible by a line of sight that does not pass through that transparency.

Complementation has such a strong effect on reference point alignment precisely because the complement is fully prefigured by the head, which provides the "lens" through which the complement is viewed. This viewing arrangement is sketched in Figure 7.14(a). Heavy lines indicate the profiled main-clause relationship, one of whose participants is the relationship designated by the complement clause (unprofiled at the composite structure level). The arrangement is such that the only path to the complement's projection (represented by the smaller dashed box) leads through the projection of the head (the larger dashed box), whose focal point is the profiled process. Since the complement is accessed via the main-clause process, it is virtually inevitable that a central participant in that process will establish itself as a reference point vis-à-vis an element of the subordinate clause, rather than conversely. This results in the well-formedness of (20)a and (22)a, in contrast to (20)b and (22)b.

(a) Complement Clause Construction

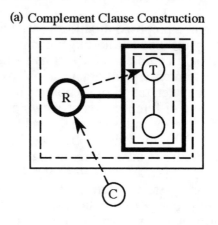

(b) Modifier Clause Construction   (c) Modifier Clause Construction

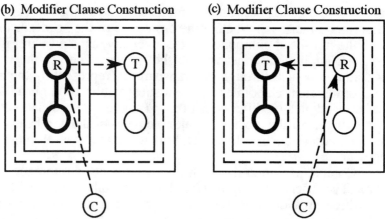

Figure 7.14

With a modifier construction, on the other hand, the head's projection is subsumed by that of the modifier, as shown in Figures 7.14(b) and (c). Suppose, for sake of concreteness, that the modifier is a *because*-clause. The horizontal line in these diagrams then represents the *because* relationship, whose trajector is elaborated by the main clause, and its landmark by the subordinate clause. The main clause is the one whose profile prevails at the composite structure level. Because the main-clause process is still the point of focus, one of its participants can perfectly well establish itself as a reference point, as in diagram (b). This results in sentences like (21)a and (23)a, where the target is a participant in the unprofiled subordinate process. It is not the case, however, that all elements of the modifier are saliently prefigured by the head and hence accessible only via that route. Since the modifier's projection extends beyond the head's, portions of it can be reached directly by a path that does not go through the head. Under the proper circumstances, therefore, a non-head element has the potential to establish itself as a reference point, as in diagram (c). Sentences like (23)b arise in this fashion.

7. Conclusion

I hardly need emphasize the preliminary, even impressionistic nature of certain ideas presented in this chapter. At the same time, I feel it raises valid issues of broad scope and fundamental importance. There are few linguists who have not been tempted to speak of "viewing" (or something comparable) in regard to aspects of language structure that do not involve vision in any literal sense, and few aspects of linguistic structure for which some such description has not suggested itself. I have tried to present a way of conceiving and talking about such phenomena in a coherent, integrated manner. It has, I hope, been demonstrated that specific constructs relating to viewing can in principle be devised, used for the explicit characterization of linguistic data, and empirically justified by their descriptive utility.

Chapter 8
Generic constructions

It is well known that generic sentences can assume a variety of forms, some of which are exemplified in (1).*

(1) a. *Cats stalk birds.*
 b. *A cat stalks a bird.*
 c. *Every cat stalks birds.*

One of my objectives is to reconcile the overt forms of these expressions with their meanings. I suggest that they have different meanings, even when each is used to make a generic statement of universal validity. Another objective is to explain a rather striking difference in their grammatical behavior. With a plural generic, it is possible to use the progressive to signal that the generic property holds for only a limited span of time, as specified by the adverb *these days* in (2)a. A progressive with this import is not however possible with singular generics, as seen in (2)b. Such expressions are also bad with *every*, though not to the same degree.

(2) a. *Cats are being born with extra toes these days.*
 b. **A cat is being born with extra toes these days.*
 c. *?*Every cat is being born with extra toes these days.*

1. Higher-order entities

An expression profiles either a *thing* or a *relationship*, each term being understood in an abstract technical sense (FCG1: part II; CIS: ch. 3). Abbreviatory notations are given in Figure 8.1. Especially important here is our manifest ability to conceive of *higher-order* things and relationships. Clearly, we are able to construe a number of component things as collectively constituting a higher-order thing that functions as a unitary entity for linguistic purposes. Such an entity functions, for example, as the profiled referent of terms like *group, stack, pile,* etc. Likewise, we are able to conceive of a number of component relationships (events, states, etc.) as collectively constituting a higher-order relationship; e.g. *Three boys ran up the hill* profiles a higher-order event comprising three component events.

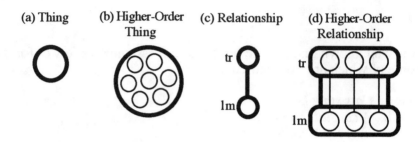

Figure 8.1

Recall that the participants in a relational expression are accorded varying degrees of prominence. One participant is singled out as the *trajector* (tr), i.e. as the primary figure in the profiled relationship. At the clausal level, the trajector is manifested by the subject. Often another participant is accorded a lesser degree of focal prominence. This is called a *landmark* (lm), i.e. the secondary figure in a profiled relationship. A clausal object manifests the landmark at that level. Importantly for our purposes, the trajector (or the landmark) of a higher-order relationship is the higher-order thing comprising the trajectors (or the landmarks) of the component relationships. This is shown in Figure 8.1(d).

The relationship profiled by a verb or a finite clause is called a *process*. As described in the preceding chapter (section 4), a process can either be *perfective* or *imperfective*, depending on whether it is construed as being temporally bounded within the immediate scope of predication. The progressive construction derives an imperfective from a perfective by imposing on the latter a more restrictive immediate scope that excludes its endpoints. The processual profile is necessarily limited to what appears in the immediate scope, and the progressive construes it as being internally homogeneous (in accordance with the mass-like character of imperfectives). Important for us is the fact that a higher-order process can also be either perfective or imperfective, as shown in Figure 8.2. A higher-order process of either type comprises an indefinite number of perfective event instances, which are not individually profiled and do not occupy any specific position along the temporal axis; internally, the higher-order process is mass-like, whether it is bounded or unbounded. If it is bounded and hence perfective, it can take the progressive, which imposes an "internal perspective" on the higher-order process just as it does on a simple event.[1]

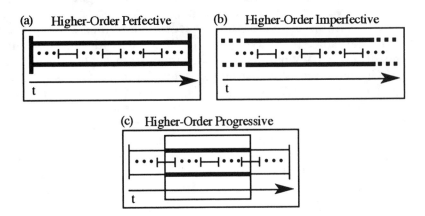

Figure 8.2

2. Plural generics

I analyze habituals, repetitives, and plural generics as profiling higher-order relationships. We have already noted that generics can profile either a perfective or an imperfective process, as respectively exemplified in (2)a and (1)a. Habituals as well can either be perfective or imperfective, indicating temporary vs. open-ended habituality. If perfective, they require the progressive for present-time reference:

(3) a. *My cat stalks that bird every morning.*
     b. *My cat is stalking that bird every morning again.*

By contrast, a repetitive is always construed as bounded. For present-time reference, the progressive is therefore necessary:

(4) a. *At this very moment, Jane is repeatedly ringing the doorbell.*
     b. **At this very moment, Jane repeatedly rings the doorbell.*

For a variety of reasons (discussed more fully in Langacker 1997d), generics and habituals can be grouped as *general validity predications*. The situation they describe may hold for either a bounded or an unbounded span of time, i.e. their validity has a temporal scope. An indefinite, potentially open-ended set of instances of the basic event type can occur within that scope. General validity predications do not however profile these instances, but rather the higher-order relationship (of genericity/habituality) that they constitute or manifest.

This initial characterization needs to be refined and clarified. In particular, since repetitives also profile higher-order relationships, we need to specify what distinguishes them from generics and habituals. Crucial here is a distinction argued for by Goldsmith and Woisetschlaeger (1982: 80): "...Use of the progressive marks a distinction which we shall call the 'structural/phenomenal' distinction, and which corresponds to two rather different types of knowledge about the world...One may describe the world in either of two ways: by describing what things happen in the world, or by describing how the world is made that such things may happen in it." They claimed that one value of the progressive is to express *phenomenal* (as opposed to *structural*) knowledge:

(5) a. <u>Phenomenal</u>: *This engine isn't smoking anymore.*
            [actual or temporarily structural]
      b. <u>Structural</u>: *This engine doesn't smoke anymore.*
            [structural (indefinite scope)]

They are making basically the right distinction, but I believe they are wrong in attributing it to the progressive per se. Note that (5)a can in fact be either phenomenal or structural, i.e. an actual ongoing occurrence or a temporary habitual. Thus my own descriptions of the examples are given below in brackets. I will use the word *actual* in lieu of "phenomenal".

On my account, the progressive is merely symptomatic of perfectivity (bounding), rather than directly coding the actual/nonactual (or phenomenal/structural) contrast. That contrast is not specifically marked in English by any morphological element. The notion of non-actuality ("structural knowledge") reflects an idealized cognitive model to be called the *structured world model*: the notion that the world has a stable structure providing a kind of framework for the occurrence of actual events. One obvious manifestation of this ICM is in science. The western scientific tradition is based on the notion that the world works in a certain way, that there is such a thing as scientific truth, that some claims about the world are false, and that valid experimental results can be replicated.

For representational purposes, I will distinguish between the *actual plane* and the *structural plane*. Instances of a given event type can be found on either plane. The actual plane comprises event instances that are conceived as actually occurring. Crucially, however, the requisite notion of actuality is independent of time and modal status: an actual event's occurrence may be a matter of either past reality or future potentiality, it may be asserted or denied, etc. On the other hand, the structural plane comprises event instances with no status in actuality. These instances are conceived merely for purposes of characterizing "how the world is made". They have no existence outside the structural plane, which can be thought of metaphorically as "blueprints" for the world's structure.

Event instances in the structural plane will be described as *arbitrary*. An arbitrary instance of a type is one "conjured up" just for some local purpose, with no status outside the *mental space* (in the sense of Fauconnier 1985) thus created. Arbitrary instances figure in numerous linguistic phenomena (FCG2). Consider (6), for example.

(6) *Zelda wants to buy a fur coat.*

On the non-specific interpretation, there is no particular coat that Zelda wants to buy. The instance referred to is an arbitrary one, an instance "conjured up" just for purposes of characterizing the nature of Zelda's desire. It has no existence or status outside the mental space representing her desire. Similarly, events in the structural plane represent arbitrary instances conjured up just for purposes of characterizing the world's structure.

We are now able to characterize the similarities and differences among the sentence types in (7):

(7) a. <u>Repetitive</u>: *My cat repeatedly stalked that bird.*
     b. <u>Habitual</u>: *My cat stalks that bird every morning.*
     c. <u>Plural generic</u>: *Cats stalk birds.*

A *repetitive* profiles a higher-order event residing in the actual plane, whereas habituals and plural generics—grouped as general validity predications—profile higher-order events in the structural plane. The basic structure of a repetitive, like (7)a, is diagrammed in Figure 8.3.

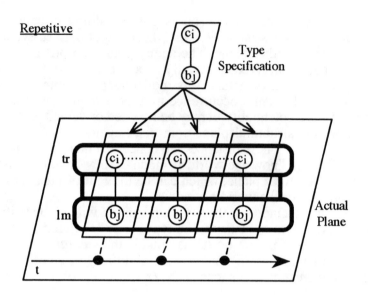

Figure 8.3

The sentence profiles a higher-order event comprising multiple instances of the same event type, namely *my cat stalk that bird*. Observe that the common type specification of these event instances refers to specific individuals: a particular cat (c_i) and a particular bird (b_j). Dotted correspondence lines indicate that the same individual functions as the trajector of each component event instance, and the same individual as the landmark of each such instance. Because these event instances belong to the actual plane, they are anchored to particular points in time. It is however the higher-order event that is profiled; (7)a does not designate a single, atomic instance of bird-stalking, but a complex event consisting of multiple component instances.

The basic structure of habitual expressions like (7)b is sketched in Figure 8.4. Once again the event type specifies an interaction between particular individuals, so the same individuals figure in each component event instance. And it is once more the higher-order relationship that is profiled. The contrast with repetitives lies in the fact that this profiled relationship occupies the structural rather than the actual plane. Hence the component events are not anchored to any particular points in time. It is merely specified that the occurrence of multiple instances of the type *my cat stalk that bird* is characteristic of the world's structure.

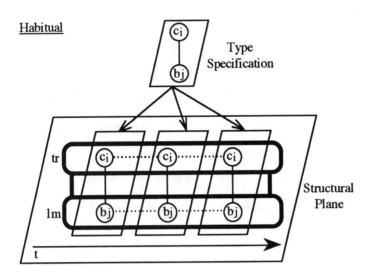

Figure 8.4

Lastly, a plural generic like (7)c has the structure shown in Figure 8.5. Here the type specification does not refer to particular individuals, but only to the thing types *cat* (c) and *bird* (b). There are no correspondence lines because there is no supposition that any two event instances have the same trajector or the same landmark. Otherwise a plural generic is analogous to a habitual, profiling a higher-order relationship in the structural plane. That is, one facet of the world's structure is the occurrence of multiple instances of the event type *cat stalk bird.*

Observe that, in regard to number, the forms of these sentences fall out from their semantic characterizations. The singular subjects and objects in (7)a-b reflect the incorporation in the type specification of reference to specific individuals. Because the trajectors and landmarks of the component events thus collapse to a single cat and a single bird, respectively, the higher-order trajector and landmark each consist of just a single individual. This is not so with a plural generic, where different individuals presumably participate in each event instance. In that case the higher-order trajector consists of multiple cats, and the higher-order landmark of multiple birds.

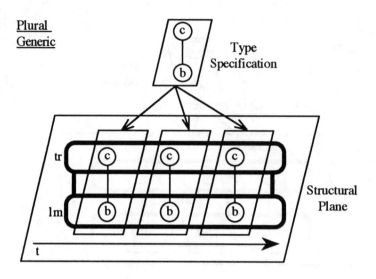

Figure 8.5

3. Quantifier constructions

Let us now return to the fact that generic statements assume a variety of forms, as seen in (1). I presume that these differences in form correspond to subtle differences in meaning, even though all three kinds of sentences make universal statements about the members of a class. These kinds of generics impose different construals, i.e. they use different strategies for indicating that the ascription of a property has general validity for the class in question. While all of them evoke the structured world model, they differ in what they choose for their profile and focal participants. I will try to show that the differential ability of generic constructions to take the progressive (for indicating temporary genericity) falls out from the semantic characterization suggested by the contrasting grammatical forms.

The examples in (2) actually represent only part of a broader pattern. Plural generics with a zero determiner belong to a paradigm with those taking the quantifiers *all*, *most*, and *some*. As seen in (8), these pattern alike in allowing both open-ended generics and temporary generics signaled by the progressive:

(8) a. *{All/Most/Some/Ø} cats die before the age of 15.*
   b. *{All/Most/Some/Ø} cats are dying before the age of 15*
      these days.

By contrast, singular generics with the indefinite article belong to a paradigm with those taking the quantifiers *every* and *any*. From (9), we see that these only allow open-ended generics; temporary generics in the progressive are precluded.

(9) a. *{Every/Any/A} cat dies before the age of 15.*
   b. *{?*Every/*Any/*A} cat is dying before the age of 15*
      these days.

Why *every* works better in this construction than *any* or *a* can also be explained in terms of the proposed description.

The description hinges on a proper conceptual analysis of the semantics of these quantifiers (FCG2: ch. 3). *All, most, some,* and *Ø* are *proportional quantifiers*. They profile a set of entities (P) characterized as some proportion of the *reference mass* (R_T), i.e. the set of all instances of the nominal category (T). In the case of *all*, P coincides with R_T. With *most*, the boundaries of P approximate those of R_T. *Some* indicates that P is non-empty. *Ø* is neutral in regard to proportion, allowing a universal construal (P = R_T) as a special case.

These notions are sketched in Figure 8.6, taking *most* as a specific example. The two conceived masses P and R_T each consist of instances of the thing type T. *Most* indicates that P comes close to exhausting R_T but does not quite match its full extension.

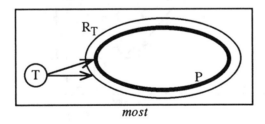

most

Figure 8.6

On the other hand, *every, any,* and *a* are *representative-instance quantifiers*. That is, they profile a single, arbitrary instance of the category, but one which is somehow guaranteed to be representative of it. Universal coverage is achieved indirectly, via this notion of representativeness, even though just one member of the class is actually mentioned. *Any* implies random selection from the reference mass (if an instance from R_T is chosen at random, it will exhibit the property in question). *Every* specifically construes the profiled instance against the background of a set of equivalent instances conceived as exhausting R_T. *A* is more neutral but allows the construal of representativeness as a special case.

A representative-instance quantifier is diagrammed in Figure 8.7, with *every* chosen for illustration. The box on the left is taken as specifying a type of relationship, and the circle on the right (T), a type of thing. Only one instance of that thing type is actually profiled by *every* (or by a nominal such as *every cat*), but that instance is specifically conceived against the background of other instances construed as being exhaustive of R_T. Besides instantiating the same thing type, they are equivalent in the sense that each participates in an instance of the same type of relationship. In this way the arbitrary instance of T singled out for profiling achieves the representativeness responsible for the quantifier's universality.

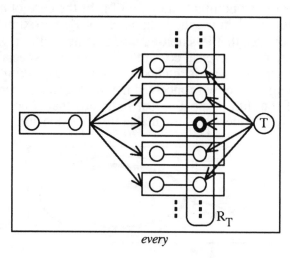

every

Figure 8.7

The crucial point is that proportional quantifiers profile a set of entities, whereas representative-instance quantifiers profile a single, albeit representative instance. Directly reflecting this difference is the plural vs. singular contrast in the nouns they quantify. Their use in generics, where they quantify the subject of a clause, is respectively diagrammed in Figures 8.8 and 8.9. Figure 8.8 corresponds to sentences like those in (8), where the profiled higher-order process can either be bounded or open-ended (hence the heavy dashed lines). Note that the trajector is characterized as a proportion of the reference mass, the specific proportion depending on the quantifier chosen. The point to observe is that the profiled relationship is the higher-order, collective process, and that this process may—as one option—be bounded (perfective), yielding a temporary generic. Under this option the progressive appears with the present tense, as in (8)b, in accordance with regular patterns of English.

Generic Construction: Proportional Quantifier

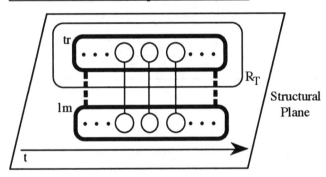

Figure 8.8

On the other hand, Figure 8.9 exemplifies the generic use of representative-instance quantifiers, with *every* chosen once more for specific illustration. A sentence like *Every cat dies before the age of 15* profiles a single, arbitrary instance of dying in the structural plane (on the part of a single, arbitrary cat), but portrays this event (and this cat) as being representative. The expressions in (9)a are therefore possible as full generics. However, the configuration in Figure 8.9 does not support the progressive, which takes an internal perspective on a profiled perfective process. Here only a single instance of the basic event type is profiled; the notion of a higher-order process remains implicit and unprofiled. Because the progressive cannot impose its internal perspective on the higher-order process constituting a bounded episode of genericity, expressions like (9)b are not available as temporary generics.

Generic Construction: Representative-Instance Quantifier

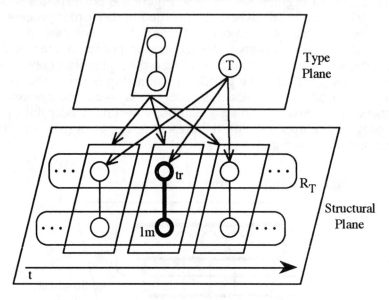

Figure 8.9

Why does *every* work better than *any* or *a*, as indicated in (9)b? The reason is that *every* makes salient reference to multiple event instances, implying a higher-order event, even though only one component event is in profile. Strictly speaking, the progressive requires a profiled perfective process on which to impose its limited temporal scope, but at least with *every* a higher-order relationship is present, since the profiled event is specifically construed in relation to others of the same type. By contrast, *any* (involving the notion of random selection) and *a* (intrinsically singular) focus exclusively on just one event instance. Their representativeness implies the possibility of other instances, but any notion of a higher-order event comprising multiple instances remains latent or at least farther in the background.

Observe that singular generics in the progressive improve when the object is made plural:

(10) a. *?Every cat is stalking birds these days.*
      b. *??Any cat is stalking birds these days.*
      c. *?*A cat is stalking birds these days.*

The reason, I think, is that a generic statement usually implies habituality on the part of any given individual. In saying that cats stalk birds, it is contemplated that a single cat does so habitually. Hence there are multiple instances of bird-stalking on the part of a single cat, distributed through time, and collectively these instances can be construed as constituting a higher-order event of the sort required for the progressive. With a plural object, this latent higher-order event is brought to the fore, since the plurality reflects multiple instances of the event type. In other words, the progressive in (10) may pertain in some fashion to the habituality ascribable to each member of the set of cats, rather than to the genericity per se. The judgments are clearest when this possibility is eliminated, when the nature of the event is such that any one member of the class can participate in just one instance of the event type, as in (2) [*be born with extra toes*] and (9) [*die before the age of 15*]. However, a much more extensive and systematic survey of actual data will be needed to clarify the status and interpretation of such examples.

Chapter 9
Grouping and pronominal anaphora

A CG account of pronominal anaphora was discussed at some length in Chapter 7 (section 6).* The present chapter continues the discussion by exploring pronoun-antecedent relationships in sentences involving "special" phenomena such as genericity, quantifier scope, and "sloppy identity". It reinforces the basic claim that restrictions on the location of a pronoun vis-à-vis its antecedent are best described in terms of conceptual (rather than purely syntactic) configurations. Crucial to semantic and grammatical organization are various kinds of conceptual groupings that need not coincide with the ones accorded the status of syntactic constituents.

1. Interaction, grammar, and discourse

As a primary instrument of thought and communication, language is grounded in both cognition and social interaction. These facets of its dual basis are intimately related and ultimately indissociable. Communication takes place between cognizing individuals who apprehend their interaction and tailor their utterances to accommodate what they believe their interlocutors know and are capable of understanding. Conversely, much of our thought occurs through actual or imagined dialog and presupposes vast stores of knowledge established in large measure via linguistic interaction. Hence cognitive linguistics and functional linguistics (with its emphasis on discourse and social interaction) should be regarded as complementary and mutually dependent aspects of a single overall enterprise.

1.1. Negotiation and contextual understanding

From the outset, CG has strongly emphasized the contextual and interactive basis of language structure. It maintains that linguistic elements are learned through a process of progressive decontextualization, as features that recur across a series of *usage events* (i.e. apprehensions of actual utterances in their full phonetic detail and contextual understanding) are reinforced and thus abstracted from the remainder. Any facet of the interactive context has the potential to recur and thus establish itself (in schematized form) as either a central or peripheral aspect of an element's conventional value: affective factors, relation to the preceding discourse, social status of the interlocutors, etc. Moreover, the values of conventional units are neither static nor fully predetermined. A lexical item, for example, is quite unlike its standard metaphorical conception as a "container" holding a fixed quantity of a substance called "meaning"—it is better conceived as evoking certain realms of knowledge and experience (*cognitive domains*) in a flexible, open-ended manner (Reddy 1979; Haiman 1980). The precise value it assumes on a given occasion reflects the influence of surrounding elements (*accommodation*) and is negotiated by the interlocutors on the basis of their full, contextually grounded understandings.

The same holds for novel expressions assembled in accordance with conventional grammatical patterns. Language exhibits only *partial compositionality*: often if not always, the actual meaning of a complex expression is more elaborate than anything regularly derivable from the meanings of its component elements. It is therefore misleading to think of components as "building blocks" from which the meaning of the whole is constructed—their function is rather to evoke and symbolize certain facets of the integrated composite conception the speaker has in mind. Through general and contextual knowledge, the addressee can usually overcome the discrepancy between conventionally determined value and how an expression is actually understood. The gap is often substantial: the notions coded overtly may be quite limited compared to the implicit conceptual substructure providing their support and coherence.

Numerous theoretical constructs have been devised with reference to various aspects of this conceptual substratum. For my own purposes, it is useful to posit a mental space comprising those elements and relations construed as being shared by the speaker and addressee as a basis for communication at a given moment in the flow of discourse; I call this the *current discourse space* (FCG2: 3.1.1). The entities that constitute this space fall within the realm of current discussion and are immediately available to both interlocutors, who are either consciously aware of them or have ready access to them (e.g. by association or simple inference, or as obvious facets of general knowledge). The content of the current discourse space naturally changes as the discourse unfolds; new specifications are continually added, while others slowly fade from awareness. The situation that obtains at a given moment is roughly depicted in Figure 9.1, where the spaces labeled K_S and K_H represent the total knowledge of the speaker and the hearer. The current discourse space (CDS) consists of those portions of their knowledge which is both shared and immediately available.

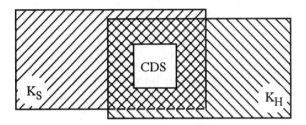

Figure 9.1

Another set of constructs pertain to the conceptualizations that function as the meanings of linguistic expressions. I use the term *maximal scope* (MS) for the full extent of the conceptual content an expression (e) evokes or presupposes as the basis for its meaning. As shown in Figure 9.2, an expression's maximal scope (MS_e) represents some portion of the speaker's knowledge (K_S); its relation to the hearer's knowledge and the current discourse space will be considered shortly. Within an expression's maximal scope, there is often a privileged subpart—called the *immediate scope* (IS)—comprising the content of direct current relevance. The immediate scope can be described metaphorically as the "onstage region", i.e. the general locus of attention. The term *profile* is used for the specific focus of attention. An expression's profile is the entity it designates, its referent within the conceptual *base* provided by its scope.

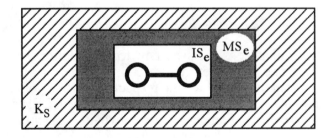

Figure 9.2

The connection between these two sets of constructs is shown initially in Figure 9.3. In using an expression, the speaker intends to evoke or convey a certain range of conceptual content that constitutes its maximal scope (at least as the speaker understands it). Whereas this conceptualization is necessarily part of the speaker's knowledge (K_S), it has no fixed position with respect to that of the hearer (K_H). The scope indicated in the diagram is probably typical of expressions exhibiting any substantial complexity: portions of it fall within the current discourse space (being active or immediately accessible); other portions represent dormant hearer knowledge that the utterance serves to activate; and still others were previously unknown. To the extent that the hearer apprehends the expression along the lines intended by the speaker, both hearer knowledge and the current discourse space expand to incorporate the newly available material. There is of course no guarantee that the hearer will actually understand it in this manner — the content of the current discourse space and the expression's import in relation to it are subject to disagreement and negotiation.

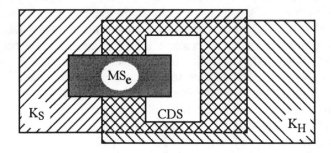

Figure 9.3

1.2. Incrementing the current discourse space

Various theoretical constructs pertain to the relation between an expression's scope and the current discourse space. The terms *given* and *new* are often employed for the respective portions of an expression's content that are and are not subsumed by the CDS, as sketched in Figure 9.4(a). Parts of an expression conveying content that is new and salient are collectively referred to as its *focus*. Here it will be convenient to adopt additional terms describing analogous facets of the evolving CDS. As shown in 9.4(b), *anchor* will indicate the content already part of the CDS which the expresssion evokes anew. Content which it adds to the CDS will be called the *increment*.

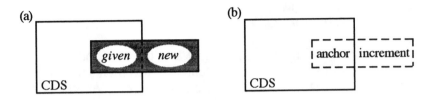

Figure 9.4

Consider the following simple (if not simplistic) example:

(1) *A boy and a girl were playing in the yard with their dog. The boy saw a cat.*

The first sentence establishes a current discourse space that incorporates several *participants* (the boy, the girl, and the dog) as well as a *setting* (the yard). Using circles for things and lines for relations, the CDS at this stage is depicted abstractly in the lefthand diagram of Figure 9.5. The middle diagram represents the apprehension of the second sentence, which profiles a relationship involving the boy and a cat. The effect of the utterance, shown in the righthand diagram, is to add this relation to the CDS. With respect to the meaning of the sentence (one facet of which is its construal in relation to the preceding discourse), we can say that the conception of the boy is given, whereas the event of seeing the cat is new. With respect to the CDS, the boy is the anchor providing the point of attachment for the increment, namely the process of seeing the cat in which the boy participates.

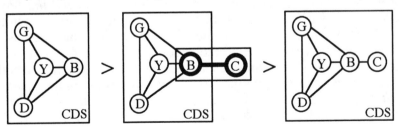

Figure 9.5

Naturally, either the anchor or the increment can be multi-faceted. Consider the discourse in (2):

(2) *A girl and a boy were walking together in the woods. The girl showed the boy some flowers.*

As represented in Figure 9.6, the girl and the boy both anchor the relationship with which the second sentence increments the CDS established by the first. That relationship is itself complex: the girl sees the flowers and communicates with the boy, who is thereby induced to see the flowers as well.

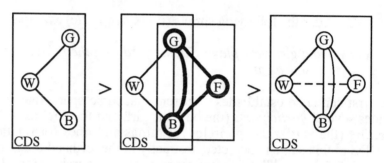

Figure 9.6

This example also illustrates partial compositionality and the essential contribution of general knowledge. The sentence in question would normally be understood as indicating that the flowers were in the woods; the dashed line in the derived CDS represents this relationship. This information is not however explicitly given in either sentence, nor can it be deduced by purely logical inference. Observe that if the second sentence were instead *The girl showed the boy a new constellation,* it would not follow that the constellation was in the woods. Moreover, it could be the case that the girl and boy were walking at the very edge of the woods, with the flowers in an adjoining meadow. The more usual interpretation—which places the flowers in the woods—emerges from interaction between the meaning of *show* (implying that the object shown is visible to both animate participants) and general knowledge of various kinds: knowing that flowers grow in the ground rather than the sky; default assumptions about the experience of walking in the woods; and canonical expectations about how far one can see as well as the relative size of the entities concerned.

1.3. Role of the composite conception

The speaker understands an expression in a certain way and intends for the addressee to interpret it in a comparable manner. The speaker's understanding of it constitutes an integrated conceptualization—the expression's maximal scope (MS_e)—whose relation to the current discourse space and hearer knowledge was diagrammed in Figure 9.3. The hearer's interpretation draws on multiple resources: the CDS, which provides an anchor for new information; general knowledge (including default expectations and inferencing ability); apprehension of the physical, social, and linguistic context; and the conventionally determined contribution of the expression itself. This contribution may be more limited than is generally assumed. As viewed in CG, an expression's *compositional* semantic value at best approximates its *actual* semantic value (i.e. the speaker's or the addressee's version of the MS_e). Conventional patterns of composition, applied to established values of component elements, yield a hypothetical structure (of uncertain cognitive status) that usually greatly underspecifies an expression's actual meaning. From this skeletal compositional value, the hearer uses the other resources listed above to arrive at the actual value, ideally the one the speaker intends. It is primarily this integrated conceptualization that provides the expression's coherence and determines the specific values attributed to the component elements.

A metaphor useful in thinking about partial compositionality was proposed in Chapter 7. Diagrammed in Figure 7.3, it involves a "viewer" (V) examining the integrated composite conception as if it were projected on a screen. Within this composite conception, the viewer's attention is focused on some entity (the profile). The component structures are drawn on plastic transparencies, which the viewer looks through in gazing at the composite image. Each transparency projects to a portion of the composite conception. The transparencies are not constitutive of the composite image but merely reinforce the elements subsumed by their projections and thus enhance their salience for the viewer. Typically the composite conception incorporates elements not included on either transparency. The components project to portions of the composite structure that generally overlap but fail to exhaust its content (the expression's maximal scope).

In terms of the transparency metaphor, the notion of *correspondence* reduces to something more basic: what it means for two component entities to correspond is that they project to the same entity in the composite conception. It is that conception which has primacy; the component structures are derivative in the sense of being artificially extracted from the integral whole to be individually symbolized for communicative purposes. Usually only selected portions are accorded this privilege: those deemed sufficient by the speaker to evoke the desired conception in the addressee, given the total discourse situation. As seen in Figures 9.5 and 9.6, they generally include both incremental knowledge and an anchor in the current discourse space to which the increment attaches.

We now have some of the apparatus needed to characterize pronominal anaphora. The "coreference" between a pronoun and its antecedent is basically a matter of their profiles projecting to the same entity in an overarching composite conception. The situation is depicted abstractly in Figure 9.7:

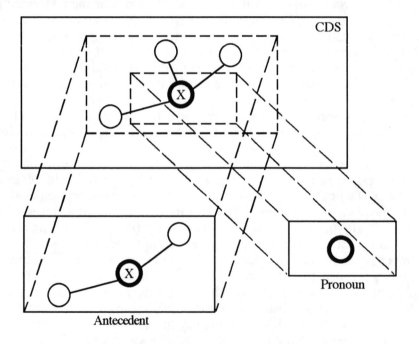

Figure 9.7

The antecedent and the pronoun are nominal expressions, each of which profiles a thing. The antecedent usually has lexical content (X in the diagram) and may specify relationships the referent bears to other entities. The semantic pole of the pronoun is quite schematic by comparison. It does however incorporate the supposition that its profile projects to an entity already salient in the current discourse space (whether established there by an antecedent expression, or merely apparent from the context). For a pronoun's use to be felicitous, the CDS must contain such an entity, whose specifications include those contributed by the antecedent (if there is one) as well as any others apparent from the context or general knowledge. This entity serves as the anchor for purposes of interpreting the pronoun. Usually, though, the pronoun fails to supply an increment— virtually as a matter of definition, the content of an anaphoric element is fully subsumed by its anchor.

2. Spaces, planes, and groupings

The standard approach to anaphora is to formulate constraints on the position of a pronoun vis-à-vis its antecedent in terms of classical constituent structure (Langacker 1969; Reinhart 1983). It was argued in Chapter 5, however, that classical constituency is neither fundamental nor consistently manifested. Rather it emerges as a special case from the more basic phenomena of conceptual grouping, phonological grouping, and symbolization. As described in Chapter 7 (section 6), a detailed CG account of pronominal anaphora— based on conceptual grouping rather than constituency— has been provided by van Hoek (1995, 1997a) and shown to be empirically advantageous. The reason syntactic tree structures seem relevant to anaphora is that constituency (when it emerges) represents an especially potent basis for conceptual grouping.

2.1. Spaces and constituency

By and large, "classical" constituents conform to the dictum that elements which "belong together semantically" tend to "occur together syntactically" (Behaghel's law). Their semantic togetherness resides in *conceptual overlap* involving salient substructures of the component elements. This usually involves a correspondence between (parts of) the component structure profiles, i.e. their projection to the same entity at the composite structure level (Figure 5.7). Syntactic togetherness is a matter of elements being contiguous and rhythmically cohesive in the phonological string. A classical constituent emerges just in case a conceptual grouping based on overlap happens to be symbolized by a phonological grouping based on linear contiguity. A standard constituency hierarchy (tree structure) results when classical constituents emerge at every level of organization and exhaust an expression's explicit content. However, not every potential conceptual grouping necessarily emerges, and those that do may not be symbolized in the classical manner, if at all. Numerous conceptual groupings that are not symbolized in any obvious or canonical way are nonetheless important to semantic and grammatical organization.

One kind of conceptual grouping is a *mental space*, defined by Fauconnier (1985: 16) as a structured set of elements and relations between them, such that new elements and new relations can be added as discourse unfolds. The CDS is one such object. Other clear examples are the world created by a fictive work, the hypothetical situation established by a conditional clause, and the space representing someone's thought, belief, or desire:

(3)   a. *In this novel, linguists rule the world.*
      b. *If the bus is late, we'll have to take a cab.*
      c. *With a supercomputer I believe we can solve that problem.*

Mental spaces need not coincide with grammatical constituents. In (3)b, for instance, the hypothetical space comprises everything following *if* (i.e. *the bus is late we'll have to take a cab*), which is not a syntactic constituent on anybody's account. In (3)c, the content of the belief space is manifested discontinuously (*with a supercomputer... we can solve that problem*).[1]

2.2. *Type plane*

For certain kinds of conceptual groupings (or mental spaces), it is perspicuous to speak metaphorically of distinct *planes* of representation (analogous to "tiers" in phonology). The groupings in question involve different sorts of generalizations abstracted from actuality (Langacker To appear-c). Along one dimension, we can distinguish between a *type plane* and an *instance plane*. Along another dimension, we need to distinguish various kinds of instance planes, among them the *actual plane* and the *structural plane* (Chapter 8).

The distinction between types and instances correlates with the grammatical contrast between lexical nouns and verbs, on the one hand, and full nominals and finite clauses, on the other. The former make *type specifications*: by itself, a lexical noun simply names a type of thing, and a lexical verb, a type of process. Thus *cat* and *love* respectively characterize a thing type and a process type; their role is merely classificatory. In contrast, a nominal or a finite clause has the discourse-related role of singling out an instance of the thing or process type and specifying its relation to the *ground* (the speech event and its participants). Tense and the modals effect the grounding of finite clauses in English. For nominals, grounding elements include the demonstratives, the articles, and certain quantifiers. Personal pronouns and proper names occur without such elements because a specification of their relation to the ground (person and definiteness) is inherent in their meaning.

Figure 9.8(a) shows the instantiation of a single thing type (T) by three thing instances (t_i, t_j, and t_k):

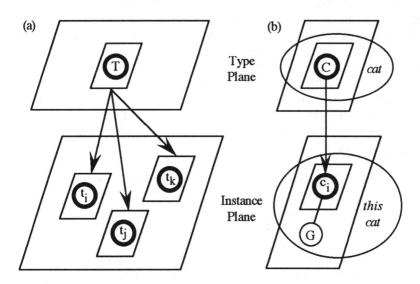

Figure 9.8

Their individual graphic depiction should not be taken as implying that the two planes are wholly distinct or necessarily have separate cognitive representations; indeed, a type specification is both abstracted from and immanent in the conception of instances. Proper linguistic description nevertheless requires the ability to refer to either the type or the instance level. Grounding pertains to instances, as shown in Figure 9.8(b), where G stands for the ground, and the line between

G and c_i indicates the grounding relationship (e.g. one of definiteness). A full nominal such as *this cat* therefore codes the lower configuration in 9.8(b), whereas a noun like *cat* by itself (or when incorporated as the first element of a compound, e.g. *cat-lover*) merely lexicalizes a type specification.

A type specification need not be limited to the simple conception of a thing or process. For example, the compound *cat-lover* lexicalizes a complex type specification that incorporates the content of three simpler ones: the thing type *cat*; the process type *love*; and the abstract thing type *-er*, which designates the trajector of a process specified only schematically. Regular nominalization and compounding patterns effect the integration of these elements to yield a higher-order type specification whose profile (conceptual referent) may then undergo instantiation and grounding. Alternatively, this higher-order type can be incorporated as part of an even more complex type specification, such as *cat-lover hater* ('hater of cat lovers'). There is clearly no limit, as we can go on to form ungrounded compounds evoking type specifications of indefinite complexity (e.g. *cat-lover hater behavior modification school instructor*).

The metaphor of "planes" must not obscure the fact that type and instance specifications intermingle in various ways. Within expressions, their manifestations do not always coincide with grammatical constituents and may even be discontinuous. Consider the following sentences:

(4) a. *On Christmas morning, three boys found lumps of coal in their stockings.*
     b. *On Christmas morning, three boys found a lump of coal in their stocking.*

While both sentences have multiple interpretations, we need only concern ourselves with the most likely one, in which each boy finds a single lump of coal in his own stocking. There are, then, three instances of the event type 'X find a lump of coal in X's stocking'. Example (4)a conflates these instances into a single complex event involving three boys, multiple lumps of coal, and multiple stockings. The plural nouns designate the participants in this higher-order event; each is a higher-order thing comprising multiple instances of the basic thing type (e.g. *boys* profiles a complex entity comprising multiple instances of the basic type *boy*). By contrast, (4)b evidences a mixture of two lexicalization strategies. Parts of the sentence—notably *three boys*, *their*, and arguably *found*—lexicalize facets of the higher-order event and thus occur in the plural. However, other parts—*a lump* and *stocking*—unexpectedly occur in the singular even though multiple instances of each basic type are understood to be involved. I analyze them as lexicalizing facets of the type specification ('X find a lump of coal in X's stocking') common to the three event instances that constitute the higher-order event. Clearly, those portions of the sentence which directly manifest the type specification do not form a constituent.

We observe another kind of intermingling between the type and instance planes in cases where a type specification refers to an instance of another type. In (5)a, for example, three women participated individually in separate instances of the process type 'X admire this sweater', each instance involving the same member of the *sweater* category.

(5)   a. *Those three women each admired this sweater.*
      b. *Every Charger fan remembers Dan Fouts.*

Likewise, (5)b ascribes an instance of the process type 'X remembers Dan Fouts' to every member of the class of Charger fans (Dan Fouts being the unique instance of the type invoked by the proper noun). A type specification incorporating reference to a specific individual is not in any way unnatural or problematic. A type is merely an abstraction representing what is common to a set of instances. When the commonality observable across a set of occurrences includes the participation of the same individual in all of them, reference to that individual is naturally incorporated as part of the type specification they are taken as instantiating.

Type specifications are essential to the meaning of certain quantifiers. To describe their meanings we need the notion of a *reference mass* (R_T), defined as the maximal extension of a type (T).[2] *Proportional quantifiers*, such as *all, most*, and *some*, profile a mass (possibly the "particulate" mass described by a plural) characterized as representing some proportion of the reference mass for a given type (Figure 8.6). *Representative-instance quantifiers*, including *every, each*, and *any*, are commonly described as universal quantifiers, since they ascribe a property to all members of a class. It is therefore striking that they behave grammatically as singulars.[3] They are singular by virtue of profiling just a single, *arbitrary* instance of the thing type specified by the head noun. The instance is arbitrary in the sense that it is "conjured up" by the speaker just for the local purpose of ascribing a property, and has no status outside the mental space created to do so. It is thus an imagined instance of the type rather than any actual instance known to the speaker on independent grounds.

Despite profiling only a single instance, an arbitrary one at that, these quantifiers achieve universality because that instance is conceived as being *representative* of the class with respect to the property in question. In the case of *any*, representativeness derives from the notion of random selection: the essential import of *Any cat likes tuna* is that, by choosing at random from the set of cats (its reference mass), the one chosen is bound to have the property of liking tuna. A property confidently ascribed to an arbitrary, randomly selected instance can with equal confidence be ascribed to all instances of the category. In the case of *every* (diagrammed in Figure 8.7), the profiled instance is specifically conceived against a background of other instances, exhaustive of the reference mass, all of which simultaneously exhibit the same property.

2.3. Instance planes

Let us now turn to the instance plane. In Chapter 8, we found reason to distinguish between the *structural plane*, representing generalizations about the "structure of the world", and the *actual plane*, the phenomenal level where actual events occur. Importantly, this is not the same as the distinction between the type and instance planes, for it is part of our conception of the world's structure that particular types have multiple instantiations. The structural and actual planes should rather be thought of as two facets of the instance plane, or two levels within it. As shown in Figure 9.9, the actual plane comprises *reality* —the history of what has actually happened up through the present, where the ground (G) is located—together with whatever may or will happen in the future; it is the domain of actual occurrences, whether real or potential. Events in the actual plane are anchored to particular points in time (t), which can in principle be located with respect to G.

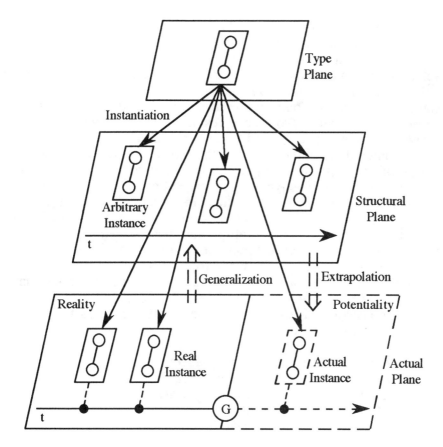

Figure 9.9

By contrast, event instances in the structural plane have no specific temporal location. These are arbitrary instances, conjured up just for purposes of expressing a generalization, namely that occurrences of the event type in question constitute one aspect of the world's structure and can thus be expected under appropriate circumstances. Multiple instances do then figure in the characterization of what the world is like, but these conjured instances do not project to particular locations in actual time, nor is there any specific number of them. The generalization they embody concerning the world's nature does however afford some basis for extrapolating the future evolution of reality in the actual plane.

Arbitrary event instances are therefore characteristic of the structural plane, and actual event instances — whether real or only potential—of the actual plane. Whether arbitrary, real, or potential, they are instances (rather than types), being expressed by finite clauses.

Thus (6)a describes an actual and real delivery event involving actual participants, and (6)b an actual though potential event also involving actual individuals. By contrast, (6)c profiles an arbitrary instance of delivering, one "conjured up" to describe a facet of the world's general nature, so it occupies the structural plane. The messenger and the package referred to are also arbitrary instances of those types, conjured up for the same reason. In (6)d, the subject and object are plural: each profiles a higher-order thing comprising multiple instances of their respective thing types. But neither the higher-order things nor their constitutive entities are actual—they reside in the structural plane and do not represent any specific individuals. What the sentence conveys is that multiple instances of delivering, involving multiple messengers and multiple packages, are characteristic of the world's structure. Finally, while (6)e invokes a specific messenger (an actual individual), it indicates a habitual practice rather than any actual event. As described in Chapter 8, it profiles a higher-order process consisting of arbitrary instances of the process type 'this messenger deliver (a) package on time'.

(6) a. *A messenger just delivered a package.*
    b. *A messenger will deliver a package this afternoon.*
    c. *A messenger always delivers a package on time.*
    d. *Messengers deliver packages.*
    e. *This messenger delivers packages on time.*

It needs to be noted that the quantification effected by proportional and representative-instance quantifiers can pertain to either the structural or the actual plane. Because they invoke a reference mass (all instances of a type), they lend themselves naturally to structural statements, as in (7):

(7) a. *Most Americans graduate from high school.*
    b. *Every millionaire dies with a guilty conscience.*

Thus (7)a profiles a higher-order process in the structural plane (Figure 8.8), comprising multiple instances of the process type 'American graduate from high school'. Its trajector is a higher-order thing consisting of the trajectors of the component event instances, and is further characterized as coming close to exhausting the reference mass (i.e. the set of all Americans). This being a structural statement, the space fictively examined to find the reference mass is unrestricted—for as long as the world exhibits this structural property, the set of Americans constituting R_T is maximally inclusive and not subject to contextual delimitation. The search space for finding the reference mass is likewise unrestricted in (7)b, which profiles a single, arbitrary instance of dying on the part of an arbitrary millionaire. This imagined individual is however construed as being representative of its type with respect to the process type 'die with a guilty conscience' (Figure 8.9). Indirectly, then, (7)b ascribes to the world, as a stable aspect of its structure, the property that dying with a guilty conscience is universal for the set of millionaires, that set being maximally inclusive and contextually unrestricted.

Nonetheless, these quantifiers are often used in the description of actual events. When they are, the reference mass may still be construed as maximally inclusive.[4] In (8), for instance, the denunciation of atheists extends to all conceivable members of the class.

(8) *All atheists were denounced by the fiery preacher.*

More typically, however, R_T is contextually delimited. In (9), the set of atheists and the set of believers in question are taken as being just those who were in the philosophy building when the lightning bolt struck:

(9) *When a lightning bolt destroyed the philosophy building, all*
    atheists escaped unharmed but every believer was injured.

These examples show that universal quantification, even unrestricted, does not per se imply that a statement pertains to the structural plane.

I should mention in passing that generalizations expressed in terms of arbitrary event instances are not confined to the structural plane. Often such an instance is conjured up to capture a local regularity of an ad hoc nature. Consider (10):

(10) *Three times, a member of the audience asked a dumb question.*

On the relevant interpretation, three different members of the audience were involved, and three different questions were asked. Yet the nominals describing these participants are singular. Evidently, the sentence profiles an arbitrary instance of the ad hoc event type 'a member of the audience ask a dumb question', abstracted to characterize the common nature of three actual events. The adverb *three times* then specifies how the arbitrary instance maps onto the actual ones of ultimate concern.

Finally, let me call attention to one further basis for grouping, namely association with a conceptual reference point (Chapter 6). A reference point implicitly defines a *dominion* consisting of all its potential targets (i.e. all the entities to which it affords mental access). Usually, in fact, a given reference point establishes numerous dominions pertaining to different linguistic functions or dimensions of conceptual organization.[5] We will see that reference points and their dominions are relevant to pronominal anaphora in multiple ways.

3. Antecedence and grouping

According to van Hoek (1995, 1997a), a pronoun portrays its referent as being immediately accessible in the current discourse space, whereas a full nominal implies the opposite. To be accessible, in her analysis, is to be in the dominion of a currently active reference point (Figure 7.13). When interpreted in that context, a pronoun with appropriate specifications can be construed as coreferential to the reference point (Figure 9.7). Semantic anomaly results when the inherent semantic value of a nominal or a pronoun (with respect to discourse status) conflicts with the reference point organization imposed by other grammatical and discourse factors.[6]

3.1. Role of dominions

Of course, mere occurrence of a pronoun in a reference point's dominion does not establish antecedence, if only because a given nominal anchors multiple dominions accessed for different purposes. In Chapter 7 (section 6.1) I distinguished a nominal's *referential dominion* from its *structural dominion*. The former was broadly characterized as the set of things to which the nominal profile gives mental access and which themselves have the potential to functional as nominal referents. The latter was characterized as the structural context over which an entity holds sway as the primary reference point for a particular purpose. A thing occurring in a nominal's referential dominion need not be coreferential to it (this dominion includes its subparts and associated entities such as possessions or kin). Instead, coreference represents the special case in which mental access from the reference point to the target is most immediate, namely the case where they coincide. Hence this identity is built into the meaning of a pronoun as a separate specification.[7]

A relationship of *antecedence* obtains when, in addition, a pronoun occurs in the structural dominion of a full nominal which profiles the reference point in question. The critical problem, which van Hoek examines in great depth and detail, is thus to elucidate the factors influencing the choice of a reference point and the extent of its structural dominion. She shows that a variety of factors interact dynamically to determine local and global reference point organization. They include both discourse considerations and the kinds of conceptual factors embodied in grammatical structure—e.g. viewpoint, relative salience, and conceptual overlap. It is precisely because they are characterized with respect to such factors that syntactic notions like subject, object, main vs. subordinate clause, and complement vs. modifier are relevant to the description of possible pronoun-antecedent configurations.

Van Hoek's analysis correctly predicts that well-formedness judgments pertaining to pronoun-antecedent relationships should often be graded. The viability of anaphoric expressions depends on an appropriate antecedent (or the entity it profiles) establishing itself as a prominent reference point whose structural dominion includes the pronoun. The salience of a reference point and the strength of its influence are intrinsically matters of degree; numerous factors are capable of affecting them.

Van Hoek's account has the additional desirable feature of not being limited to examples where an explicit antecedent occurs in the same sentence as the pronoun. The sentence has no privileged status in CG. There is no reason why a reference point's structural dominion cannot extend across sentence boundaries, though we naturally expect its influence to wane as distance increases. It is in fact not the occurrence of an overt antecedent that matters, but rather the existence of a salient reference point in the CDS. Once a nominal has established such a referent, it has served its purpose and need not be invoked for subsequent processing—the mere existence of an appropriate reference point in the CDS is sufficient to satisfy a pronoun's semantic requirements. Furthermore, a pronoun can be used felicitously even when there is no explicit antecedent at all, the reference point being supplied by the extra-linguistic context.

This CG analysis can be seen as implementing a "radical" proposal made some time ago by Orin Gensler: that all anaphora is non-syntactic (Gensler 1977). What ultimately counts is the availability of a suitable conceptual antecedent, irrespective of whether this is directly coded by a structural antecedent in the form of a full nominal. Gensler gives examples to show that the requisite conceptual antecedent can arise in various ways from the discourse context and bear various kinds of relationships to overtly occurring linguistic material. He notes in particular that almost any sub-element in an established frame has the potential to anchor an anaphoric relationship. He gives (11)a as an illustration:

(11) a. *Remember Mary's party? Wasn't **he** just the neatest guy you ever saw?*
  b. ***Alice** says **she** needs a vacation.*

Though linguistic theorists might put a star or at least two question marks in front of the second sentence, the sequence strikes me as being a rather normal instance of actual language use. There is, I think, a valid difference to be noted between expressions like this and those involving canonical antecedence, as in (11)b, but it has to be considered one of degree. The sorts of examples to which most theoretical discussions confine themselves—sentences where a full nominal directly mentions the entity construed as the pronoun's referent— are properly seen as a special case within a much broader spectrum of possibilities.

Still, it is in some sense a privileged case. If we want to achieve a comprehensive understanding of language and its functional motivation, we cannot afford to level such distinctions; treating all the data as equivalent would be no less misleading than focusing on just a small portion of it. I will therefore draw a distinction between *strict* and *metonymic antecedence*. In strict antecedence, an overt nominal directly names (i.e. profiles) the entity construed as the referent (i.e. the profile) of the pronoun. Strict antecedence represents the canonical, the optimal, or the most straightforward way of establishing the reference point a pronoun requires. On the other hand, metonymic antecedence relies on metonymy to establish a referent that is not per se explicitly mentioned. Metonymy, of course, is itself a natural and ubiquitous reference point phenomenon. It produces metonymic antecedence when a nominal's usual referent evokes a target in its referential dominion that in turn functions as the reference point required by a pronoun. In constructions which permit this, the pronoun's referent is consequently not identified with the profile of an overt nominal, but rather with some entity it readily evokes.

Metonymic antecedence is broadly defined and thus subsumes a wide variety of expression. Example (11)a involves metonymy between an overall frame and a particular element within it. "Anaphoric island" violations (Postal 1969a) provide another class of cases:

(12)   a. *He speaks excellent **French** even though he's never lived **there**.*
       b. *The **French** invasion of Algeria proved **it** was a peace-loving country.*

Though (12)a seems more acceptable than (12)b, both anaphors are plausibly construed as referring to France, which the noun and the adjective *French* evoke but do not directly name. Illustrated in (13) are two kinds of cases where the explicit antecedent is not a full nominal but rather a noun incorporated as part of a compound; as such, it merely names a thing type, as opposed to profiling one or more instances of that type.

(13)   a. *The **duck** situation is getting serious. **They** leave droppings all over my living room.*
       b. *Jane is a **cat**-lover because **they** are so cuddly.*

Strictly speaking, then, *they* has no antecedent in either example. The incorporated noun does however establish metonymic antecedence by naming the type with respect to which the pronoun is construed. In (13)a, *they* refers to a set of actual instances of the *duck* category. On the other hand, since *they* is construed as referring generically to cats in (13)b, it designates a set of arbitrary instances which inhabit the structural plane (Figure 8.5).

3.2. In the wrong space at the wrong time

We can now explore some of the complex ways in which pronominal anaphora interacts with various kinds of conceptual groupings. Let us start with the well-known difference between specific and non-specific indefinites in regard to their ability to serve as an antecedent. In a sequence like (14)a, the felicity of interpreting *a Porsche* as the antecedent of *it* depends on whether Zelda has a specific Porsche in mind, or whether she merely intends to become a Porsche owner. The contrast is made explicit in (14)b-c, where *certain* forces the specific reading, and *any* the non-specific one.

(14) a. *Zelda is willing to buy **a Porsche**. **It** is red.*
     b. *Zelda is willing to buy **a certain Porsche**. **It** is red.*
     c. **Zelda is willing to buy **any Porsche**. **It** is red.*

The fact that *any* has the same effect as the non-specific *a* suggests the existence of a broader phenomenon that cannot be handled just by positing alternate senses for the indefinite article. A far more satisfactory account has been proposed by Fauconnier (1985) using his notion of mental spaces. From examples like (15) we see that even a non-specific nominal can establish a discourse referent and antecede a pronoun, under the proper circumstances.

(15) *Zelda is willing to buy {a/any} Porsche. It has to be red,
      though.*

The problem with (14)c and the parallel interpretation of (14)a is not that the pronoun lacks a proper antecedent, but rather that the two component sentences are inconsistent concerning the mental space in which the common referent resides. In Fauconnier's analysis, a predicate like *willing* sets up a mental space representing the situation favorably contemplated by its subject. The conception evoked by *Zelda is willing to buy a Porsche* thus includes two mental spaces: reality (where the ground is located), and the space Zelda envisages (cf. Figure 2.1).
     On either interpretation, Zelda has a role in both spaces: the speaker portrays her as part of reality, and she herself figures in the conception she entertains. The Porsche also figures in the latter space, which features the event of Zelda buying it. The contrast between the specific and non-specific interpretations hinges on whether the Porsche is conceived as residing in reality as well, or whether the envisaged situation is its only residence. This matters because the following sentence—*It is red*—itself puts the pronoun's referent in reality (primarily due to the finite verb inflection and the absence of a modal). A construal of coreference is therefore consistent only with the specific reading; since the non-specific reading denies the Porsche any status outside the realm of Zelda's thoughts, it is inconsistent with a statement ascribing a color to it in reality. The continuation in (15)—*It has to be red, though*—is however permissible owing to its modal character. The *have to* construction indicates that the color

specification pertains to a non-real space, which is easily identified with the one Zelda envisages. We see that with the proper cues such a space is able to extend across sentence boundaries and host a recurring discourse referent.

Similar observations can be made for general validity predications, which profile relationships in the structural as opposed to the actual plane. Construing *A cat stalks a bird* generically (the only likely interpretation), the sequence in (16)a is semantically anomalous. The first sentence profiles a relationship residing in the structural plane. It constitutes an arbitrary but representative instance of the cat-stalk-bird process type, involving arbitrary instances of the *cat* and *bird* categories that are conjured up just for purposes of describing what the world is like. By contrast, *It just flew away* locates the profiled event in reality (primarily due to *just*), so its trajector—the referent of *it*—has to be an actual instance of some category. A construal of coreference is thus anomalous, for it is inconsistent to identify an arbitrary instance of *bird* in the structural plane with an actual individual.

(16) a. **A cat stalks **a bird**. It just flew away.*
     b. *A cat stalks **a bird** but seldom succeeds in catching **it**.*

There is no such problem in (16)b because both conjuncts are readily interpretable as general validity predications. They are taken as describing two facets of a single generic specification. The entire complex action thus belongs to the structural plane, its participants being arbitrary but representative instances of their categories. A consistent interpretation emerges when the profiles of *a bird* and *it* are construed as projecting to the same entity in that plane.

The habituals in (17) are roughly analogous:

(17) a. *??Every day, my cat catches and eats **a mouse**. It is delicious.*
     b. *Every day, my cat catches and eats **a mouse**. It is invariably delicious.*

In each case the first sentence profiles a higher-order process that resides in the structural plane. It consists of indefinitely many instantiations of the complex event type 'my cat catch and eat a mouse'. Whereas the type specification makes reference to a specific cat, the victim is an arbitrary instance of the *mouse* category, one conjured up just for purposes of describing the kind of event whose recurrence is portrayed as being part of the world's structure (albeit a minor one). Since the referent of *a mouse* has no status in actuality, coreference with *it* yields a consistent conceptualization just in case the latter's referent is also confined to the type specification and its instantiations in the structural plane. For *It is delicious* in (17)a, such an interpretation is possible but marginal. The adverb *invariably* does however force this reading in (17)b, which is therefore unproblematic.

We have so far examined cases involving actual conceptual inconsistency as to the location of a referent vis-à-vis certain kinds of conceptual groupings (or mental spaces). The inconsistencies do not pivot on the specific semantic properties of personal pronouns, so they do not disappear when the pronoun is replaced by another kind of coreferring expression, e.g. a simple definite nominal. The sequences in (18) thus exhibit the same anomaly as those in (14)c, (16)a, and (17)a, respectively.

(18) a. **Zelda is willing to buy **any Porsche**. **The Porsche** is red.*
   b. **A cat stalks **a bird**. **The bird** just flew away.*
   c. *??Every day, my cat catches and eats **a mouse**. **The mouse** is delicious.*

We will now look at some examples where just the opposite is true. The semantic problems they pose are less a matter of actual inconsistency than of the requisite antecedent having insufficient salience to be easily invoked as a reference point. Moreover, replacing the pronoun with a simple definite nominal does change acceptability. This difference in grammatical behavior will be seen as following from the semantic contrast between definite and pronominal anaphors.

4. Antecedents and reference points

A distinction was made previously between two kinds of quantifiers that function as grounding predications. The following section explores the interaction of these grounding quantifiers with pronominal anaphora (see also van Hoek 1996).

4.1. Anaphora with grounding quantifiers

Proportional quantifiers, exemplified by *all*, *most*, and *some*, identify their referent as some proportion of the reference mass (R_T), i.e. the maximal extension of a type (T). Representative-instance quantifiers, such as *any* and *every*, profile an arbitrary instance of T that is also conceived as being representative of its class with respect to the ascription of a property. This contrast in the nature of their profiles (Figures 8.6 and 8.7) accounts straightforwardly for their different grammatical behavior. A proportional quantifier profiles a mass, including the special kind of "particulate" mass named by a plural (comprising indefinitely many instances of a basic thing type). Accordingly, it acts grammatically as either a singular or a plural (*Most chocolate is sweet*; *Most kittens are playful*). It cannot, however, occur with a singular count noun (*most kitten). On the other hand, since *every* profiles a single instance of T specifically construed in relation to other, distinct instances, it can only occur with singular count nouns (*every {kitten/*kittens/*milk}*). *Any* achieves its representativeness by random selection from R_T, and since either a discrete object or some portion of a mass is readily conceived as being pulled out randomly for examination, it occurs with both count and mass nouns (*any {kitten/kittens/milk}*).

Proportional quantifiers lend themselves naturally to generic statements, as in (19)a, but they can also be used for actual occurrences. In such uses, e.g. (19)b, the reference mass is usually identified with a contextually determined set (the maximal extension of the category in the CDS).

(19) a. *{All/Most/Some} cats die before the age of 15.*
      b. *Despite the intensity of the blaze, {all/most/some} occupants escaped unharmed.*

Either kind of use is sufficient to establish a reference point for purposes of pronominal anaphora:

(20) a. ***{All/Most/Some} kittens** are playful. **They** especially like to chase a piece of string.*
      b. ***{All/Most/Some} occupants** escaped unharmed. **They** got out through a rear window.*

It is only necessary that the profiles of the antecedent and the pronoun project to the same mental space (the structural or the actual plane).

Although they resemble *all* in their universal character, representative-instance quantifiers behave rather differently. Such quantifiers can establish an antecedent under the proper circumstances:

(21) *{Every/Any} kitten is playful. **It** especially likes to chase a piece of string.*

Observe that *it* refers to the same arbitrary yet representative instance profiled by *every* or *any*. Both sentences describe this conjured instance in the structural plane and thereby make a complex specification about one facet of the world's structure. But despite the universality thus achieved, neither quantifier succeeds in establishing the antecedent required for a plural pronoun:

(22) *{??Every/*Any} kitten is playful. **They** especially like to chase a piece of string.*

The sequences in (22) might well occur and even be considered acceptable. They would, however, represent cases of metonymic antecedence. Strictly speaking, the quantified nominal fails to introduce the plural reference point presupposed by the plural pronoun.

The problem in (22) is that the antecedent nominal, while evoking the class of kittens as a whole (R_T) as part of its characterization, specifically profiles only a single, representative member. Using a nominal of the form *every N* to antecede a plural pronoun is less than fully optimal because it requires a metonymic shift from the entity explicitly mentioned (the profiled instance t_i) to one that is only implicit and relatively non-salient, namely the maximal set (R_T) with respect to which t_i is construed as being representative. From the judgments marked in (22), it appears that this shift is somewhat easier with *every* than with *any*. This can be predicted from their semantic characterizations. With *every*, the profiled t_i is representative by virtue of being conceived in relation to other, unprofiled instances of T, all of them construed as equivalent in regard to the property being ascribed. The multiplicity of instances presupposed by *they* can therefore at least be discerned within the scene—they merely lack the salience afforded by profiling. With *any*, however, the notion of multiple instances lies farther in the background. The basic conception is one of random choice within R_T; only one instance is examined and specifically ascribed the property in question. More effort is thus required to evoke and shift the focus to the multiplex reference point required for *they*.

Turning now to the actual plane, we find—rather strikingly— that representative-instance quantifiers are not very effective in establishing antecedents for either singular or plural pronouns. With plurals the results are variable but never quite optimal. Consider the following:

(23) *It's so clear I can see {?every/?*each/*any} peak in this mountain range. **They** are more jagged than I had imagined.*

As before, *they* might be used and judged acceptable, but only on the basis of metonymic antecedence. More interesting are the degrees of acceptability afforded by the different universal quantifiers. As previously noted, the metonymic shift from the profiled instance to the reference mass is most easily accomplished with *every*, which specifically portrays t_i against the background of multiple instances conceived as exhausting R_T. *Each* is quite similar to *every*, but adds the nuance that the various instances are being examined sequentially rather than simultaneously (FCG2: 114-115). It is therefore harder to evoke them collectively to provide the multiplex reference point required by *they*. The sequence is once again least acceptable with *any*, since the notion of random selection draws all the attention to a single instance.

The acceptability of such examples is clearly a matter of degree, lending credence to the claim that it depends on the relative salience and accessibility of an appropriate reference point. Observe in this regard that acceptability can be improved by factors that do not affect logical properties or the structural configuration of the pronoun and antecedent. For instance, adding *all* to the second clause makes all the examples better, to the point that *every* yields a judgment of virtually full acceptability:

(24) *It's so clear I can see {every/?each/??any} peak in this mountain range. **They** are all more jagged than I had imagined.*

The reason, of course, is that *all* highlights the reference mass and thus enhances its ability to serve as a reference point.

Despite the fact that representative-instance quantifiers function grammatically as singulars, they are even less successful anteceding a singular pronoun (in the actual plane) than a plural one. Let us focus on *every*, since the universal *any* resists a non-generic reading. The following examples are all quite bad, though animacy slightly cushions their jarring impact:

(25) a. **It's so clear I can see **every peak** in this mountain range.
       It is quite jagged.*
   b. **It's so clear I can see **every peak** in this mountain range.
       I would like to climb **it**.*
   c. *?*Despite the intensity of the barnyard blaze, **every duck**
       escaped unharmed. **It** got out through a gap in the fence.*
   d. *?*Despite the intensity of the barnyard blaze, **every duck**
       escaped unharmed. The farmer's wife carried **it** to safety.*

This class of cases is similar to those discussed in the previous section. The basic problem is that *every* profiles an arbitrary instance of the type specified by the head noun, whereas the second sentence in each sequence designates a specific event or situation, so that *it* is construed as referring to a particular instance. Why the second sentence has to be construed in this fashion—and not as part of the relational type specification evoked by *every* (Figure 8.9)—is a difficult question that I cannot pursue here.

   The problem posed by representative-instance quantifiers pertains specifically to pronouns. It disappears when the pronoun is replaced by a simple definite nominal:

(26) a. *It's so clear I can see {every/each/any} peak in this
       mountain range. **The peaks** are more jagged than
       I had imagined.*
   b. *Despite the intensity of the barnyard blaze, **every duck**
       escaped unharmed. **The ducks** got out through a
       gap in the fence.*

We can explain this in terms of the semantic difference between these two kinds of expressions. Following van Hoek, I have argued that a personal pronoun carries the expectation of there being a salient reference point in the current discourse space to which it can be construed as being identical. A plural pronoun requires a plural reference point, which a representative-instance quantifier cannot supply because it profiles a single instance and is therefore singular. No such problem arises with a definite plural, such as *the peaks* or *the ducks* in (26), since the definite article does not share with pronouns the expectation of a reference point. Instead, it presupposes uniqueness of the specified type in the current discourse space (Hawkins 1978; FCG2: 3.1.1). An expression like *every peak in this mountain range* is sufficient to introduce into the CDS—if the context has not already done so—a set of peaks that collectively may satisfy this requirement.[8] It does not profile such a set, but does evoke it, as we have seen. Provided that no other peaks are in view or under discussion, that set will be unique in the CDS.

A singular definite nominal does not however overcome the infelicity of using a singular pronoun with an antecedent grounded by a representative-instance quantifier:

(27) a. **It's so clear I can see **every peak** in this mountain range. **The peak** is quite jagged.*
   b. **Despite the intensity of the barnyard blaze, **every duck** escaped unharmed. **The duck** got out through a gap in the fence.*

If anything, (27)b is even worse than (25)c. We should expect this result, since replacing *it* with *the peak* or *the duck* does nothing to obviate the discrepancy between an arbitrary and a particular instance that caused the problem in (25). With a singular noun the definite article in fact compounds the problem, for it implies that there is only one instance of *peak* or *duck* in the CDS, while *every* intimates just the opposite.

4.2. *Quantifier scope*

We have concentrated so far on sentences with just a single quantifier, and found that the possibility of pronominal antecedence depends in part on the extent of a processual type specification. In (21), for example, we saw that *every kitten* is a strict antecedent of *it* because the second sentence (*It especially likes to chase a piece of string*) is construed as belonging to the complex processual type ('X is playful; X especially likes to chase a piece of string') that *every* ascribes to all members of the *kitten* category. On the other hand, *every peak* cannot antecede *it* in (25)a-b, since the second sentence pertains to actuality and is thus excluded from the processual type specification that *every* distributes to category members. A construal of coreference involves the profiles of the antecedent and the pronoun projecting to the same entity in the current discourse space (Figure 9.7). They must therefore occur in the same conceptual grouping (e.g. a type specification).

In sentences with two quantifiers, questions of "scope" arise. For instance, sentence (28)a has three interpretations: (i) A total of two cats and a total of three birds were involved in stalking activity. Neither quantifier has the other "in its scope". (ii) A total of two cats stalked, and each did so with respect to three birds. *Two* has *three* in its scope. (iii) A total of three birds were stalked, each by two cats. *Three* has "wide scope", *two* has "narrow scope". Various kinds of salience—including accent, discourse prominence, and the inherent salience of subject status—facilitate a quantified nominal achieving wide scope. Thus, while *two* tends to have wide scope in (28)a, *three* is favored in (28)b-c.

(28)   a. *Two cats stalked three birds.*
       b. *How many birds were stalked by two cats?*
          Two cats stalked THREE birds.
       c. *Three birds were stalked by two cats.*

Conceptually, scope is a matter of one quantifier being incorporated as part of a processual type specification distributed across the members of a set quantified by the other (FCG2: 3.3.2). Consider Figure 9.10(a), which diagrams the normal construal of (28)a, where *two* has wide scope. The processual type specification is 'X stalk three birds', which incorporates the quantity *three* applied to *birds*. Participation in an instance of that process type is distributed across a set of cats, whose size is specified by the other quantifier. In the case at hand, just two cats are ascribed this property. Figure 9.10(b) represents the construal in which *three* has wide scope, as in (28)b-c. Here the processual type specification is 'two cats stalk X' (or 'X be stalked by two cats'). The property of participating in an instance of that process type is distributed across a set comprising three birds.

These sentences further illustrate a phenomenon discussed earlier in regard to (4)b, namely the coexistence of portions that lexicalize a shared type specification with others that code the actual complex situation being described. When (28)a is construed in the manner of Figure 9.10(a), the actual number of cats involved is two, and the actual number of birds as many as six. The subject *two cats* reflects the complexity of the actual situation, whereas the remainder of the sentence—or at least the object, *three birds*—instead lexicalizes the processual type specification (hence the number *three*, rather than *six*). Conversely, if (28)c is construed in the manner of 9.10(b), *three birds* reflects the actual situation, whereas *(be stalked by) two cats* codes a facet of the shared process type.

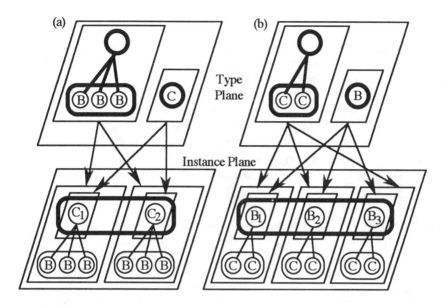

Figure 9.10

Thus, when two quantified sets participate in a scope relationship, it is only the one with wide scope whose actual extension receives explicit mention. Recall now that explicit mention (profiling) is the canonical way of establishing a salient reference point that can serve as an antecedent. We can therefore predict that a reference point introduced only indirectly, via narrow scope quantification, should not be able to engage in direct antecedence. Consider (29), where the *only*-construction reinforces the tendency for the subject to be interpreted as having the object in its scope.

(29) *??Only two of the women speak **three languages**.*
    ***They** are ergative.*

A non-linguist would naturally understand (29) as meaning that the women are ergative (whatever that might be). A linguist might well construe *they* as referring to the full set of (up to six) languages spoken by the women, but only as a case of metonymic antecedence; that set is not profiled or directly mentioned. It is however latent in the current discourse space, being established by the first sentence. Using the full set of languages as the antecedent for *they* presupposes a metonymic shift that accords it sufficient salience as an entity in its own right to function as a reference point.

Since the first sentence does introduce a set of languages into the CDS, referring back to them with a simple definite nominal is unproblematic, as we see in (30)a.

(30) a. *Only two of the women speak **three languages**.*
    ***The languages** are all ergative.*
  b. *??Only two of the women are trilingual. **The languages**
    are all ergative.*
  c. **Only two of the women are trilingual. **They** are all
    ergative.*

The judgments in (30)b-c are also as expected. Although *trilingual* does imply that three languages are spoken, there is no direct mention of them, let alone of the full set of (up to) six. Despite the presence of *all*, which facilitates a collective construal, the languages in their totality are insufficiently salient in the CDS even for simple definite reference. The metonymic shift required for pronominal reference hardly seems possible at all. It is evident that we are dealing here with matters of prominence and accessibility (which are matters of degree) as opposed to logical inconsistency. The antecedence in (29) and (30) poses no problem of logical or conceptual consistency, since the languages referred to in the first and second sentences of each sequence are all located in actuality. The problem is rather that the overall set of (up to) six languages designated by *they* or *the languages* is not specifically mentioned in the first sentence, but has to be inferred.

4.3. Type specifications and "sloppy identity"

The same problem arises in other cases where only a shared type specification is lexicalized. Observe first that, in sentence (31), *right hand* occurs in the singular even though several distinct hands are involved.

(31) *At the teacher's insistence, several boys held up their
    right hand and examined **it**.*

The reason is that portions of the sentence lexicalize the common type specification 'X hold up X's right hand and examine it', rather than the actual scene in its full complexity. The pronoun *it* is permissible here because the type specification incorporates both the pronoun and its antecedent: the type of action ascribed to each of the boys is one in which the body part raised and the object examined are the same. In other words, their coreference is an internal specification of the type description itself.[9] Of course, within the type specification the hand referred to represents an arbitrary instance of *right hand* rather than any actual one.

So far so good. In fact, we can go even further and add a coreferential pronoun in another clause:

(32) *At the teacher's insistence, several boys held up their **right*** *hand and examined **it**, finding that **it** was dirty.*

The additional material, including the stipulation of coreference, is all construed as part of the shared type specification, now quite complex, involving three references to the same hand. The problem comes when the added material is in a separate sentence:

(33) a. *?*At the teacher's insistence, several boys held up their* *right hand and examined **it**. **It** was dirty.*
      b. *?*At the teacher's insistence, several boys held up their* *right hand and examined **it**. **They** were dirty.*

Though a type specification can sometimes extend across sentence boundaries (as in (21)), here it evidently cannot. The sequence in (33)a is thus ill-formed because the second occurrence of *it* represents an actual instance of *right hand*, yet the preceding context fails to single out any particular instance to serve as a reference point. In (33)b we find that a plural pronoun fares no better. The first sentence does introduce multiple instances of *right hand* in the current discourse space, but as in previous examples, there is no direct mention of the higher-order entity comprising them. Though latent in the scene, this complex entity does not have enough salience to be readily evoked as a reference point for *they*.

Let me note in passing that a slight modification will rescue (33)a:

(34) *At the teacher's insistence, several boys held up their **right*** *hand and examined **it**. In each case, **it** was dirty.*

The effect of adding *in each case* is to reinforce the notion of multiple events that instantiate the same process type. This proves sufficient to extend the processual type specification across the sentence boundary. The example is interesting if only because the entire clause—*it was dirty*—lexicalizes the type description. There is nothing in the clause itself which tells us that multiple instances of hands being dirty are actually being referred to.

The last phenomenon to be considered is the one often called "sloppy identity", exemplified in (35).

(35) *Jeff raised his hand, and Bill did so too.*

The sentence is ambiguous between the situation where Bill also raised Jeff's hand and the far more likely scenario in which he instead raised his own. The latter reading has been regarded as theoretically problematic because the antecedent *raised his hand* and the verb-phrase anaphor *did so* are not, strictly speaking, identical: the first refers to Jeff's hand, and the second to Bill's. To some extent the same phenomenon can be observed with pronominal anaphors. The examples in (36) show that acceptability varies (assuming in each case the "sloppy" interpretation).

(36) a. *??Jeff raised **his hand**, and Bill raised **it** too.*
　　 b. *Jeff closed **his eyes**, and Bill closed **them** too.*
　　 c. **Jeff wrote **his daughter**, and Bill wrote **her** too.*
　　 d. *The man who gave **his paycheck** to his wife was wiser than the man who gave **it** to his mistress.* [Karttunen 1969]

We cannot concern ourselves here with the factors that influence these judgments. Our sole objective will be to determine the essential character of such constructions.

In a sentence like (36)b, both clauses designate actual events involving specific participants. *Jeff* and *Bill* are referentially distinct, as are *his eyes* and *them*. The clauses are however parallel in their conceptual and grammatical organization. In particular, the events they describe are instances of the same event type, 'X close X's eyes', in which the subject and possessor are identical. We have already seen that portions of a sentence may lexicalize a type specification, even when actual instances of that type are being described. I propose that sloppy identity be analyzed as a special manifestation of this general potential. More specifically, it is a matter of the anaphor being the only element to lexicalize the type specification rather than one of its parallel instantiations.

Suppose we replace the pronoun in (36)b with a full nominal:

(37) *Jeff closed his eyes, and Bill closed his eyes too.*

Here we would not speak of sloppy identity, but merely of two analogous clauses, each describing a distinct instantiation of the same event type ('X close X's eyes'). The two occurrences of *his eyes* are referentially distinct, so long as we confine our attention to the instance plane. It should by now be clear, however, that expressions often shift between the type and the instance planes, even within a single constituent (e.g. *their right hand* in (34)). Moreover, in referring to an instance we also invoke a type—rather than being separate and discrete mental entities, type conceptions are immanent in their instantiations. To some extent, therefore, using a sentence like (37) involves two occurrences of the type conception 'X close X's eyes', and thus of 'X's eyes'. Construed in the type plane, there need be no referential distinction between these occurrences; it is precisely by abstracting away from such distinctions that type conceptions emerge. At the requisite level of abstraction, each occurrence of 'X's eyes' simply refers to a "role" within the event type 'X close X's eyes', and it is of course the same role (hence the same abstract referent) in both cases.

"Sloppy identity" reflects an abstract construal of this sort. It results from lexicalizing the second occurrence of the role conception in accordance with the identity observable at the appropriate level of abstraction. In this respect it is comparable to the anaphora observed in (31), except that the antecedent occurrence is not directly coded.[10] It is however accessible by virtue of being immanent in the description of a specific instantiation. In (36)b, *his eyes* designates Jeff's eyes in particular, but it does harbor the role conception which *them* refers to anaphorically.

5. Conclusion

This chapter has dealt with numerous difficult phenomena in a preliminary, even cursory manner. I believe it does however demonstrate the grammatical importance of conceptual groupings that do not necessarily coincide with classical constituents, as well as the conceptual basis of restrictions on pronoun-antecedent configurations. Certainly the possible configurations are in large measure determined by language-specific conventions, which in CG assume the form of constructional schemas. However, this does not in any way diminish the extent of their semantic and functional motivation. For the most part, the patterns that emerge can be seen as "falling out" from the interaction of various conceptual and communicative factors. Prominent among these are the semantic values of the elements that participate in anaphoric relationships (e.g. full nominals vs. simple definites vs. personal pronouns). They further include the myriad semantic and interactive factors which influence the nature and extent of conceptual groupings, in particular the dominions associated with the reference points that rise and fall in salience as discourse proceeds. The essential point I hope to have made is that it is both possible and necessary to describe such entities in explicit detail, and to posit specific constructs for that purpose.

Chapter 10
Subjectification and grammaticization

The contrast between subjective and objective construal (Chapter 7) is manifested diachronically in the process called *subjectification*.* Our objective here is to refine an earlier characterization of this process (CIS: chapter 12) and examine its consequences for *grammaticization*, i.e. the evolution of grammatical elements from lexical sources.

1. Subjectification, attenuation, and transparency

Subjectification is a shift from a relatively objective construal of some entity to a more subjective one. The cases considered here involve *attenuation* in the degree of control exerted by an agentive subject. When carried to extremes (as it is in highly grammaticized forms), attenuation results in the property of *transparency*, which has important grammatical consequences (Chapter 11).

1.1. The nature of subjectification

An entity is construed objectively to the extent that it is put onstage as a focused object of conception. By definition, an expression's profile is construed with a high degree of objectivity, being the focus of attention within its immediate scope (Figure 7.1). At the opposite extreme, an offstage conceptualizer is subjectively construed to the extent that it functions as the subject of conception without itself being conceived. Maximal subjectivity attaches to a tacit locus of consciousness, an implicit conceptualizing presence that is not itself an object of conception. So defined, subjectivity/objectivity is a matter of vantage point and role in a viewing relationship.[1]

With respect to the meanings of linguistic expressions, the primary conceptualizers (subjects of conception) are the speaker and hearer. As such, they are canonically offstage and subjectively construed. They have this tacit role in grounding predications, which evoke them as viewers (with their spatial and temporal locations as vantage points) without ever mentioning them explicitly (Figures 7.5-

6). Facets of the ground can however be put onstage as focused targets of conception, being profiled by expressions like *I, you, here,* and *now.* When explicitly mentioned, the speaker or hearer has a dual role as both subject and object of conception.

I have previously characterized subjectification in terms of replacement: some relationship within the objective situation under description is replaced by a comparable but subjectively construed relationship inherent in the very process of conception (CIS: 325-326). However, as suggested by Verhagen (1995) and Harder (1996: 352), I have come to believe that this subjective component is there all along, being immanent in the objective conception, and simply remains behind when the latter fades away. This revised notion of subjectification is represented abstractly in Figure 10.1.

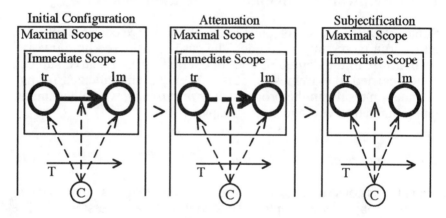

Figure 10.1

In the initial configuration, the solid arrow in bold depicts an objectively construed, profiled relationship. The direction of the arrow indicates some kind of objective asymmetry which motivates the choice of trajector; the trajector is in some sense more active—typically as an agent, experiencer, or mover. The solid arrow labeled T stands for processing time. The import of the diagram is that the conceptualizer, C, does some kind of mental scanning from the trajector to the landmark in conceiving of the profiled relationship (i.e. the trajector functions as a "starting point" or initial point of access in conceptualizing it). The dashed arrows represent the conceptualizer's mental activity, carried out through processing time. In the second diagram, the bold arrow representing the profiled relationship is given in dashed lines to indicate attenuation, involving both the objectively conceived relationship and the trajector's role in it. Although the conceptualizer continues to carry out the same or a comparable mental scanning as in the initial configuration, the objective situation now offers less motivation for it. We will be investigating the progressively more tenuous objective basis for both the relationship and for the trajector's selection as primary focal participant.

Finally, the last diagram indicates the full disappearance of any objective basis for the conceptualizer's mental scanning. A relationship is still established between the trajector and landmark, but the basis for it now resides exclusively in the conceptualizer's activity. This relationship is subjectively construed because it inheres in the process of conceptualization itself, rather than being an onstage object of conception. To the extent that the same mental operations figured in the initial configuration, we can say that the subjective relationship was immanent in the objective one. Observe that subjectification per se need not have any effect on the choice of focal participants (trajector/landmark alignment). It merely removes any objective basis for selecting the trajector as initial point of access.

1.2. Dimensions and degrees of attenuation

A first example is the semantic extension relating the two senses of *across* exemplified in (1):

(1) a. *The child hurried across the street.*
     b. *There is a mailbox right across the street.*

In (1)a, the trajector of *across* (instantiated by *the child*) has that status by virtue of being a mover, successively occupying all of the points along a spatial path traversing the static landmark. This is shown in the first diagram of Figure 10.2. In (1)b, on the other hand, the trajector of *across*—the mailbox—is static, as seen in the second diagram; it occupies only a single position vis-à-vis the landmark (equivalent to the final position in (1)a). This illustrates attenuation with respect to both the objective relationship and the basis for the choice of trajector. The profiled relationship is less inclusive and less dynamic in this second sense of *across*, and the trajector does not stand out as primary focal participant by virtue of moving.

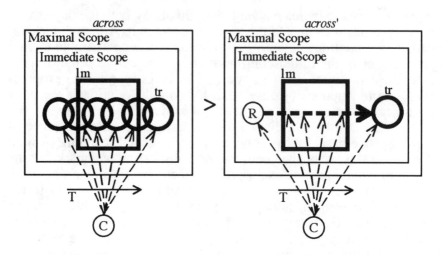

Figure 10.2

In conceiving of the trajector following the objective spatial path in (1)a, the conceptualizer necessarily scans mentally along the same path as an inherent aspect of tracking the subject's motion. Although objective motion is lacking in the derived sense of *across*, we see from the second diagram in Figure 10.2 that the conceptualizer nonetheless follows the same path subjectively in locating the trajector with respect to a reference point (R). Once the objective motion is stripped away, the subjective mental scanning becomes more apparent. Observe that this fading away of the objective motion does not inherently involve any change in trajector/landmark alignment; only the extent the trajector's role is modified. Instead of successively occupying *all* the locations constituting a spatial path, it occupies only the *final* location.

Although I consider this to be a case of subjectification, I have left a dashed arrow to show that an objective basis for the conceptualizer's scanning along the spatial path has not disappeared entirely; usually some vestige of it remains. It might appear that the transition connecting the two senses of *across* would have to be discrete: the trajector either traverses all the locations constituting the spatial path, or occupies only the final location, but there is no intermediate sense in which, say, it traverses only a portion of the path. But the *extent* of the motion is only one dimension of possible variation—other dimensions involve the *status* of the motion as well as *who* does the moving. Differences along these parameters provide a series of cases that are intermediate between that of profiled, objective motion by the trajector, and at the other extreme, that of purely subjective motion by the conceptualizer imposed with no objective basis. Such a series is given in (2).

(2) a. *The child hurried across the busy street.* [profiled objective movement by trajector]
   b. *The child is safely across the street.* [static location resulting from unprofiled, past, actual movement of trajector]
   c. *You need to mail a letter? There's a mailbox just across the street.* [static location as goal of unprofiled, potential, future movement of addressee]
   d. *A number of shops are conveniently located just across the street.* [static location as goal of potential movement by a generalized or generic individual]
   e. *Last night there was a fire across the street.* [static location, no physical movement necessarily envisaged at all]

   Only in (2)a is movement along the entire spatial path put in profile. This constitutes an important and discrete difference: since the other sentences profile only a single, static configuration, they are imperfective and take the verb *be*. There nevertheless remains a vestige of objectively construed motion. It undergoes a change in *status* from profiled to unprofiled, and from actual to potential to generic. The *mover* also changes, from being an objectively construed participant (the trajector) to being subjectively construed (the unmentioned addressee), and from a specific mover to a generalized or unspecified one. It is only in the last example, (2)e, that the conception of physical movement may be entirely absent, leaving only subjective motion by the conceptualizer, who mentally traces along the path in order to specify the trajector's location.

   Thus I do not envisage attenuation and eventual full subjectification as occurring in a single step. It is more likely a gradual evolutionary process involving small steps along a number of possible parameters. This will usually result in the coexistence of alternative values at a given diachronic stage, with gradual shifts in preference being responsible for changes that in retrospect appear to be discrete (cf. Heine 1992).

   Attenuation can be observed with respect to at least four parameters (the grouping is somewhat arbitrary). We have already noted change in *status*: from actual to potential, or from specific to generic. A second parameter is change in *focus*, i.e. the extent to which parti-

cular elements stand out as focus of attention, notably in terms of profiling. We saw that actual motion by the trajector is profiled in (2)a,
but unprofiled in (2)b, which designates only the final locative configuration resulting from that motion. Full elimination, exemplified by
the absence of any objective movement in (2)e, might be thought of as
the extreme case of defocusing. A third kind of attenuation is a shift in
domain, e.g. from a physical interaction to a social or experiential
one, as in the evolution of modals (Sweetser 1982, 1990). The final
parameter is change in the *locus of activity* or *potency*. This is illustrated in (2) by the change in mover: from a focused onstage participant (the trajector) to an offstage one (the addressee), or from a
specific mover to a non-specific, generalized one.

1.3. Attenuation and transparency

Let us next consider the common evolution of a verb meaning 'go'
into a marker of futurity, as with the English *be going to* construction.
We can first observe that a sentence like (3) is ambiguous. It may
indicate actual movement through space by the subject, in order to initiate an action at the endpoint of the spatial path. It can also indicate
the futurity of the infinitival event, with no implication of spatial
motion; in this case I posit subjective movement through time by the
conceptualizer.

(3) *Sam is going to mail the letter.* [physical, objective movement
       through space by the subject OR subjective movement through
       time by the conceptualizer]

The two senses of *be going to* are sketched in Figure 10.3. In
the first sense, the trajector follows a spatial path, at the end of which
he intends to initiate some activity, which constitutes a relational landmark.[2] The movement of course takes place through time (t). In the
future sense of *be going to*, the conceptualizer traces a mental path
along the temporal axis and situates the infinitival event downstream
in the flow of time relative to some reference point. As we saw before
with *across*, there is no change in trajector. The trajector does however have a diminished role in the profiled relationship: since it no
longer moves through space, its activity is confined to whatever it
does in the landmark event. While this may seem peculiar, it is actually quite common (see Chapter 11). Moreover, it is unproblematic in

CG because the trajector is characterized as primary focal participant, not in terms of any particular semantic role.

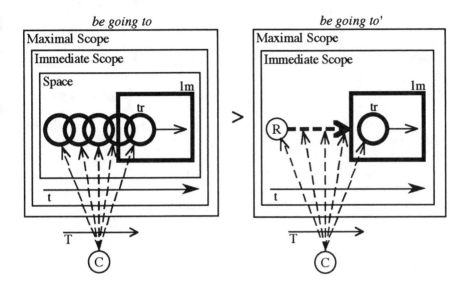

Figure 10.3

This clearly qualifies as subjectification as defined above. In following the subject's movement through space, which unfolds through time, the conceptualizer implicitly traces a mental path through time—the same path which stands alone as the profiled temporal configuration in the future sense of *be going to*. The conceptualizer's subjective motion through time is immanent in the conception of the subject's objective motion through space, and remains behind when the latter fades away. Once more, the heavy dashed arrow in the second diagram of Figure 10.3 indicates that the relationship is not purely subjective; some vestiges remain of the original objective basis for the conceptualizer's mental path. We can discern a number of intermediate stages:

(4) a. *Sam was going to mail the letter but couldn't find a mailbox.*
   b. *Sam was going to mail the letter but never got around to it.*
   c. *If Sam isn't careful he's going to fall off that ladder.*
   d. *Something bad is going to happen—I just know it.*
   e. *It's going to be summer before we know it.*

In the physical motion sense of (4)a, the subject does not just move but also has the intention to carry out the infinitival event at the end of the spatial path. This intention perseveres in many non-motion uses, as seen in (4)b. The trajector thus continues to be a locus of activity tending toward realization of the infinitival process. The activity is however attenuated by virtue of having lost its physical component; only its mental aspect remains. We can regard this as either a change in focus (an extreme case, resulting in the full absence of physical motion) or else a change in domain (from physical to mental/experiential).

Intention is a sort of potency directed toward realizing the envisaged event. One prevalent kind of attenuation involves progressive diffusion in the locus of potency. We see this in examples like (4)c, where the future event is conceived as being accidental; the subject does not act with the specific intent of bringing it about. He is nonetheless still plausibly attributed a certain amount of responsibility for the falling. Given the overall circumstances in which the subject finds himself, his other actions and/or his inattentiveness create the potential and even the likelihood of the event being realized. In short, the locus of potency is no longer concentrated and specifically identified with the subject, but is much more diffuse. It resides in a combination of factors merely associated with the subject (e.g. degree of attentiveness) and the external circumstances in which the subject's activity takes place. Naturally, the specifics vary greatly from one example to the next.

In (4)d, the subject is no longer even a locus of responsibility; in fact, the subject does not exist at the reference time (R) and is incapable of responsibility. It is rather just some aspect of the present circumstances that induces in the conceptualizer an expectation of the future event. The source of this expectation may be quite diffuse, a matter of speaker assessment that cannot be tied to any specific objective elements. Finally, (4)e approximates the limiting case of a purely temporal relationship. At the extreme, the profiled relationship resides solely in the conceptualizer temporally locating the situation by mentally scanning forward through time from the reference point.[3]

Towards the end of this attenuation process—in cases like (4)d-e where the subject no longer has any role in bringing about the infinitival event—we have the situation I call *transparency*: anything eligible to be the subject of the infinitival complement is also eligible to be the subject of the entire expression, as seen by the so-called "dummy" or "expletive" subjects in (5). This is the kind of situation that was dealt with in transformational grammar by positing a rule of Subject-to-Subject Raising.

(5) a. *There is going to be another storm tonight.*
    b. *Tabs are going to be kept on all the dissidents.*

We will see in the next chapter that raising rules are super-fluous in a CG description. What we find in this construction, and in others to be examined, is progressive attenuation and diffusion in the locus of control, as seen in (4). Such attenuation does not per se have any effect on the choice of trajector, but only on the extent of the objective motivation for this choice. Beyond a certain point, therefore, the trajector of the profiled relationship no longer has any role in effecting that relationship, so it need not have any particular properties (as it does when it is still construed as a mover or as having intention or responsibility). What the trajector actually does, in such extreme cases, is limited to whatever is implied by virtue of its status as trajector of the process temporally downstream from the reference point. Hence all restrictions on its choice are determined by the infinitival complement. I reiterate that in CG it is unproblematic for the trajector of a relationship to have no direct role in it—trajector status is characterized in terms of primary focal prominence, and the "spot-light" of focal prominence can in principle be directed wherever desired.

Progressive diffusion in the locus of potency is nothing out of the ordinary. We can observe it in the normal range of variation per-mitted with virtually any agentive verb in regard to the specific role of the subject. Consider the examples in (6), where the nature of the subject's involvement is described in brackets:

(6) a. *Edward frightened the hikers by jumping out of the bushes and shouting at them.* [source of volitional physical action]
    b. *Edward frightened the other hunters by accidentally firing his rifle.* [source of non-volitional physical action]
    c. *Edward frightened the priest by believing in satan.* [locus of mental attitude]
    d. *Edward frightened the children by being so ugly.* [locus of property reacted to by others]
    e. *Edward frightened his parents by not being among the children getting off the bus.* [mere association with circumstance reacted to by others]

Edward has a fully agentive role in (6)a, but in (6)b his agentivity is attenuated through absence of volitionality. In (6)c Edward's participation shifts from the physical to the mental domain, and changes from a temporally bounded action to a steady-state attitude. Also, the person being frightened now has a greater proportion of the responsibility for the fright being induced; holding a belief is not frightening per se, but only if someone finds its content objectionable. In (6)d-e the subject's responsibility diminishes still further, while the object's increases. In (6)d, Edward is merely the passive and unwilling locus of a static property. And in (6)e, even that is lacking—it is only due to someone else's expectations that Edward is even associated with the fright-inducing circumstance.

This is not yet a case of full transparency. One cannot, for example, say (7):

(7) **Tabs frightened civil libertarians by being kept on all the dissidents.*

Thus even in (6)e there is some tenuous respect in which Edward is still held responsible for inducing the fright. But it may be quite tenuous indeed. This illustrates the great flexibility we usually have in construing agentivity or responsibility; the individual put in focus as trajector or subject may in fact be only metonymically related to the actual locus of potency.

2. Grammaticization

Full transparency results when attenuation of subject control and diffusion of responsibility are carried to their ultimate conclusion. Thus it tends to be characteristic of highly grammaticized forms. At any one stage, of course, a particular form is likely to have a spectrum of uses representing various degrees of grammaticization. In its motion sense, for instance, *be going to* is not at all transparent—only with a temporal interpretation are the sentences in (5) acceptable.

2.1. Uses of have

The verb *have* is an especially interesting example but can be mentioned here only in passing (cf. Brugman 1988). As a main verb taking nominal complements, *have* shows a broad range of uses with varying degrees of attenuation in subject control:

(8) a. *Be careful—he has a knife!* [source of immediate physical control]
   b. *I have an electric saw (but I seldom use it).* [source of potential physical control]
   c. *They have a good income from investments.* [locus of experience, abstract control]
   d. *They have three children.* [locus of social interaction, generalized responsibility]
   e. *He has terrible migraine headaches.* [passive locus of experience]
   f. *We have some vast open areas in the United States.* [locational reference point, diffuse locus of potential experience]

Yet some vestige of subject involvement always remains. Even in examples like (8)f (Figure 6.6), where a generalized subject functions mainly as a locative reference point, there is still a vague notion of possible experiential consequences. Hence the main verb *have* is non-transparent. The auxiliary verb *have* in the perfect construction is fully transparent, however:

(9) a. *There may have been a serious breach of security.*
   b. *Tabs should have been kept on those dissidents all along.*

This construction represents a considerably more advanced stage of grammaticization and no longer implies any necessary subject involvement.[4]

2.2. English modals

The English modals are likewise highly grammaticized and for the most part transparent, as seen in (9). They have evolved from main verbs with meanings like 'want', 'know how to', 'have the strength to', etc. Observe that such verbs have two crucial properties both reflected in grammaticized modals: they are *force-dynamic* (Sweetser 1982, 1990; Talmy 1988a); and the action serving as target of the force vector, i.e. the event expressed by the verb's complement, remains *potential* rather than being actual. The profiled relationship involves some kind of effectiveness or *potency* tending toward realization of the type of action expressed by the complement, but no actual instantiation of that action is implied. I cannot go into the details of either the synchronic analysis of the modals or their diachronic evolution (see Langacker 1990c, FCG2: 6.3). Here I will simply note that their development illustrates the attenuation of subject control, in that the locus of potency is no longer identified with the subject.

Consider first the root or deontic interpretations of modals. As noted by Talmy and Sweetser, root modals generally convey force-dynamic relationships in the domain of social interaction. This shift from physical to social force constitutes attenuation in regard to domain. Moreover, the source of potency is no longer identified with the subject, but is implicit and subjectively construed. It may be the speaker but need not be, as seen in (10). It is not necessarily any specific individual, but may instead be some nebulous, generalized authority. In other words, the source of potency is highly diffuse.

(10) a. *You may not see that movie—I won't allow it!*
  b. *You must go home right away—your wife insists!*
  c. *Passengers should arrive at the airport two hours before their flight.*
  d. *You must not covet your neighbor's wife.*

Nor is the subject necessarily the target of the potency, which is also diffuse. Although the modal force may be directed at a specific individual—be it the subject, the addressee, or some third party—we see from (11) that this is not always the case. The force is simply directed toward realization of the target event, to be apprehended by anyone who might be in a position to respond to it. Because the subject is usually not the source of potency, and need not be its target, the root modals exhibit transparency.

(11) a. *The next patient can come in now.*
  b. *This fence must be painted by tomorrow—you had better get busy.*
  c. *This fence must be painted by tomorrow—you had better tell Harry.*
  d. *There may not be any alcohol served at the party.*
  e. *Tabs must be kept on those dissidents!*

What about epistemic modals, as in (12)?

(12) a. *They should be able to find what they need.*
      b. *Tabs will probably be kept on all the dissidents.*
      c. *There may be some rain tonight.*

Epistemic modals are maximally diffuse in regard to the source and target of potency, hence transparent. I have described their potency as inhering in the *evolutionary momentum* of reality itself, as assessed by the speaker/conceptualizer: given how reality has been evolving up through the present, what is the likelihood of it continuing to evolve in such a way as to "reach" the target process? This is basically equivalent to saying that the conceptualizer carries out a *mental extrapolation* of ongoing reality, projecting into the future, and senses the degree of force impelling this mental extrapolation in the envisaged direction, or the degree of resistance encountered in projecting it through to the target. In other words, the force dynamics are inherent in the conceptualizer's mental activity, hence subjectively construed in a strong sense.

2.3. *Spanish* estar

Let us next consider the frequent path of grammaticization whereby verbs of motion or posture evolve into auxiliary verbs roughly translated as 'be'. A case in point is Spanish *estar*, whose etymological value was 'stand'. Like English *be*, it takes various types of relational expressions as complements, including adjectives, prepositional phrases, and active participles:

(13) a. *Está enfermo.* 'He is ill.'
      b. *Está en la cocina.* 'He is in the kitchen.'
      c. *Está trabajando.* 'He is working.'

What exactly is the meaning of an auxiliary verb like Spanish *estar* or English *be*? Elsewhere (FCG1, 1987c) I have argued that the characteristic property of a verb or a finite clause—the property that distinguishes them from non-verbal relations like adjectives, prepositions, and participles—is a subjective factor, namely whether the conceptualizer follows the profiled relationship's temporal evolution *sequentially* or construes it in *summary* or *holistic* fashion. A *be*-type auxiliary verb embodies this subjective factor, but does not specify any particular relationship for its profile, i.e. the objectively construed relationship it follows through time is highly schematic. *Be*-type verbs can thus be used in constructions like those in (13), in which they combine with a non-verbal element to form the complex head of a finite clause. When the schematic but sequentially viewed relationship profiled by the auxiliary is equated with the specific relationship profiled by the non-verbal complement, it lends to the complement the sequential viewing required for the head of a finite clause.

The historical evolution leading from a motion or posture verb to a *be*-type auxiliary clearly involves attenuation. Let us consider it in regard to a participial construction, as in (13)c. The initial configuration is shown in the first diagram of Figure 10.4. In this construction, the onstage profiled relationship is that of the trajector maintaining a certain posture. Since 'stand' is a verb, the relationship is scanned sequentially by the conceptualizer (note the arrow labeled T, for processing time). The import of using 'stand' in this participial construction is that maintaining the posture accompanies and perhaps even renders possible another activity, carried out at the same time by the same individual (Langacker 1998a). This is shown diagrammatically by the dotted correspondence line equating the two trajectors, as well as the double arrow, which indicates that maintaining the posture enables the participial activity to occur. The resulting expressions are roughly comparable to (14)a. Expressed by the participle, the accompanying activity is offstage and unprofiled—(14)a profiles the standing, not the looking—and since sequential viewing requires a high degree of focus, the offstage activity is viewed holistically, in summary fashion.[5]

(14) a. *He stood there looking over the fence.*
      b. *The clock stood ticking on the table.*
      c. *The cup was leaking.*
      d. *It was raining.*
      e. *Tabs were being kept on all the dissidents.*

The second diagram in Figure 10.4 represents attenuation with respect to both the nature of the profiled process and its role in effecting the accompanying activity. In (14)b, for instance, *stand* is attenuated due to being predicated of an inanimate subject. Whereas a person exerts muscular control in order to maintain a vertical orientation, a clock stands passively, merely by virtue of having a certain shape. The effective relationship between *stand* and the participial activity is also greatly attenuated; presumably the clock will tick in any orientation.

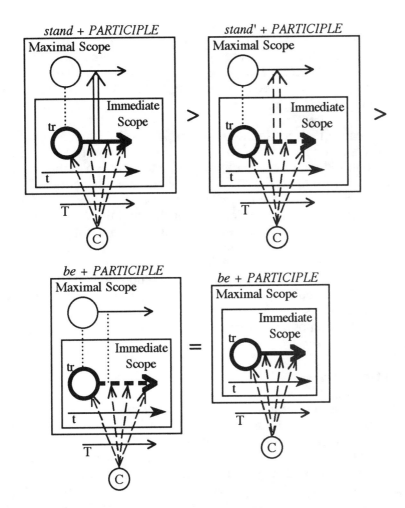

Figure 10.4

Carried to its extreme, attenuation of subject control erases
even the orientational specifications of a verb like *stand*. Nothing then
remains of any specificity—all that is left onstage is the highly
schematic notion of the trajector being involved in some wholly unspecified relationship followed sequentially through time. This is the
value ascribed to a *be*-type verb, as described above. Moreover, since
the profiled process no longer has any specific properties that would
distinguish it from the activity expressed by the participle, these come
to be equated, as indicated by the additional correspondence line in the

third diagram of Figure 10.4. In other words, *be* profiles a schematic process followed sequentially through time, and the participle describes the same process in more specific terms. Hence the two relationships collapse into one, as seen in the final diagram. The *be*-type verb contributes the sequential viewing required for the head of a finite clause, resulting in a progressive construction, as in (13)c or (14)c.

Because the profiled relationship is wholly schematic, it imposes no restrictions on its trajector. And since the profiled relationship is identified with the one expressed by the participle, the participial subject is *ipso facto* the subject of the entire construction. This is a situation of full transparency, as seen in (14)d-e. It is also a case of full overlap between the profiled relationship and that of its complement: owing to attenuation, nothing is left onstage that is not subsumed by the complement. This is a common outcome of grammaticization, which in general leads to greater overlap between the grammaticized element and the structure it combines with (Langacker 1992a, 1995b). Needless to say, this is additionally a case of subjectification, since the sequential viewing which remains as the only essential contribution of *be* was immanent in the original value of *stand*.

2.4. Get-*passives*

Finally, consider the grammaticization of *get* in combination with a passive participial complement. In (15), we find a series of expressions representing an evolutionary path not unlike the one leading to the progressive *be*. In each example, *get* is a finite verb, hence it profiles a process viewed sequentially, whereas the passive participial complement is non-finite and viewed holistically. The evolution of *get* involves progressive attenuation in both the nature of the profiled relationship and the degree of control exercised by its subject. The result is that *get* comes close to being just a passive auxiliary, like *be*, serving only to provide the sequential viewing required for the head of a finite clause. It has not gone quite that far, however.

(15) a. *Sue got (herself) appointed to the governing board.*
     b. *Ralph got fired again.*
     c. *All my books got stolen.*
     d. *Another bank got robbed last night.*

In all the examples, the main clause subject—the trajector of the finite verb *get*—is also the trajector of the complement. And since the complement is based on a passive participle, its trajector is the same element which functions as landmark (or patient) of the verb stem from which the participle derives. Our interest, though, lies in the trajector's role in the main clause relationship. In (15)a, the trajector and subject (*Sue*) is construed as a volitional agent who manages to bring about the participial event, and who also, secondarily, is an experiencer who enjoys the benefits of its occurrence. This volitional construal is almost necessary with the reflexive *herself*, but it is at least possible in the simpler construction without the reflexive. That is our starting point, sketched in Figure 10.5(a).

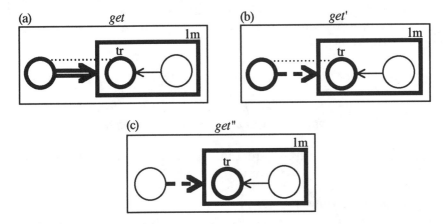

Figure 10.5

More typical are examples like (15)b, where the subject is not a volitional agent with respect to the participial complement. The subject may still be responsible in some way—Ralph may have been fired because of what he did or did not do, or simply because his boss recognized certain undesirable qualities in him—but not necessarily. He is still however an experiencer in regard to the participial event, as shown by the dashed arrow in Figure 10.5(b). But under any of these construals, the subject's primary role is that of passive undergoer of the complement event. Its external, specifically main clause role has been attenuated and now ranges from some indeterminate kind of responsibility to merely that of an experiencer.

If the main clause subject in (15)b is the locus of experience, this cannot be true in (15)c, where the subject is inanimate. We have further attenuation in the degree of subject control, for the experiencer is no longer the subject per se, but rather an individual associated with the subject, the possessor in this example. Moreover, even further diffusion is possible, as the locus of the experience need not be overtly specified or clearly delimited. Thus (15)d does not imply any particular experiencer, which may be construed as the owners or employees of the bank, or perhaps just lawful members of society who feel menaced by the rising level of crime. Hence in Figure 10.5(c) the experiencer is not identified with the trajector, nor is it put in focus as a specified, profiled participant.

The passive *be* in English merely adds sequential viewing to the participial complement. The passive *get* may come close to this, but so long as any vestigial notion of experience remains, the relationship it profiles is not merely a schematic representation of the participial relationship. Moreover, *get*-passives approximate but do not quite achieve full transparency:[6]

(16) a. *?A lot of headway got made last night.*
      b. *??Tabs got kept on all the dissidents.*
      c. *?*It got claimed that there are wombats on Venus.*
      d. **There got claimed to be wombats on Venus.*

Get-passives are non-transparent in that the subject must in some way be implicated in the experiential relationship, not necessarily as the locus of experience, but maybe just by providing a link to the implicit experiencer. *Headway* is easily associated experientially with those who make it, but with *tabs* the matter is less clear (*keep tabs on* is less analyzable than *make headway*). Although I believe that *it* and *there* are also meaningful, their value is more abstract and does not pertain to the objective situation under description (Chapter 11). Thus they are not readily implicated in an experiential relationship as examples like (16)c-d would imply.

3. Conclusion

Let me conclude by acknowledging certain limitations of this account. In articulating some general patterns observable in the evolution of numerous grammatical constructions, I have naturally been unable to examine any one construction in full depth and detail. In particular, I have not attempted to determine how many distinct conventional values have to be attributed to a particular element or construction at a given historical stage to account for the variety of contextual interpretations it displays. I should also emphasize that this work has not been based on serious historical investigation. In presenting series of examples representing progressive degrees of attenuation, I have not intended to suggest that they necessarily correspond to the actual order of diachronic development, which clearly has to be established in its own terms. On the positive side, I have offered a unified account of diverse phenomena usually considered in isolation from one another. Attenuation in subject control has been shown to be a pervasive, multifaceted phenomenon that plays a major role in certain kinds of grammaticization, with important consequences for synchronic analysis and description.

Further examples of attenuation in subject control are readily found. A case in point is the contrast between the main verb *do*, implying some degree of subject responsibility, and the auxiliary verb *do*, which is fully transparent. Another is the relationship between the so-called "equi" and "raising" senses of verbs like *promise, threaten,* and many others (cf. Ruwet 1991: ch. 2; Traugott 1993; Farrell 1995; Verhagen 1995).

(17) a. *Felix promised to get rid of his trombone.*
     b. *There promises to be a bright future for all of us.*

In the former, as in (17)a, the subject has to be capable of volition, planning, and communicative interaction. By contrast, (17)b merely expresses the speaker's assessment based on an overall appreciation of the current situation, hence there are no restrictions on the subject. The overall pattern documented here suggests that the so-called "raising" constructions are best seen as the limiting case of "equi" constructions, representing the extreme situation where attenuation of subject control (or its counterpart in the object-raising constructions) results in transparency (cf. Newman 1981, 1982). An analysis along these lines will be presented in the following chapter.

Chapter 11
Raising and transparency

Pivotal to the derivational analyses of transformational syntax were a set of operations generally referred to as "raising" rules.* Raising is crucial to Chomsky's classic example of the contrast between *expect* and *persuade* (1965: 22-3), figured prominently in some of the foundational works of generative grammar (e.g. Rosenbaum 1967), and was regularly exploited in arguments for the transformational cycle (cf. Soames and Perlmutter 1979). While these rules are no longer uniformly adopted in generative descriptions, the phenomena they were meant to accommodate retain their interest and pose a worthwhile challenge for cognitive and functional theories.

1. Previous accounts

Concerning *expect* and *persuade*, Chomsky argued that sentences like (1)a and (2)a have to be distinguished grammatically despite their superficial parallelism. The difference becomes apparent when the subordinate clause is passivized: whereas (1)a and (1)b are "cognitively synonymous", no relationship of "even weak paraphrase" holds between (2)a and (2)b.

(1) a. *She expected a specialist to examine her mother.* =
     b. *She expected her mother to be examined by a specialist.*

(2) a. *She persuaded a specialist to examine her mother.* ≠
     b. *She persuaded her mother to be examined by a specialist.*

Chomsky attributed this difference to "logical" grammatical relations. Thus in (2)a *a specialist* is both the logical object of *persuade* and the logical subject of *examine*, while in (2)b *her mother* is the logical object of both verbs. In (1), by contrast, neither *a specialist* nor *her mother* bears any "logical" relation to *expect*—the former functions exclusively as the logical subject of *examine* in both (1)a and (1)b, and the latter as its logical object.

1.1. The classic raising analysis

In the transformational model then current (Chomsky 1965), deep structures were posited to provide a consistent representation of logical grammatical relations. Thus the "cognitively synonymous" examples in (1) were both derived by "raising" from the deep structure shown in (3),[1] whereas the sentences in (2) were assigned the respective underlying structures roughly sketched in (4).

(3) *she expected [a specialist examine her mother]*   [⇒ (1)a-b]

(4) a. *she persuaded a specialist [a specialist examine her mother]*
         [⇒ (2)a]
     b. *she persuaded her mother [a specialist examine her mother]*
         [⇒ (2)b]

Sentence (2)a was then derived from (4)a by the transformational rule that came to be known as "Equi-NP Deletion", which erased the complement subject under certain conditions of identity (today, of course, one would speak of "control" and "coindexing" rather than deletion). Sentence (2)b was likewise derived by "Equi" from (4)b once Passivization in the subordinate clause gave rise to the configuration needed for its application. The choice between (1)a and (1)b depends solely on whether Passivization applies to the embedded clause in (3). To this very day it is usual to speak of "equi" (or "control") verbs like *persuade* in opposition to "raising" verbs like *expect*.[2]

The factors Chomsky cited—paraphrase and "logical" relations—are basically semantic in nature. They indicate that the NP which follows a raising verb participates in the semantic role structure of the subordinate clause but not, apparently, in that of the main clause. Later generative accounts presented other kinds of evidence in support of two further claims: (i) that this NP functions grammatically as the direct object of the main-clause verb, and (ii) that it assumes its object function by virtue of a syntactic rule which moves, reattaches, or relabels the subordinate-clause subject. The rule which accomplished this was accordingly known as "Subject-to-Object Raising".

Arguments that the NP in question bears (derived) grammatical relations in the main clause include its ability to undergo such rules as Passivization and Reflexivization, shown independently to be monoclausal in scope. Note these examples with the raising verb *believe*:

(5) a. *The witness was believed to be untrustworthy.*
     b. *Zelda believes herself to be virtuous.*

That the NP originates in the complement clause seemed evident from examples involving "idiom chunks" and "syntactic dummies", e.g. the *it* that occurs with weather verbs:

(6) a. ***Tabs** are believed to have been **kept on** all the radicals.*
     b. ***It** is expected to **rain** this afternoon.*

The surveillance *tabs* and the meteorological *it* do not occur freely; outside of raising constructions, the former is limited to the idiomatic sequence *keep tabs on*, and the latter can only be the subject of verbs like *rain*. Since these contexts are found in the subordinate clause, *tabs* and *it* must originate there despite their surface role as main-clause subject. Moreover, the discrepancy between surface position and motivating context has to be ascribed to the application of a syntactic rule, for the same discrepancy is exhibited by an element generally accepted as being inserted by such a rule, namely the existential *there*:

(7) ***There** are believed to **be** wombats orbiting Jupiter.*

We can describe the crucial difference between "raising" and "equi" verbs by saying that the former display a kind of *transparency*: any element which could occur as the subject of the complement clause can also function as the raising verb's object in the main clause; the raising verb itself imposes no restrictions on this element, whose structural motivation is entirely due to the complement. By contrast, equi verbs impose their own restrictions on their surface arguments. Elements like *tabs*, *it*, and *there* are consequently infelicitous with *persuade*:

(8) a. **She persuaded *tabs* to be kept on all the radicals.*
     b. **She persuaded *it* to rain this afternoon.*
     c. **She persuaded *there* to be wombats orbiting Jupiter.*

Clearly, the object of *persuade* has to be sentient and potentially volitional.
    The classic transformational analysis involved not just one argument-raising rule but three. Although they have gone by various names at different times, the most perspicuous labels are "Subject-to-

Object Raising" (SOR), "Subject-to-Subject Raising" (SSR), and "Object-to-Subject Raising" (OSR).

(9) a. *I expect [**David** criticize this plan]* ⇒ (SOR)
         *I expect **David** [to criticize this plan]*
  b. *[**David** criticize this plan] is likely* ⇒ (SSR)
         ***David** is likely [to criticize this plan]*
  c. *[David criticize **this plan**] is easy* ⇒ (OSR)
         ***this plan** is easy [for David to criticize]*

While it is SOR that has so far concerned us, the case for SSR is if anything even stronger, since the putative change in clause membership is rendered visible by a difference in linear order. This construction also exhibits transparency:

(10) a. ***Tabs** are likely to be kept on all the radicals.*
    b. ***It** is likely to rain this afternoon.*
    c. ***There** are likely to be wombats orbiting Jupiter.*

With OSR, the situation is less straightforward. On the one hand, flexible idioms like *keep tabs on* and *make headway* behave as expected:

(11) a. ***Tabs** are easy to **keep on** antiabortion protesters.*
    b. ***Headway** was tough to **make** against that fierce wind.*

On the other hand, acceptable examples involving *it* and *there* prove impossible to construct. Since these "dummies" originate as subjects, they could in any case undergo OSR only in complex expressions where they function as derived objects owing to a previous occurrence of SOR, as in (12).

(12) a. *I expect **it** [to rain]*
    b. *we believe **there** [to be wombats on Jupiter]*

However, embedding them to an appropriate predicate and applying the OSR rule invariably yields an ungrammatical result:

(13) a. ****It** is easy for me to expect to rain.*
    b. ****There** is tough for us to believe to be wombats on Jupiter.*

If one posits this rule to derive the sentences in (11), some kind of restriction is needed to block those in (13).

1.2. Critique of the classic analysis

Granted the working assumptions of transformational syntax, there is no denying that this analysis elegantly accounted for a broad array of data. It is for good reason that raising figured so prominently in presentations of generative theory and demonstrations of syntactic argumentation.[3] I will demonstrate, however, that comparable descriptive success is achievable in CG, which does not posit derivations from underlying structures.

Generative treatments have not been unproblematic. Because the autonomy of syntax is a foundational claim of generative theory, it is hardly surprising that a number of the shortcomings pertain to the semantic aspects of raising. For example, it is widely accepted that the *to* which occurs in raising and equi constructions is a meaningless grammatical marker induced by the absence of an overt subject (Kiparsky and Kiparsky 1970). Although the meanings of *to* and the other "complementizers" will not be our focus here, I would argue—in accordance with the principles of CG—that they are in fact meaningful and contribute to the conceptual import of the constructions in which they occur (see Langacker 1987c, FCG2: 10.2.1; Achard 1998; Wierzbicka 1988: ch. 1). There has likewise been no really serious attempt to characterize the meanings of raising predicates. In the absence of detailed semantic descriptions, arguments for raising based on "logical grammatical relations" have to be regarded with caution. A revealing account of raising constructions must also ascertain the degree and nature of the semantic coherence exhibited by their sets of governing predicates, and afford some basis for understanding why each construction selects the predicates it does.

Another semantic problem is that sentences supposedly derived by raising sometimes differ in meaning from their unraised counterparts. For instance, Borkin (1973) pointed out that (14)a could be used for a judgment based on indirect evidence (e.g. the results of a consumer survey), whereas the raising sentence (14)b suggests that the basis for judgment is more direct, and (14)c (derived by a further rule deleting *to be*) implies that the speaker has actually sat in the chair.[4]

(14) a. *I find that this chair is uncomfortable.*
 b. *I find this chair to be uncomfortable.*
 c. *I find this chair uncomfortable.*

Postal (1974: ch. 11) acknowledges such differences, observing for example that (15)a indicates some kind of perceptual experience of Julius Caesar, while (15)b might occur in a present-day discussion of Rome and famous Romans.

(15) a. *Julius Caesar struck me as honest.*
 b. *It struck me that Julius Caesar was honest.*

One could of course adopt the unenlightening (and I think erroneous) position that subtle semantic contrasts like these are of no concern in a purely syntactic analysis. Postal does not go quite that far, but the solution he adopts—the suggestion that rule applications are sometimes linked to "assumptions" that "are not part of the core meanings of sentences"—is decidedly ad hoc.
 A different kind of problem is the difficulty of distinguishing between equi and raising constructions in the first place. The parallelism of their surface forms (e.g. *She {persuaded/expected} a specialist to examine her mother*) forces the analyst to distinguish them on the basis of logical grammatical relations and the behavior of dummy elements. In practice, however, both kinds of tests run into problems. It is hard to feel secure about evaluating semantically unanalyzed expressions with respect to a nebulous, unexplicated notion of "logical grammatical relations", and to the extent that speakers have some intuitive idea of what is intended, judgments are often uncertain. For instance, while Postal (1974: 316) suggests that (16)a is derived by raising, Newman (1981: 104) observes that Melvin is as much the object of perception as is the action involving him, and that the occurrence could simply be reported by (16)b given the appropriate context.

(16) a. *Everyone heard Melvin enter the building.*
 b. *Everyone heard Melvin.*

Nor does the "dummy" test yield consistent and unambiguous results:

(17) a. **I heard there be a party going on in the next room.*
 b. *I heard it raining.*

It is also unclear whether the NP following a verb of causation should be regarded as its "logical object".[5] The test of "cognitive synonymy" under passivization suggests that *have, make,* and *force* are equi verbs (i.e. passivization induces a change in meaning).

(18) a. *She {had/made/forced} a specialist (to) examine her mother.*
b. *She {had/made/forced} her mother (to) be examined by a specialist.*

But while *cause* arguably acts like a raising verb in this respect, intuitions are less than clear-cut; it is just not evident whether (19)a-b should or should not be considered synonymous.

(19) a. *She caused a specialist to examine her mother.*
b. *She caused her mother to be examined by a specialist.*

The behavior of these verbs with "dummies" is also hard to assess:

(20) a. *She {caused/*had/?made/??forced} there (to) be a riot.*
b. *Zeus {caused/had/made/?forced} it (to) rain.*

Judgments are graded, and to the extent that they allow a line to be drawn between raising and equi verbs, it does not coincide with the division based on paraphrase.

Other factors render the putative distinction between equi and raising even more elusive. Both Bolinger (1967) and Borkin (1974) have cited data suggesting that sentences supposedly involving raising are sometimes more acceptable if the derived main clause is a well-formed expression in its own right, and if the proposition conveyed by the latter is compatible with the one expressed by the complement:

(21) a. *I believe the report to be true.*
b. *?I believe the rain to be falling.*
c. *I believe Jennifer to be telling {the truth/?a lie}.*
d. *We confirmed the rumor to be essentially {true/?*false}.*

An additional factor, discussed by Perlmutter (1970) for *begin,* is the occurrence of the same verb in both equi and raising constructions:

(22) a. *There began to be a commotion.*
b. *Zeke began to scrutinize the documents.*

In his study of raising vs. equi in French, Ruwet (1991: ch. 2) established that such ambivalence is not limited to a handful of predicates but represents a widespread pattern with interesting semantic correlations. He concludes that the boundary between raising and equi constructions is fuzzy at best, that traditional tests for distinguishing them are open to question, and that the data reflects subtle and pervasive semantic considerations that the classic analysis does not even begin to deal with (see also Lamiroy 1987). Likewise, Newman (1981) presents a variety of reasons for viewing equi and raising constructions as forming a continuum. In his conception — akin to the one pursued here — clear instances of "raising" represent the limiting case in which the NP referent's direct participation in the main-clause relationship approximates zero.

One of the strongest arguments for a raising analysis has been its ability to account for the displacement of "idiom chunks" from their expected position within fixed idiomatic sequences, as in (6)a, (10)a and (11). Even within the generative tradition, however, it has been known for many years that movement rules cannot account for all instances of discontinuous idioms. Bresnan and Grimshaw (1978: 388) cited a number of cases of idiom chunks in positions where no plausible rule could have put them:

(23) a. *We didn't **make** the amount of **headway** that was expected of us.*
      b. *We were fired because they expected more **headway** from us than we were able to **make**.*
      c. *Unfortunately, we **made** what the President considered to be insufficient **headway** on that problem.*

Therefore, they conclude, "the assumption that idiomatic verb-object constructions must always be base-generated together is false". Yet the idiom-chunk argument for raising rests squarely on that assumption. More generally, the arguments based on idioms and dummies were not grounded in the extensive investigation and clear understanding of the nature of those phenomena that would be necessary to render them secure.

As a final observation, let us note the existence of sentences that seem directly parallel to those for which raising has been posited, yet which lack a subject- or object-complement clause from which the NP in question could have been extracted. OSR provides the widest array of examples. In (24), the relationship between the main-clause subject and predicate is apparently unaffected by omission of the subordinate clause:

(24) a. *A 5K is easy (to run).*
     b. *Trivial Pursuit is fun (to play).*
     c. *Portraits are tough (to paint).*

In the proper context, such expressions are susceptible to an open-ended set of possible interpretations regarding the activity to which the judgment pertains. An adverbial clause may supply that context:

(25) *When it comes to {fixing/cleaning/selling/stealing/lifting} them,*
     Volkswagens are really easy.

With SSR and SOR, the possibilities are much more limited. Examples can however be found:

(26) a. *Another war is {certain/sure/likely} (to break out).*
     b. *When would you {like/want/expect} us (to arrive)?*

Data like this suggests that the expressions supposedly derived by these rules instantiate a considerably broader phenomenon for which a raising analysis cannot be made to work in general.

Despite its apparent insight, therefore, the classic analysis is seriously problematic in multiple respects. Its limitations ought to instill the suspicion that the phenomena it was designed to handle might also be accommodated in ways that are not dependent on the theory-bound mechanisms of transformational syntax. They prove in fact to be straightforwardly characterized from the perspective of CG.[6]

2. Logical grammatical relations

Although "logical grammatical relations" were important in establishing the classic raising analysis (and deep structures in general), for the most part that notion was simply taken for granted, remaining unexamined and unexplicated. The basis for the notion is less than obvious given the assumption that subject and object are grammatical relations, the view that grammar is autonomous, as well as the supposed inadequacy of natural language as the vehicle of logical deduction. The lack of a clear understanding and theory-independent motivation of these putative relations persists to this very day, and in practice linguists often disagree in assigning them (e.g. Postal vs. Newman in regard to (16)a).

2.1. A fallacious argument

Be that as it may, I suggest that the argument for raising based specifically on logical grammatical relations is fallacious. I say this in retrospect, for in earlier years I accepted it and used it quite effectively in the classroom. With the following kind of reasoning, I succeeded in convincing many students of the need for an abstract deep structure and hence the need for a raising rule:

(27) (i)   Consider the sentence *Don is likely to leave.*
     (ii) Logically, the subject of *likely* is not a person—we do not say **Don is likely*—but rather an event (as in *That Don will leave is likely*).
     (iii) To capture this logical relationship, we must posit an abstract structure of the form *[Don leave] is likely.*
     (iv) Thus a raising rule is needed to derive the surface form.

Step (ii) asserts the existence and non-existence of particular logical relations, primarily on the basis of analogy to other linguistic expressions. This move rests on the implicit assumption that the meaning and logical relationships inherent in one use of a predicate, in a particular construction, are the ones it must also have in other constructions. Thus the tacit reasoning of step (ii) goes as follows:

(28) (i)   In the construction *X is likely*, the subject can be an event (*That Don will leave is likely*) but not a person (**Don is likely*).
     (ii) This construction establishes the meaning (and hence the logical relationships) of *likely* in all its uses.
     (iii) *Likely* must therefore exhibit the same meaning and logical relationships in sentences such as *Don is likely to leave.*
     (iv) In this latter construction, however, the surface subject of *likely* is a person rather than an event.
     (v)   There is thus a discrepancy between the surface and logical grammatical relations of *likely* in this construction.

The problem again lies in step (ii), which amounts to a denial of polysemy. This ignores the possibility that the same predicate might have alternate but related senses in different constructions, with the consequence that different kinds of entities might function as its "true", "semantic", or "logical" subject or object. Basic tenets of CG lead to a different interpretation of the data. It is claimed, first, that polysemy represents the usual situation for a common lexical item. In the case of relational elements, one aspect of lexical meaning resides in the choice of participants accorded focal prominence as trajector and landmark (primary and secondary relational figure). It is thus to be expected that the senses of a relational expression often differ in the choice of focal participants ("argument structure"), even within the same conceptual base. Moreover, one sense of a lexical item is commonly perceived as basic (prototypical), others as secondary (extensions). It can also happen that a particular lexical variant (with an extended meaning and resulting argument structure) has limited distribution, perhaps occurring in just a single construction responsible for inducing the extension.

2.2. A case of polysemy

The points just made have all been established independently in CG and are not even particularly controversial. They can all be illustrated by a concrete verb like *wash*:

(29) a. *I washed the car.*
     b. **I washed the mud.*
     c. *I washed the mud off the car.*

Reasoning directly analogous to (27) could be used to argue that *wash* is a kind of raising verb. Normally things like *mud* cannot be the object of *wash*, but only things like cars. Consequently, (29)c must derive from an underlying structure like (30), where the subordinate clause describes the result of the main-clause action (rather than being the logical object of *wash*, which is unspecified).

(30) *I washed Δ [the mud ({be/go}) off the car]*   [⇒ (29)c]

Thus, if the argument from logical grammatical relations is taken seriously and systematically applied, raising will have to be far more widespread than generally believed, involving many different raising rules.

However, basic tenets of CG permit a very different and perfectly viable analysis that does not posit any raising operation. It holds that *wash* is polysemous, having the alternate senses sketched in Figures 11.1(a)-(b). These two lexical variants have the same conceptual base (content): a volitional agent, somehow employing a water-like substance, applies force to an object's surface containing a dirt-like substance, resulting in the latter's removal and the object's change of state (from dirty to clean). Within this common base, the two variants choose the same trajector but different landmarks—the object which undergoes the change of state in 11.1(a), and the dirt-like substance in 11.1(b). Because landmark status is a matter of focal prominence, conferring that status on a given participant tends to highlight any relationship directly involving it; the patient's change of state is therefore rendered salient in the first variant (it can be considered part of the profiled relationship), and the mover's change of location in the second. These alternate choices of landmark and the resultant contrast in relational prominence constitute a difference in meaning between the two variants. Moreover, the one in 11.1(a) is felt to be basic, and that in 11.1(b) secondary. The latter can only be used in a construction which renders explicit (hence salient) the removal of the dirt-like substance, as in (29)c.

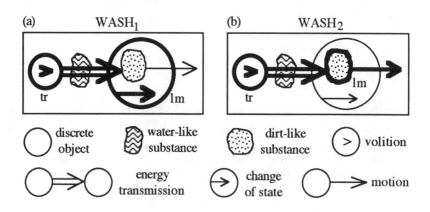

Figure 11.1

A precisely analogous account suggests itself for "raising" constructions. The predicate *likely*, for example, would be considered polysemous and attributed the two related senses sketched in Figure 11.2. The meaning diagrammed in 11.2(a) is the one it exhibits with sentential subjects (e.g. *That Don will leave is likely*). Very roughly, we can say that this variant situates a process within a certain region on a scale of probability. Its processual trajector is specified by the sentential subject, while the scalar region, being uniquely identified by the predicate itself, is not separately coded. Figure 11.2(b) diagrams the semantic value *likely* assumes in the raising construction (*Don is likely to leave*). It has the same conceptual content as 11.2(a). The difference resides in its choice of trajector: rather than according this focal status to the process overall, it confers it on the most salient participant in that process (its trajector). This tends to highlight that participant's role in the overall relationship; e.g. *Don is likely to leave* encourages the interpretation that Don's volition is critical, whereas *That Don will leave is likely* is more neutral in this regard. Moreover, the first sense is felt to be more basic: it is only in the context of the special construction involving both a subject and an infinitival complement that the alternate meaning emerges.

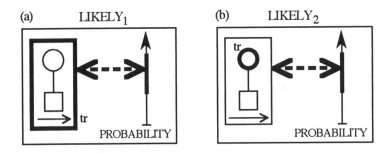

Figure 11.2

A certain objection might be raised at this juncture. It does not seem too implausible to claim that, in (29), either the car or the mud can be construed as "logically" being an object of *wash*. But there is no sense (so the argument would go) in which *Don* could be the logical subject of *likely*—likelihood can only be assessed of events or situations, not of people. However, this argument simply has no force in the absence of any explicit characterization of "logical" relations and the independent demonstration that they are criterial for grammatical relations, at least in "underlying" structure.

CG claims that the notion of underlying structure in the generative sense is erroneous, and that the subject and object relations are first and foremost matters of prominence, not of any specific conceptual content (logical or otherwise). A subject is characterized as a clause-level trajector, i.e. the primary figure within the profiled relationship, and an object as clause-level landmark (secondary figure). Prototypically the subject is an agent, and the object a patient, but there is no specific semantic role or conceptual content that a subject or object has to instantiate. Trajector and landmark status are better thought of as spotlights of focal prominence that can be directed at various entities within a scene. Certain elements exert a natural attraction for this highlighted status; notably, an agent—being animate and an initial energy source—has intrinsic cognitive salience and tends to attract the stronger spotlight. These tendencies can however be overridden, particularly by discourse considerations. If trajector status is basically a matter of prominence, there is no inherent reason why, in Figure 11.2(b), the trajector of *likely* cannot be identified as the primary participant in the process located on the scale of probability, instead of the process per se. Indeed, that participant will usually resemble a prototypical subject more closely than does a process or a proposition.

2.3. The active-zone analysis

Another objection might be raised to the polysemy account. Not just anything (it might be argued) can be illuminated by the "spotlights of focal prominence". The choice has to be constrained. The most natural way to constrain it is to require that the entities selected as trajector and landmark have to participate directly in the profiled relationship. This is so with the putative extended meaning of *wash*, but not that of *likely*. That is, while the landmark of *wash*—namely the mud—is easily thought of as being directly involved in the activity, a comparable remark cannot be made for the supposed trajector in Figure 11.2(b): there is no sense in which a person (Don in this case) directly interacts with the scale of probability.

It is simply not true, however, that trajector or landmark status is limited to entities participating directly in a profiled relationship. Instead, as noted in Chapter 2 (section 4), there is usually some discrepancy between the entities that participate most directly in such a relation and the entities profiled by its subject and object nominals. It is typically not the subject's or object's profile per se, but rather some associated entity—called its *active zone*—that actually or most crucially participates (Figure 2.10). While the active zone is often a subpart (e.g. *She blinked*), it can equally well be referentially distinct (*I'm in the phone book*).

Discrepancy between a nominal profile and its active zone is not just common but represents the normal situation. It can be recognized as a special case of metonymy, a ubiquitous and natural phenomenon with a clear functional motivation: it allows us to focus attention on entities which have the greatest cognitive salience, and at the same time—by invoking them as reference points—to establish mental contact with the intended targets (Chapter 6, section 4.3). Profile/active-zone discrepancy can thus be characterized as metonymy in the choice of focal participants in a profiled relationship. Rather than being puzzling or pathological, from a functional standpoint it is both natural and expected.

These considerations invalidate the hypothetical objection to the proposed account of raising. It is not a general characteristic of subjects and objects that their profiles invariably participate directly in the profiled relationship—quite the contrary. Hence there is nothing in principle objectionable about the configuration sketched in Figure 11.2(b), where the trajector of *likely* is not itself assessed for degree of probability (and thus does not interact directly with the probability scale). In fact, since clauses do not make very good subjects, and a process is not very natural as a reference point, this configuration might be considered better motivated than the one in 11.2(a). While this latter may seem more "logical", because profile and active zone coincide, this advantage is at best a small one, profile/active-zone discrepancy being quite routine and unproblematic. Subject and object status is not a matter of logic but of focal prominence.

The proposed analysis assumes that a participant's active zone with respect to a profiled relationship need not be a *thing*, but can also be *another relationship* in which it figures. This is precisely what is being claimed for the trajector of LIKELY$_2$ in Figure 11.2(b): its active zone with respect to the scale of probability—the entity that *mediates* its interaction with that scale—is some process in which the trajector engages (in *Don is likely to leave*, the process of Don leaving). This kind of situation is covered by the characterization of active zones, since a process in which a nominal referent engages is clearly associated with that referent. Moreover, the possibility of a relationship functioning as active zone can be independently established.

One construction in which a relationship (and specifically a process) functions in that capacity is exemplified in (31):

(31) *She {began/continued/finished} the novel.*

Since *begin*, *continue*, and *finish* are aspectual in nature, they do not directly engage the novel as a physical or even an intellectual entity. Mediating their interaction is some implicit process involving the novel, such as reading, writing, or reciting it (cf. Newmeyer 1970). A process can also mediate a noun's participation in the relationship profiled by an adjective:

(32) a. *That {car/runner/printer/barber/surgeon} is really fast.*
  b. *When it comes to {suturing/deciding to operate/sending his bill}, that surgeon is really fast.*

In (32)a, the processual active zone is left implicit because the noun itself is sufficient to evoke it—there is one characteristic thing that a car, runner, printer, barber, or surgeon does that would most obviously justify its placement on a scale of rapidity. The process in question can however be made explicit when it does not represent a default and is not apparent from the context. Thus the adverbial clause in (32)b specifies the surgeon's active zone with respect to *fast*.

3. Complex constructions

The central idea having been presented, we can begin examining the active-zone analysis in greater structural detail. It will be helpful, though, to start with a non-raising example to make sure that certain basic concepts and notations are clearly grasped.

Consider (29)c, *I washed the mud off the car*, diagrammed in Figure 11.3.[7] It involves the secondary sense of *wash* (WASH$_2$), which takes as its landmark, not the entity being cleaned, but rather the dirt-like substance initially attached to it. The verb is the clausal head (hence enclosed in a heavy-line box), which in this case is elaborated by three component structures functioning as complements. As defined in CG, the pronoun *I* is the subject because it elaborates the trajector of the profiled process. Similarly, *the mud* is the clausal object because it elaborates the landmark. The elaboration sites are marked by hatching and connected with a solid arrow to the elaborating component. Dotted correspondence lines connect elements construed as being identical (i.e. they project to the same composite structure element).

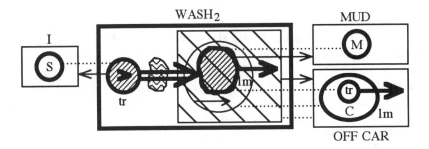

Figure 11.3

There is in addition a third elaborative relationship, responsible for the third complement of *wash*: the prepositional phrase *off the car*. Part of the meaning of WASH$_2$ is that the dirt-like substance follows a path which removes it from its initial position on the surface of the entity being cleaned. This path functions as an e-site which the prepositional phrase *off the car* spells out in finer detail (particularly in regard to the object the substance initially adheres to). Of course, the prepositional phrase has its own internal structure. The mover functions as its trajector, and the trajector's initial location as its landmark, already elaborated by *the car* at a lower level of organization.

As observed in Figure 11.3, a complex expression generally subsumes numerous profiled relationships, their status as conceptual referent prevailing within different component structures or at different levels of organization. Each of these relationships—when examined individually—makes its own trajector/landmark assignment (as an intrinsic part of its semantic value).[8] The same conceived entity can therefore function simultaneously as the trajector or landmark of multiple relationships. In diagrams, these multiple roles are reflected in correspondence lines, which indicate that entities shown separately as participants in distinct relations are actually the same individual.

In the case of WASH$_2$, we see that the dirt-like substance functions simultaneously as the action-chain tail, as the mover with respect to the resultant change of location, and as the entity initially located on the surface of the patient. It is to the first of these roles—as the target of the agent's exertions—that this substance owes its selection as the landmark (spelled out by the clausal object, *the mud*). Observe, now, that the two non-agentive participants are also focal participants of the relationship profiled by the prepositional phrase, *off the car*, where the mover functions as trajector, and the initial location as landmark. Correspondence lines indicate, moreover, that the landmark of *wash* is the same conceived entity as the trajector of the prepositional phrase, while the unprofiled patient of *wash* (the object being cleaned) is equated with the prepositional landmark. It is entirely unproblematic for the same entity to have multiple values in regard to focal prominence, e.g. by simultaneously being the land-mark of one relation and the trajector of another. There is no contra-diction because the relations in question pertain to different levels of conceptual and structural organization.

When we turn now to raising constructions, we find that no-thing is required for their description which has not already been in-troduced and motivated on independent grounds. Consider first SSR, illustrated by the contrast between *That Don will leave is likely* and *Don is likely to leave.* The two senses of *likely* were previously dia-grammed (Figure 11.2). Shown now in Figure 11.4 are essential as-pects of the complex constructions that they head.[9]

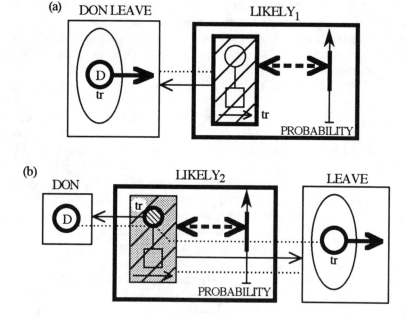

Figure 11.4

The structure depicted in 11.4(a)—representing the sentence *That Don will leave is likely*—is quite straightforward. Functioning as

the sole e-site is the trajector of *likely*, a schematic process. It is elaborated by the finite clause *that Don will leave*, which is consequently
the subject of *likely* and of the complex sentence as a whole. Our interest however lies with the "raising" example, *Don is likely to leave*,
diagrammed in Figure 11.4(b). The overall head (profile determinant)
is LIKELY$_2$. Its trajector is a thing, whose location on the probability
scale is mediated by a process in which it participates (also as trajector); this schematic process is thus the trajector's active zone for the
scale. There are two elaborative relationships: the noun phrase *Don*
elaborates the trajector of *likely*, and the infinitival expression *to leave*
specifies the active zone.[10] Correspondence lines indicate that *Don*
functions simultaneously as the trajector both of *likely* and of *leave*.

Let us next examine OSR. The contrast between such pairs as
To like Don is easy and *Don is easy to like* is once again handled by
positing two related senses of the governing predicate. As shown in
Figure 11.5(a), EASY$_1$ has a processual trajector elaborated by the
infinitival clause *to like Don*, which is consequently the subject of the
former sentence.[11]

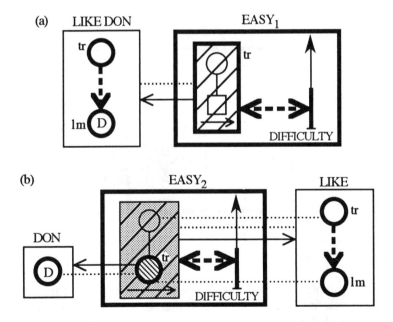

Figure 11.5

The raising sentence is sketched in 11.5(b). The trajector of EASY$_2$ is a thing, whose placement on the difficulty scale is mediated by a schematic process (its active zone with respect to that scale). The difference between this construction and the one involving LIKELY$_2$ (Figure 11.4(b)) is that the trajector of EASY$_2$ is the landmark of this schematic process instead of its trajector; for this reason one speaks of Object-to-Subject (rather than Subject-to-Subject) Raising. By tracing the correspondences in 11.5(b), we see that *Don* is simultaneously the object of *like* and the subject of *easy*.

Finally, exemplifying SOR is the distinction between *I expect that Don will leave* and *I expect Don to leave*, shown in Figure 11.6(a):

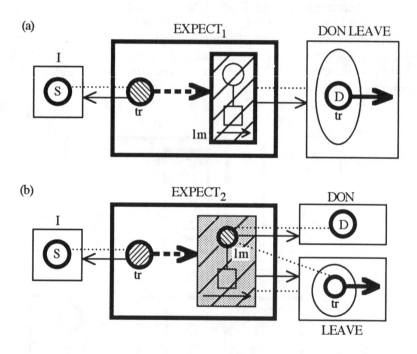

Figure 11.6

EXPECT$_1$ profiles a mental relationship between a sentient trajector and a processual landmark. The former is elaborated by the subject nominal, and the latter by a finite clause which is consequently the main-clause object. EXPECT$_2$ incorporates the same conceptual content but construes it differently by conferring secondary focal prominence—landmark status—on a different entity: the trajector of the en-visaged process, rather than that process per se (which is however the landmark's active zone in regard to the expectation). As seen in 11.6(b), the subject and object of *expect* (so identified because they elaborate its schematic trajector and landmark) are *I* and *Don*, respectively. The infinitival complement *to leave* specifies the active zone. By virtue of correspondences, we see that *Don* functions simultaneously as the landmark of *expect* and the trajector of *leave*. I regard it as the "true" object of *expect* even though it does not participate directly in the profiled relationship.

4. General properties of raising constructions

We have seen in some detail how raising constructions are analyzed in CG. Their characterization is perfectly straightforward granted general principles of the theory and independently established linguistic phenomena. The next task is to show systematically how the proposed treatment accommodates the various considerations which originally appeared to support the raising analysis, and how it avoids the problems which arose in that analysis.

4.1. Grammatical relations

The classic raising analysis neatly captured certain facts concerning overt and "logical" grammatical relations in raising sentences and in their semantically equivalent non-raising counterparts. The same observations are straightforwardly captured in the CG account. To see this, let us focus on SSR, contrasting *Don is likely to leave* with its non-raising counterpart *That Don will leave is likely*. Properly interpreted, the observations are directly discernible in Figure 11.4—they can simply be "read off" the two diagrams.

(i) The raised NP bears a certain overt grammatical relation in the main clause. *Don* is the overt subject of *likely* in *Don is likely to leave*. This is directly apparent in Figure 11.4(b) from the fact that *Don* elaborates the schematic trajector of LIKELY$_2$.

(ii) The raised NP bears the same semantic relation in the subordinate clause that it has overtly in the non-raising counterpart sentence. *Don* bears the same semantic relation to *leave* that it has overtly in the counterpart sentence *That Don will leave is likely*.

Tracing the correspondences in 11.4(b) reveals that *Don* is the trajector of *leave* (its "logical" or "semantic" subject).

(iii) <u>The subordinate clause bears the same semantic relation to the main clause that it has overtly in the counterpart sentence.</u> In *Don is likely to leave*, the infinitival clause *[Don] to leave* is the semantic subject of *likely*, the same relation that the subordinate clause has overtly in *That Don will leave is likely*. We observe this diagrammatically by noting that the infinitival complement in 11.4(b) (labeled LEAVE) and the finite complement in 11.4(a) (labeled DON LEAVE) both elaborate the same substructure: the schematic process that *likely* situates with respect to a scale of probability.

(iv) <u>The raised NP bears the same overt relation in the main clause that the subordinate clause has semantically, and has overtly in the counterpart sentence.</u> *Don* is the overt subject in *Don is likely to leave*, the same relation that the subordinate clause has semantically, and has overtly in the counterpart *That Don will leave is likely*. In other words, the raised NP appears to "replace" the subordinate clause out of which it is lifted, for it assumes overtly the same relation which the clause bears semantically to the main-clause predicate.[12] From Figure 11.4, we can see that this apparent replacement reflects the metonymic relationship between the trajector and the schematic process which functions as its active zone with respect to the probability scale: the semantic extension producing the "raising" predicate resides in a shift in focal prominence (trajector status) from the process as a whole to a salient participant in that process. Because the trajector is a participant in the schematic process—which would itself have focal prominence were it not for the metonymy—the NP that elaborates the trajector appears to replace, as main-clause subject, the infinitival clause which specifies its active zone.

4.2. Semantic non-equivalence

One drawback of the classic analysis is that sentences supposedly derived from the same deep structure are often not precisely the same in meaning (e.g. (14)-(15)). The differences are subtle and largely beyond the scope of this presentation. However, a basic notion of CG is that semantic nuances like these cannot be safely ignored in grammatical analysis—in fact, they are the very essence of grammar.

Raising sentences and their non-raising counterparts are not derived from the same underlying structure, nor one from the other.

They instantiate separate and parallel constructions, each representing its own way of construing and symbolizing situations that may in some cases be the same. These differences in construal are nonetheless genuine differences in meaning, construal being central and essential to linguistic semantics. Every lexical and grammatical choice has semantic import, and the import of grammatical elements resides largely in the construal they impose on conceptual content. The semantic non-equivalence of raising sentences and their counterparts is attributable to two factors: the meanings of the grammatical elements they contain (e.g. *that, to, will, -ing*), and the prominence accorded to the "raised" NP.

For brief illustration of the first factor, consider just one point of contrast between *That Don will leave is likely* and *Don is likely to leave*: the occurrence of the modal *will* in the first, and the infinitival *to* in the second. Although both elements can be future oriented, they have different conceptual import. Here I will merely observe (following Talmy 1988a and Sweetser 1990) that the modals are force-dynamic in nature. On one account (FCG2: 6.3), *will* invokes the "evolutionary momentum" of reality and places an event (*Don leave*) in the projected path of its future evolution. By contrast, *to* imposes a holistic (atemporal) construal on the envisaged event, and probably also places it in the future with respect to a temporal reference point (Wierzbicka 1988: ch. 1), but it is not force-dynamic and does not focus on the evolutionary momentum of reality.[13]

The prominence accorded to the raised NP has two facets. One facet is the focal prominence inherent in its status as main-clause trajector or landmark. We can observe this in Figures 11.4-6 by comparing the salience—within the main-clause predicate—of the participant corresponding to the profile of *Don*. In the (a) diagrams (the non-raising constructions), this entity has no particular main-clause salience, being merely a participant in a conceptually subordinated process. At the main-clause level, focal prominence is conferred on that process as a whole, not on its individual participants. By contrast, in the (b) diagrams (the raising constructions) this same participant is focused within the main clause by virtue of standing metonymically for the subordinated process.

Metonymy being a reference point phenomenon, the second facet of the raised NP's prominence is its status as reference point with respect to the infinitival complement. For instance, LIKELY$_2$ portrays its trajector as a reference point which enables the conceptualizer to access the process being located on the probability scale.

The trajector readily fulfills that function, because it is the most salient participant in the mediating process, and the focal participants of a process are obvious and natural reference points for it (Chapter 6, section 3.1). Thus, in *Don is likely to leave*, it is claimed that Don functions as a reference point with respect to the process of his leaving: the notion of leaving is accessed via the conception of Don and conceived in relation to that individual. This reference point relationship is absent in the corresponding sentence *That Don will leave is likely*, which consequently has a slightly different meaning. The raised NP can be thought of as a kind of local topic, i.e. a topic for purposes of ascertaining the actual (or direct) participant in the profiled main-clause relationship (*Don* calls to mind a process involving Don, and such a process can be assessed for likelihood). This makes the prediction that raised NPs should tend to exhibit greater "topicality" than their unraised counterparts.

4.3. Optionality of the complement clause

A potential problem for the classic analysis was illustrated previously in (24)-(26): sentences whose main clause would appear to be semantically and grammatically parallel to that of so-called raising sentences, but which lack a complement clause from which the "raised" NP could have been extracted. There is no obvious difference, for example, between (33)a and the main clause of (33)b, supposedly derived by OSR. The former would be perfectly felicitous (and non-elliptic) in the proper context, e.g. if uttered during an employee interview in a marsupial-washing facility. If *wombats* in (33)b is the logical object of *wash*, becoming the subject of *easy* only through raising, then the subject in (33)a has no apparent source. The classic raising rule would likewise fail to derive the subject of (33)c.

(33) a. *Wombats are easy.*
    b. *Wombats are easy to wash.*
    c. *As for washing them, wombats are easy.*

In the analysis proposed here, such examples are completely unproblematic.[14] They are merely sentences where the processual active zone, which is normally elaborated by an infinitival complement, remains unelaborated because its nature is evident by other means. Thus (33)a employs the predicate $EASY_2$ and is directly parallel to the construction in Figure 11.5(b), except that only the trajector is elaborated; its active zone with respect to the difficulty scale is deemed apparent and consequently left implicit. As a general point, the complement clause in raising constructions functions as a periphrastic device allowing the raised NP's active zone to be spelled out explicitly when required. In this regard it is comparable to the adverbial clauses in (25) and (32)b, the topic construction in (33)c, the prepositional phrases in (34)a, and the "extra" argument in (34)b.

(34) a. *He accidentally poked me in the eye with his thumb.*
　　 b. *She blinked (her big blue eyes).*

The omissibility of the complement specifying the active zone depends on how predictable or evident the nature of this process is. It is readily omitted in (24)—*A 5K is easy*; *Trivial Pursuit is fun*; *Portraits are tough*—since the process in question represents a default with respect to the subject: what one normally does in regard to a 5K is to *run* it; the canonical activity associated with Trivial Pursuit is *playing* it; and the only difficult thing we typically think of doing in relation to a portrait is to *paint* it. With SSR and SOR, there is usually no default, so the infinitival clause cannot in general be left out.[15] It can in certain instances, however. The complement clause is omissible in (35), because occurring is the most basic thing a war can do, and occurrence is also central to the meaning of *likely*.

(35) *Another war is likely (to {occur/happen/break out}).*

If the speaker envisages a more elaborate scenario, e.g. the probability of another war causing a rise in the price of gold, that would have to be specified overtly.
　　 People are more versatile than wars, so a human subject usually requires specification of the processual active zone. Still, the exchanges in (36) represent conventional patterns:

(36) a. **Q:** *Who is coming to your party?* **A:** *Well, Tom is likely, and Sally is certain.*
　　 b. **Q:** *Who is coming to your party?* **A:** *I expect Tom and Sally.*

The question indicates that the event at issue is that of attending or appearing on the scene; since this is also quite close to the notion of occurrence central to the meaning of *likely*, *certain*, and *expect*, it need not be specified in the answer. On the other hand, we see in (37) that a complement describing more than just appearance on the scene is not omissible:

(37) a. **Q:** *Who will win the lottery?* **A:** **Tom is {likely /certain}.*
  b. **Q:** *Who will get married next?* **A:** **I expect Tom and Sally.*[16]

4.4. Transparency

A basic argument for the classic analysis was what I have called *transparency*: the fact that any element which can occur in the appropriate position in the subordinate clause can likewise occur in "raised" position in the main clause. The main clause itself imposes no constraints on the raised NP—its structural motivation comes from its role in the subordinate clause.

This transparency is automatic in the proposed analysis given appropriate semantic characterizations of the governing predicates. Consider the raising sense of *expect*, as represented in Figure 11.6(b) and repeated in Figure 11.7(a). We have already observed that the entity focused as the landmark of *expect* is simultaneously the trajector of another process (typically elaborated by an infinitival complement). This schematic process functions as the landmark's active zone with respect to the profiled relationship. Crucially, the trajector of *expect* does not directly interact with the landmark per se—their interaction is mediated by the processual active zone. More specifically, the trajector entertains an expectation concerning the occurrence of a process, and the landmark is invoked as a reference point by virtue of being the trajector of that process. But what it takes to be the trajector of a process is solely determined by that process itself: no constraints are imposed on its trajector just because the process constitutes someone's expectation. In short, the inherent constraints imposed by *expect* are limited to there being some process (of an unspecified nature) which the trajector can envisage and anticipate. That process will itself have a trajector, which *expect* puts in focus as landmark, but this predicate is quite neutral concerning its possible character.

(a) EXPECT₂

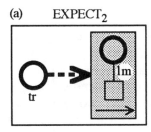

(b) PERSUADE

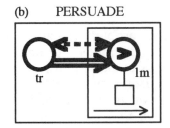

Figure 11.7

Contrast *expect* with *persuade*, diagrammed in Figure 11.7(b). The landmark of *persuade* is also envisaged as engaging in another process (specified by an infinitival complement). However, this predicate further designates a complex *direct* interaction between the trajector and landmark. There is some kind of communicative, typically verbal exchange (represented in the diagram by the double-headed dashed arrow). Through this exchange, moreover, the trajector exerts social or psychological force on the landmark (indicated by the double arrow). As a result of this direct interaction, the landmark has an attitude of intention or volitionality toward the envisaged process (shown as a wedge). These specifications of *persuade* impose a number of constraints on the landmark above and beyond its role as major participant in the infinitival process: it must be capable of envisaging a process, of engaging in a communicative exchange, of succumbing to social/psychological pressure, and of intending to do something. Hence the lack of transparency—the object nominal has to satisfy these specifications, in addition to those imposed by the subordinate clause.

The example, I believe, is representative, though full justification of this account would of course require detailed semantic analysis of all the raising predicates. Section 5 will examine in general terms the kinds of meanings exhibited by the predicates governing each raising construction. While the semantic characterizations are preliminary, they will in each case enable us to see precisely how transparency emerges.[17]

4.5. *Idioms and syntactic "dummies"*

One major problem remains: the behavior of "idiom chunks" and "syntactic dummies", exemplified in (6)-(8) and (10)-(11). The working assumption in transformational grammar was that elements like *tabs, headway, it,* and *there* have no independent semantic value and only occur as part of fixed sequences (*keep tabs on, make headway, it rain, there be*). If there is no movement operation, how can these dummy elements wind up separated from the sequences in question, in the main clause, when the remainder is found in the subordinate clause? Why can they occur apart from the motivating sequences just in those places where hypothesized movement rules can put them? With respect to the proposed analysis, it might further be asked how semantically empty elements can be invoked as conceptual reference points.

The basic response is that the working assumption is simply false—these elements are indeed meaningful, and they do not occur only as part of completely fixed sequences. The original notion that idiom chunks are individually meaningless was theoretically grounded rather than empirically justified: it followed from the building-block metaphor and the assumption that, for an expression to be analyzable into meaningful components at all, it has to exhibit full analyzability and full compositionality. This is an untenable assumption based on a linguistically inappropriate metaphor. CG allows degrees of analyzability and takes partial compositionality to represent the usual situation. Hence there is no question that elements like *tabs* and *headway* ought to be considered meaningful (even if limited to certain larger structural contexts): *tabs* means something like 'surveillance' or 'contact' with the entity being watched, and *headway* means roughly the same as *progress*.[18]

To the extent that an idiom is analyzable and a particular "chunk" is attributed a certain semantic value, it has the potential to be used as permitted by that value. We should not anticipate complete freedom, since idioms—being lexical items—are indeed fixed expressions, hence not automatically and indefinitely flexible. Whether departures are permitted from the canonical manifestation of an idiom depends on such factors as its degree of analyzability, what specific value a speaker attributes to a chunk, and how that value relates to the semantic requirements of particular constructions. If these factors create the potential for variation, whether that potential is actually exploited still depends on precedent, convention, and level of speaker tolerance. All these considerations interact to produce the extraordinary complexity of the situation empirically encountered.

For us, though, the essential point is simply that idiomatic variation, including the occurrence of idiom chunks in raising constructions, is readily accommodated in CG. The only semantic requirements that a raising construction imposes on an element like *tabs* or *headway* (apart from those internal to the idiom) is that it be capable of receiving focal prominence and being invoked as a reference point. There is no inherent reason why an element meaning 'surveillance' or 'progress' could not serve in these capacities—one can perfectly well have an expectation in regard to surveillance, as in (38)a, or make an assessment of likelihood in regard to progress, as in (38)b.

(38)　a.　*They expected **tabs** to be **kept on** all dissenters.*
　　　 b.　***Headway** is not likely to be **made** soon.*
　　　 c.　**We persuaded {**tabs** to be **kept on** all dissenters
　　　　　　/**headway** to be **made**}.*
　　　 d.　***The bucket** is easy to **kick**.*

However, since *tabs* and *headway* are not sentient creatures, they cannot be the object of *persuade*; the examples in (38)c are therefore deviant. A further prediction is that those idiom chunks which are *not* attributed any independent meaning should resist occurrence in raising constructions. The classic example, of course, is the object of *kick the bucket*. Thus, in contrast to *tabs* and *headway* (cf. (11)), *the bucket* cannot undergo OSR, so (38)d is ill-formed.

It has long been known that not all manifestations of an idiom can invariably be derived from a single, fixed underlying sequence (cf. (23)). Independently of the proposed account of raising, it has to be recognized that an idiom (like any other lexical item) represents a complex category comprising multiple variants. Typically there is indeed a central variant (or prototype) realized phonologically as a contiguous sequence (e.g. *keep tabs on; make headway*). We should nonetheless anticipate finding other variants, perhaps limited to certain larger constructions, in which the component elements exhibit other orders and possible discontinuity. The prototype and its various extensions may well give rise to a schematized representation which abstracts away from any particular way of integrating the phonological components.

As a concrete illustration, Figure 11.8 diagrams the schematic variant of *keep tabs on*. The details of the semantic structure need not detain us; the important point is that each component of the idiom is meaningful, and that particular substructures are linked by correspondences (as in any construction).[19] At the phonological pole, the schema merely specifies how each semantic element is symbolized, individually. It is unspecified as to the temporal ordering and possible contiguity of *keep, tabs, on,* and the prepositional object. The prototypical variant will of course make these additional specifications (*keep tabs on* ...), and certain other specific variants (notably one with *tabs* preposed and discontinuous) may also be entrenched as units.

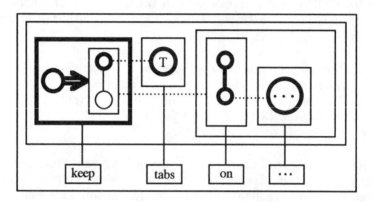

Figure 11.8

There remains the argument that idiom chunks can only occur separately in those places where hypothesized movement rules can put them. It should first be noted that the argument has no trustworthy factual basis; examples like (23) show that plausible movement rules cannot account for all the departures from the basic forms of idioms. In the absence of a massive survey based on attested data, one cannot even be confident of a strong correlation between the position of idiom chunks and their possible landing sites (granted generally accepted movement operations). But even if a non-negligible correlation were empirically established, the alternative analysis proposed here could also account for it (as well as the cases not derivable by movement).

In CG, there are no movement rules, only alternate constructions. Constructions are based on correspondences, and productive constructions — those describing passive and raising sentences, for instance — embody conventional, well-rehearsed patterns of correspondence among their component elements. These patterns enable a speaker to recognize a lexical item like *keep tabs on* (in a schematized variant) even when the components occur discontinuously or in a non-canonical order. Positing movement rules to derive atypical manifestations of idioms is both unnecessary and insufficient. Instead, we need only admit that entrenched constructions specify semantic relationships permitting the recognizable use of lexical items despite perturbations in their temporal arrangement.

The argument concerning syntactic "dummies" is exactly analogous, so it will not be presented in detail. Elements like *it* and *there* have abstract meanings, and are basically confined to specific structural configurations (described by constructional schemas), in which they have a particular semantic and grammatical role.[20] Granted schematic variants of these constructions—which preserve the essential correspondences while abstracting away from details of linear order— the essential semantic and grammatical relationships can be recognized even when the component elements are discontinuous. In *I expect it to rain*, for instance, *it* functions simultaneously as the landmark of *expect* and the trajector of *rain*, just as, in *I expect Don to leave*, *Don* is both the landmark of *expect* and the trajector of *leave* (Figure 11.6(b)). Correspondences inherent in the raising construction establish the relationship between *it* and *rain* that the former requires.

If elements like *it* and *there* are meaningful, what are their meanings? These are harder to characterize than the meanings of *tabs* and *headway*, being more schematic and more abstract. I have argued (FCG2: 8.1.3.4) that they designate *abstract settings*, i.e. settings (as opposed to *participants*) characterized with the minimum possible specificity, hence schematic even with respect to their domain of application. Rather than being specifically spatial or temporal, therefore, they should probably be thought of as abstract presentational frames serving to announce the intention of subsequently introducing something in those frames.[21] With such an analysis, it is perfectly understandable that *it* and *there* should serve as reference points: a setting constitutes a natural and obvious reference point for the elements that occur within it.

5. Specific properties of raising constructions

For further corroboration of the analysis, as well as a deeper understanding of the raising constructions, we need to examine more extensively the meanings of the governing predicates. In particular, what is the source of their transparency? Why can any element whatever occur as subject or object of the main clause provided that it is capable of bearing a certain grammatical relation in the subordinate clause? A general answer has already been proposed: basically, the referent of the "raised" NP does not participate directly in the profiled main-clause relationship, which therefore imposes no constraints on its character (Figure 11.7(a)). Its involvement in the main-clause relationship is wholly mediated by another process (its active zone), usually specified by an infinitival complement.

5.1. Subject-to-Object Raising

From a broader examination of SOR verbs, this basic explanation appears to be borne out. Here is a representative sample:[22]

(39) <u>Some SOR predicates</u>:
    a. *like, prefer, want, need, mean, intend*
    b. *believe, expect, think, assume, feel, know, find, hold, imagine, recognize, judge, take*
    c. *allege, state, acknowledge, certify, decree, say, declare, proclaim, specify, stipulate*

The governing predicates include verbs of need, desire, or intention with respect to a situation, as in (39)a. Many of them express some degree of commitment to the reality of a situation, as in (39)b. Others, as in (39)c, are primarily verbs of communication serving to inform the addressee about a situation or to effect it by virtue of the speech act named.

    Strikingly, all of these verbs imply a conceptualizer (the active-voice subject) who conceives of a situation and assumes some stance or attitude in relation to it. More importantly, they do not specify any direct interaction between the conceptualizer and a participant in that situation—the profiled relationship links the conceptualizer to the conceived situation per se. In the verbs of communication, for example, the raised NP is not the addressee; thus (40)a does not entail any statement to the person being evaluated (who may be locked up in a mental hospital)—the incompetent is not portrayed as the target of communication.

(40) a. *The judge declared him to be mentally incompetent.*
      b. *The judge told him to remain silent.*
      c. **The judge told there to be silence.*

When the referent of the object NP is indeed portrayed as the addressee, as in (40)b, the resulting grammatical behavior is that of a "control" (or "equi") construction rather than a "raising" construction, as observed in (40)c.

There are of course intermediate cases, where it is not so obvious whether the subject merely interacts with the conceived situation, or whether there is also some direct interaction with the object NP. Verbs of perception and causation tend to be harder to pin down in this regard, and are probably subject to variable construal. It is not surprising, then, that such verbs resist simple, unambiguous classification as either raising or control verbs. We saw this earlier in regard to (16)-(20).

Although a finer-grained semantic analysis of the entire range of data is obviously needed, a preliminary conclusion does seem warranted: clear-cut examples of SOR predicates consistently have the semantic property shown to be responsible for transparency in the case of *expect*. Namely, there is no significant interaction between the conceptualizing subject and the raised NP, hence no constraints are imposed on the latter. Apart from being invoked as a reference point, its interaction with the subject is entirely mediated by the infinitival process, which it stands for metonymically.

5.2. Subject-to-Subject Raising

The predicates appearing in SSR constructions are more variegated grammatically. They include auxiliary elements, listed in (41)a; diverse atemporal relations, listed in (41)b; and verbs, in (41)c:[23]

(41) <u>Some SSR predicates:</u>
      a. *may, will, must, can, be, have, do, used to*
      b. *sure, certain, liable, (un)likely, apt, bound, destined,*
          supposed, set, gonna, about
      c. *seem, appear, tend, chance, turn out, prove, happen,*
          promise, threaten, fail, get, begin, start, come,
          continue, cease, keep (on), persist, quit, stop, end up

Semantically, these predicates once more show a surprising degree of coherence and commonality. By and large, they are reasonably characterized as modal or aspectual in nature (those being the primary domains covered by auxiliaries). What modals and aspectuals have in common is that they pertain to the very existence of a process, its actual or potential manifestation in reality or in some other mental space: modals pertain to the likelihood of its manifestation, and aspectuals to its temporal contour (CIS: ch. 12; FCG2: chs. 5-6).

It is also striking that these predicates—in contrast to the SOR verbs—do not make reference to an overtly specified, onstage conceptualizer. The exceptions here are *seem* and *appear*, which allow an indirect object:

(42) *There {seems/appears} (to me) to be a problem.*

These are the two predicates in this class which focus not so much on reality per se, but rather on how it presents itself to some viewer. Even with *seem* and *appear*, however, the conceptualizer is usually not overtly specified; most often the viewer is only potential, remains offstage, or is construed generically or in a generalized fashion. It is worth noting that verbs which highlight the mental reaction to a situation, and thus render the conceptualizer more salient, do not occur as raising predicates, as shown in (43):

(43) a. *For there to be a problem would {surprise/shock*
              /astound/astonish/infuriate} me.
       b. **There would {surprise/shock/astound/astonish /infuriate}*
              me to be a problem.

Especially interesting are *promise* and *threaten*, which have an "axiological" component (Krzeszowski 1993), indicating a prospect that is positive or negative for the potential experiencer. In their basic use, exemplified in (44)a-b, the experiencer is put in focus as an object.

(44) a. *You promised us that you would be more considerate.*
       b. *He threatened us with retaliation.*
       c. *There {promises/threatens} (*us) to be another rainstorm.*

We observe in (44)c, however, that as raising predicates they do not even allow the conceptualizer to be overtly expressed.

Thus, while some kind of conceptualizer is always implied, the SSR predicates tend very strongly to keep it offstage and unmentioned, as an implicit conceptualizing presence rather than an explicit, focused participant. In other words, the conceptualizer tends to be subjectively construed. This is important in regard to grammatical relations and transparency, since by definition a subject and object are objectively construed, the focal elements within a profiled (hence onstage) relationship. A subjectively construed conceptualizer is not even a candidate to be considered for focal prominence.

The transparency of SSR predicates is a consequence of the aforementioned semantic properties, namely that the modal or aspectual relationship pertains merely to the manifestation of a process, and that the conceptualizer is construed subjectively, remaining offstage and unprofiled. Together these properties imply the absence of any natural candidate for the status of trajector, other than the trajector of the "target" process, i.e. the one whose manifestation is being modally or aspectually qualified. The conceptualizer's subjectivity makes it ineligible to serve as trajector, and while the target process can sometimes be reified and accorded focal prominence, as in (45)a, a clause is anything but a prototypical subject.

(45) a. *For wallabies to still inhabit this area would be quite*
         unlikely.
      b. *Wallabies would be quite unlikely to still inhabit this area.*

Therefore, given that the spotlight of focal prominence has to be directed at some onstage element, the most likely candidate—the one favored by prototypicality and general principles of cognitive salience—is the central participant of the target process (as opposed to that process itself). The result, of course, is a SSR construction, as in (45)b. It is nevertheless the target process whose manifestation is at issue: the modal or aspectual qualification pertains to that process as a whole, not to the focused trajector taken individually. Because the modal/aspectual relationship involves the trajector only indirectly (via the target process), it imposes no constraints on its possible nature.

In short, the basic source of transparency with SSR predicates is the absence of any likely candidate for focal prominence distinct from the focal elements of the complement clause. If the main-clause subject is properly characterized as having the highest degree of focal prominence, it stands to reason that this status would be conferred in such cases on the accessible entity with the greatest intrinsic cognitive salience, namely the trajector of the complement process. Since the choice is based on prominence, the search for a suitable candidate can perfectly well extend to entities that do not directly participate in the modal/aspectual relationship, and opting for such a candidate renders a predicate transparent.[24]

5.3. Object-to-Subject Raising

Some predicates that govern OSR are listed in (46). These predicates describe the quality of the experience engendered by the subject in someone who interacts with it in the way specified by the infinitival complement. They pertain either to the degree of ease or difficulty the experiencer encounters in carrying out the activity, as in (46)a, or else how pleasureful or unpleasureful the experience is, as in (46)b-c. These predicates are mostly adjectives but also include noun phrases describing comparable experiences.

(46) <u>Some OSR predicates</u>:
    a. *tough, easy, hard, difficult, impossible*
    b. *pleasant, enjoyable, nice, fun, a joy, a pleasure*
    c. *unpleasant, unenjoyable, disagreeable, terrible, a bitch*

Even from this initial characterization, certain peculiarities of the OSR construction can be explained. First, the centrality of engendered experience is reflected in the option of explicitly mentioning the experiencer in a *for*-phrase:

(47) a. *These diagrams are easy for anyone to interpret.*
     b. *The retirement village was fun for the architect to design.*

To be sure, the *for*-phrase tends to be omitted; the construction is typically used in general statements where the experiencer is construed generically. A second peculiarity is that *impossible* readily occurs in this construction, whereas its positive counterpart, *possible*, cannot:

(48) *Those wombats are {impossible/*possible} to wash.*

Akatsuka (1979: 6) was on the right track in claiming that the difference stems from the latter predicate being "totally devoid of emotional coloration", not being based on "private evaluation" or "actual experience". I would however amend this by emphasizing the distinct force-dynamic natures of the two predicates. If force-dynamic at all, *possible* merely indicates the absence of a barrier to something happening; it is quite neutral as to potential degree of difficulty (so that we can say either *quite possible* or *barely possible*). By contrast, *impossible* evokes an insurmountable barrier and thus has definite implications about the degree of resistance encountered by an experiencer trying to carry out the action, as well as the quality of the resulting experience (cf. *You're just impossible!*).

Since adjectives predominate in this construction, the semantics of the adjective class should be pertinent to its further elucidation.[25] Adjectives are commonly described as designating properties, and these properties are thought of as inhering in the adjectival subjects. I believe this characterization to be correct and important, although it does conceal certain subtle and complex issues. For example, the notion that a property inheres in an entity cannot mean, in general, that no other entity is involved in its manifestation. Adjectival properties occupy the full spectrum of possibilities in regard to how saliently they invoke the conception of other entities. Reference to other entities is relatively non-salient with adjectives (usually considered prototypical) that designate inherent physical properties such as size, shape, and color. Toward the opposite extreme, however, adjectives like *cooperative, shy, visible,* and *user-friendly* describe properties that focus precisely on interactions with other entities. Adjectives also vary in the extent to which the designated property is defined in reference to a specific kind of interactive process, and how prominently that process figures in their conception. For instance, a color term like *blue* involves the process of seeing—if there were no vision there would be no color terms. Yet we think of color as characteristic of an object per se, which has it independently of whether anybody sees it; there is thus a real sense in which seeing is non-salient in the meaning of *blue*. With *visible*, on the other hand, the process of seeing is central and highly prominent.

Ultimately, I believe that most if not all adjectival properties are best characterized with respect to some activity or process involving the entity ascribed the property—what varies is how specific and how salient that process is. Consider the adjective *hard* (as in *hard surface*, or *This ice cream is hard*). To say that an object is *hard* indicates its substantial resistance to anything tending to penetrate its surface or deform it. The notion 'resistance to deformation' evokes a force-dynamic process with the potential to result in deformation, and this in turn invokes a source of energy, the default being a human agent. The notion of 'resistance' implies an intent to deform that may not succeed, and the notion of degree presupposes some kind of comparison over objects and potentially deforming events, such that success in some cases requires a greater expenditure of energy than in others. Lurking in the background, then, is an implicit, generalized human agent/experiencer who has the intention of deforming, provides energy for that purpose, experiences the outcome associated with a given level of exertion, and assesses the experience in relation to other actions of the same type.

I would thus describe *hard* as profiling the inherence of a property in the entity focused as its trajector. That property is however characterized in terms of a schematic interactive process (not per se profiled) with respect to which the adjectival trajector functions as the target or patient. Several factors contribute to the property being conceived as inherent in its trajector. For one thing, the interactive process is usually generic and potential (rather than specific and actual) in terms of both type and the agent/experiencer it implies. Moreover, instead of being transient or instantaneous, the property's association with the trajector is generally stable over a period of time (and often permanent). Finally, some facet of the trajector is thought of as determining the nature of the interaction and the experience it engenders. In the case of *hard*, for instance, the object's physical constitution is such that it tends to maintain its configuration when pressure is applied that would be sufficient to effect the penetration or deformation of other objects. The ascribed property involves the capacity to offer resistance to such forces.

If this characterization has any validity, we can begin to understand why adjectives form the nucleus for the OSR construction. The key point is that the ascribed property makes implicit reference to an interactive process, and usually to some aspect of human experience engendered by it.[26] This process and the experience it engenders come to the fore in the raising sense of *hard* and *tough*, as well as the primary sense of adjectives like *easy, difficult, pleasant, fun, terrible*, etc. One way in which a raising sense differs from a physical -property sense is that the defining interaction is more salient, more schematic, and more extrinsic to the trajector. Concomitantly, there is more focus on the experience of the agent, and less on the trajector's inherent constitution. Because the interaction is prominent but highly schematic, its specification by an infinitival complement is nonredundant and generally necessary. A further consequence of its schematicity is that the trajector need not be physical, and can instantiate any semantic role that the complement verb imposes on its object (see

Figure 11.5(b)). But despite the greater emphasis on the quality of the agent's experience, this more abstract sense still involves the conception of a property and ascribes that property to the trajector. I suggest, moreover, that the trajector is still conceived as being in some sense responsible for the nature of the experience engendered in the agent.

I am hardly the first to propose that the subject of an OSR sentence is viewed as being in some way responsible for the complement process. For instance, Berman (1973) and Akatsuka (1979) cite examples like the following, which show that the engendered experience cannot be due to external circumstances beyond the subject's control or having nothing to do with its nature:

(49) a. *That book is impossible for Paul to read—he can't understand the technical terms.*
     b. **That book is impossible for Paul to read—it's in the bindery.*

(50) a. *Tony has been impossible to live with—he's been churlish, irritable, and short-tempered.*
     b. **Tony has been impossible to live with—he's been in prison for the last five years.*

Still, the trajector's responsibility is not always entirely evident. In this respect it is important to bear in mind that the adjective itself is quite schematic concerning the interactive process. Because of this schematicity, and because the process may be quite extrinsic to the trajector, the latter's responsibility is largely undetermined—it can take almost any form and may be very abstract or tenuous in nature.

The interaction may still be physical, as in (51)a: physical properties of the wheel are responsible for the agent encountering substantial resistance to its efforts. In (51)b, more abstract properties of the diagrams play some role in the agent's pleasureful reaction— for example, they may be complex enough to be challenging, yet not too complex to be frustrating.

(51) a. *This wheel is hard to turn.*
     b. *These diagrams are fun to draw.*
     c. *A 1934 penny is hard to find.*

But what about cases like (51)c? Can a penny be held responsible for someone's difficulty in locating it? I think it reasonably can. Since the process of finding a penny is quite extrinsic to it, we can expect the nature of its responsibility to be rather tenuous. The statement is generic, so the subject stands metonymically for 1934 pennies as a class. If we assume that such pennies are now quite rare, their scarcity can be held responsible for rendering difficult the successful completion of the search.[27]

A few examples hardly prove the point; they are only meant to indicate how abstractly and flexibly this notion of responsibility must be interpreted. The trajector's influence on the interaction and the engendered experience need not reflect any facet of it that is salient, objectively discernible, or central to its characterization. Rather, the adjectival construction *imposes* the conception of the trajector's influence, which the conceptualizer can then construe in any way that makes sense in terms of the scene evoked. Tenuous though it may be in some cases, this notion of responsibility is semantically and grammatically important. It is the basis for ascribing a property to the trajector, for seeing that property as inhering in the trajector, and thus for the target of the interaction being chosen as trajector in the first place. It is a vestige of the adjective category prototype that survives the extension of the class to encompass these non-central members.

The schematicity of the interactive process and the extreme flexibility it affords in construing the trajector's responsibility can now be cited as the source of the transparency exhibited by OSR predicates. Apart from being the landmark of the complement process, the only constraint the adjective imposes on its subject is that somehow—in any way the speaker can imagine—an agent's experience in carrying out that process might be influenced by something associated with its landmark (the adjectival trajector). The requisite notion of responsibility is so flexible that it amounts to hardly any constraint at all; few entities will be wholly excluded. At least some idiom chunks will pass the test, as we saw with *headway* and *tabs* in (11): it is not far-fetched to think of 'progress' or 'surveillance' having intrinsic characteristics that contribute to the experience of making or maintaining it being easy, difficult, or (un)pleasureful.

Still, the ascription of responsibility for inducing a certain kind of experience is not a totally vacuous notion. It goes beyond the mere capacity to serve as a conceptual reference point (which is all the "raised" NP has to do in the other constructions). In particular, I see in this notion a way of explaining the failure of the "dummy" *it* and *there* to occur in the OSR construction, as shown in (13). The reason they cannot be used, I suggest, is that they are too *subjective*, belonging more to the construal of the scene than to the scene itself. These elements are meaningful. They designate schematic abstract settings and have the discourse function of establishing a presentational frame in which an event or situation will be introduced. This enables them to serve as reference points in the SSR and SOR constructions. But the OSR construction demands something more, however slight: its subject must have some influence on the experience engendered in the agent by the complement process. The abstract settings profiled by *it* and *there* cannot have such influence because they are external to the situation under discussion—they pertain to the presentation of a situation rather than being a part of it. Since they reside exclusively in the viewing of a situation, it is hard to think of them as having consequences within it.

6. Final matters

Let me conclude by briefly addressing a number of general issues. These include the relationship of the raising constructions to one another, their relationship to control constructions, the role of functional considerations in linguistic analysis, and the characterization of subject and object.

To what extent do the three "raising" constructions constitute a unified phenomenon meriting parallel treatment? In government-binding theory, they have generally been considered quite distinct and handled in very different ways.[28] The proposed CG analysis offers a more unified account. To be sure, SSR, SOR, and OSR represent distinct constructions, each described by its own constructional schema (in fact, a family of schemas and subschemas). It is also the case that OSR stands slightly apart from SSR and SOR by virtue of attributing some measure of responsibility (not merely reference point function) to the referent of the "raised" NP. The constructions are nonetheless alike in that the NP in question is analyzed as the true subject or object of the main clause, both syntactically and semantically. In each case, moreover, the nominal referent stands metonymically for its processual active zone vis-à-vis the main-clause relation. The functional motivation advanced for raising constructions suggests that they do in fact represent a unified phenomenon. This does not of course imply their full identity or the absence of conventionally determined idiosyncrasies.

The transparency of raising constructions results from the nominal referent not having any direct role in the profiled main-clause relationship; its participation in that relationship is wholly mediated by the processual active zone for which it serves as reference point. I would emphasize that full transparency and full non-participation in the profiled relation represent the limiting case, the endpoint in a continuous spectrum of possibilities (Chapter 10). Since an entity's involvement in a relationship is often multifaceted and subject to variable construal, participation may be a matter of degree, zero participation being a privileged special case. The qualitative distinctness of the limiting case (in particular, the transparency it engenders) has led theorists to posit distinct raising constructions which stand sharply opposed to control constructions. The superficial parallelism of raising and control constructions is then unanticipated, and the difficulty of distinguishing them empirically looms as problematic. If raising and control constructions are instead analyzed as forming a continuum, with classic examples of raising occupying one extremity, such problems evaporate. This has the advantage of not forcing an arbitrary dichotomization (involving substantially different grammatical structures) on examples that vary continuously or are distinguished only by subtle semantic nuances.

The basic point of contention between "formal" and "functional" schools of linguistics is whether functional considerations are *subsidiary* to the investigation of language structure, hence properly undertaken after the latter has been studied independently and described autonomously; or whether they are *foundational* to the enterprise, in that linguistic structures cannot be understood or correctly described in the first place without a clear appreciation of their function. If the foregoing discussion has been at all convincing, it strongly suggests that functional considerations cannot be relegated to subsidiary status.

I have proposed an analysis of raising that I believe to be not only more adequate descriptively than those inspired by theories of autonomous syntax, but also more straightforward, coherent, and revealing. Based squarely on meaning and function, this analysis could never have been arrived at were these not seen as the critical factors from the very outset. In particular, raising was claimed to be just one manifestation of a far more general, even typical phenomenon characterized in terms of two semantic constructs: profile/active-zone discrepancy. That in turn was seen to be a special case of metonymy, with which it shares the cognitive/communicative function of allowing an entity to be evoked through the explicit mention of another that is more salient, of greater interest, or more easily coded. Metonymy instantiates our basic cognitive ability to invoke one conceived entity as a reference point for purposes of establishing mental contact with another.

Pivotal to this and previous analyses of raising is the perennially contentious issue of how to characterize subjects and objects. Attempts to define these notions semantically are usually considered hopeless, since there is clearly no semantic role that all subjects or all objects instantiate. Hence linguists think of these as purely "syntactic" notions and seek to define them in terms of grammatical behaviors. This is of course problematic, since the behaviors vary considerably from one language to the next, to the point that some theorists have questioned the universality of the subject and object relations (e.g. Schachter 1976; Foley and Van Valin 1977). In my view this line of thought is doubly mistaken. First, the appropriate semantic characterization of subjects and objects is most essentially a matter of prominence (an aspect of construal) as opposed to semantic roles (or any other specific conceptual content). Second, the grammatical behaviors in question are symptomatic of the prominence constitutive of subject and object status, rather than being definitional for these grammatical relations. Entities that stand out as the primary and secondary figures in a profiled relationship tend—precisely because of that salience—to be recruited for various grammatical purposes, and each language evolves its own array of conventional constructions which involve them in some way. Semantic roles have the ancillary function of determining which relational participants are most naturally accorded focal prominence in canonical circumstances.

The case for autonomous syntax rests in no small measure on the apparent impossibility of providing general semantic characterizations of basic grammatical notions, subject and object being prime examples. Clearly, however, a proper assessment of the issue requires an appropriate view of linguistic semantics, which I take to be a conceptualist semantics that recognizes the fundamental importance of construal. From this perspective the suggested characterization of subjects and objects is not only plausible but well supported. The descriptive constructs trajector and landmark (primary and secondary relational figure) are necessary just to give an explicit account of the semantic difference between numerous pairs of lexical items (e.g. *before* and *after*) that evoke the same content and profile the same relationship. Because this asymmetry in the prominence of relational elements is manifested at every level of organizational complexity, it is both reasonable and economical to identify the notions subject and object as its clause-level manifestations.[29]

The characterization of subjects and objects in terms of focal prominence accounts for both the variability of the semantic roles they instantiate and the existence of unmarked choices in this regard, not to mention their high degree of accessibility for participation in grammatical relationships (cf. Keenan and Comrie 1977). The existence of "dummy" subjects in no way contravenes the analysis once it is recognized that the elements in question are actually meaningful. Indeed, granted that *there* and *it* designate abstract settings, it seems perfectly natural to claim that these presentational frames are themselves selected for primary focal prominence in constructions serving to introduce a new participant into the scene, or which lack a suitable participant to put in focus (e.g. with weather verbs). Finally, this characterization of subjects and objects dovetails with the analysis of raising as a special case of metonymy, whose general function is to ensure the linguistic prominence of intrinsically salient entities.[30]

As a last remark, I would like to reiterate certain virtues of the proposed analysis. For one thing, it captures the insights and generalizations that motivated the classic transformational account, but without adopting underlying structures or derivations. At the same time, it avoids the many problems of the classic description. Furthermore, no theoretical innovations or special devices are required just to handle raising; the framework and all the theoretical constructs employed (profile, trajector, active zone, setting, subjectivity, etc.) have independent motivation. An additional feature is that the surface grammar of raising constructions directly reflects their semantic characterization. From this characterization, moreover, numerous properties of these constructions fall out as automatic consequences. I believe these advantages are non-trivial and offer considerable support for the CG framework.

Chapter 12
Dynamic conceptualization

In presenting CG, I have often encountered the supposition that conceptual representations are necessarily static and insular entities, hence unable to accommodate the dynamics of connected discourse emerging from contextually grounded social interaction.* In fact, however, I have never regarded conceptualization as being either static or insular. I have always defined it in the broadest possible terms, to encompass novel conceptions, sensory and emotive experience, and apprehension of the physical, linguistic, social, and cultural context. I have also consistently emphasized its inherently *dynamic* nature: conceptual structure emerges and develops through *processing time*; it resides in *processing activity* whose temporal dimension is crucial to its characterization. A dynamic view of conceptualization is essential to a principled understanding of grammar and how it serves its discourse and interactive functions.

1. Previous applications

Previous discussions of CG have in fact emphasized the dynamic nature of conceptual structure. In the scheme described in FCG1, mental experience resides in *cognitive events*, defined as neurological occurrences of any degree of complexity. Cognitive events are *coordinated* when they are incorporated as facets of a more inclusive, higher-order event. When temporal sequencing figures in the coordination of two events, A and B, there is said to be a *transition* between them: A > B. A particular kind of transition is an act of *comparison*, which results in either recognition or the detection of discrepancies. Comparison (including *categorization* as a special case) is presumably ubiquitous in all facets and at all levels of cognitive processing. A *chain* of comparisons (A > B > C > D > ...) effects the *scanning* of a domain of experience, registering either continuity or change. Although discontinuity is required as the basis for experience, *structure* emerges as cognitive events recur, so that comparison at higher levels of organization results in recognition.

    I have further speculated (I think quite plausibly) that any conception involving *ordering* or *directionality* at the experiential level implies some kind of seriality at the processing level, i.e. it incorporates the sequenced occurrence of cognitive events as one facet of its neural implementation (Langacker 1986). This sequencing in the neurological processing is taken as being *constitutive* of the conceptual ordering. For example, our conception of the alphabet as an ordered series of letters resides in part in our well-rehearsed ability to go through them in sequence, whether vocally or just mentally.

A basic kind of sequenced mental occurrence is the observation of events as they happen in real time. As we follow an event through time, we observe (through processing time) a continuous series of minimally different configurations. These constitute a coherent, integrated experience because we conceive of each in relation to its immediate predecessor, noting either constancy or change. These conceptions form a comparison chain, whereby we track an evolving relationship by scanning through time. I call this mode of processing *sequential scanning*. Through memory, we also have the ability to mentally superimpose the successive stages of such an event, progressively building up a more and more elaborate conception in which the various stages come to be experienced as a simultaneously available gestalt. I refer to this as *summary scanning*. I have used these modes of scanning to explicate the linguistic constrast between verbs and finite clauses on the one hand, and participles, infinitives, and non-finite clauses on the other (CIS: ch. 3). The holistic view afforded by summary scanning also figures in the conceptual reification by virtue of which an event is coded with a noun and can even be characterized by a shape-specifying adjective, as in *straight flight* or *zig-zag trajectory*.

I must emphasize the extraordinary complexity of any actual conceptualization. It is essential not to oversimplify by assuming that a conception resides exclusively in a single mode of processing or involves just a single ordering of elements. Instead, we have to acknowledge the multifaceted character of conceptualizations, typically comprising numerous cognitive domains, many structural dimensions, and multiple levels of organization. Consider an expression like *downward trajectory*, which imposes a summary view on an event originally observed sequentially in real time. The summary conception is itself multifaceted, having two essential levels of organization: a sequenced "build-up phase", in which the ordered stages of the event are successively superimposed, as well as the holistic, gestalt-like conception that results. The first level of organization provides the expression's directionality (a *downward trajectory* is not the same as an *upward trajectory*), and the second is reflected in its nominal form.

Inspired by DeLancey (1981), MacWhinney (1977), and Talmy (1988a), I have also described clause structure and transitivity in dynamic terms (CIS: ch. 9; FCG2: chs. 7-9). In particular, I define a *natural path* as any cognitively natural ordering of the elements of a complex structure, and a *starting point* as the origin of such a path. Transitive clauses involve a number of natural paths, including (i) the transmission of energy from participant to participant along an *action chain*, (ii) the temporal sequence of events or event components, (iii) the temporal order of words in the expression, and (iv) access to clausal participants on the basis of their relative prominence. The respective starting points of these natural paths are (i) the agent, (ii) the initial event component, (iii) the first word, and (iv) the subject. There is a tendency for natural paths to "harmonize" or coalign, and clauses which maximize such coalignment are generally recognized as being neutral or unmarked. Thus, in a canonical transitive clause like (1)a, *Floyd* is the starting point with respect to all the paths mentioned. In the corresponding passive (1)b, however, we find conflicting alignments of natural paths, with each clausal participant serving as starting point for two of them.

(1) a. *Floyd broke the glass.*
     b. *The glass was broken by Floyd.*

I have further characterized ergative/absolutive organization in terms of a natural path based on *conceptual autonomy*.[1]

Dynamic conceptualization is also apparent in the notion of *reference points* (Chapter 6). The reference point ability—that of invoking the conception of one entity for purposes of establishing mental contact with another—was proposed as an abstract conceptual basis for numerous linguistic phenomena. Among these are possessives, topic constructions, metonymy (including profile/active-zone discrepancy), and pronominal anaphora. I further take a whole as an inherent reference point for the conception of its parts, a setting or salient landmark for purposes of locating something in space, and focal participants for the conception of a profiled relationship. Most broadly, we can speak of a reference point relation whenever one entity is *mentally accessed* via another.

Invoking a reference point relation is thus an inherently dynamic process involving a shift in focus from the more readily acces-

sible reference point to a target accessed through it. Since the target is
then in focus, it has the potential to function in turn as reference point
in its own right, giving access to another target. We thus encounter
chains of reference point relations, as sketched in (2)a.

(2) a. $R_1 > T_1/R_2 > T_2/R_3 > T_3/R_4 > T_4/R_5 > ...$
      b. *my friend's cousin's wife's sister's lawyer*
      c. *In the kitchen, on the counter, next to the toaster sat a cute*
          little mouse.
      d. *Nicole, Pierre, elle le déteste.* 'Nicole, Peter, she hates him.'
      e. *body > arm > hand > finger > knuckle*
      f. **A famous economist who has won the Nobel Prize**
          will be honored at a luncheon next week. The
          *theories of **this economist** have been very*
          *influential. **The scholar** is known world-wide.*
          She *has published several books.*

The most obvious example is a chain of possessives, as in (2)b. Illustrated in (2)c is a chain of locational reference points, which can be
identified as either the landmarks of the successive locative expressions or else the search domains defined in terms of them (Chapter 2,
section 3); the final target is the entity whose location is being specified (the mouse). Chains of topics are sometimes encountered, as in
(2)d, from spoken French (Lambrecht 1996). Exemplified in (2)e is a
chain of whole/part relations, where the profile of each expression
provides the immediate scope for the one that follows. We also find
chains of anaphoric relationships, as in (2)f.
     Metonymy as well is commonly based on chains of mental
associations. For instance, *I'm in the phone book* does not mean that
the speaker as such is in the phone book, nor even this person's
name, address, and telephone number (since these are abstract), but
rather a graphic representation of this information. Moreover, if focal
participants are correctly viewed as reference points for the conception
of a profiled relationship, the trajector/landmark asymmetry implies
the chain *trajector > landmark > relationship*.

2. Unification

Over many years of investigation, numerous theoretical constructs
have been introduced in CG and justified by their descriptive utility
(Chapter 2). Some of these show tantalizing similarities to one an-

other.[2] There is in fact a substantial amount of linguistic evidence pointing to special affinities among them. They suggest the possibility of a general formulation which treats them as manifestations—in different structural dimensions or at different levels of organization—of a single basic phenomenon.

Two factors in particular point to a general scheme and suggest its nature. The first is the notion of chaining, which is common (if not characteristic) in reference point relationships. The second recurring factor is the focusing of attention on some element observed within a broader context. For instance, an expression's profile stands out as a focus of attention within its conceptual base (Figure 1.1). In locative expressions, the trajector—as the target of search—stands out as focus of attention within the search domain (Figure 2.4). In a reference point relation, the reference point and target are successive foci of attention, the latter found in the former's dominion (Figure 6.1). I likewise regard trajector and landmark as successive foci of attention in the context of a profiled relationship (Langacker 1998c).

The general scheme I propose is sketched in Figure 12.1. I will speak of a *focus chain*, i.e. a series of successive foci of attention, each occurring in some context. Directing attention to a particular focus, in a given context, changes the circumstances and thereby creates or evokes a new context, within which the next focus may be found. No real distinction is being drawn between a focus chain and a reference point chain. The terms and notation in Figure 12.1 do however make the chaining of foci more explicit and may facilitate broader comparisons. Nor is there any sharp distinction between a focus chain and a natural path (any cognitively natural ordering). The latter, though, is more inclusive since it is not required that the ordered elements be individually focused or even salient.[3]

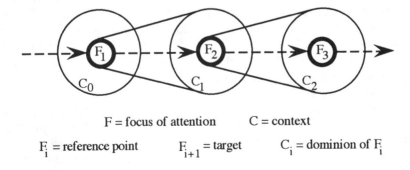

F = focus of attention   C = context

F_i = reference point F_{i+1} = target C_i = dominion of F_i

Figure 12.1

Let us see how some descriptive constructs instantiate this general scheme. With respect to a reference point relationship, F_1 is the initial reference point, C_1 is its dominion, and F_2 the initial target (which may in turn serve as a reference point). In a possessive construction, for instance, F_1 is the possessor, and F_2 the possessed. In the case of a topic construction, F_1 is the topic, C_1 is the domain of knowledge it anchors, and F_2 the proposition to be integrated in that domain. For locative expressions, F_1 is a spatial landmark, C_1 is the associated search domain, and F_2 is either the next landmark in a chain (as in (2)c) or else the final target of search.

What about profiling? Here I think it reasonable to equate F_1 with the form of an expression (i.e. its phonological pole). An expression constitutes an instruction to evoke an array of conceptual content—its base, and in particular its immediate scope—and within that to focus attention on a certain substructure, the profile. The form F_1 is thus an initial point of access, which evokes a context C_1 (the immediate scope), within which the profile stands out as the focused entity, F_2. We can then describe metonymy as carrying this process one step further: F_2 evokes its own context, C_2, in which a new focus, F_3, stands out as the expression's actual intended referent. If *Sue loves Chomsky* is interpreted metonymically, the form *Chomsky* is F_1, the well-known political activist is F_2, and his writings (the actual object of love) are F_3.[4]

More subtle is the focus-chain characterization of trajector and landmark. A relationship is *conceptually dependent* on its participants, in that their conception is requisite to its own. The trajector and landmark (if there is one) are therefore reference points with respect to a profiled relationship by virtue of providing mental access to its full conception. Hence the focal participants and the relationship overall constitute a focus chain in which the trajector is F_1, the landmark F_2, and the relationship F_3. Since a reference point's dominion is the set of potential targets it gives access to, and the final target is the profiled relationship, the context evoked by a focal participant is identifiable as the set of relationships it is capable of anchoring (the profiled relationship standing out as the one actually chosen).[5]

The focus-chain scheme achieves substantial conceptual unification in the descriptive apparatus of CG. It reveals a common, psychologically plausible basis for a variety of independently justified constructs originally devised for different kinds of linguistic phenomena. Of course, this abstract commonality does not negate the existence or distinctive character of its varied manifestations, as determined by the level or dimension of structure they pertain to. We can however look for evidence that constructs claimed to be analogous in this scheme are indeed related in some fashion. There are in fact numerous indications of their special affinity.

Consider first the practice, extremely prevalent across languages, of using possessive constructions to specify the focal participants of a nominalized verb or clause (as in *your complaining* or *Helen's selection by the nominating committee*). This is clear indication that the relation between possessor and possessed is somehow analogous to the relation between focal participants and a profiled process. Possession is characterized schematically as a reference point relation between two things, with the possessor as reference point and the possessed as target (Chapter 6). Analogously, focal participants are described schematically as reference points providing access to a profiled target process. When a verb or clause is nominalized, the process it designates undergoes conceptual reification, creating an abstract thing. The reference point relation between a focal participant and a process is thereby transformed into a reference point relation between two things, which is precisely how possession is defined. The cross-linguistic prevalence of possessive periphrasis is thus predicted.

Further evidence is afforded by constraints on the position of a pronoun vis-à-vis its antecedent. In the CG account of anaphora (Chapters 7 and 9), a pronoun has to occur in the dominion of a salient reference point, to which it is construed as being coreferential (Figure 7.13). Relevant here are the various factors elucidated by van Hoek (1995, 1997a) as determining the likelihood of a particular nominal referent establishing itself as a reference point, and the extent of its structural dominion.

The strongest factors turn out to be those which independently confer the status of reference point (or focus) on the nominal in question. For instance, a topic is a reference point with respect to the following proposition:

(3) a. ***This computer**, I really like **it**.*
     b. **It**, I really like **this computer**.*

In accordance with the focus-chain characterization of trajector and landmark, the subject functions as anaphoric reference point with respect to all other clausal participants, and a direct object for all participants other than the subject:

(4) a. ***Tom*** *likes **his** mother.*
    b. ****He** likes **Tom's** mother.*
    c. *Jenny put **the kitten** in **its** box.*
    d. **Jenny put **it** in **the kitten's** box.*

Also important is the difference between main and subordinate clauses. Main-clause status allows an antecedent to overcome the awkwardness of following a pronoun in the temporal sequence:

(5) a. *Everyone [who meets **Sally**] really likes **her**.*
    b. *Everyone [who meets **her**] really likes **Sally**.*

The distinction between a main and a subordinate clause is that the former's profile is inherited at the composite structure level. Recall now that a profile is one kind of focus. There is thus a correlation among a number of grammatical roles all described in terms of focusing: antecedent, topic, profile, and focal participant.

Let us now consider some constructs all characterized as contexts in which a focus occurs: dominion, search domain, and immediate scope. In terms of Figure 12.1, each of these functions as a context, C_1, which is evoked by an initial focus, F_1, and hosts a subsequent focus, F_2. In the case of a dominion (e.g. for possession), F_1 is a reference point and F_2 a target. For a locative search domain, F_1 is a spatial landmark, F_2 being the target of search. With respect to symbolization, an expression's form is an initial focus, F_1, which evokes an immediate scope containing its profile, F_2. Is there evidence supporting the parallel treatment of these seemingly different kinds of contexts? It turns out that for any two of them we can find linguistic grounds for their identification.

A special connection between dominion and immediate scope is apparent from the frequent and natural use of possessive constructions for the expression of whole/part relations: *Bill's leg, the car's engine, the door's hinges, the book's final chapter,* etc.[6] Possessives are canonical examples of reference point constructions, the possessed standing out as focused target (F_2) in the possessor's dominion. A part term evokes as its immediate scope the conception of the whole with respect to which the part is characterized; within this conceptual base the part stands out as the profile. When possessives are used for whole/part relations, the reference point and dominion coincide: the whole affords mental access to its parts, which collectively constitute it. The possessor's dominion is thus the possessor itself, as a whole, the target being the focused part. In expressions like *Bill's leg*, consequently, there are two correspondences linking the possessive to the head noun. In addition to the usual correspondence equating the possessive target with the head noun's profile, a second correspondence identifies the possessor—hence also its dominion—with the whole functioning as the head noun's immediate scope.

There are likewise constructions in which a possessive dominion corresponds to a locative search domain. Two such cases were described in Chapter 6. The first, quite common, is the description of possession by means of spatial metaphor, as in this well-known Russian example:

(6) *U menja kniga.* (at me book) 'I have a book.'

A spatial relationship functions as the source domain of the metaphor, and a possessive reference point relation as the target domain. The correspondences linking the two domains were shown previously in Figure 6.3: the spatial landmark and trajector correspond respectively to the possessive reference point and target; but more importantly here, an additional correspondence equates the locative search domain with the possessive dominion. In other words, the possessor's sphere of control is spatially construed.

A correspondence between dominion and search domain was also observed in Figure 6.6, for expressions like the following:

(7) a. *We have coyotes in these parts.*
    b. *They have a lot of snakes in Florida.*

The subject in this *have*-construction is construed in generalized fashion as the inhabitants of some region, which is their dominion in the sense that they determine its extent and have the potential to experience anything that occurs within it. The locative phrase describes this region more concretely, i.e. spatially rather than experientially. In particular, the dominion implied by *have* is equated with the search domain of the locative.

We have seen a construction where dominion corresponds to immediate scope, and others where dominion corresponds to search domain. Can we also find a construction in which a correspondence identifies an immediate scope with a search domain? Obviously we can (or I would not have posed the question). We find it in the "nested locative" construction, as in (8), previously diagrammed in Figure 2.9.

(8) *The mustard is in the pantry, on the top shelf, behind the*
     mayonnaise.

The essential feature of nested locatives—the source of their "zooming in" effect—is that the search domain of one locative constitutes the immediate scope of the next (i.e. the spatial region in which the profiled relation is realized). In (8), for instance, *in the pantry* defines a search domain consisting of the pantry's interior. The construction specifies that this is the only region that need be examined to find the relation profiled by the next locative, *on the top shelf.*

3. Back to clause structure

Dynamic conceptualization is important in all areas of linguistic structure. This is especially evident in the case of clause structure, where it helps resolve numerous classic problems.

The importance of dynamicity was first suggested in Chapter 1 (section 2.3) with the appeal to natural paths in explicating nominative/accusative vs. ergative/absolutive organization. The former reflects the natural path defined by energy transmission from agent to theme along an action chain. Motivating the latter is a natural path based on conceptual autonomy: starting from a conceptually autonomous thematic process—a minimal event conception with a single participant (a theme)—the path is defined by successively adding layers of causation, each step resulting in a longer, conceptually autonomous action chain incorporating another participant.[7] The starting points on these coexisting natural paths are an agent and a theme, respectively. When the paths are exploited for case marking, the starting point is typically marked by zero. In a nominative/accusative system, it is therefore the nominative case—prototypically associated with the agent—that tends to be the zero form. In an ergative/absolutive system, absolutive case usually marks the theme and is virtually always zero.

We have also noted certain advantages to characterizing trajector and landmark as the first and second foci evoked in arriving at the conception of a profiled relationship. This dynamic characterization accounts for both their prominence and their inherent asymmetry. It is directly reflected, I suggest, in the well-known tendency for subjects to be highly accessible grammatically, and objects somewhat less so (as witnessed by their role in pronominal anaphora). It is also reflected in the cross-linguistic tendency for subjects to precede objects in neutral word order. We saw earlier that their status as reference points predicts the use of possessives to specify the trajector and landmark of a nominalized verb or clause. It is further predicted—correctly I believe—that there is no landmark unless there is also a trajector: a second focus presupposes a first.[8] For this reason a sentence like *The wax melted* has a subject rather than an object, despite its object-like semantic role (cf. *The heat melted the wax*).

By describing a trajector in dynamic terms, as the initial focus and point of access in the conception of a profiled relationship, we can see the basis for the long-noted affinity between subjects and topics (Li and Thompson 1976; Langacker 1998c). Both a subject and a clause-external discourse topic, as in (3)a, function as reference point with respect to a target process. The difference resides in the level of organization at which this function obtains. In a topic construction, where the target stands alone as a full finite clause, a sense of sequenced mental access—with the topic focused initially, then the clausal process—is almost palpable.[9] An analogous mental sequencing is being imputed to the clause-internal relation between a subject and the profiled process (and at a still lower level of organization, between the trajector and processual profile of a verb). In the case of a subject, however, the target clause does not exist independently from the reference point. In accordance with its clause-internal status, the subject functions as starting point for the very purpose of conceptualizing the profiled clausal process. In short, a topic's reference point relation with a clause is *extrinsic* to the latter, while a subject's is *intrinsic*.[10]

A clause is the lowest level of organization for which we can posit a discourse topic (in the usual sense), and also the highest level for which we can posit a processual trajector (expressed by the subject nominal). This convergence at the clause level is responsible for the descriptive and theoretical difficulties encountered in properly distinguishing topics and subjects. It is not the case that topics and topic-like relationships are always external and extrinsic to a clause. Languages have a variety of means for allowing a single clause to accommodate both a subject and a topic.

In a sentence like (9)a, we observe a neat partitioning between the topic nominal and the comment clause containing a subject. The topic serves the discourse function of specifying the domain of know-ledge to which the clausal proposition pertains. The subject has a clause-internal role as starting point for the very conception of that proposition.

(9) a. *Lawyers, I really admire them.*
   b. *Lawyers I really admire.*

There is no such partitioning in (9)b, a single-clause expression that incorporates a discourse topic and marks it by clause-internal means. *Lawyers* functions simultaneously as the verb's direct object (corre-sponding to its landmark) and as discourse topic for the very clause in which it appears.

This construction is sketched in Figure 12.2:

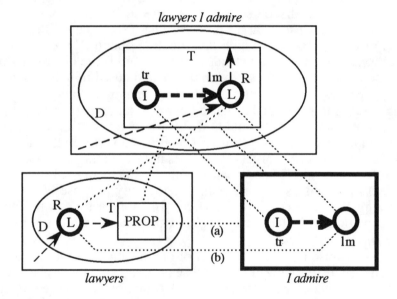

Figure 12.2

Observe that *lawyers* profiles a thing construed as reference point for a schematic proposition; this represents its topic function. Two corre-spondences effect its integration with the partially specified finite clause *I admired*. Correspondence (a) identifies the clause with the target proposition; this is the same correspondence found in a clause-external topic construction, such as (9)a. Correspondence (b) identifies the topic with the schematic landmark of the finite clause; this is the same correspondence found in a normal direct object construction. The construction in question is thus a conflation of two others which exist independently.[11] This conflation appears at the composite structure level as the coexistence of two distinct relationships, in both of which *lawyers* participates: the profiled relation of admiring, where it functions as landmark; and the unprofiled reference point relation which, as a discourse topic, it bears to the clause containing it.

A different sort of conflation is found in the expressions, very common cross-linguistically, often called "double-subject" constructions. Consider this example from Japanese:

(10) *Rokugatu ga   ame ga   yoku furu.*
     June   SUBJ rain SUBJ often fall
     'June always has a lot of rain.'

Both nominals, *Rokugatu* 'June' and *ame* 'rain', act in some ways as subjects (e.g. both take the subject marker *ga*), and the portion after the first nominal (*ame ga yoku furu*) can stand alone as a clause. Yet the entire expression functions as one clause, with *Rokugatu* as its subject. The structure I ascribe to it is given in Figure 12.3.[12]

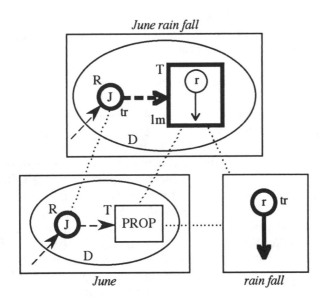

Figure 12.3

At the component structure level, *ame ga yoku furu* 'rain often falls' is in fact a clause, with *ame* 'rain' as its trajector. This clause is further identified as a proposition in the dominion of the reference point *Rokugatu* 'June', which thus has topic-like function. Indeed, were the profile of *ame ga yoku furu* to be inherited at the composite structure level, this would simply be a clause-external topic construction, analogous to (9)a. But it is not. Instead, the composite structure profiles the reference point relation between topic and proposition.[13] As first and second foci in this reference point relation, now profiled, the reference point and target are by definition the trajector and landmark of the higher-level clause.

Granted the possibility of a new clausal profile, with a new trajector, emerging at the composite structure level, the question arises whether a comparable analysis might be proposed for other "atypical" clausal constructions. The matter obviously has to be decided for each individual construction on the basis of specific evidence. A case in point is a preposed locative construction of English, as in (2)c and (11)b:

(11) a. *A motorcycle stood beside the shed.*
      b. *Beside the shed stood a motorcycle.*

The locative (or locative sequence) occupies the position normally reserved in English for the subject, and certainly the location it specifies functions as a kind of reference point. Yet there is no real evidence that *beside the shed* is the subject in (11)b. All the usual tests indicate that the post-verbal nominal, *a motorcycle*, retains this role.[14]

How, then, can we characterize this construction and the semantic contrast between (11)a and (11)b? Locative expressions involve an inherent tension between two different paths of access, each natural in its own way. One of them focuses on a mover, as a kind of agent, and follows its actions as it moves through space in relation to other entities. By this *agentive principle*, the mover is the initial focus, or trajector, and a salient object it moves in relation to is focused as a landmark (e.g. *She entered the shed*). To be sure, a mover is not an archetypal agent, and in static situations there is no actual motion. I nonetheless take the agentive principle as motivating trajector/landmark alignment in sentences like (11)a, as well as in prepositions and prepositional phrases. Though static, the trajector is still a potential mover and the entity whose motion and location are at issue. We might perhaps see this as a limiting, degenerate case of motion. Be that as it may, (11)a profiles a relationship—motivated by the agentive principle—which takes the potential mover as initial point of access. The subject is thus *a motorcycle*.

The alternate path of access, which leads in the opposite direction, reflects our quotidian experience of finding things in space. We commonly do this by first locating a salient spatial reference point, then searching through a contiguous area until we find what we are looking for. By way of narrowing the search, we may in fact access a series of reference points, and a series of progressively smaller search domains, until the target is finally located. This *locational principle* is reflected in nested locative constructions, as in (8). It defines a natural path whose initial focus is the initial point of reference, the last focus being the target of search.

Despite their opposite directions, these natural paths coexist in any given locative relationship.[15] They can however have different degrees of prominence. In a sentence like (11)a, the agentive principle prevails. The agent-based path defines the trajector/landmark organization of the profiled process as well as the prepositional phrase. Moreover, the temporal ordering reinforces the motorcycle's status as initial focus, it being the first element mentioned. What about (11)b? The agent-based path is still in profile, so the subject is still *a motorcycle*. But at the same time the opposite path, reflecting the locational principle, has greater prominence than it does in (11)a. Its salience is heightened by coalignment with temporal ordering, which leads us through the situation from spatial landmark—even through a series of spatial landmarks, as in (2)c—to the final target of search. Although *beside the shed* is not the subject in (11)b, it is nonetheless the initial focus with respect to an unprofiled yet salient relationship that coexists with the profiled process.

I would offer a similar analysis for sentences like (12), from German (Smith 1993):

(12) *Mir zittern die Hände.* (to me shake the hands)
     'My hands are shaking.'

The initial pronoun in (12) is in the dative case, which typically marks an experiencer. Experiencers tend to establish themselves as reference points, as one natural path leads from experiencer to object of experience. From agreement and case marking, the subject in (12) appears to be *die Hände* 'the hands'. In accordance with the agentive principle, the process of shaking is profiled, its trajector being the closest analog to an agent (the moving hands). The experiencing of hands shaking is however another, non-trivial aspect of this situation. We can reasonably posit a coexisting experiential path that takes the experiencer as initial focus. Though unprofiled, this path is quite salient by virtue of dative case marking and coalignment with word order.

There is no reason to expect that the agent-based path will always emerge victorious. In a given language, a sentence analogous to (12) can perfectly well accord greater prominence to the experiential path instead. The result is then a "dative-subject" construction, since the profiled relationship is defined by the path whose initial focus is the experiencer. Diachronically, expressions like (12) can easily be reanalyzed as dative-subject constructions: the essential step is merely a shift in profile from one of two coexisting relationships to the other, i.e. a straightforward instance of metonymy. Whichever path is profiled, its initial reference point is by definition the clausal trajector, and the nominal expressing it is by definition the clausal subject. Similar reanalyses can put a locational path in profile, resulting in setting-subject or location-subject constructions.[16]

4. Looking ahead

Although dynamic conceptualization has been part of CG from the very outset, its extensive ramifications are only starting to be investigated. I expect to find it relevant, if not pivotal, to every aspect of linguistic structure. Articulating the dynamic nature of conceptual and grammatical structure leads us inexorably to the dynamics of discourse and social interaction. While these too have been part of CG from the very outset, they have certainly not received the emphasis they deserve. This is gradually changing as the implications of dynamicity are being explored. I anticipate an increasingly closer and more transparent relationship between CG descriptions of language structure and its discourse-pragmatic function. We should strive for a unified account of structure and function, revealing in seamless fashion how the structures described are shaped by the necessities and affordances of communicative interaction.

Notes

Chapter 1: Clause structure

*   This chapter is a slight revision of an article titled "Clause structure in cognitive grammar", which appeared in *Studi Italiani di Linguistica Teorica e Applicata* 22: 465-508, 1993. It is reprinted with permission.

1. See, for example, FCG1-2, CIS; Lindner 1981; Tuggy 1981; Casad 1982; Hawkins 1984; Rice 1987a; Smith 1987; Cook 1988a; Vandeloise 1991; Maldonado 1992; Manney 1993; Rubba 1993; Doiz-Bienzobas 1995; van Hoek 1995, 1997a; Achard 1998; Israel 1998; F. Kumashiro 1999; T. Kumashiro 1999.

2. Consider, for instance, a field of dots all of which are black, except for three that are red. We immediately discern and group the red dots on the basis of their common distinctive color, and can easily see them as forming a triangle (a higher-order unitary entity).

3. I claim that a verb designates a relationship whose evolution through time is scanned sequentially. Infinitives and participles view such a relationship in summary fashion, as do nominalizations, which further involve conceptual reification. (FCG1: part II; CIS: ch. 3.)

4. Whereas Johnson and Lakoff take image schemas as being experientially derived, I myself tend to see them as reflections of inborn abilities that make it possible for structured experience to arise in the first place. And though I recognize the critical importance of these fundamental conceptions, I do not necessarily see them as comprising a homogeneous or well-delimited class.

5. This is called the *invariance hypothesis*. See Turner 1993 for clarification concerning its precise formulation.

6. Known as *encyclopedic semantics*, this view rejects the standard but inappropriate metaphor which portrays a lexical item as a "container" holding a limited quantity of semantic "substance", e.g. a small set of semantic features (cf. Reddy 1979; Haiman 1980). One consequence of encyclopedic semantics is that a lexical item takes on a subtly different value every time it is used, depending on which array of associated conceptions it happens to evoke on a given occasion, and the specific level of activation they achieve. For an argument against the encyclopedic view, see Wierzbicka 1995.

7. For example, the conception of a feather is not evoked by *tree*, even though birds are associated with trees, and feathers with birds—'tree' and 'feather' are

related only indirectly, via 'bird'. Conceptual reference is discussed below under the rubric of *profiling*.

8. Instead of *construal*, I have often used the term *imagery*. The latter term does not (in this usage) specifically indicate our ability to form and manipulate visual images, nor does it imply that all conceptual structure reduces to such images.

9. See Langacker 1985 and CIS: ch. 12. The notion of subjectivity/objectivity is most easily grasped with respect to perception (a special case of conception). When I direct my gaze at an external object, I construe it objectively (as the object or target of visual perception), whereas I construe myself subjectively (I do the perceiving but am not myself perceived). Maximal objectivity thus attaches to an explicitly mentioned focus of attention "onstage", and maximal subjectivity to an implicit, "offstage" viewing presence. Note that the vantage points implied by *upstairs*, *outside*, *yesterday*, and *soon* are offstage and subjectively construed.

10. That is, the boundary may be "fuzzy" rather than precise. The evidence for bounding is presented in Chapter 2.

11. Of course, among our conceptualizations is one that we identify (correctly, I assume) as representing "reality" (the world "out there" that we actually live in). Hence a conceptual notion of reference can accommodate the classical notion (reference in the world) as a special case.

12. We will see later that some focal elements are not construed as *participants* but rather as *settings* or *locations* (Langacker 1987b).

13. The notions usually contemplated—concepts like 'event' and 'physical object'—are insufficiently abstract to serve as schematic characterizations applicable to all class members. Furthermore, since members of different classes can apparently incorporate precisely the same conceptual content (e.g. *collide* vs. *collision*, or *round* vs. *circle*), content-based schematic definitions must be ruled out in principle.

14. The same description was offered previously for the senses of a lexical item. Cognitive linguistics claims that most linguistic categories exhibit this kind of complexity (cf. Lakoff 1987; FCG1:ch. 10; Taylor 1995).

15. Actually, since lexical items are themselves complex categories, each lexical *variant* functions as a node in the overall network.

16. What about the phonological pole? Perhaps we can say that a prototypical noun comprises a segment sequence containing at least one syllable. And for

the class of nouns as a whole? There is probably no specific phonological trait that all nouns share without exception, in which case the noun-class schema is maximally schematic (essentially vacuous) at the phonological pole. This should not be considered odd: although nouns are symbolic elements, their crucial distinguishing property is a semantic one.

17. A preposition's landmark is specified by the prepositional object, and the trajector of an adjective or adverb by the element it modifies. It follows that an adjective modifies a noun, whereas an adverb modifies a verb, preposition, adjective, or another adverb. A preposition or prepositional phrase can itself be considered adjectival or adverbial depending on whether its trajector is a thing or a relationship.

18. These assemblies are quite different from the tree structures of generative grammar, which are generally conceived as autonomous syntactic objects devoid of intrinsic semantic or phonological content. Observe that each "node" in Figure 1.4(b) is a symbolic structure with both a semantic and a phonological pole. At a given level of organization, grammatical class is determined by the composite structure's profile (*sharpen* is thus a verb, *sharpener* a noun, etc.), in contrast to the "syntactic" (hence semantically empty) node labels of generative phrase trees. Another difference is that the symbolic elements in 1.4(b) are not linearly ordered with respect to one another (i.e. the hierarchical structure is more like a mobile than a tree with fixed branches). So-called "linear" order is actually temporal order, which each symbolic element specifies internally as part of its phonological characterization. (For discussion of constituency, see Chapter 5.)

19. This *building-block metaphor* is ubiquitous, unavoidable, and useful up to a point. It is not altogether appropriate, however, and if taken too seriously it leads to conceptual and theoretical difficulties that in actuality are merely artifacts of the metaphor itself. It has led, for example, to analyzability being almost completely neglected in linguistic theory and description (since building blocks are either present in a structure or absent—they cannot be there to a certain degree).

20. *Full compositionality* can be seen as the special, limiting case in which non-compositional specifications are completely absent. I believe, however, that partial compositionality represents the norm for expressions of all sizes, both fixed and novel.

21. The pictorial representations at the semantic pole merely abbreviate complex sets of semantic specifications. They are not offered as formal descriptions.

22. Likewise, at the phonological pole *jar* elaborates the e-site identified schematically as the word directly preceding *lid*.

23. My ultimate claim, of course, is that all grammatical elements are properly regarded as meaningful in all of their uses.

24. As noted earlier, symbolic complexity is further resolvable into the number of component symbolic elements and their degree of analyzability. We can likewise distinguish between schematicity at the semantic and at the phonological pole. Other parameters include the extent to which symbolic structures are conventional (within a speech community) and entrenched (for a given speaker).

25. In this respect CG is essentially equivalent to construction grammar (cf. Fillmore 1988; Fillmore, Kay, and O'Connor 1988; Goldberg 1995; Michaelis and Lambrecht 1996). The basic difference between the theories is that the latter does not attempt the full reduction of grammar to assemblies of symbolic structures.

26. As a general term, noun phrase is unfortunate because not all instances of the category are phrases, nor do they all contain a head noun (as that notion is traditionally understood). Some examples: *you*; *several*; *those with money*; *which of them?*; *being on time [is important]*; *that so many people are depending on us [is frightening]*.

27. This point is not at all obvious and has to be interpreted in the context of an overall analysis of nominal structure (see FCG2: part I).

28. The discussion must still be quite succinct. For more extensive treatment, see CIS: ch.9, FCG2: part II; Achard 1998; Cook 1988a, 1993a, 1993b; T. Kumashiro 1999; Maldonado 1988, 1992, 1993; Manney 1993; Rice 1987a, 1987b, 1993; Smith 1987, 1993.

29. I analyze the adjective as profiling an atemporal relation, which *be* (a schematic verb) extends through time to form an imperfective process that functions as the clausal head (Langacker 1987c). There are of course other ways to accommodate this archetype. Languages vary to some extent in regard to both the inventory of basic clause types and their specific structural properties.

30. Compare, for example, *Na va'ai le tama 'i le fale* (PAST see the boy to the house) 'The boy saw the house' and *Na alu le tama 'i le fale* (PAST go the boy to the house) 'The boy went to the house'.

31. The term object is used more broadly (we speak of prepositional objects, as well as indirect objects), but the subject and direct object of a finite clause are what we are presently trying to characterize.

32. For preliminary efforts to this end in the context of CG, see FCG2: 7.3.1.3, Langacker 1998c, and Chapter 6.

33. These archetypes are analogous to the "deep cases" of case grammar (Fillmore 1968) or the "thematic roles" employed in various contemporary theories. In CG, they are viewed as pre-linguistic, experientially grounded conceptions of sufficient cognitive salience that linguistic categories are likely to coalesce around them.

34. Absolute construal is a matter of degree and pertains to how a situation is conceptualized. It is therefore not precluded that some kind of force or energy might be involved (e.g. heat in the case of *melt*, gravity for *rise*). The essential factor is whether the notion of force remains submerged in the background or is somehow brought into focus. Even a process that is clearly energetic in objective terms may be construed as absolute by virtue of conforming to the "normal course of events". (See Langacker 1989, FCG2: 7.1.2; Maldonado 1988, 1993.)

35. The term *causal chain* is used by Croft (1991), whose view of clause structure is quite similar to the one presented here.

36. I believe an indirect object is revealingly characterized as an active experiencer in the target domain, and thus as a kind of semantic role, not a grammatical relation akin to subject and direct object. By this definition, it is possible for a nominal to function simultaneously as a direct and an indirect object (as does *him* in *I showed him the picture*). For discussion and justification, see FCG2: 7.3.3.

37. Examples (4)c and (5)c are open to variable construal in regard to whether an agent and instrument are included within their scope. Likewise, (5)b need not be construed as involving an agent, in which case the "instrument" becomes more agent-like (Nishimura 1993).

38. These definitions are based on conceptual factors (correspondence, profiling, figure/ground organization), not on structural configuration. They are consequently independent of grammatical constituency, i.e. the order in which a complex symbolic structure is assembled out of smaller components. (See Chapter 5, section 1, for discussion and illustration.)

39. In Newari, for example, dative case can also mark experiencer subjects and animate direct objects (Cook 1988b; Hung 1988).

40. This relational/nominal distinction is to some degree independent of whether the element in question is manifested phonologically as a separate particle, an affix, or a morphological inflection.

41. For example, verb-stem suppletion operates on an ergative/absolutive basis in the Uto-Aztecan family of American Indian languages: intransitive stems agree in number with the subject, and transitive stems with the object. Case marking in this family follows the nominative/accusative pattern.

42. Kindred ideas are explored in MacWhinney 1977, DeLancey 1981, and Chafe 1994. Observe that there are other kinds of natural paths, including word order, topicality, event order, the empathy hierarchy, etc. For a comprehensive account of pronominal anaphora based on this notion, see van Hoek 1995, 1997a.

43. Though it has not been emphasized here, *autonomy* vs. *dependence* is seen in CG as a pervasive and fundamental aspect of linguistic structure (FCG1). Within a syllable, for example, the vocalic nucleus is autonomous, and the associated consonants dependent. An affix is morphologically dependent with respect to the autonomous stem it attaches to.

44. It is not claimed that every complex event displays a clear-cut layering of this sort (e.g. what is the single-participant thematic process in *She kissed him?*), only that it represents an archetypal arrangement providing the motivation for certain grammatical phenomena.

45. As a concomitant property, a thematic process is generally richer in conceptual content than other links in an action chain (cf. Keenan 1984). The verbs called "unaccusative" in relational grammar (Perlmutter 1978) can be characterized as those which profile a thematic process construed in absolute fashion. Their single participant is not an underlying direct object but rather a thematic trajector whose construal is basically non-energetic.

46. For discussion of this point as well as a comprehensive CG description of the English passive, see CIS: ch. 4. In brief, the passive participial morpheme is analyzed as both atemporalizing the process designated by the verb and imposing on it an alternate choice of trajector; *be* then serves to retemporalize the participial relationship and thus derive the higher-order processual head. This is, of course, just one of the strategies languages use in passive or passive-like constructions (cf. Shibatani 1985).

47. See Langacker 1976 and FCG2: 8.3.3 for examples, as well as discussion of how unspecified-argument markers are related to reflexive markers and to noun incorporation.

48. *Location* is the local term corresponding to the global notion setting. A location is a fragment of the overall setting, e.g. the portion of the setting that is occupied by a single participant.

49. Simple location (i.e. merely being somewhere) is one basic kind of thematic process; its participant instantiates the zero role archetype. Motion is likewise a thematic process, and its participant simply a mover, provided that it is limited to change of location per se, comprising only a series of positions manifested at successive points in time. An energetic construal becomes more likely to the extent that the conception is expanded to encompass additional factors such as the manner and rate of movement, which are intimately associated with the force-dynamic notion of propulsion. Hence the participant in a process like *run* or *crawl* combines the roles of mover and agent. As a symptom of this putative contrast between motion construed in absolute and in energetic fashion, consider a well-known fact of French: purely directional motion verbs (*aller* 'go', *venir* 'come', *monter* 'ascend', *descendre* 'descend', etc.) take the auxiliary *être* 'be' in forming the perfect, whereas verbs that incorporate manner and/or rate (e.g. *nager* 'swim', *courir* 'run', *voler* 'fly') instead take *avoir* 'have'.

50. For example, we might perceive the same display as comprising either two dots of light projected on a dark surface, or else—with some effort—as a dark sheet with holes in it, through which a light background is visible.

51. A setting is a special kind of reference point, and setting-subject constructions belong to a broader class of *reference-point-subject constructions*. Many languages exhibit "double subject constructions" that fall in this class. (FCG2: 8.1.3; Langacker 1993d, To appear-b; T. Kumashiro 1999.)

Chapter 2: Evidence for descriptive constructs

* This chapter is adapted with substantial revisions from "Grammatical traces of some 'invisible' semantic constructs", which appeared in *Language Sciences* 15: 323-355, 1993. It is reprinted with permission.

1. On the specific reading, the description *a Norwegian* pertains to a real individual but is applied to an element in the subordinate clause representing Xavier's desire. This analysis lets us avoid positing the same ambiguity for other indefinite determiners (as in *I'm looking for {some/Ø} tall marines*).

2. Further examples and discussion can be found in Chapters 7 and 8. (See also CIS: 52-55, 94-97.)

3. These facets include zero derivation, a productive derivational pattern affecting whole phrases, and a semantic contrast effected via profile shift. These are all exemplified in the productive use of complex path expressions to indicate static location at the end of the path (e.g. *She hiked across the field, through the*

woods, over the hill vs. *She lives across the field, through the woods, over the hill*).

4. It is least obvious how *um* fits into this pattern. Smith plausibly suggests that the notion of completion inherent in path-goal is related to the notion of a full circular path canonically associated with *um* (note the expression *come full circle*).

5. Recall that for 'in' the search domain is the landmark's interior, hence its boundary may coincide with the landmark.

6. Chapter 11 will show that profile/active-zone discrepancy is the key to a cogent analysis of "raising" constructions, e.g. (15)d.

7. Recall the canonical event model discussed in Chapter 1 (section 2.1).

8. For some interesting examples in Mandarin, see Shen 1996.

9. Thus passivizability cannot be specified merely by lexically listing a set of eligible verbs. Nor is transitivity simply a matter of a verb being directly followed by a nominal in object position.

10. Other setting-subject constructions were briefly discussed in Chapter 1 (see examples (18)-(21)). As predicted, in each case a passive is infelicitous.

Chapter 3: The meaning of of

*   This chapter is slightly revised from "The symbolic nature of cognitive grammar: The meaning of *of* and of *of*-periphrasis", which appeared in Martin Pütz (ed.), *Thirty Years of Linguistic Evolution: Studies in Honour of René Dirven on the Occasion of his Sixtieth Birthday*, 483-502, Amsterdam / Philadelphia, John Benjamins, 1992. It is reprinted with permission.

1. The present discussion deals only with cases where both the trajector and the landmark are nominal in character. I have not investigated how the analysis could be extended to uses with relational arguments.

2. The definite articles are ignored (see FCG2: 3.1.1).

3. Observe that it is possible to interpret (10)b, but not (10)a, as referring to a father accompanied by children who are not his own.

4. The essential notions were discussed in Chapter 1 (section 2.3).

5. For a more precise and detailed description, see Langacker 1987c and FCG2: ch. 1.

Chapter 4: A dynamic usage-based model

* This chapter is slightly revised from one with the same name that appeared in Michael Barlow and Suzanne Kemmer (eds.), *Usage Based Models of Language*, 1-63, Stanford, CSLI Publications, 1999. It is reprinted with permission.

1. Regarding the issue of innate specification I make no apriori claims. I do however subscribe to the general strategy in cognitive and functional linguistics of deriving language structure insofar as possible from more general psychological capacities (e.g. perception, memory, categorization), positing inborn language-specific structures only as a last resort. I anticipate, moreover, that any such structures would constitute specialized adaptations of more general abilities, and thus be continuous with them rather than separate and *sui generis*.

2. This is, I think, equivalent to Bybee's (1988) notion of "connections" established between overlapping portions of stored units.

3. Observe that here the thickness of boxes corresponds to level of activation rather than entrenchment.

4. This tendency is however less than absolute (Bybee and Moder 1983).

5. They fail to establish that grammar is "autonomous" in the sense of requiring descriptive devices not reducible to symbolic assemblies.

6. The pattern [N_{an} [PRON-P]] would then have to be dealt with separately.

7. For a detailed account of the latter in CG, see van Hoek 1997a.

8. While I cannot not yet claim to have seriously dealt with phonology in CG, insightful preliminary studies have been done by Farrell (1990) on Spanish stress, by Rubba (1993) on modern Aramaic, and by F. Kumashiro (1999) on the importance of phonotactics in a usage-based phonology. I would also subscribe in both spirit and detail to Bybee's prolegomena for a cognitive/ functional phonology (Bybee 1994). Kemmer and Israel (1994) discuss phonological variation from a usage-based perspective.

9. For some differences between derivation and categorization, see FCG1: 443-444.

10. These are analogous to patterns of semantic extension, e.g. the metonymic pattern whereby the name for a location is used for a noteworthy event associated with it: *the Alamo, Pearl Harbor, Yalta, Vietnam, Woodstock, Watergate, Oklahoma City*, etc.

11. Here I must acknowledge the visionary work of Joan Bybee (1985; 1988; Bybee and Slobin 1982), who was advocating a usage-based approach long before that term was coined. Many of her ideas have direct analogs in the conception presented here, including the extraction of schemas, the storage of specific complex forms (even some that appear to be regular), degrees of entrenchment and ease of activation ("lexical strength"), and the importance of viewing morphological structure as networks of "connections" (as opposed to discrete "building blocks"). I must also highlight the more recent contribution of Jo Rubba (1993), who has given extensive thought to how traditional morphological problems can be handled in CG, providing illustration with a detailed description of verb morphology in modern Aramaic.

Chapter 5: Conceptual grouping and constituency

*   This chapter is adapted with substantial revisions from "Conceptual grouping and constituency in cognitive grammar", which appeared in Ik-Hwan Lee (ed.), *Linguistics in the Morning Calm 3*, 149-172, Seoul, Hanshin, 1995. It is reprinted with permission.

1.   Grammatical structure is not however limited to this strictly hierarchical kind of organization. It is a special (if privileged) case within the wide spectrum of configurations symbolic assemblies can assume.

2.   The term direct object is usually reserved for clauses that are transitive, in addition to having a nominal landmark. Transitivity is a global semantic property of the clause as a whole (see Rice 1987a, 1987b).

3.   No attempt is made in this diagram to indicate the status of *Bill* as a clause-internal topic (see Langacker 1998c, To appear-b).

4.   Recall Behaghel's law: elements that belong together semantically tend to occur together syntactically.

5.   This is not a necessary assumption. A plausible alternative (which I do not specifically reject) would be to claim that multiple conceptual constituents regularly emerge, but that when they cross-cut, only one of them is singled out for symbolization by means of a phonological constituent. According to this alternative, for instance, both groupings shown in Figure 5.7 emerge for

the sentence *Bill Alice saw*, but only the subject-verb constituent receives direct symbolization (by *Alice saw*).

6. Similar phenomena are discussed in Lambrecht 1988 and Langacker 1997b.

Chapter 6: Reference point constructions

* This chapter is adapted from "Reference-point constructions", which appeared in *Cognitive Linguistics* 4: 1-38, 1993. It is reprinted with permission.

1. Cognitive abilities are discussed in Chapter 1, section 1.1, and conceptual archetypes in section 2.1. The former might be identified with some of the *image schemas* posited by Johnson (1987) and by Lakoff (1987). For instance, the source-path-goal image schema can be thought of as the ability to scan mentally from one point to another in any kind of representational space. For Johnson and Lakoff, however, image schemas are not innate but abstracted from everyday bodily experience.

2. For extensive discussion of dynamicity, see Chapter 12.

3. Being mainly concerned with possessives as a manifestation of the reference point phenomenon, I make no pretense of offering a comprehensive account of the many interesting problems associated with possessive constructions, in English or cross-linguistically. Deane 1987 deals insightfully with the choice between possessive determiners and *of*-phrases. Nikiforidou 1991 examines genitives as a radial category, both cross-linguistically and diachronically. These analyses complement the one presented here (see also Langacker 1995c) and appear to be compatible with it. Taylor 1996 pursues the reference point analysis of English possessives in considerable detail, comparing this CG approach to generative treatments.

4. Other analyses are conceivable, e.g. the proposal by Taylor (1996) that only the target is profiled. Since the profile of POSS is overridden by that of the modified noun at a higher level of organization, the choice has no evident consequences for present purposes.

5. The possessive morpheme exhibits a comparable value in sentences like *I'm dining at my aunt's tonight*. Here the dominion is understood to be the reference point's usual spatial locus (residence or place of occupation).

6. A setting (or location) lends itself quite naturally to reference point function, and represents a special case in which the reference point itself delimits the scope of search. The reference point is thus a "container" with respect to potential targets (FCG2: 351).

7. Observe that the possessor precedes the head in such cases. By their very nature, reference points can be predicted to exhibit a strong cross-linguistic tendency to precede their targets, especially when their relationship remains implicit rather than being coded morphologically. This prediction appears to be borne out by topics and pronominal antecedents, which I also analyze as reference points.

8. In this context, the relevant dominion is the reference point itself (i.e. the body as a whole, the target being one of its subparts). Cf. Figure 6.7.

9. Hence the crucial semantic relationships are accommodated without positing any rule akin to "possessor ascension". (Cf. Tuggy 1980; Velázquez-Castillo 1996; Dąbrowska 1997.)

10. The relation between topics, subjects, and possessors in CG is explicated in Langacker 1998c.

11. Corroborating this suggested relationship between possessives and topics are expressions like *ship's cook* and *potter's wheel*, where the possessive ending attaches to a noun (rather than a full noun phrase) to form a complex head noun (which is likewise not itself an NP—for NP status a determiner must be added, e.g. *a ship's cook*). In such combinations the possessor noun does not refer to a particular individual but merely provides a type specification (FCG2: ch. 2). Like the topic *sakana* 'fish' in (17), it is a reference point in the sense that it specifies a domain of knowledge that must be accessed in order to properly interpret the second noun (the target).

12. Penhallurick 1984 discusses the discourse motivation of such constructions in terms compatible with the present account. (See also Birner and Ward 1993.)

13. It therefore represents a dimension of *conceptual grouping*, in the sense of Chapter 5. We will return to van Hoek's analysis at various points in later chapters.

14. Active zones were discussed in section 4 of Chapter 2 (see also CIS: ch. 7).

Chapter 7: Viewing in cognition and grammar

* This chapter is adapted with substantial revisions from "Viewing in cognition and grammar", which appeared in Philip W. Davis (ed.), *Alternative Linguistics: Descriptive and Theoretical Modes*, 153-212, Amsterdam / Philadelphia, John Benjamins, 1995. It is reprinted with permission.

1. Talmy's term "ception" has a similar motivation (Talmy 1996).

2. Here, of course, there are usually two observers, whose interaction with one another is a consequential aspect of such experience even when their attention is directed elsewhere. How two interlocutors accommodate their divergent perspectives, and negotiate the adaptation of conventional patterns to the idiosyncratic complexity of the immediate context, are foundational questions of linguistic theory.

3. Linguistic evidence for the constructs maximal and immediate scope was provided in Chapter 2.

4. The speaker's location can also be considered a reference point, just as the reference time in (2) can be considered a temporal vantage point. The difference between these closely related notions is a matter of whether we construe the location in question as being *occupied* by a viewer or as being *evoked* by a viewer to locate a target.

5. Whether the target domain of a metaphor is immediate to the conceptualizer in some comparable fashion is much less obvious.

6. See Chapter 1, section 2.4, and Chapter 2, section 5 (also Langacker 1987b).

7. This arrangement greatly diminishes the asymmetry on which subjectivity /objectivity is based. The pronoun *I* construes the speaker quite objectively compared to its normal subjectivity, but less so than is usual for the profiled entity.

8. Arrows have been omitted from many previous diagrams, as have "vertical" correspondence lines and even the composite structures. Owing to the complexity of constructions, any particular diagrammatic representation has to abstract away from numerous details and focus on those of immediate relevance.

9. An analogous viewing metaphor can be used for metaphor itself. The source- and target-domain configurations can be thought of as being drawn on separate transparencies, with the former placed on top. Viewing the target through the "lens" of the source tends to produce an integrated "hybrid" domain that the conceptualizer may not even perceive as being metaphorical (cf. Fong 1988). This hybrid structure is referred to as a *blend* in recent work (e.g. Fauconnier 1997, 1998; Fauconnier and Turner 1998; Turner and Fauconnier 1995).

10. Indeed, once a complex expression is established as a fixed unit, it tends to undergo a loss of analyzability, i.e. we grasp its composite value with progressively less awareness of the semantic contributions—and even the existence—of its components (Figure 4.12).

11. This is another way of saying that, in typical constructions like Figure 7.2, integration hinges on a correspondence between the profile of one component structure and some portion of the other component's profile. Naturally, if we go beyond the profiles of the two components to consider their full, encyclopedic semantic descriptions, cases where one projection is wholly included in the other will be relatively few.

12. For detailed arguments to this effect, see Langacker 1985, 1990c, 1993b, 1997a, and FCG2: 2.4.

13. We employ this latter ability, for example, when we mentally reconstruct the flight of a ball and visualize its successive positions as defining a certain shape (e.g. *curve*, *slider*, *sinker*).

14. The terms "active" and "stative" are perhaps more common. The distinction does not represent a rigid lexical partitioning: although most verbs have a default-case value, categorization in a given expression is flexibly and globally determined.

15. The many non-present uses of the "present tense" are analyzed in terms of proximity in the context of a special viewing arrangement. For more extensive analysis and discussion, see FCG1: 6.2, and also Langacker To appear-c. Doiz-Bienzobas 1995 describes the contrast between the Spanish preterite and imperfect in terms of viewing.

16. The "play-by-play" mode of speech hinges on the conventional fiction that the commentator is able to pull this off, or at least minimize the time delay to the point of making it negligible. It is not irrelevant that the events reported in this mode are quite brief and tend to be rather stereotypical.

17. Causative verbs like *make* and *let* also take zero-marked complements, but they do not imply the strict temporal coincidence that we find with perception verbs. The zero marking may however reflect some notion of proximity (at least compared to the infinitival complements of *cause* and *allow*), thus corresponding to the schematic value of the "present-tense" morpheme. Parallelism between verbs of perception and causation is also observed in French. I suspect that Achard (1996, 1998) is on the right track in suggesting that in both cases the subject exercises "control" over the subordinate-clause process.

18. For diagrammatic convenience, component structures are shown on the left, and composite structures on the right.

19. In a more detailed treatment, the object of viewing would be characterized not just as a situation, but as a thing—the referent of the object nominal—ob-

served within a situation. The object nominal would be a third component structure, its profile corresponding to landmark of *see* and the trajector of *Ving* or $\emptyset + V$.

20. Supporting this characterization are sentences like the following: *I saw the factory burning an hour ago, and I still see it burning now.* The overall act of seeing the factory in flames continues over an extended time period, and each conjunct segments out a limited portion for profiling. The referent of the first conjunct is an episode of seeing prior to the time of speaking, while the second conjunct refers to an episode coincident with the speech event.

21. This much could also be said of definite determiners (cf. Postal 1969b; FCG2: 3.1). Here we are only considering definite personal pronouns.

22. Strictly speaking, it is the nominal referent—the profiled thing instance—which functions as the reference point; the nominal expression per se is the reference point only metonymically. A nominal's *referential* dominion will be distinguished from its *structural* dominion, the structural context over which it holds sway. These two kinds of dominion represent distinct dimensions of reference point organization both of which are essential to pronominal anaphora.

23. This antecedence does however provide a point of overlap which allows the contents of the proposition to be integrated in the domain of knowledge evoked by the topic. It is this domain of knowledge—rather than a set of potential nominal referents—that constitutes the topic's non-structural dominion. This distinguishes topics from both pronominal antecedents and possessors.

24. A sentence like (16)c may be acceptable when the topic is used contrastively to redirect attention to a referent already introduced: *Jill has a crazy husband— SHE's very calm, but HIM, he's always out of control.* The construction is also permissible with first- and second-person pronouns, since the speech-event participants are always accessible: *JILL is very calm, but ME, I'm always out of control.* The semantic conflict alluded to results when the topic pronoun itself bears the brunt of introducing and singling out the intended referent.

25. Van Hoek's analysis achieves a unified account of pronoun-antecedent relationships as manifested within sentences and in longer stretches of discourse, and further accommodates bound anaphora as well as reflexives. It successfully handles many kinds of examples that have been problematic in other approaches (cf. Langacker 1969; Reinhart 1983; McCawley 1984).

26. Such examples are not easy to render fully acceptable, since linear order and the asymmetry between main and subordinate clause still motivate the opposite choice of reference point. There may however be counterbalancing factors, e.g. the foreground/background alignment associated with the perfective/ imperfective aspectual contrast. The following sentence thus seems reasonably natural (Harris and Bates 1990): *He had been staring at the control panel for an hour when **Jack** got a message from his commander*. All that matters here is that there is some discernible difference between cases involving complements and non-complements.

27. This is actually the *definition* of correspondence: entities correspond when they project to the same element of the composite image.

Chapter 8: Generic constructions

*   This chapter is adapted from "A constraint on progressive generics", which appeared in Adele E. Goldberg (ed.), *Conceptual Structure, Discourse and Language*, 289-302, Stanford, CSLI Publications, 1996. It is reprinted with permission.

1. Observe that the format used in Figure 8.2 represents aspectual properties of a verb or clause, whereas the format of Figure 8.1 represents participants. A full representation has to include both kinds of information.

Chapter 9: Grouping and pronominal anaphora

*   This chapter is adapted with substantial revisions from "Conceptual grouping and pronominal anaphora", which appeared in Barbara Fox (ed.), *Studies in Anaphora*, 333-378, Amsterdam / Philadelphia, John Benjamins, 1996. It is reprinted with permission.

1. Fauconnier's definition of a mental space is quite broad, and the notion of a conceptual grouping is admittedly vague. It may well be that the terms are coextensive. The former emphasizes the partitioning of our mental world into semi-autonomous zones, while the latter highlights their internal cohesiveness.

2. In the case of count nouns, the reference mass is the set of all instances. In the case of mass nouns, it is the union of all instances (since any subpart of a mass-noun instance is itself an instance of the category). The space fictively examined to find "all instances" is variable and subject to contextual determination.

3. *Any* can also occur with mass nouns, including plurals.

4. At least this is so for proportional quantifiers. With representative-instance quantifiers the situation is less clear. It is hard not to interpret *Every atheist was denounced by the fiery preacher* as pertaining to a contextually limited set of atheists. Even a sentence like *Bill loves {every/any} woman* seems to evoke a reference mass restricted to the set of women Bill might potentially encounter.

5. For instance, a person can be invoked as reference point for many purposes, each setting up a different dominion: as the owner or possessor of a set of objects; as "ego" in a network of kinship relations; as a physical whole with respect to which various parts are identified (here the reference point and dominion are the same); as a discourse topic (its dominion being the associated domain of knowledge); and so on.

6. See the discussion of example (16) in Chapter 7.

7. Note the dotted correspondence line in Figure 7.13.

8. Technically, I analyze *the peaks* as designating a single instance of the thing type *peaks*, derived by pluralization from the more basic type *peak*.

9. Example (21) is analogous in this respect.

10. It can also be thought of as a special case of metonymic antecedence, in which an instance-level nominal expression provides mental access to a type-level antecedent immanent in it.

Chapter 10: Subjectification and grammaticization

*   This chapter is adapted from "Losing control: Grammaticization, subjectification, and transparency", which appeared in Andreas Blank and Peter Koch (eds.), *Historical Semantics and Cognition*, 147-175, Berlin / New York, Mouton de Gruyter, 1999. It is reprinted with permission.

1. See Langacker 1985, 1986, 1990c, 1993b, 1997a, FCG2. In contrast, Traugott (e.g. 1986, 1989) uses the terms subjectivity and subjectification with respect to a general tendency toward greater pragmaticization of meaning, subsuming (i) the shift from externally based descriptions to internally grounded assessments, (ii) extension to textual and metalinguistic uses, and (iii) increased involvement of speaker judgment. Rather than *perspective*, these pertain primarily to the *domain* in which a property or relationship is

manifested. Traugott's version of subjectivity and my own will both figure in an overall account of grammaticization.

2. This landmark is specified by the infinitival complement, and the trajector by the subject noun phrase, at higher levels of grammatical organization.

3. Observe that this account is not based on metaphor. Contrary to my own previous discussion of *be going to* (1986), as well as Sweetser's (1988), there is no transfer from the spatial to the temporal domain, but merely the retention of a temporal relationship that was there all along. Moreover, it is specifically *not* claimed that the subject of *be going to* is metaphorically construed as moving along a temporal path (analogous to a spatial path) — only the conceptualizer is claimed to move along a temporal path, mentally and subjectively.

4. For detailed analysis, see Langacker 1990c, FCG2: 5.2.3; Carey 1994.

5. This holistic construal is one semantic contribution of the participial inflection; another—ignored here—is the "internal perspective" imposed by a progressive construction (Chapter 7, section 4.3).

6. Observe that all of these sentences are well formed if *get* is replaced with *be*.

Chapter 11: Raising and transparency

* This chapter is adapted with substantial revisions from "Raising and transparency", which appeared in *Language* 71: 1-62, 1995. It is reprinted with permission.

1. Chomsky himself did not propose any kind of raising rule for such examples, but after Rosenbaum 1967 a raising analysis became completely standard in transformational grammar. In 1973, however, Chomsky rejected raising in such examples in favor of an account treating the nominal in question as the subject of the complement clause.

2. Of course, *expect* can also act as an equi verb (e.g. *They expect to finish on time*). Numerous predicates can function in either capacity.

3. I cannot undertake a full review of the characterization and implications of raising over the history of generative grammar. While SSR is still widely accepted, the rejection of SOR was pivotal in the development of government and binding theory (Chomsky 1973; Massam 1984; cf. Authier 1991). OSR (commonly known as "*Tough* Movement") has long been problematic. The construction exhibits mixed properties, which have spawned considerable

debate as to whether and how movement figures in its derivation (e.g. Postal and Ross 1971; Akmajian 1972; Lasnik and Fiengo 1974; Jackendoff 1975; Chomsky 1977, 1981; Oehrle 1979; Jones 1983; Brody 1993). Nanni (1980) proposed a treatment in terms of complex adjectives. For raising analyses in relational grammar (involving a variety of languages), see Frantz 1980, Perlmutter and Postal 1983, Seiter 1983, and Legendre 1986. Sadock 1992 discusses raising in the context of autolexical syntax.

4. See Newman 1982 for further relevant data and insightful discussion, including the identification of semantically grounded regularities in the complements that occur with different kinds of predicates.

5. This suggests a non-trivial semantic parallelism between perception and causation verbs, as proposed by Achard 1996.

6. Partial presentations of the CG account were given in Langacker 1984, 1990c, 1993d, FCG2; cf. Farrell 1995. For a generativist response, see Nakajima 1997.

7. To simplify matters here and in later diagrams, I will omit the representation of tense markers, articles, and complementizers. All of these are described in FCG2. I will also be ignoring constituency, which is non-essential (Chapter 5), and omitting any explicit representation of the composite structure. For our purposes it is enough to know which element functions as the clausal head, and which components elaborate its substructures.

8. Of course, the trajector/landmark assignment made at the composite structure level is the one that counts for most higher-level purposes.

9. For our purposes, the semantic contribution of *be* can be ignored (see CIS: chs. 3-4).

10. Observe that the schematic process in Figure 11.4(b) is both shaded, to signal its role as an active zone, and hatched, to mark it as an elaboration site.

11. The single-headed dashed arrow stands for a relationship of mental contact: the meaning of *like* implies that its trajector conceives of the landmark and has a certain mental/emotional attitude in regard to it.

12. In relational grammar, the "relational succession law" stipulates that a raised NP can only assume the grammatical relation of the clause out of which it ascends. This law was proposed as a syntactic universal in Perlmutter and Postal 1983.

13. One should bear in mind that the heuristic diagrams used here are not intended to capture this difference, and that I have oversimplified matters in consistently referring to subordinate clauses as processes. Technically, an infinitival clause does not profile a process but rather a complex atemporal relation derived by construing a process holistically. A more precise representation would show an infinitival complement (as well as the corresponding e-site in the governing predicate) as imposing this atemporal construal on a processual base. I suspect, in fact, that subject-complement clauses and perhaps *that*-clauses go one step further and construe the base process as an abstract thing (by conceptual reification). Such refinements do not affect the basic points of this chapter.

14. For a proposed solution in the context of government-binding theory, see Pesetsky 1987.

15. This difference reflects the semantics of the raising constructions and their governing predicates. Observe that the OSR construction is mostly limited to adjectival predicates. I will argue later that an adjective ascribes a property to its trajector, and consequently that the OSR construction portrays the subject as responsible for the infinitival process engendering a certain experience. By its very nature, then, the construction tends to focus attention on a process intrinsic to the characterization of the subject.

16. Either response is rendered felicitous by the addition of *to*, which is analyzed (in accordance with general principles of CG) as a schematic infinitival complement. The judgment in (37)b assumes a continuous intonation contour: with a pause (*I expect, Tom and Sally*), the response is acceptable but is interpreted as being elliptic (cf. *Tom and Sally, I expect*).

17. In Chapter 10 we saw how transparency arises diachronically through a natural process of attenuation, giving rise to new raising predicates.

18. Fraser 1970 is a classic transformational account of idioms based explicitly on the assumption of unanalyzability. Gorbet 1973 provides strong evidence that neither their unanalyzability nor their fixed character can be maintained. In the generative tradition, Bresnan and Grimshaw 1978 demonstrated that the insertion of idioms as fixed sequences cannot account for all their manifestations (recall the examples in (23)). A subtle and detailed examination of French idioms led Ruwet (1991: ch. 5) to conclude that they could not validly be used for the justification of movement rules (see also Jones 1983). The now commonplace idea that the "deformability" of an idiom correlates with its analyzability goes back to Chafe 1968. In more recent work, Nunberg, Sag, and Wasow 1994 reinforces the conclusion that many idioms are analyzable, while

O'Grady 1998 (interpreted along the lines of Chapter 5) indicates the possibility of discontinuous idioms nonetheless forming conceptual groupings.

19. The import of the ellipses in Figure 11.8 is that the idiom is analyzed as containing a schematic prepositional object (see FCG1: 313-316).

20. The fact that *it* and *there* are limited to particular structural configurations does not render them sharply distinct from other lexical items. Part of the characterization of every lexical item is a set of structural frames (constructional schemas) in which it conventionally occurs. The richer conceptual content of a typical lexeme lets it occur in a wider and more diverse array of symbolic assemblies, but the difference is one of degree.

21. Some of the evidence was presented in Chapter 1 (section 2.4). This characterization is similar to proposals made by Bolinger (1973; 1977: chs. 4-5), as well as the description of Dutch *er* advanced by Kirsner (1979). Pinker (1989: 147) hints at something comparable. In Achard 1998 (ch. 7), the referent of French *il* is specifically identified as the *immediate scope* of an existential predication.

22. This list does not pretend to be exhaustive, nor is it evident that a definitive, well-delimited inventory could be established. Postal (1974) provides a more inclusive listing and documents the limitations certain predicates exhibit when used in a raising construction. With some of them, for example, the main clause has to be passive (*He is said to be a thief/*They say him to be a thief*). Others prefer a modal (*I would like you to do that/??I like you to do that*). Some of the predicates listed go better with *-ing* than with *to* (*The board certified him {as being/?to be} fully qualified*).

23. The raising analysis of auxiliaries goes back to Ross 1967a, and while it is not universally accepted, they do exhibit transparency. Some auxiliary elements combine with a bare verb stem (for an explanation, see FCG2: 6.1). Most of the aspectual verbs in (41)c allow or require *-ing* instead of *to*. The atemporal predicates in (41)b include adjectives, participles, and the preposition *about*. Describing a predicate as atemporal does not indicate that time is irrelevant to its characterization, but only that it views a relationship holistically, as a single gestalt (whereas a verb is "temporal" or "processual" in the sense of tracking or rendering salient its evolution through time).

24. To be sure, the complement's trajector will not invariably have great intrinsic salience (it may, for instance, be a setting, as in (42) and (44)c). It is not claimed that the functional considerations being appealed to are necessarily active and operate *de novo* every time a raising sentence occurs. Rather, they are seen as motivating the emergence and conventionalization of the raising

construction, which is then available for broader use. In any case, the raising of elements like *there* and *it* has its own functional motivation, since an abstract setting (presentational frame) makes a natural reference point and *starting point* (MacWhinney 1977) for the complex sentence as a whole.

25. Obviously, these remarks will be partial and provisional at best. For some varied but cogent discussions, see Dixon 1977, Givón 1979 (8.6), Wierzbicka 1988 (ch. 9), and Croft 1991.

26. That process is sometimes made explicit, e.g. *This suitcase is heavy (for my mother) to lift*. These sentences are formally indistinguishable from instances of OSR. In a classic paper, Bolinger (1961) cited this formal coincidence as a case of "syntactic blending". The extraordinary proliferation of distinct yet similar and clearly related constructions is handled in cognitive linguistics by treating constructions as complex categories, i.e. networks of constructional variants linked by categorizing relations. (See Chapter 4, as well as Lakoff 1987 (case study 3), Brugman 1988, Langacker 1988, and Goldberg 1995.)

27. Observe that adjectives like *rare* and *scarce* invoke a more specific process— one of finding or acquisition—and directly name a property responsible for impeding its accomplishment.

28. In fact, only SSR is usually analyzed in raising terms. Standard for SOR constructions since Chomsky 1973 has been an account that eschews raising and treats the NP in question as the subject of the complement clause. As for OSR, the basic analysis since Chomsky 1977 claims that the main-clause subject originates as such, but that WH-movement (of an empty operator) figures in the complement.

29. Newmeyer (1990: 65 [fn. 5]) therefore misinterprets the inherent logic of the enterprise (Chapter 2) when he states that CG "simply...build[s] a great deal of syntactic structure directly into...conceptual structures". Instead, certain semantic constructs (in the case at hand, trajector and landmark) are first introduced and justified independently as necessary for the explicit characterization of lexical meanings. It is then argued that certain grammatical notions (in this case subject and object) are revealingly described as manifestations of those constructs, the apparent need to treat them as syntactic primitives being attributable to the failure of linguistic semantics to recognize or accommodate construal.

30. For further justification of this characterization of subject and object, see Langacker 1998b, 1998c, and To appear-a.

Chapter 12: Dynamic conceptualization

*   This chapter is a condensed and greatly revised version of "A dynamic account of grammatical function", which appeared in Joan Bybee, John Haiman, and Sandra A. Thompson (eds.), *Essays on Language Function and Language Type Dedicated to T. Givón*, 249-273, Amsterdam / Philadelphia, John Benjamins, 1997. It is reprinted with permission.

1. See Chapter 1 (section 2.3) as well as Langacker 1989.

2. E.g. many people have intuitively likened the focal prominence of trajector and landmark in a relational expression to the salience of a profile within its conceptual base.

3. Consider the mental scanning inherent in following (or imagining) the flight of a baseball. While the position of the ball at successive points in time defines a natural path through space, we can scan through it without focusing attention on any single location.

4. Especially with metonymy, C_1 and C_2 need not be sharply distinct. In the present example, C_1 might feature a conception of the political landscape, in which Chomsky has a particular role. Once accessed as F_2, he can then evoke a context, C_2, relating more specifically to his own affairs (such as his writings). In this case C_1 and C_2 represent different "takes" on the encyclopedic semantics of the same expression (FCG1: 4.2).

5. For elaboration on this point, see Langacker 1998c, which further argues that the trajector/landmark asymmetry has a temporal component (as implied by the focus-chain model).

6. This particular construction favors a "topical" possessor (Deane 1987), so with inanimates a non-possessive alternative using a prepositional phrase is commonly preferred (*?that house's roof; the roof of that house; ??this watch's stem; the stem on this watch*). The *have*-construction shows greater flexibility (*That house has a leaky roof; This watch has a stem*). It is not crucial that a possessive dominion sometimes correlates with maximal rather than immediate scope (e.g. *my left ankle* vs. *??my left leg's ankle*), since both function as contexts for a part term's profile.

7. See Chapter 1, examples (10)-(11).

8. I realize that the correctness of this prediction is far from obvious, and I cannot yet furnish the detailed explication and analyses required to make it so.

9. It is not claimed that this sequencing necessarily correlates with the temporal ordering of speech. Instead, an inherent conceptual ordering is being imputed to the topic function per se. Its strong correlation with word order represents the tendency for natural paths to coalign. Comparable remarks can be made regarding the linear order of subject, object, and verb.

10. This intrinsicness renders the mental sequencing less evident at the level of conscious awareness, as does the more compressed time scale at which it occurs. These factors are even more pronounced for the relation between trajector and processual profile at the verb level.

11. That is, it "inherits"—or constitutes an "extension"—from them both.

12. For supporting arguments, see Langacker To appear-b and T. Kumashiro 1999. The latter examines Japanese double-subject constructions in great detail (as well as the superficially identical but grammatically distinct "complex predicate constructions").

13. Hence neither component structure qualifies as profile determinant. The construction, in other words, is *exocentric.*

14. E.g. the preposed locative does not control agreement, nor is question inversion permitted: *Beside the shed {are/*is} two motorcycles; *Was beside the shed a motorcycle?.* See Birner and Ward 1993 for discussion of this construction from the standpoint of information structure.

15. They are not unlike (and not unrelated to) the natural paths motivating nominative/accusative vs. ergative/absolutive organization, which lead in opposite directions along an action chain. Phenomena reflecting the two paths commonly coexist in a single clause.

16. See Chapter 1, section 2.4, and Chapter 2, section 5.

References

Achard, Michel
    1996   Two causation/perception constructions in French. *Cognitive Linguistics* 7: 315-357.
    1998   *Representation of Cognitive Structures: Syntax and Semantics of French Sentential Complements.* (Cognitive Linguistics Research 11.) Berlin / New York: Mouton de Gruyter.

Akatsuka, Noriko
    1979   Why tough-movement is impossible with *possible. Papers from the Regional Meeting of the Chicago Linguistic Society* 15: 1-8.

Akmajian, Adrian
    1972   Getting tough. *Linguistic Inquiry* 3: 373-377.

Anderson, John M.
    1971   *The Grammar of Case: Towards a Localistic Theory.* (Cambridge Studies in Linguistics 4.) Cambridge: Cambridge University Press.

Authier, J.-Marc
    1991   V-governed expletives, case theory, and the projection principle. *Linguistic Inquiry* 22: 721-740.

Behaghel, Otto
    1923-32   *Deutsche Syntax.* (Germanische Bibliothek 1.10.) Heidelberg.

Berman, Arlene
    1973   A constraint on tough-movement. *Papers from the Regional Meeting of the Chicago Linguistic Society* 9: 34-43.

Bever, Thomas G. and Peter S. Rosenbaum
    1970   Some lexical structures and their empirical validity. In: Jacobs and Rosenbaum (eds.), 3-19.

Birner, Betty and Gregory Ward
    1993   There-sentences and inversion as distinct constructions: A functional account. *Proceedings of the Annual Meeting of the Berkeley Linguistics Society* 19: 27-39.

Bloomfield, Leonard
    1933   *Language.* New York: Holt.

Bolinger, Dwight
    1961   Syntactic blends and other matters. *Language* 37: 366-381.
    1967   Apparent constituents in surface structure. *Word* 23: 47-56.
    1973   Ambient *it* is meaningful too. *Journal of Linguistics* 9: 261-270.
    1977   *Meaning and Form.* London / New York: Longman.

Borkin, Ann
    1973   *To be* and not *to be. Papers from the Regional Meeting of the Chicago Linguistic Society* 9: 44-56.
    1974   Raising to object position: A study in the syntax and semantics of clause merging. Ph.D. dissertation, Department of Linguistics,

University of Michigan.

Bresnan, Joan and Jane Grimshaw
    1978   The syntax of free relatives in English. *Linguistic Inquiry* 9: 331-391.

Brody, Michael
    1993   q-theory and arguments. *Linguistic Inquiry* 24: 1-23.

Browman, Catherine P. and Louis Goldstein
    1992   Articulatory phonology: An overview. *Phonetica* 49: 155-180.

Brugman, Claudia
    1983   The use of body-part terms as locatives in Chalcatongo Mixtec. *Survey of California and Other Indian Languages* 4: 235-290.
    1988   The syntax and semantics of HAVE and its complements. Ph.D. dissertation, Department of Linguistics, University of California, Berkeley.

Bybee, Joan L.
    1985   *Morphology: A Study of the Relation Between Meaning and Form.* (Typological Studies in Language 9.) Amsterdam / Philadelphia: John Benjamins.
    1988   Morphology as lexical organization. In: Hammond and Noonan (eds.), 119-141.
    1994   A view of phonology from a cognitive and functional perspective. *Cognitive Linguistics* 5: 285-305.

Bybee, Joan L. and Carol Lynn Moder
    1983   Morphological classes as natural categories. *Language* 59: 251-270.

Bybee, Joan L. and Dan I. Slobin
    1982   Rules and schemas in the development and use of the English past tense. *Language* 58: 265-289.

Cantrall, William R.
    1974   *Viewpoint, Reflexives, and the Nature of Noun Phrases.* The Hague: Mouton.

Carey, Kathleen
    1994   Pragmatics, subjectivity and the grammaticalization of the English perfect. Ph.D. dissertation, Department of Linguistics, University of California, San Diego.

Casad, Eugene H.
    1982   Cora locationals and structured imagery. Ph.D. dissertation, Department of Linguistics, University of California, San Diego.

Casad, Eugene H. (ed.)
    1996   *Cognitive Linguistics in the Redwoods: The Expansion of a New Paradigm in Linguistics.* (Cognitive Linguistics Research 6.) Berlin / New York: Mouton de Gruyter.

Chafe, Wallace
    1968   Idiomaticity as an anomaly in the Chomskyan paradigm. *Foundations of Language* 4: 109-127.

1987   Cognitive constraints on information flow. In: Russell S. Tomlin (ed.), *Coherence and Grounding in Discourse*, 21-51. (Typological Studies in Language 11.) Amsterdam / Philadelphia: John Benjamins.

1994   *Discourse, Consciousness, and Time: The Flow and Displacement of Conscious Experience in Speaking and Writing*. Chicago / London: University of Chicago Press.

Chapin, Paul G.

1967   On the syntax of word-derivation in English. MITRE Corporation. Information System Language Studies, Report no. 16.

Chomsky, Noam

1965   *Aspects of the Theory of Syntax*. Cambridge, MA: MIT Press.

1970   Remarks on nominalization. In: Jacobs and Rosenbaum (eds.), 184-221.

1973   Conditions on transformations. In: Stephen R. Anderson and Paul Kiparsky (eds.), *A Festschrift for Morris Halle*, 232-286. New York: Holt.

1977   On WH-movement. In: Peter W. Culicover, Thomas Wasow and Adrian Akmajian (eds.), *Formal Syntax*, 71-132. New York: Academic Press.

1981   *Lectures on Government and Binding*. Dordrecht: Foris.

Cook, Kenneth W.

1988a   A cognitive analysis of grammatical relations, case, and transitivity in Samoan. Ph.D. dissertation, Department of Linguistics, University of California, San Diego.

1988b   The semantics of Newari case-marking distinctions. *Linguistic Notes from La Jolla* 14: 42-56.

1993a   A cognitive account of Samoan case marking and cliticization. *Studi Italiani di Linguistica Teorica e Applicata* 22: 509-530.

1993b   A cognitive account of Samoan *lavea* and *galo* verbs. In: Geiger and Rudzka-Ostyn (eds.), 567-592.

Croft, William A.

1991   *Syntactic Categories and Grammatical Relations: The Cognitive Organization of Information*. Chicago: University of Chicago Press.

Cruse, D. A.

1979   On the transitivity of the part-whole relation. *Journal of Linguistics* 15: 29-38.

Culicover, Peter W. and Michael Rochemont

1983   Stress and focus in English. *Language* 59: 123-165.

Cutrer, Michelle

1994   Time and tense in narrative and in everyday language. Ph.D. dissertation, Department of Linguistics, University of California, San Diego.

Dąbrowska, Ewa
  1997   *Cognitive Semantics and the Polish Dative.* (Cognitive Linguis-
            tics Research 9.) Berlin / New York: Mouton de Gruyter.
Davis, Philip W. (ed.)
  1995   *Alternative Linguistics: Descriptive and Theoretical Modes.* (Cur-
            rent Issues in Linguistic Theory 102.) Amsterdam / Philadelphia:
            John Benjamins.
Deane, Paul
  1987   English possessives, topicality, and the Silverstein hierarchy.
            *Proceedings of the Annual Meeting of the Berkeley Linguistics
            Society* 13: 65-76.
  1991   Limits to attention: A cognitive theory of island phenomena. *Cog-
            nitive Linguistics* 2: 1-63.
  1992   *Grammar in Mind and Brain: Explorations in Cognitive Syntax.*
            (Cognitive Linguistics Research 2.) Berlin / New York: Mouton
            de Gruyter.
DeLancey, Scott
  1981   An interpretation of split ergativity and related phenomena. *Lan-
            guage* 57: 626-657.
Dixon, R. M. W.
  1977   Where have all the adjectives gone? *Studies in Language* 1: 19-80.
Doiz-Bienzobas, Aintzane
  1995   The preterite and the imperfect in Spanish: Past situation vs. past
            viewpoint. Ph.D. dissertation, Department of Linguistics, Univer-
            sity of California, San Diego.
Dryer, Matthew S.
  1986   Primary objects, secondary objects, and antidative. *Language* 62:
            808-845.
Elman, Jeffrey L.
  1990   Finding structure in time. *Cognitive Science* 14: 179-211.
Elman, Jeffrey L. and James L. McClelland
  1984   Speech perception as a cognitive process: The interactive activa-
            tion model. In: Norman Lass (ed.), *Speech and Language*, Volume
            10, 337-374. New York: Academic Press.
Farrell, Patrick
  1990   Spanish stress: A cognitive analysis. *Hispanic Linguistics* 4: 21-
            56.
  1995   Lexical binding. *Linguistics* 33: 939-980.
Fauconnier, Gilles
  1985   *Mental Spaces: Aspects of Meaning Construction in Natural
            Language.* Cambridge, MA / London: MIT Press / Bradford.
  1997   *Mappings in Thought and Language.* Cambridge: Cambridge Uni-
            versity Press.
  1998   Mental spaces, language modalities, and conceptual integration. In:
            Tomasello (ed.), 251-279.

Fauconnier, Gilles and Eve Sweetser (eds.)
  1996   *Spaces, Worlds, and Grammar.* Chicago / London: University of
            Chicago Press.
Fauconnier, Gilles and Mark Turner
  1998   Conceptual integration networks. *Cognitive Science* 22: 133-187.
Fillmore, Charles J.
  1968   The case for case. In: Emmon Bach and Robert T. Harms (eds.),
            Universals in Linguistic Theory, 1-88. New York: Holt.
  1988   The mechanisms of "construction grammar". *Proceedings of the
            Annual Meeting of the Berkeley Linguistics Society* 14: 35-55.
Fillmore, Charles J., Paul Kay and Mary Catherine O'Connor
  1988   Regularity and idiomaticity in grammatical constructions: The case
            of *let alone. Language* 64: 501-538.
Foley, William A. and Robert D. Van Valin, Jr.
  1977   On the viability of the notion "subject" in universal grammar.
            *Proceedings of the Annual Meeting of the Berkeley Linguistics
            Society* 3: 293-320.
  1984   *Functional Syntax and Universal Grammar.* Cambridge: Cam-
            bridge University Press.
Fong, Heatherbell
  1988   The stony idiom of the brain: A study in the syntax and semantics
            of metaphors. Ph.D. dissertation, Department of Linguistics, Uni-
            versity of California, San Diego.
Frantz, Donald G.
  1980   Ascensions to subject in Blackfoot. *Proceedings of the Annual
            Meeting of the Berkeley Linguistics Society* 6: 293-299.
Fraser, Bruce
  1970   Idioms within a transformational grammar. *Foundations of Lang-
            uage* 6: 22-42.
Friedrich, Paul
  1985   Review of Paul J. Hopper (ed.), Tense-aspect: between semantics
            and pragmatics. *Language* 61: 182-187.
Geiger, Richard A. and Brygida Rudzka-Ostyn (eds.)
  1993   *Conceptualizations and Mental Processing in Language.* (Cogni-
            tive Linguistics Research 3.) Berlin / New York: Mouton de
            Gruyter.
Gensler, Orin D.
  1977   Non-syntactic antecedents and frame semantics. *Proceedings of the
            Annual Meeting of the Berkeley Linguistics Society* 3: 321-334.
Givón, Talmy
  1979   *On Understanding Grammar.* (Perspectives in Neurolinguistics and
            Psycholinguistics.) New York: Academic Press.
  1984   *Syntax: A Functional-Typological Introduction*, Volume 1. Am-
            sterdam / Philadelphia: John Benjamins.

Goldberg, Adele E.
1992   The inherent semantics of argument structure: The case of the English ditransitive construction. *Cognitive Linguistics* 3: 37-74.
1995   *Constructions: A Construction Grammar Approach to Argument Structure.* Chicago / London: University of Chicago Press.
Goldberg, Adele E. (ed.)
1996   *Conceptual Structure, Discourse and Language.* Stanford: CSLI Publications.
Goldsmith, John and Erich Woisetschlaeger
1982   The logic of the English progressive. *Linguistic Inquiry* 13: 79-89.
Gorbet, Larry
1973   The isthmus of anaphor (and idiomaticity). *Stanford Occasional Papers in Linguistics* 3: 25-34.
Haiman, John
1980   Dictionaries and encyclopedias. *Lingua* 50: 329-357.
1983   Iconic and economic motivation. *Language* 59: 781-819.
Halle, Morris
1959   *The Sound Pattern of Russian.* The Hague: Mouton.
Hammond, Michael and Michael Noonan (eds.)
1988   *Theoretical Morphology: Approaches in Modern Linguistics.* San Diego: Academic Press.
Hankamer, Jorge and Ivan Sag
1976   Deep and surface anaphora. *Linguistic Inquiry* 7: 391-428.
Harder, Peter
1996   *Functional Semantics: A Theory of Meaning, Structure and Tense in English.* (Trends in Linguistics Studies and Monographs 87.) Berlin / New York: Mouton de Gruyter.
Harris, Catherine and Elizabeth Bates
1990   Functional constraints on backwards pronominal reference. *Proceedings of the Twelfth Annual Meeting of the Cognitive Science Society,* 635-642. Hillsdale, NJ: Erlbaum.
Hawkins, Bruce W.
1984   The semantics of English spatial prepositions. Ph.D. dissertation, Department of Linguistics, University of California, San Diego.
Hawkins, John
1978   *Definiteness and Indefiniteness: A Study in Reference and Grammaticality Prediction.* London: Croom Helm.
Heine, Bernd
1992   Grammaticalization chains. *Studies in Language* 16: 335-368.
Hockett, Charles F.
1958   *A Course in Modern Linguistics.* New York: Macmillan.
Hopper, Paul J. and Sandra A. Thompson
1980   Transitivity in grammar and discourse. *Language* 56: 251-299.

Householder, Fred W., Jr.
  1971   *Linguistic Speculations*. Cambridge: Cambridge University Press.
Huck, Geoffrey J. and Almerindo E. Ojeda (eds.)
  1987   *Syntax and Semantics*, Volume 20, *Discontinuous Constituency*.
             Orlando: Academic Press.
Hudson, Richard A.
  1984   *Word Grammar*. Oxford: Basil Blackwell.
  1987   Zwicky on heads. *Journal of Linguistics* 23: 109-132.
Hung, Tony
  1988   Case and role in Newari: A cognitive grammar approach. *Ling-
             uistic Notes from La Jolla* 14: 95-107.
Israel, Michael
  1998   The rhetoric of grammar: Scalar reasoning and polarity sensiti-
             vity. Ph.D. dissertation, Department of Linguistics, University of
             California, San Diego.
Itkonen, Esa and Jussi Haukioja
  1996   A rehabilitation of analogy in syntax (and elsewhere). In: András
             Kertész (ed.), *Metalinguistik im Wandel: Die 'Kognitive Wende'
             in Wissenschaftstheorie und Linguistik*, 131-177. Frankfurt am
             Main / New York: Peter Lang.
Jackendoff, Ray
  1975   *Tough* and the trace theory of movement rules. *Linguistic Inquiry*
             6: 437-447.
  1977   *X-Bar Syntax: A Study of Phrase Structure*. Cambridge, MA /
             London: MIT Press.
Jacobs, Roderick A. and Peter S. Rosenbaum (eds.)
  1970   *Readings in English Transformational Grammar*. Waltham, MA:
             Ginn.
Johnson, Mark
  1987   *The Body in the Mind: The Bodily Basis of Meaning, Imagination,
             and Reason*. Chicago / London: University of Chicago Press.
Jones, Michael A.
  1983   Getting "tough" with Wh-movement. *Journal of Linguistics* 19:
             129-159.
Karttunen, Lauri
  1969   Pronouns and variables. *Papers from the Regional Meeting of the
             Chicago Linguistic Society* 5: 108-116.
Keenan, Edward L.
  1976   Towards a universal definition of "subject". In: Li (ed.), 303-333.
  1984   Semantic correlates of the ergative/absolutive distinction. *Linguis-
             tics* 22: 197-223.
Keenan, Edward L. and Bernard Comrie
  1977   Noun phrase accessibility and universal grammar. *Linguistic In-
             quiry* 8: 63-99.

Kemmer, Suzanne
    1993   *The Middle Voice.* (Typological Studies in Language 23.) Amsterdam / Philadelphia: John Benjamins.
Kemmer, Suzanne and Michael Israel
    1994   Variation and the usage-based model. *Papers from the Regional Meeting of the Chicago Linguistic Society* 30.2: 165-179.
Kiparsky, Paul and Carol Kiparsky
    1970   Fact. In: Manfred Bierwisch and Karl Erich Heidolph (eds.), *Progress in Linguistics*, 143-173. The Hague: Mouton.
Kirsner, Robert S.
    1979   *The Problem of Presentative Sentences in Modern Dutch.* (North-Holland Linguistic Series 43.) Amsterdam: North-Holland.
Kirsner, Robert S. and Sandra A. Thompson
    1976   The role of pragmatic inference in semantics: A study of sensory verb complements in English. *Glossa* 10: 200-240.
Klaiman, M. H.
    1981   Toward a universal semantics of indirect subject constructions. *Proceedings of the Annual Meeting of the Berkeley Linguistics Society* 7: 123-135.
Kluender, Robert
    1992   Deriving island constraints from principles of predication. In: Helen Goodluck and Michael Rochemont (eds.), *Island Constraints: Theory, Acquisition and Processing*, 223-258. Dordrecht: Kluwer Academic Publishers.
Krzeszowski, Tomasz P.
    1993   The axiological parameter in preconceptual image schemata. In: Geiger and Rudzka-Ostyn (eds.), 307-329.
Kumashiro, Fumiko
    1999   Phonotactic interactions: A non-reductionist approach to phonology. Ph.D. dissertation, Department of Linguistics, University of California, San Diego.
Kumashiro, Toshiyuki
    1999   The conceptual basis of grammar: A cognitive approach to Japanese clause structure. Ph.D. dissertation, Department of Linguistics, University of California, San Diego.
Kuno, Susumu
    1987   *Functional Syntax: Anaphora, Discourse and Empathy.* Chicago: University of Chicago Press.
Lakoff, George
    1970a   *Irregularity in Syntax.* New York: Holt.
    1970b   Repartee, or a reply to "Negation, conjunction and quantifiers". *Foundations of Language* 6: 389-422.
    1987   *Women, Fire, and Dangerous Things: What Categories Reveal About the Mind.* Chicago / London: University of Chicago Press.

1990   The invariance hypothesis: Is abstract reason based on image-schemas? *Cognitive Linguistics* 1: 39-74.

Lakoff, George and Mark Johnson
1980   *Metaphors We Live By*. Chicago / London: University of Chicago Press.

Lambrecht, Knud
1988   There was a farmer had a dog: Syntactic amalgams revisited. *Proceedings of the Annual Meeting of the Berkeley Linguistics Society* 14: 319-339.
1996   On the formal and functional relationship between topics and vocatives. Evidence from French. In: Goldberg (ed.), 267-288.

Lamiroy, Béatrice
1987   The complementation of aspectual verbs in French. *Language* 63: 278-298.

Langacker, Ronald W.
1968   Observations on French possessives. *Language* 44: 51-75.
1969   On pronominalization and the chain of command. In: Reibel and Schane (eds.), 160-186.
1976   *Non-Distinct Arguments in Uto-Aztecan*. (University of California Publications in Linguistics 82.) Berkeley / Los Angeles: University of California Press.
1982   Space grammar, analysability, and the English passive. *Language* 58: 22-80.
1984   Active zones. *Proceedings of the Annual Meeting of the Berkeley Linguistics Society* 10: 172-188.
1985   Observations and speculations on subjectivity. In: John Haiman (ed.), *Iconicity in Syntax*, 109-150. (Typological Studies in Language 6.) Amsterdam / Philadelphia: John Benjamins.
1986   Abstract motion. *Proceedings of the Annual Meeting of the Berkeley Linguistics Society* 12: 455-471.
1987a   *Foundations of Cognitive Grammar*, Volume 1, *Theoretical Prerequisites*. Stanford: Stanford University Press.
1987b   Grammatical ramifications of the setting/participant distinction. *Proceedings of the Annual Meeting of the Berkeley Linguistics Society* 13: 383-394.
1987c   Nouns and verbs. *Language* 63: 53-94.
1988   A usage-based model. In: Rudzka-Ostyn (ed.), 127-161.
1989   Absolute construal. In: F. J. Heyvaert and F. Steurs (eds.), *Worlds Behind Words: Essays in Honour of Prof. Dr. F. G. Droste on the Occasion of His Sixtieth Birthday*, 65-75. Leuven: Leuven University Press.
1990a   *Concept, Image, and Symbol: The Cognitive Basis of Grammar*. (Cognitive Linguistics Research 1.) Berlin / New York: Mouton de Gruyter.

1990b   The rule controversy: A cognitive grammar perspective. *CRL Newsletter* 4.3: 4-15.

1990c   Subjectification. *Cognitive Linguistics* 1: 5-38.

1991   *Foundations of Cognitive Grammar*, Volume 2, *Descriptive Application*. Stanford: Stanford University Press.

1992a   Prepositions as grammatical(izing) elements. *Leuvense Bijdragen* 81: 287-309.

1992b   The symbolic nature of cognitive grammar: The meaning of *of* and of *of*-periphrasis. In: Martin Pütz (ed.), *Thirty Years of Linguistic Evolution: Studies in Honour of René Dirven on the Occasion of his Sixtieth Birthday*, 483-502. Philadelphia / Amsterdam: John Benjamins.

1993a   Clause structure in cognitive grammar. *Studi Italiani di Linguistica Teorica e Applicata* 22: 465-508.

1993b   Deixis and subjectivity. In: S. K. Verma and V. Prakasam (eds.), *New Horizons in Functional Linguistics*, 43-58. Hyderabad: Booklinks Corporation.

1993c   Grammatical traces of some "invisible" semantic constructs. *Language Sciences* 15: 323-355.

1993d   Reference-point constructions. *Cognitive Linguistics* 4: 1-38.

1995a   Conceptual grouping and constituency in cognitive grammar. In: Ik-Hwan Lee (ed.), *Linguistics in the Morning Calm 3*, 149-172. Seoul: Hanshin.

1995b   A note on the Spanish personal "a". In: Peggy Hashemipour, Ricardo Maldonado and Margaret van Naerssen (eds.), *Studies in Language Learning and Spanish Linguistics in Honor of Tracy D. Terrell*, 431-441. New York: McGraw-Hill.

1995c   Possession and possessive constructions. In: John R. Taylor and Robert E. MacLaury (eds.), *Language and the Cognitive Construal of the World*, 51-79. (Trends in Linguistics Studies and Monographs 82.) Berlin / New York: Mouton de Gruyter.

1995d   Raising and transparency. *Language* 71: 1-62.

1995e   Viewing in cognition and grammar. In: Davis (ed.), 153-212.

1996a   Conceptual grouping and pronominal anaphora. In: Barbara Fox (ed.), *Studies in Anaphora*, 333-378. (Typological Studies in Language 33.) Amsterdam / Philadelphia: John Benjamins.

1996b   A constraint on progressive generics. In: Goldberg (ed.), 289-302.

1997a   Consciousness, construal, and subjectivity. In: Maxim I. Stamenov (ed.), *Language Structure, Discourse and the Access to Consciousness*, 49-75. (Advances in Consciousness Research 12.) Amsterdam / Philadelphia: John Benjamins.

1997b   Constituency, dependency, and conceptual grouping. *Cognitive Linguistics* 8: 1-32.

1997c   A dynamic account of grammatical function. In: Joan Bybee, John Haiman and Sandra A. Thompson (eds.), *Essays on Language*

Function and Language Type Dedicated to T. Givón, 249-273. Amsterdam / Philadelphia: John Benjamins.

1997d   Generics and habituals. In: Angeliki Athanasiadou and René Dirven (eds.), *On Conditionals Again*, 191-222. (Current Issues in Linguistic Theory 143.) Amsterdam / Philadelphia: John Benjamins.

1998a   Cognitive grammar meets the Yuman auxiliary. In: Leanne Hinton and Pamela Munro (eds.), *Studies in American Indian Languages: Description and Theory*, 41-48. (University of California Publications in Linguistics 131.) Berkeley: University of California Press.

1998b   Conceptualization, symbolization, and grammar. In: Tomasello (ed.), 1-39.

1998c   Topic, subject, and possessor. *Linguistic Notes from La Jolla* 19: 1-28.

1999a   A dynamic usage-based model. In: Michael Barlow and Suzanne Kemmer (eds.), *Usage Based Models of Language*, 1-63. Stanford: CSLI Publications.

1999b   Losing control: Grammaticization, subjectification, and transparency. In: Andreas Blank and Peter Koch (eds.), *Historical Semantics and Cognition*, 147-175. (Cognitive Linguistics Research 13.) Berlin / New York: Mouton de Gruyter.

To appear-a   Assessing the cognitive linguistic enterprise.

To appear-b   Double-subject constructions.

To appear-c   Virtual reality.

Lasnik, Howard and Robert Fiengo

1974   Complement object deletion. *Linguistic Inquiry* 5: 535-571.

Lees, Robert B.

1960   *The Grammar of English Nominalizations.* (Publication 12.) Bloomington: Indiana University Research Center in Anthropology, Folklore, and Linguistics. [*International Journal of American Linguistics* 26.3, Part II.]

Legendre, Géraldine

1986   Object raising in French: A unified account. *Natural Language and Linguistic Theory* 4: 137-183.

Li, Charles N. (ed.)

1976   *Subject and Topic.* New York: Academic Press.

Li, Charles N. and Sandra A. Thompson

1976   Subject and topic: A new typology of language. In: Li (ed.), 457-489.

Lindner, Susan

1981   A lexico-semantic analysis of English verb-particle constructions with UP and OUT. Ph.D. dissertation, Department of Linguistics, University of California, San Diego.

Lyons, John
    1967   A note on possessive, existential and locative sentences. *Foundations of Language* 3: 390-396.

MacWhinney, Brian
    1977   Starting points. *Language* 53: 152-168.
    1987   The competition model. In: Brian MacWhinney (ed.), *Mechanisms of Language Acquisition*, 249-308. Hillsdale, NJ / London: Erlbaum.

Maldonado, Ricardo
    1988   Energetic reflexives in Spanish. *Proceedings of the Annual Meeting of the Berkeley Linguistics Society* 14: 153-165.
    1992   Middle voice: The case of Spanish 'se'. Ph.D. dissertation, Department of Linguistics, University of California, San Diego.
    1993   Dynamic construals in Spanish. *Studi Italiani di Linguistica Teorica e Applicata* 22: 531-566.

Manney, Linda
    1993   Middle voice in Modern Greek. Ph.D. dissertation, Department of Linguistics, University of California, San Diego.

Massam, Diane
    1984   Raising an exceptional case. *Papers from the Regional Meeting of the Chicago Linguistic Society* 20: 281-300.

Matsumoto, Yoshiko
    1988   Semantics and pragmatics of noun-modifying constructions in Japanese. *Proceedings of the Annual Meeting of the Berkeley Linguistics Society* 14: 166-175.

McCawley, James D.
    1982   Parentheticals and discontinuous constituent structure. *Linguistic Inquiry* 13: 91-106.
    1984   Anaphora and notions of command. *Proceedings of the Annual Meeting of the Berkeley Linguistics Society* 10: 220-232.

McClelland, James L. and Jeffrey L. Elman
    1986a   Interactive processes in speech perception: The TRACE model. In: McClelland and Rumelhart (eds.), 58-121.
    1986b   The TRACE model of speech perception. *Cognitive Psychology* 18: 1-86.

McClelland, James L. and David E. Rumelhart (eds.)
    1986   *Parallel Distributed Processing: Explorations in the Microstructure of Cognition*, Volume 2, *Psychological and Biological Models*. Cambridge, MA / London: MIT Press / Bradford.

Michaelis, Laura A. and Knud Lambrecht
    1996   Toward a construction-based theory of language function: The case of nominal extraposition. *Language* 72: 215-247.

Miller, George A. and Philip N. Johnson-Laird
    1976   *Language and Perception*. Cambridge, MA: Harvard University Press / Belknap.

Nakajima, Heizo
    1997   A generativist view of the cognitive analysis of *raising*. In: Masatomo Ukaji, Toshio Nakao, Masaru Kajita, and Shuji Chiba (eds.), *Studies in English Linguistics: A Festschrift for Akira Ota on the Occasion of His Eightieth Birthday*, 474-491. Tokyo: Taishukan.

Nanni, Deborah L.
    1980   On the surface syntax of constructions with *easy*-type adjectives. *Language* 56: 568-581.

Newman, John
    1981   The semantics of raising constructions. Ph.D. dissertation, Department of Linguistics, University of California, San Diego.
    1982   Predicate adjuncts. *Australian Journal of Linguistics* 2: 153-166.

Newmeyer, Frederick J.
    1970   On the alleged boundary between syntax and semantics. *Foundations of Language* 6: 178-186.
    1990   Some issues in language origins and evolution. *Studies in the Linguistic Sciences* 20.2: 51-68.

Nikiforidou, Kiki
    1991   The meanings of the genitive: A case study in semantic structure and semantic change. *Cognitive Linguistics* 2: 149-205.

Nishimura, Yoshiki
    1993   Agentivity in cognitive grammar. In: Geiger and Rudzka-Ostyn (eds.), 487-530.

Nunberg, Geoffrey, Ivan A. Sag and Thomas Wasow
    1994   Idioms. *Language* 70: 491-538.

O'Grady, William
    1998   The syntax of idioms. *Natural Language and Linguistic Theory* 16: 279-312.

Oehrle, R. T.
    1979   A theoretical consequence of constituent structure in *tough* movement. *Linguistic Inquiry* 4: 583-593.

Pawley, Andrew
    1985   On speech formulas and linguistic competence. *Lenguas Modernas* 12: 84-104.

Pawley, Andrew and Frances Hodgetts Syder
    1983   Two puzzles for linguistic theory: Nativelike selection and nativelike fluency. In: Jack Richards and Richard W. Schmidt (eds.), *Language and Communication*, 191-225. London: Longman.

Penhallurick, John
    1984   Full-verb inversion in English. *Australian Journal of Linguistics* 4: 33-56.

Perlmutter, David M.
    1970   The two verbs *begin*. In: Jacobs and Rosenbaum (eds.), 107-119.

1978   Impersonal passives and the unaccusative hypothesis. *Proceedings of the Annual Meeting of the Berkeley Linguistics Society* 4: 157-189.

Perlmutter, David M. (ed.)
1983   *Studies in Relational Grammar 1*. Chicago / London: University of Chicago Press.

Perlmutter, David M. and Paul M. Postal
1983   The relational succession law. In: Perlmutter (ed.), 30-80.

Pesetsky, David
1987   Binding problems with experiencer verbs. *Linguistic Inquiry* 18: 126-140.

Pinker, Steven
1989   *Learnability and Cognition: The Acquisition of Argument Structure*. Cambridge, MA / London: MIT Press / Bradford.

Pinker, Steven and Alan Prince
1991   Regular and irregular morphology and the psychological status of rules of grammar. *Proceedings of the Annual Meeting of the Berkeley Linguistics Society* 17: 230-251.

Postal, Paul M.
1969a   Anaphoric islands. *Papers from the Regional Meeting of the Chicago Linguistic Society* 5: 205-239.
1969b   On so-called "pronouns" in English. In: Reibel and Schane (eds.), 201-224.
1974   *On Raising: One Rule of English Grammar and Its Theoretical Implications*. (Current Studies in Linguistics 5.) Cambridge, MA / London: MIT Press.

Postal, Paul M. and John R. Ross
1971   ¡Tough movement sí, tough deletion no! *Linguistic Inquiry* 2: 544-546.

Reddy, Michael J.
1979   The conduit metaphor—A case of frame conflict in our language about language. In: Andrew Ortony (ed.), *Metaphor and Thought*, 284-324. Cambridge: Cambridge University Press.

Reibel, David A. and Sanford A. Schane (eds.)
1969   *Modern Studies in English: Readings in Transformational Grammar*. Englewood Cliffs, NJ: Prentice-Hall.

Reinhart, Tanya
1983   *Anaphora and Semantic Interpretation*. Chicago: University of Chicago Press.

Rice, Sally
1987a   Towards a cognitive model of transitivity. Ph.D. dissertation, Department of Linguistics, University of California, San Diego.
1987b   Towards a transitive prototype: Evidence from some atypical English passives. *Proceedings of the Annual Meeting of the Berkeley Linguistics Society* 13: 422-434.

1993   The so-called pseudo-passive revisited (by a cognitive linguist). *Studi Italiani di Linguistica Teorica e Applicata* 22: 567-599.

Robinson, Jane J.
1970   Dependency structures and transformational rules. *Language* 46: 259-285.

Rosenbaum, Peter S.
1967   *The Grammar of English Predicate Complement Constructions.* (Research Monograph 47.) Cambridge, MA: MIT Press.

Ross, John R.
1967a   Auxiliaries as main verbs. In: William Todd (ed.), *Studies in Philosophical Linguistics*, Volume 1, 77-102. Evanston, IL: Great Expectations.
1967b   Constraints on variables in syntax. Ph.D. dissertation, Department of Linguistics, MIT. [Published as Ross 1986.]
1986   *Infinite Syntax!* Norwood, NJ: Ablex.
1987   Islands and syntactic prototypes. *Papers from the Regional Meeting of the Chicago Linguistic Society* 23: 309-320.

Rubba, Johanna E.
1993   Discontinuous morphology in Modern Aramaic. Ph.D. dissertation, Department of Linguistics, University of California, San Diego.
1994   Grammaticization as semantic change: A case study of preposition development. In: William Pagliuca (ed.), *Perspectives on Grammaticalization*, 81-101. (Current Issues in Linguistic Theory 109.) Amsterdam / Philadelphia: John Benjamins.

Rudzka-Ostyn, Brygida (ed.)
1988   *Topics in Cognitive Linguistics.* (Current Issues in Linguistic Theory 50.) Amsterdam / Philadelphia: John Benjamins.

Rumelhart, David E. and James L. McClelland (eds.)
1986   *Parallel Distributed Processing: Explorations in the Microstructure of Cognition*, Volume 1, *Foundations*. Cambridge, MA / London: MIT Press / Bradford.

Ruwet, Nicolas
1991   *Syntax and Human Experience.* Chicago / London: University of Chicago Press.

Sadock, Jerrold M.
1992   Cyclic rules without derivations. In: Jeannette Marshall Denton, Grace P. Chan and Costas P. Canakis (eds.), *The Cycle in Linguistic Theory*, 237-262. Chicago: Chicago Linguistic Society. [*Papers from the 28th Regional Meeting of the Chicago Linguistic Society*, Volume 2, *The Parasession*.]

Saxton, Dean
1982   Papago. In: Ronald W. Langacker (ed.), *Studies in Uto-Aztecan Grammar*, Volume 3, *Uto-Aztecan Grammatical Sketches*, 93-266.

(SIL Publications in Linguistics 57.) Dallas: Summer Institute of Linguistics and University of Texas at Arlington.

Schachter, Paul

1976   The subject in Philippine languages: Topic, actor, actor-topic, or none of the above? In: Li (ed.), 491-518.

1977   Reference-related and role-related properties of subjects. In: Peter Cole and Jerrold M. Sadock (eds.), *Syntax and Semantics*, Volume 8, *Grammatical Relations*, 279-306. New York: Academic Press.

Seiter, William J.

1983   Subject-direct object raising in Niuean. In: Perlmutter (ed.), 317-359.

Sells, Peter

1987   Aspects of logophoricity. *Linguistic Inquiry* 18: 445-479.

Shen, Ya-Ming

1996   The semantics of the Chinese verb "come". In: Casad (ed.), 507-540.

Shibatani, Masayoshi

1985   Passives and related constructions: A prototype analysis. *Language* 61: 821-848.

Smith, Michael B.

1987   The semantics of dative and accusative in German: An investigation in cognitive grammar. Ph.D. dissertation, Department of Linguistics, University of California, San Diego.

1993   Aspects of German clause structure from a cognitive grammar perspective. *Studi Italiani di Linguistica Teorica e Applicata* 22: 601-638.

Soames, Scott and David M. Perlmutter

1979   *Syntactic Argumentation and the Structure of English*. Berkeley / Los Angeles: University of California Press.

Steele, Susan M.

1977   On being possessed. *Proceedings of the Annual Meeting of the Berkeley Linguistics Society* 3: 114-131.

Stemberger, Joseph Paul and Brian MacWhinney

1988   Are inflected forms stored in the lexicon? In: Hammond and Noonan (eds.), 101-116.

Sweetser, Eve E.

1982   Root and epistemic modals: Causality in two worlds. *Proceedings of the Annual Meeting of the Berkeley Linguistics Society* 8: 484-507.

1988   Grammaticalization and semantic bleaching. *Proceedings of the Annual Meeting of the Berkeley Linguistics Society* 14: 389-405.

1990   *From Etymology to Pragmatics: Metaphorical and Cultural Aspects of Semantic Structure*. (Cambridge Studies in Linguistics 54.) Cambridge: Cambridge University Press.

Talmy, Leonard
    1988a   Force dynamics in language and cognition. *Cognitive Science* 12: 49-100.
    1988b   The relation of grammar to cognition. In: Rudzka-Ostyn (ed.), 165-205.
    1996   Fictive motion in language and "ception". In: Paul Bloom, Mary A. Peterson, Lynn Nadel, and Merrill F. Garrett (eds.), *Language and Space*, 211-276. Cambridge, MA / London: MIT Press / Bradford.

Taylor, John R.
    1989   Possessive genitives in English. *Linguistics* 27: 663-686.
    1995   *Linguistic Categorization: Prototypes in Linguistic Theory.* Second edition. Oxford: Oxford University Press / Clarendon.
    1996   *Possessives in English: An Exploration in Cognitive Grammar.* Oxford: Oxford University Press / Clarendon.

Tesnière, Lucien
    1965   *Éléments de Syntaxe Structurale.* Paris: Klincksieck.

Tomasello, Michael (ed.)
    1998   *The New Psychology of Language: Cognitive and Functional Approaches to Language Structure.* Mahwah, NJ / London: Erlbaum.

Traugott, Elizabeth C.
    1986   From polysemy to internal semantic reconstruction. *Proceedings of the Annual Meeting of the Berkeley Linguistics Society* 12: 539-550.
    1989   On the rise of epistemic meanings in English: An example of subjectification in semantic change. *Language* 65: 31-55.
    1993   The conflict *promises/threatens* to escalate into war. *Proceedings of the Annual Meeting of the Berkeley Linguistics Society* 19: 348-358.

Tuggy, David
    1980   ¡Ethical dative and possessor omission sí, possessor ascension no! *Work Papers of the Summer Institute of Linguistics, University of North Dakota* 24: 97-141.
    1981   The transitivity-related morphology of Tetelcingo Nahuatl: An exploration in space grammar. Ph.D. dissertation, Department of Linguistics, University of California, San Diego.
    1986   Noun incorporations in Nahuatl. *Proceedings of the Annual Meeting of the Pacific Linguistics Conference* 2: 455-470.
    1993   Ambiguity, polysemy, and vagueness. *Cognitive Linguistics* 4: 273-290.

Turner, Mark
    1993   An image-schematic constraint on metaphor. In: Geiger and Rudzka-Ostyn (eds.), 291-306.

Turner, Mark and Gilles Fauconnier
  1995   Conceptual integration and formal expression. *Journal of Metaphor and Symbolic Activity* 10: 183-204.
van Hoek, Karen
  1993   Conceptual connectivity and constraints on anaphora. *Papers from the Regional Meeting of the Chicago Linguistic Society* 29.2: 363-375.
  1995   Conceptual reference points: A cognitive grammar account of pronominal anaphora constraints. *Language* 71: 310-340.
  1996   A cognitive grammar account of bound anaphora. In: Casad (ed.), 753-791.
  1997a   *Anaphora and Conceptual Structure.* Chicago / London: University of Chicago Press.
  1997b   Backwards anaphora as a constructional category. *Functions of Language* 4: 47-82.
van Oosten, Jeanne
  1977   Subjects and agenthood in English. *Papers from the Regional Meeting of the Chicago Linguistic Society* 13: 459-471.
  1986   *The Nature of Subjects, Topics and Agents: A Cognitive Explanation.* Bloomington: Indiana University Linguistics Club.
Vandeloise, Claude
  1991   *Spatial Prepositions: A Case Study from French.* Chicago / London: University of Chicago Press.
Velázquez-Castillo, Maura
  1996   *The Grammar of Possession: Inalienability, Incorporation and Possessor Ascension in Guaraní.* (Studies in Language Companion Series 33.) Amsterdam: John Benjamins.
Verhagen, Arie
  1995   Subjectification, syntax, and communication. In: Dieter Stein and Susan Wright (eds.), *Subjectivity and Subjectivisation: Linguistic Perspectives*, 103-128. Cambridge: Cambridge University Press.
Wierzbicka, Anna
  1988   *The Semantics of Grammar.* (Studies in Language Companion Series 18.) Amsterdam / Philadelphia: John Benjamins.
  1995   Dictionaries vs. encyclopaedias: How to draw the line. In: Davis (ed.), 289-315.
Zwicky, Arnold
  1985   Heads. *Journal of Linguistics* 21: 1-29.
Zwicky, Arnold and Jerrold M. Sadock
  1975   Ambiguity tests and how to fail them. In: John Kimball (ed.), *Syntax and Semantics*, Volume 4, 1-36. New York: Academic Press.

Index

Cognitive Linguistics Research

Edited by René Dirven, Ronald W. Langacker and
John R. Taylor

Mouton de Gruyter · Berlin · New York

This series offers a forum for the presentation of research within the perspective of "cognitive linguistics". This rubric subsumes a variety of concerns and broadly compatible theoretical approaches that have a common basic outlook: that language is an integral facet of cognition which reflects the interaction of social, cultural, psychological, communicative and functional considerations, and which can only be understood in the context of a realistic view of acquisition, cognitive development and mental processing. Cognitive linguistics thus eschews the imposition of artificial boundaries, both internal and external. Internally, it seeks a unified account of language structure that avoids such problematic dichotomies as lexicon vs. grammar, morphology vs. syntax, semantics vs. pragmatics, and synchrony vs. diachrony. Externally, it seeks insofar as possible to explicate language structure in terms of the other facets of cognition on which it draws, as well as the communicative function it serves. Linguistic analysis can therefore profit from the insights of neighboring and overlapping disciplines such as sociology, cultural anthropology, neuroscience, philosophy, psychology, and cognitive science.

1 Ronald W. Langacker, *Concept, Image, and Symbol. The Cognitive Basis of Grammar.* 1990.
2 Paul D. Deane, *Grammar in Mind and Brain. Explorations in Cognitive Syntax.* 1992.
3 *Conceptualizations and Mental Processing in Language.* Edited by Richard A. Geiger and Brygida Rudzka-Ostyn. 1993.
4 Laura A. Janda, *A Geography of Case Semantics. The Czech Dative and the Russian Instrumental.* 1993.
5 Dirk Geeraerts, Stefan Grondelaers and Peter Bakema, *The Structure of Lexical Variation. Meaning, Naming, and Context.* 1994.
6 *Cognitive Linguistics in the Redwoods. The Expansion of a New Paradigm in Linguistics.* Edited by Eugene H. Casad. 1996.
7 John Newman, *Give. A Cognitive Linguistic Study.* 1996.